The Art of Electronic Publishing

The Art of Electronic Publishing

The Internet and Beyond

by

Sandy Ressler

Prentice Hall PTR
Upper Saddle River, New Jersey 07458
http://www.prenhall.com

Ressler, Sanford
The art of electronic publishing: the Internet and beyond / Sandy Ressler.
p. cm.
Includes index.
ISBN 0-13-488172-9 (pbk.)
1. Electronic publishing. 2. Internet (Computer network)
I. Title.
Z286.E43R47 1997
686.2′2544--dc20 96-31458
CIP

Prentice-Hall, Inc.
A Division of Simon and Schuster
Upper Saddle River, NJ 07458

The publisher offers discounts on this book when ordered in bulk quantities. For more information, contact: Corporate Sales Department - Prentice Hall PTR; One Lake Street; Upper Saddle River, NJ 07458. Phone: 800-382-3419; Fax: 201-236-7141; e-mail: corpsales@prenhall.com

Printed in the United States of America

10 9 8 7 6 5 4 3 2 1

ISBN: 0-13-488172-9

Prentice-Hall International (UK) Limited, London

Prentice-Hall of Australia Pty. Limited, Sydney

Prentice-Hall of Canada Inc., Toronto

Prentice-Hall Hispanoamericana, S.A., Mexico

Prentice-Hall of India Pte. Ltd., New Delhi

Prentice-Hall of Japan, Inc., Tokyo

Simon & Schuster Asia Pte. Ltd., Singapore

Editora Prentice-Hall do Brasil, Ltda., Rio de Janeiro

In Memory of Yuri Rubinsky
(1952 - 1996)

Contents

Chapter 4 • Form and Function of Document Processors 145

Chapter 5 • Document Standards ... 175

Chapter 6 • Media and Document Integration ... 231

Preface

OH NO! .... not another book about the Web!!!

That's exactly right, this is not just another book.

I wrote this book because the explosion of activity surrounding the Internet and World Wide Web has fundamentally changed the world of electronic publishing.

This book is a complete birds–eye view of the World Wide Web, Internet, and the technologies involved in creating electronic publications from them. This book provides you with background information and practical guidance on how to surf, view, and publish material for the Web, as well as on paper. The explosion of activity surrounding the Internet and the World Wide Web requires a sane, non-hyped guide to help you navigate the sometimes treacherous waters.

Whether you are preparing a short report, a lengthy book, or Web site, electronic publishing is an interdisciplinary field. It requires many different skills. This book covers each of these fields in enough depth to give you the knowledge to find the details yourself.

The technologies surrounding the Internet and the World Wide Web are changing so rapidly that no book can be completely up-to-date for long. However, I'll explain how those technologies form a collection of integrated communications tools. Using this information and these tools, you can explore and express your ideas and follow new developments in the field.

Design, communications, data processing, and systems integration are some of the skills you must master to play the electronic document game. Even *writing* text using an electronic publishing system is different from simply typing the old-fashioned way. In fact, you must become a "document engineer." Your text will be processed by a complex document processing program. The electronic files will be assembled into a report. The electronic processing system will also compute page numbers. It will create the table of contents. It will generate and create lists of figures and tables. If you use the electronic system properly, you will accomplish all these tasks quickly and easily.

You can approach document creation in many ways. Only you can know which is appropriate for your needs. This book explains the basic approaches and gives you the background you need to decide for yourself how to proceed. Once you choose an approach, you can create the document so that its content can outlive the system on which it was created. Being able to reuse part or all of your material will save you time and money. Document standards will help you accomplish this goal. After all, it is the *content* of your publication that matters.

In this book we begin with a tour of the World Wide Web. Chapters 1 and 2 will give you the key terms and concepts, some practical suggestions on using the Web, and an overview of some promising developments and likely trends.

Next, we will explain the fundamental concepts involved in electronic documents and present some of the many ways in which you can work with and view them. Then, we will discuss document standards, management, and how standards affect the publishing process. Finally, we will learn from others. A series of case studies will demonstrate how to approach the real–world problems of document production. The book concludes with lists of helpful resources.

Throughout the book, you will find discussions of specific tools, software products, and other technologies, as well as many examples. The goal is to clarify the complexities of this exciting and valuable field to help you decide for yourself how best to meet your own document processing needs. And to help you communicate with the professional.

In many ways, this book is a second edition of my previous book, *Perspectives on Electronic Publishing*, published in 1993 by Prentice-Hall. However I never did like that name. We needed a new one.

More importantly since that time the whole field of Electronic Publishing has gone through a radical change. The biggest development has been the creation and wide acceptance of the World Wide Web. In the early 90's electronic publishing was an ambiguous and obscure term. Now everyone rightly assumes that it is concerned mainly with the Web. Thus I have expanded and extended the content, focussing on the Web as the premier electronic publishing medium.

Finally I would like to point out the existence of the:

Yuri Rubinsky Insight Foundation
CIBC (Canadian Imperial Bank of Commerce)
Att: Anne Foster, Private Banking Centre
2 Bloor Street West
Toronto Ontario Canada M4W 2G7

This foundation will commemorate Yuri's life by:

"...bringing together workers from a broad spectrum of disciplines to stimulate research and development of technologies which will enhance human access to information of all kinds. Recognizing that all human capabilities are limited in various ways, it seeks to achieve, to the fullest extent possible, equality of access for all."

Acknowledgments

Even though one name is listed as author inevitably many people contribute to the creation of books. This one is no exception.

This book had a strange genesis. I'd been thinking about updating *Perspectives on Electronic Publishing,* but never got around to doing anything. Out of the blue I got a call from a David Silverman of Innodata Corp. (whom I'd never met), who complimented me profusely and suggested that we work jointly on a related book. His ideas stimulated me, and I readily agreed. Unfortunately, David's work situation did not allow time for the project. However, I got off my rear end and started this one.

Much of my previous book forms the basis for this one. I'd like to thank many current and former colleagues at National Institute of Standards and Technology for their input: Steve Clark (FrameMaker tips), Belinda Collins and Jack Hsia (teaching me about color models), Steve Ray (electronic journal information), Pete Brown (concurrent engineering ref), Ken Manheimer (for his USENIX paper and FaceSaver), and Roy Morgan (tank photo). Kent Reed, Larry Welsch, and Yuri Rubinsky (SoftQuad) all read several chapters of the *Perspectives* draft and gave many useful comments.

Scott Bodarky provided some great quotes, Web tips and lots of good lunch company. Michele Vening put some order back into old FrameMaker files that had disintegrated into chaos. Thanks to Cherry Wunderlich (again), an amazingly thorough copy editor who helped me turn this into English.

Many thanks to Greg Doench of Prentice Hall for giving this a try one more time.

Finally, thanks of course, to my family—Faye Taxman, Elizabeth and Joseph—for living with me through "aren't–you–done–with–that–book–yet?"

The Art of Electronic Publishing

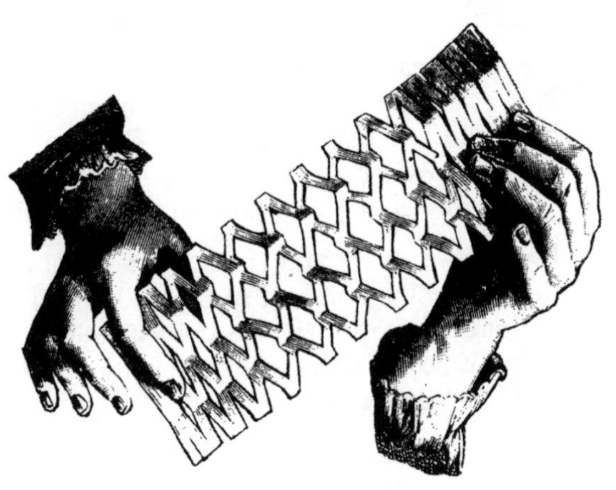

Chapter 1 • World Wide Web

"This 'telephone' has too many shortcomings to be seriously considered as a means of communication. The device is inherently of no value to us." — Western Union internal memo, 1876

1 • 1 Introduction to the World Wide Web

So what's all this fuss about the World Wide Web? What's the big deal? Why should I bother to spend my time looking at all sorts of irrelevant drivel? These questions are a typical response by the non-techie to all the hype of the World Wide Web (also known simply as the Web). In fact, most of the content *is* drivel, and it takes far too long to get useful information, but the Web *is* a big deal and it *is* worth understanding it's implications.

Perhaps the most thoughtful and profound demonstration of the impact of the Web is the recently completed "24 Hours in Cyberspace"[1] project. In that event, 100 photojournalists around the world— pho-

1. The event was held on February 8, 1996 and can still be seen at: http://www.cyber24.com.

tographed events; transmitted them to mission control in San Francisco, where editors typed up stories about the events; recorded telephone interviews with the photographers; composed the entire product into Web pages; and built the information into a robust compelling instant publication—all in 24 hours. Viewed by literally millions of people, the site had approximately four million "hits" on that first day.

It was, and still is a compelling story—how information technology is used in the daily lives of people, around the world. It used the technology to tell the story of how technology can enhance their lives. It was an elegant affair.

Is this journalism, radio, broadcasting, or what? Clearly the integration of all these technologies has created something much greater than the sum of its parts. The ability to assemble and edit information, including images and sounds, and make it available for instant reading/broadcast was phenomenal. The fundamental enabling technological glue and the cause of the Internet explosion is the World Wide Web[2]. So what is it?

Let's start in the middle of Web time with **Mosaic**. Mosaic, a Web browser, was the first "killer" Internet application. Mosaic was introduced to the net in the same way as many other university research projects. It's available for free, and, with source code, for non-profit use. Like many other applications it is a product of the Internet community, specifically, the National Center for Supercomputing Applications (NCSA). It was the product of yet another unheralded government (National Science Foundation) grant.

2. For some of the official history see http://www.w3.org/pub/WWW/WWW

Abbreviated Web History

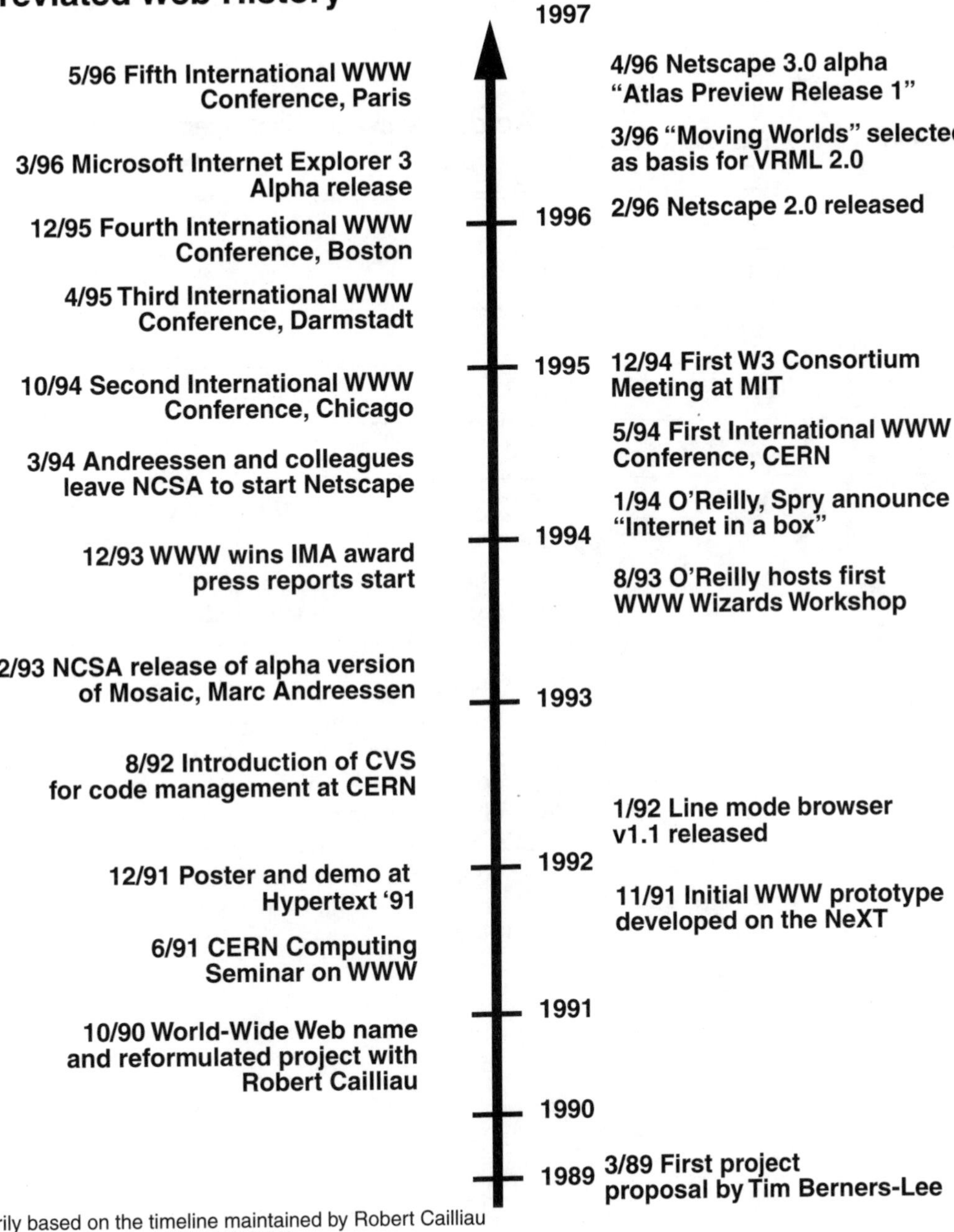
1997
5/96 Fifth International WWW Conference, Paris
4/96 Netscape 3.0 alpha "Atlas Preview Release 1"
3/96 "Moving Worlds" selected as basis for VRML 2.0
3/96 Microsoft Internet Explorer 3 Alpha release
1996
2/96 Netscape 2.0 released
12/95 Fourth International WWW Conference, Boston
4/95 Third International WWW Conference, Darmstadt
1995
12/94 First W3 Consortium Meeting at MIT
10/94 Second International WWW Conference, Chicago
5/94 First International WWW Conference, CERN
3/94 Andreessen and colleagues leave NCSA to start Netscape
1/94 O'Reilly, Spry announce "Internet in a box"
1994
12/93 WWW wins IMA award press reports start
8/93 O'Reilly hosts first WWW Wizards Workshop
2/93 NCSA release of alpha version of Mosaic, Marc Andreessen
1993
8/92 Introduction of CVS for code management at CERN
1/92 Line mode browser v1.1 released
1992
12/91 Poster and demo at Hypertext '91
11/91 Initial WWW prototype developed on the NeXT
6/91 CERN Computing Seminar on WWW
1991
10/90 World-Wide Web name and reformulated project with Robert Cailliau
1990
1989
3/89 First project proposal by Tim Berners-Lee

primarily based on the timeline maintained by Robert Cailliau at http://www.w3.org/pub/WWW/WWW

To understand the explosive growth of the Web, take a look at the number of Web sites discovered by Mat-thew Gray of net.Genesis over the past few years.

Growth of the Web

Month	No. of Web sites	% of commercial sites	Hosts per Web server
6/93	130	1.5	13,000
12/93	623	4.6	3,475
6/94	2,738	13.5	1,095
12/94	10,022	18.3	451
6/95	23,500	31.3	270
1/96	90,000	50.2	100(estimate)

The Web's exponential growth continues. As the Web becomes more widely used, it will start to impact traditional broadcast media like radio and television.

The developers of Mosaic did not try to invent everything. They built on a number of existing standards and systems. Prime among these was the Web developed at CERN, the European Laboratory for Particle Physics. In fact, most of the technological "breakthroughs" were the result of the WWW. The fuss and hoopla that surrounded Mosaic was due to the unified and reasonably pleasant interface it presents to the user.[3]

3. One could even go so far as to make a case that the single most important feature responsible for Mosaic's success was the integration of "in-line" graphics with the page. Looks count.

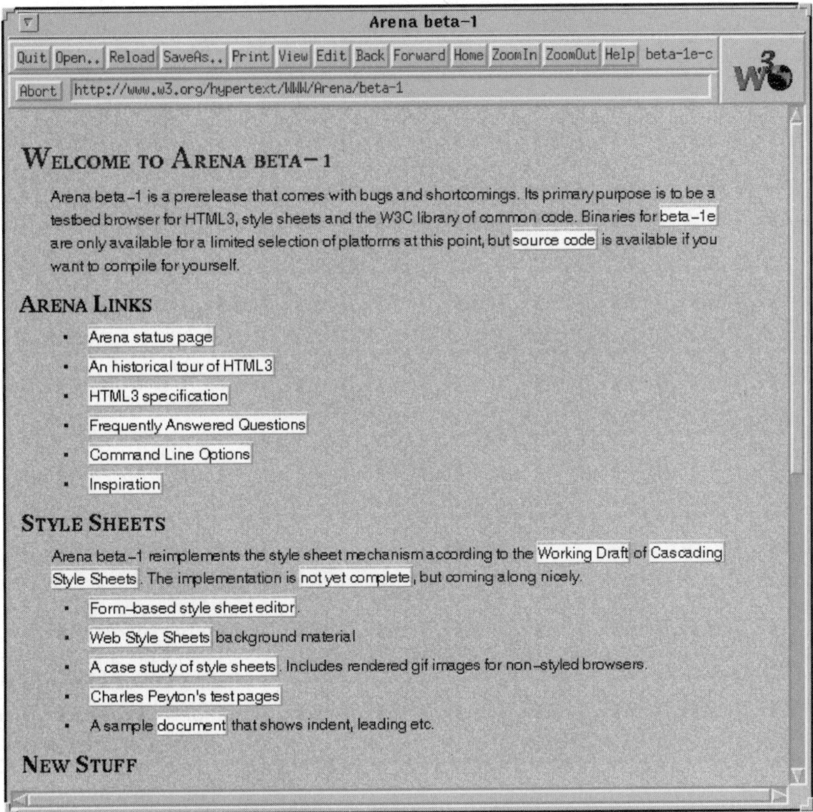

The Arena Web browser from World Wide Web Organization (W3O)

Mosaic and its commercial clones such as Netscape from Netscape Communications offer end users a view of a compound document with many types of data, images, sounds, video etc. (See *Section 3 • 4 • 1 Compound Document* in *Chapter 3 • Points of View*). Many items in the document contain links to other documents. These hypertext links allow the user to browse an entire collection of related documents easily. The documents are distributed and accessed throughout the Internet via the protocols supported by the Web. The net effect (pun intended) is to be able to read compound documents containing images and sounds with the real information sources distributed over the Internet. Web browsers have become the front end to the Internet.

Several key features make the Web extremely powerful.

- *It sits on top of the Internet's existing infrastructure.*
- *The Web protocol unites many different Internet protocols, such as ftp, telnet, gopher, mail, and news.*
- *It is based on open systems: therefore it runs on many computing platforms.*
- *It is physically and logically distributed, and thus scalable.*
- *Web browsers provide a convenient user interface, rich enough to be interesting yet simple enough to promote exploration.*

Tim Berners-Lee[4] is the acknowledged "father" of the Web. Originally from CERN he is now at the World Wide Web Organization (W3O). From his overview of the Web comes the following summary:

> *World Wide Web - Summary*
>
> The WWW (World Wide Web) project merges the techniques of networked information and hypertext to make an easy but powerful global information system.
>
> The project represents any information accessible over the network as part of a seamless hypertext information space.
>
> W3 was originally developed to allow information sharing within internationally dispersed teams, and the dissemination of information by support groups. Originally aimed at the High Energy Physics community, it has spread to other areas and attracted much interest in user support, resource discovery and collaborative work areas. It is currently the most advanced information system deployed on the Internet, and embraces within its data model most information in previous networked information systems.
>
> In fact, the web is an architecture which will also embrace any future advances in technology, including new networks, protocols, object types and data formats.

4. The acknowledged "father" of the Web originally from CERN now at the W3O.

Clients and server for many platforms exist and are under continual development. Much more information about all aspects of the web is available on-line so skip to “Getting started” if you have an internet connection.

Reader view

The WWW world consists of documents, and links. Indexes are special documents which, rather than being read, may be searched. The result of such a search is another (“virtual”) document containing links to the documents found. A simple protocol (“HTTP”) is used to allow a browser program to request a keyword search by a remote information server.

The web contains documents in many formats. Those documents which are hypertext, (real or virtual) contain links to other documents, or places within documents. All documents, whether real, virtual or indexes, look similar to the reader and are contained within the same addressing scheme.

To follow a link, a reader clicks with a mouse (or types in a number if he or she has no mouse). To search and index, a reader gives keywords (or other search criteria). These are the only operations necessary to access the entire world of data.

Information provider view

The WWW browsers can access many existing data systems via existing protocols (FTP, NNTP) or via HTTP and a gateway. In this way, the critical mass of data is quickly exceeded, and the increasing use of the system by readers and information suppliers encourage each other.

Providing information is as simple as running the W3 server and pointing it at an existing directory structure. The server automatically generates the a hypertext view of your files to guide the user around.

To personalize it, you can write a few SGML hypertext files to give an even more friendly view. Also, any file available by anonymous FTP, or any internet newsgroup can be immediately linked into the web. The very small start-up effort is designed to allow small contributions. At the other end of the scale, large information providers may provide an HTTP server with full text or keyword indexing. This may allow access to a large existing database without changing the way that database is managed. Such gateways have already been made into Oracle(tm), WAIS, and Digital's VMS/Help systems, to name but a few.

The WWW model gets over the frustrating incompatibilities of data format between suppliers and reader by allowing negotiation of format between a smart browser and a smart server. This should provide a basis for extension into multimedia, and allow those who share application standards to make full use of them across the web.

This summary does not describe the many exciting possibilities opened up by the WWW project, such as efficient document caching. the reduction of redundant out-of-date copies, and the use of knowledge daemons. There is more information in the on-line project documentation, including some background on hypertext and many technical notes.

Getting Started

If you have nothing else but an Internet connection, then telnet to info.cern.ch (no user or password). This very simple interface works with any terminal but in fact gives you access to anything on the web. It starts you at a special beginner's entry point. Use it to find up-to-date information on the WWW client program you need to run on your computer, with details of how to get it. This is the crudest interface to the web — do not judge the web by this. Just use it to find the best client for your machine.

You can also find pointers to all documentation, including manuals, tutorials and papers.

—Tim BL

1 • 2 Browsing the Web

"Surfing the Web," a phrase meaningful a short time ago only to computer geeks, has now entered the popular culture. This is one of the surest signs of the impact of the Web.

According to the WWW FAQ (Frequently Asked Questions) maintained by Thomas Boutell:

> What are WWW, hypertext and hypermedia?
>
> WWW stands for "World Wide Web." The WWW project, started by CERN (the European Laboratory for Particle Physics), seeks to build a distributed hypermedia system.
>
> The advantage of hypertext is that in a hypertext document, if you want more information about a particular subject mentioned, you can usually "just click on it" to read further detail. In fact, documents can be and often are linked to other documents by completely different authors — much like footnoting, but you can get the referenced document instantly!
>
> To access the web, you run a browser program. The browser reads documents, and can fetch documents from other sources. Information providers set up hypermedia servers which browsers can get documents from.
>
> The browsers can, in addition, access files by FTP, NNTP (the Internet news protocol), gopher and an ever-increasing range of other methods. On top of these, if the server has search capabilities, the browsers will permit searches of documents and databases.

Top Ten Reasons Why White House Staff Like The Internet

Tom Kalil, the David Letterman of the Clinton/Gore administration gave the closing keynote at INET'94/JENC5 in Prague on Friday, June 17, 1994. In his talk about National Information Infrastructure (NII) efforts in the United States, he included this list.

10. Surfing the Web is more fun than going to meetings.

9. Even reading old RFCs is more fun than going to meetings.

8. On the Internet, no one knows you're a bureaucrat.

7. It's how we get our daily marching orders from Vint Cerf, Tony Rutkowski, and Dave Farber.

6. It's hard to write your X.400 address on a cocktail napkin.

5. We get all that great electronic fan mail on the Clipper Chip.

4. We have access to the Top Secret Air Force server with cool gifs of UFOs and little green men.

3. We're still hoping to get on Carl Malamud's "Geek of the Week."

2. We love getting flamed by rabid libertarians on "com-priv."

1. We can send e-mail FROM president@whitehouse.gov.

From http://www.town.hall.org/

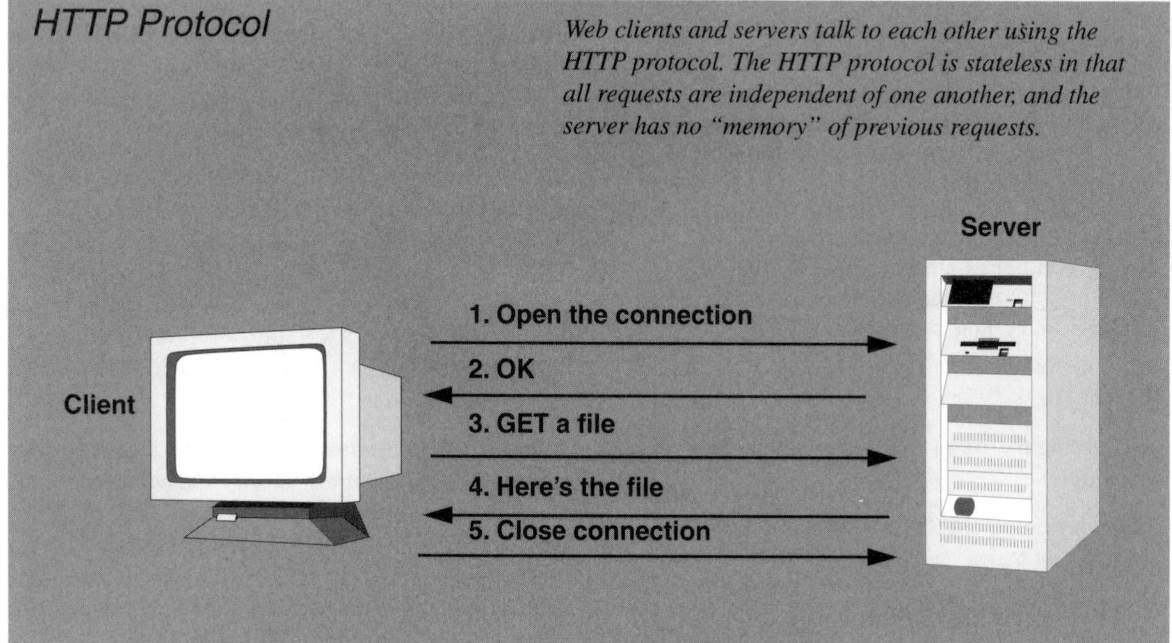

The documents that the browsers display are hypertext documents. Hypertext is text with pointers to other text. The browsers let you deal with the pointers in a transparent way: select the pointer, and you are presented with the text that is pointed to.

Hypermedia is a superset of hypertext—it is any medium with pointers to other media. This means that browsers might not display a text file, but might display images or sound or animations.

The compound document a user manipulates is "authored" using the HyperText Markup Language (HTML) which is a specific Document Type Definition (DTD) of the Standard Generalized Markup Language (SGML). In short, the WWW designers wisely chose not to invent yet another language technology and instead chose an existing standardized language.

Initially, HTML was designed simply as a convenient way to mark up text. Shortly after its creation however, the folks at CERN got wind of SGML, and the two have been struggling to stay together. HTML and SGML serve different needs and communities.

HTML is geared more toward the look of Web pages, and SGML more toward the documents structure, not how it looks. HTML has benefited greatly from the technology provided by SGML. SGML has benefited greatly from the popularity of HTML and the Web. They have a symbiotic relationship.

The developers of Mosaic used the rich foundation of WWW as a starting point. These collaborations are what make an open Internet such a valuable resource.

Web browsers all have the same basic features. They let you jump from link to link. They display some graphics. They have mechanisms to call other applications for specific media types. Web browser vendors are starting to differentiate themselves by introducing new HTML tags and features. Each vendor hopes its feature set is compelling enough to become the defacto standard for authors. This is a dangerous game and bad for the end user, because documents become tied to specific Web browsers which support the new tags. Standardization and conformance testing offer the only hope for this situation.

Navigator/browser feature comparison

	Cello v 1	NCSA X Mosaic V 2.4	NCSA Mosaic (Win) v.20-alpha3	Netscape (Win) v 1.0	Spyglass (Win) v 1.02	Air Mosaic (Win) v 3.06	Internetworks (Win) Beta 4	Win Tapes-try (Win) v 1.67	Web Explorer (OS/2) v.91
COMPLIANCE									
proxy	+	–	–	+	~	+	+	~	~
extended html	–	–	–	+	–	–	–	–	–
PERFORMANCE									
multithreading	–	–	–	+	–	–	+	+	–
dynamic linking	–	–	–	+	–	–	+	–	–
deferred image	–	–	–	+	–	+	+	+	–
multi-pane/window	–/–	–/–	–/–	–/–	–/–	–/–	+/–	–/+	–/–
CONFIGURABILITY									
kiosk mode	–	–	–	–	–	+	–	–	+
external players	–	–	–	+	–	–	+	+	+
INTEGRATION									
drag&drop to clipboard	–	–	–	–	–	+	–	+	–
spawnable players	–	~	~	+	~	+	+	~	+
search engine	–	–	–	+	–	–	–	–	–
NAVIGATION AIDS									
hotlist/bookmark	b	h	h	b	h	h	h	b	h
folders/categories	+/–	–/–	+/–	+/–	–/–	+/–	+/–	+/+	–/–
menu/button bar	–	–	+	–	–	+	–	–	–
import/export	–/+	–/–	–/–	+/+	–/+	+/+	–/–	+/–	–/–
annotation	–	+	+	+	–	–	–	+	–
auto time/date stamp	–	–	–	+	–	–	–	–	–

LEGEND: **+** indicates that feature is supported in some form

– indicates that *either* the feature is not supported *or* that we could not get it to function properly

~ indicates that the feature's support was weak by current standards

1 • 3 Web Maintenance

As the Web of HTML documents grows, maintenance of links in the documents becomes increasingly difficult. It is frustrating to select a link only to have the browser return an error message that the document doesn't exist.

New tools are helping manage and maintain Web sites. The Webtest tool suite from EIT[5] is a freely available utility. It contains a Verify Web Link tool. It starts from a URL, traverses outward, subject to a searching profile; and reports the results.

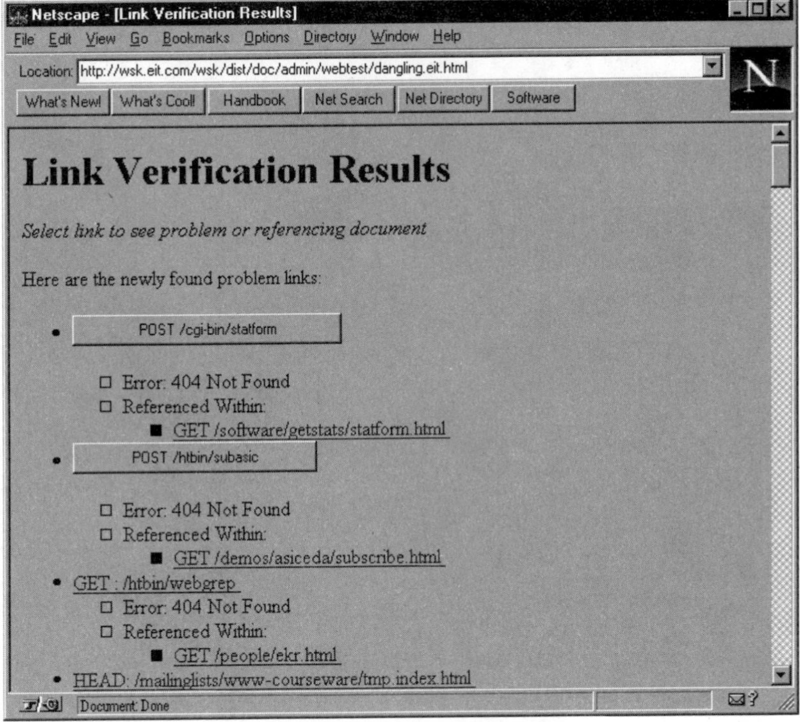

Results of Link Verification test with EIT utility

As the Web matures, vendors are catching up to the demand for Web site management products. One product by Adobe is called SiteMill. SiteMill is a

5. Find Webtest at, http://wsk.eit.com/wsk/dist/doc/admin/webtest/index.html

WYSIWYG site manager. It provides users with drag and drop controls and tools to manage links, resource usage, and error handling.

MajorHotelCorporation

File Name	Page Title	Modification Date
Farouki.html	The San Francisco Farouki, Californ	Tue, Nov 28, 1995, 7
Hotel floorplans.pdf		Thu, Nov 16, 1995, 3
images		
@spacer.gif		Thu, Sep 21, 1995, 1
Currently unused images		
emptyban.gif		Tue, Sep 26, 1995, 2
event logo.gif		Tue, Sep 26, 1995, 1
HotelLobby.gif		Tue, Sep 26, 1995, 2
mhcBG.gif		Tue, Sep 26, 1995, 1
reservationsban.gif		Tue, Sep 26, 1995, 1
rose.gif		Tue, Sep 26, 1995, 1
lobby Quicktime film.mov		Tue, Jul 25, 1995, 9
Maui.html	The Maui Mirelli Resort, Hawaii	Tue, Nov 28, 1995, 7
MHCHome.html	The Major Hotel Corporation Home F	Thu, Nov 9, 1995, 10
Planner.html	MHC Conference Planner	Tue, Sep 26, 1995, 3
Reservations.html	MHC Room Reservation form	Tue, Nov 28, 1995, 7
Titikaka.html	The Taipei Titikaka, Taiwan	Tue, Nov 28, 1995, 7
Winter event registration.pdf		Thu, Nov 16, 1995, 3

Site view displays all site resources at a glance: pages, images, directories, scripts, and other files, including PDF files created with Adobe Acrobat(R). Double-click icons to open pages and images to edit them. Name, delete, and move resources between folders—links are automatically updated. Create links by dragging a page icon from the Site view into a Page view. Each resource has pop-up menus for inbound and outbound links for easy site navigation. The Site view warns you of unreachable or unused resources.

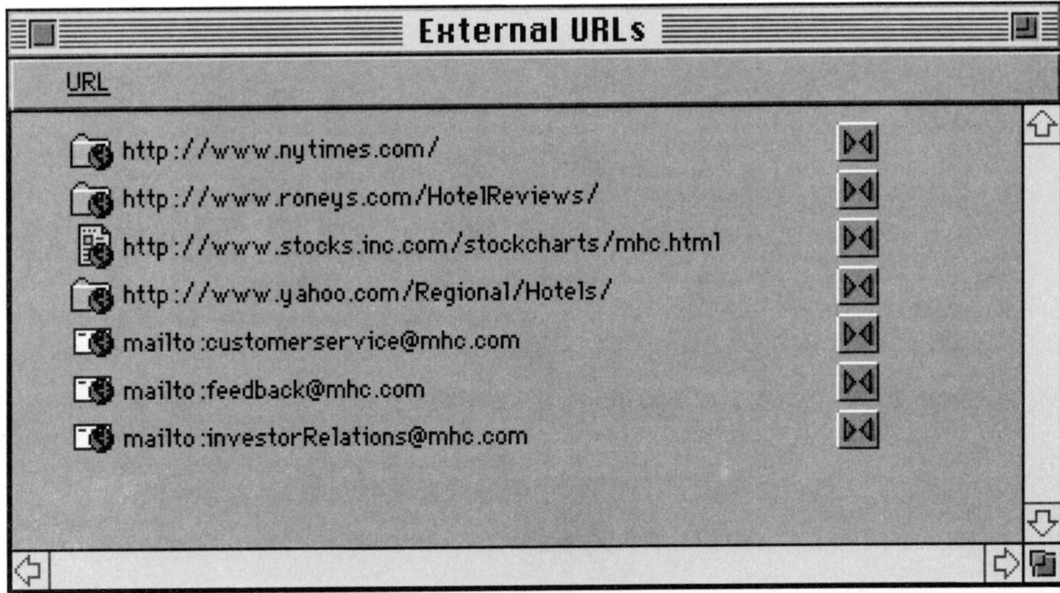

Errors in Company Site

File Name	Full Path
calendar.html	/HD/Company Site/additional/calendar.
corpindex.html	/HD/Company Site/corpindex.html
employment.html	/HD/Company Site/employment.html

SiteMill's external URL reference list and error controls

SiteMill's visually oriented tools help track down references to external URLs and locate dangling links. In the Error windows a user can drag the correct file to the missing icon; all references in the site will be updated.

Another product in this new line of Web management software is Interleaf's CyberLeaf. This system is not an authoring tool, instead it incorporates Web pages authored with whatever tool you like. Integration with the entire enterprise is another feature authoring systems are starting to support. Interleaf uses the term "Web Lifecycle" to describe the process of updating and maintaining a Web. Web authoring systems are introducing templates coupled with tools to help set up the Web site. These are similar in concept to Microsoft Wizards, which lead people through the creation of complex documents. Interleaf's long history of document processing and management systems, primarily for large organizations, is clearly evident here.

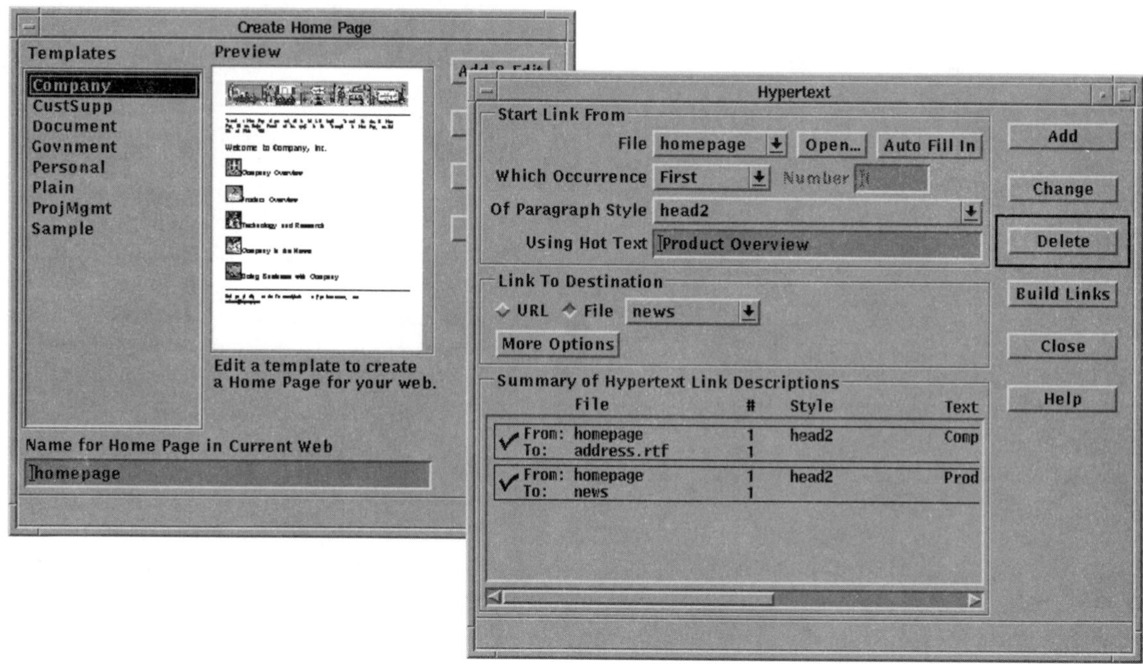

Template usage and link management dialogs from Interleaf's CyberLeaf

Web browsers are applications that run on the user's client machine. The client operating system and particular configuration of the client software and networking all play a role in the operation and behavior of the application, the browser. The availability of ancillary applications and properly configured system-wide protocols contribute to the final document's portability or lack thereof.

One important issue associated with wide distribution of HTML documents results from the Web browser's loose coupling with various applications commonly known as helper applications. Web browsers sometimes launch helper applications when the user encounters an image file[6]. The particular application launched is dependent on the data's particular MIME type (see *Section 1 • 10 • 6 MIME*); it is often dependent on the extension used for the file name as well. If, for example, the HTML document points to a JPEG formatted image, the client machine must have an application capable of displaying JPEG images and the Web browser must be configured to launch that application upon links to JPEG images. This same scenario applies to sound and video files.

Naming links is another issue related to system dependencies. There is a trade-off, when authoring, in how to name the link. Using absolute URLs (Uniform Resource Locator) is more reliable but much more painful when you have to relocate the Web documents to another directory structure or Web server. If you know that your documents will be moving, you or the authors should be careful to use only links with relative address names. Doing this will make it easy to move the documents to other locations on the same server.

This becomes important if you think you may want to encapsulate the Web for CD-ROM distribution, an increasingly popular option. Webs of documents can be distributed on CDs with the portion that must be updated obtained from the on-line Web when needed. In this way, the entire hierarchy of HTML files can be moved as a unit without concern for renaming file path names inside the documents. In addition, the relative names often must only be names in directories down from the current location. This is a security feature of the server program.

Of course, after you author your Web pages you must have them placed onto a Web server. Thousands of companies now seem to be willing to host Web pages. They offer virtually any type of service

6. Web browsers are starting to natively support more image formats, inline. However, helper applications are still necessary, and will be for quite some time.

you can imagine, albeit at a price. One particularly intriguing approach offered by AccessAbility Internet Services[7] is the concept of a self–service Web site. They provide the Web server and host, but you, the author, can do all the maintenance and updates through a controlled process. It's kind of a self–serve copy shop for the 90s.

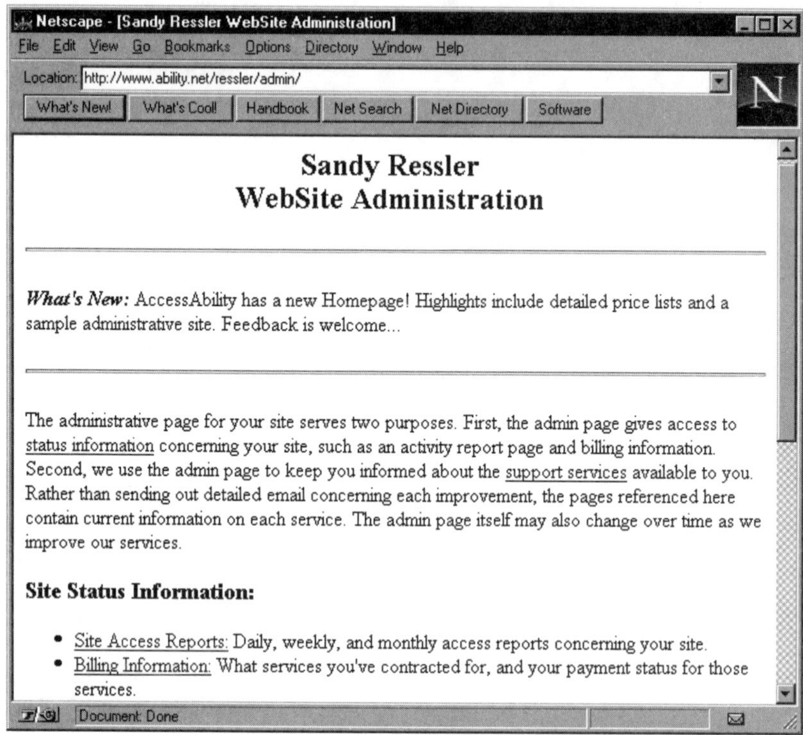

Self service Web site administration at AccessAbility

1 • 4 Worms, Spiders, and Knowbots

Web worms, spiders, robots, and knowbots are automated tools that crawl around the Web looking for information, reporting their findings. Many of the so-called Internet Starting Points use robots to scour the Web looking for new information. These automatons can be used both to search for information about a particular topic of interest or to build up databases.

7. Find AccessAbility at: http://www.ability.net.

for subsequent searching by others. (See *Section 1 • 9 Internet Starting Points* for information on searching the net.)

A **worm** is a program that moves from one site to another. The generic term "worm" has nothing to do with the Web; it simply refers to a program that seeks to replicate itself on multiple hosts. Worms are not necessarily good. The "Internet Worm" of 1988 caused a massive breakdown of thousands of systems on the Internet. But that's another story.[8]

A **knowbot** is a program or agent that, like worms, travels from site to site. However it has a flavor of artificial intelligence in that it usually follows knowledge-based rules. Another term for a knowbot might be an autonomous agent. Clear distinctions between these terms are currently not meaningful.[9] In the context of this section, finding information, we'll look below at one particular knowbot and one worm. First, however, we'll mention spiders.

Spiders, as their name implies, crawl around the Web, doing things. They can find information to build large textual databases; the WebCrawler does this. They can also maintain large Webs or collections of Webs; this is the function of the MOMspider.

Following is Brian Pinkerton's description of one Web worm, the WebCrawler:

> The WebCrawler is a web robot, and is the first product of an experiment in information discovery on the Web. I wrote it because I could never find information when I wanted it, and because I don't have time to follow endless links.

The WebCrawler has three different functions:

> It builds indices for documents it finds on the Web. The broad, content-based index is available for searching. It acts as an agent, searching for documents of particular interest to the user. In doing so, it draws upon the knowledge accumulated in its index, and some simple strategies to bias the search toward inter-

8. Check out "The Internet Worm: Crisis and Aftermath" by Eugene Spafford in Communications of the ACM, 32(6), 1989.

9. One popular "Knowbot" is the CNRI "Knowbot Information Service," which helps you find email address located at: http://info.cnri.reston.va.us/kis.html.

esting material. In this sense, it is a lot like the Fish search, although it operates network-wide. It is a test-bed for experimenting with Web search strategies. It's easy to plug in a new search strategy, or ask queries from afar, using a special protocol.

In addition, the WebCrawler can answer some fun queries. Because it models the world using a flexible, OO (*Ed.* Object Oriented) approach, the actual graph structure of the Web is available for queries. This allows you, for instance, to find out which sites reference a particular page. It also lets me construct the Web Top 25 List, the list of the most frequently referenced documents that the WebCrawler as found.

How it Works

The WebCrawler works by starting with a known set of documents (even if it is just one), identifying new places to explore by looking at the outbound links from that document, and then visiting those links.

It is composed of three essential pieces:

The search engine directs the search. In a breadth-first search, it is responsible for identifying new places to visit by looking at the oldest unvisited links from documents in the database. In the directed, find-me-what-I-want strategy, the search engine directs the search by finding the most relevant places to visit next. The database contains a list of all documents, both visited and unvisited, and an index on the content of visited documents. Each document points to a particular host, and, if visited, contains a list of pointers to other documents (links). “Agents” retrieve documents. They use CERN's WWW library to retrieve a specific URL, then returning that document to the database for indexing and storage. The WebCrawler typically runs with 5-10 agents at once.

Being a Good Citizen

The WebCrawler tries hard to be a good citizen. Its main approach involves the order in which it searches the Web. Some web robots have been known to operate in a depth-first fashion, retrieving file after file from a single site. This kind of traversal is bad. The

WebCrawler searches the Web in a breadth-first fashion. When building its index of the Web, the WebCrawler will access a site at most a few times a day.

When the WebCrawler is searching for something more specific, its search may narrow to a relevant set of documents at a particular site. When this happens, the WebCrawler limits its search speed to one document per minute and sets a ceiling on the number of documents that can be retrieved from the host before query results are reported to the user. The WebCrawler also adopts several of the techniques mentioned in the Guidelines for Robot Writers.

Implementation Status

The WebCrawler is written in C and Objective-C for NEXTSTEP. It uses the WWW library from CERN, with several changes to make automation easier. Whenever I feel comfortable about unleashing the WebCrawler, I'll make the source code available!

bp@cs.washington.edu

Brian Pinkerton

MOMspider, available for free from the University of California, Irvine, is used to help maintain Webs. It is written in PERL and runs on most UNIX systems. MOMspider was written by Roy T. Fielding and a paper titled "Maintaining Distributed Hypertext Infostructures: Welcome to MOMspider's Web"[10] was presented at the WWW94 conference in Geneva. From Fielding's paper:

> MOMspider gets its instructions by reading a text file that contains a list of options and tasks to be performed (an example instruction file is provided in Appendix A). Each task is intended to describe a specific infostructure so that it can be encompassed by the traversal process. A task instruction includes the traversal type, an infostructure name (for later reference), the "Top" URL at which to start traversing, the location for placing the indexed output, an e-mail address that corresponds to the owner of that info-

10. The paper is on the Web at: http://www.ics.uci.edu/WebSoft/MOMspider/WWW94/paper.html.

structure, and a set of options that determine what identified maintenance issues justify sending an e-mail message.

```
Appendix A
# MOMspider-0.1a Instruction File


SystemAvoid /usr/local/httpd/admin/avoid.mom
SystemSites /usr/local/httpd/admin/sites.mom
AvoidFile   /usr/grads/fielding/test/.momspider-avoid
SitesFile   /usr/grads/fielding/test/.momspider-sites
SitesCheck  7
<Site
    Name          ICS
    TopURL        http://www.ics.uci.edu/ICShome.html
    IndexURL      http://www.ics.uci.edu/Admin/ICS.html
    IndexFile     /usr/local/httpd/documentroot/MOM/ICS.html
    IndexTitle    MOMspider Index for All of ICS
    EmailAddress  www@ics.uci.edu
    EmailBroken
    EmailExpired  2
>
<Tree
    Name          MOMspider-WWW94
    TopURL        http://www.ics.uci.edu/WebSoft/MOMspider/WWW94/paper.html
    IndexURL      http://www.ics.uci.edu/Admin/MOMspider-WWW94.html
    IndexFile     /usr/local/httpd/documentroot/Admin/MOMspider-WWW94.html
    IndexTitle    MOMspider Index for Roy's WWW94 Paper
    EmailAddress  fielding@ics.uci.edu
    EmailBroken
>
<Owner
    Name          RTF
    TopURL        http://www.ics.uci.edu/~fielding/hotlist.html
    IndexURL      http://www.ics.uci.edu/~fielding/MOM/RTF.html
    IndexFile     /usr/grads/fielding/public_html/MOM/RTF.html
    EmailAddress  fielding@ics.uci.edu
    EmailBroken
    EmailChanged  3
    EmailExpired  7
>
```

Finally, rest assured that not all bots and spiders must be run from expensive workstations. An really cool product called Surfbot[11] from Surflogic LLC runs just fine on Win95 PCs. Surfbot lets you configure your own private "agents" to traverse either known Internet Starting Points or your own set of bookmarks. Its Wizard type of set up configures the agents and can produce a variety reports. This set up is simple to use.

11. Find Surfbot at: http://www.surflogic.com/.

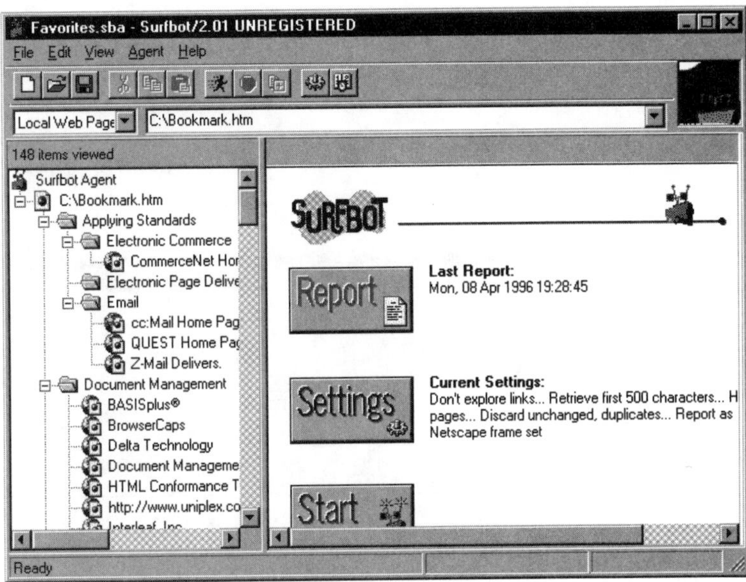

Surfbot control screen for configuring one particular agent.

One particularly nice feature is its ability to schedule the times for searching. It makes the modem connection for you and hangs up when done. You can make your agents fire up in the middle of the night so the results will be waiting for you in the morning!

1 • 5 Authoring

"Man invented language to satisfy his deep need to complain." — Lily Tomlin

Using a Web browser is easy. Authoring documents for Web publishing is relatively easy. However, sometimes it is a little tricky.

The variety and capability of Web authoring tools are exploding. Web documents must be in the HTML format. HTML is a specific application of SGML so you can purchase commercial off-the-shelf SGML products to help in the writing and analysis of Web documents. The SGML products are not necessarily the best HTML authoring tools, however.

In fact, the traditional SGML vendor community is jumping on the Web as a new market. Vendors are releasing SGML products specifically to support and aid the writing of HTML documents. The decision by the original Web developers to use SGML as the foundation for Web documents is one of the Web's great strengths.

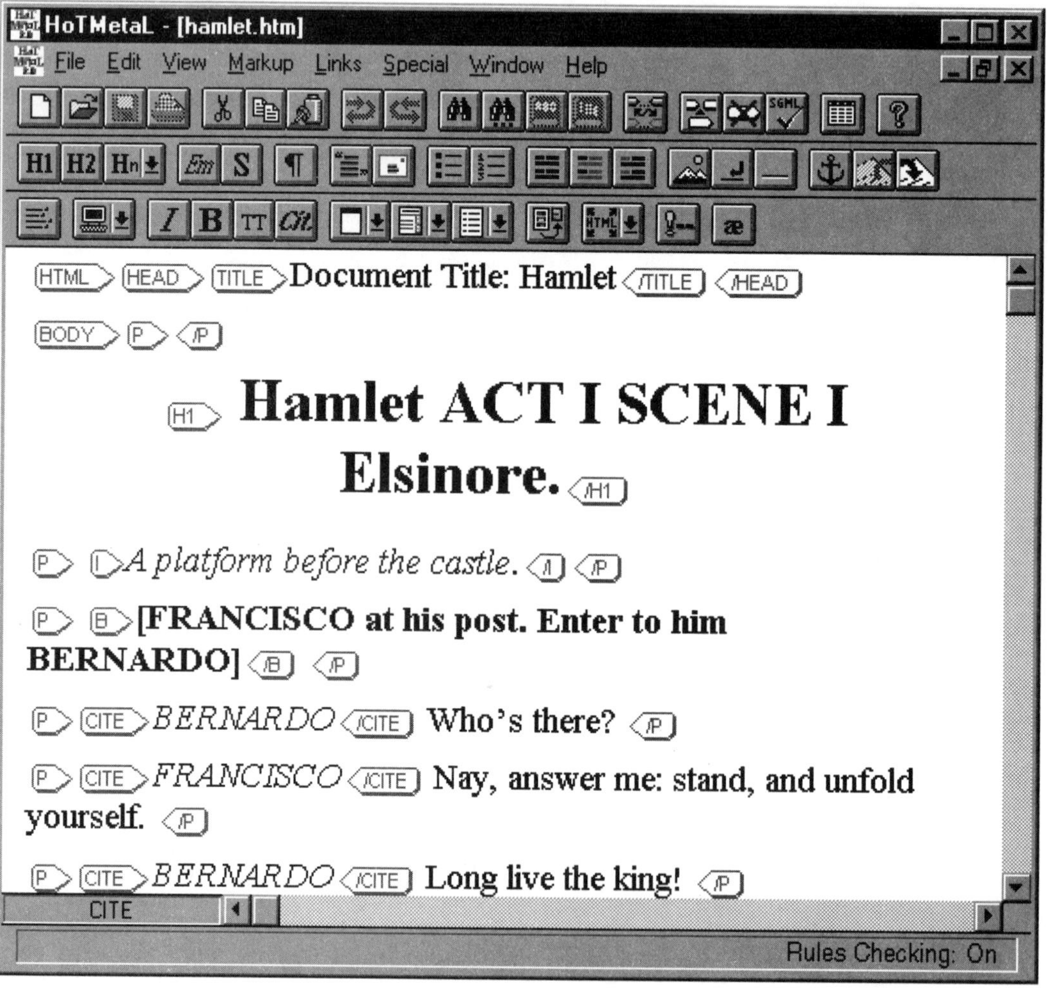

SoftQuad's HoTMetaL HTML editor

HoTMetaL[12] runs on PCs, Macs, and UNIX workstations. In addition several free-ware packages are available for PCs and the Macintosh. SimpleHTML[13] is a HyperCard–based editor for the Mac.

On UNIX workstations there is also tkWWW, an authoring tool based on the tk toolkit for X windows.

One of the most common HTML authoring methods is simply to use a text editor to write HTML directly. This "Iron Man HTML" technique can be aided by some editors, for example emacs, which provides an HTML mode to take some of the tedium away. HTML documents are readable and editable; they just require a little learning.

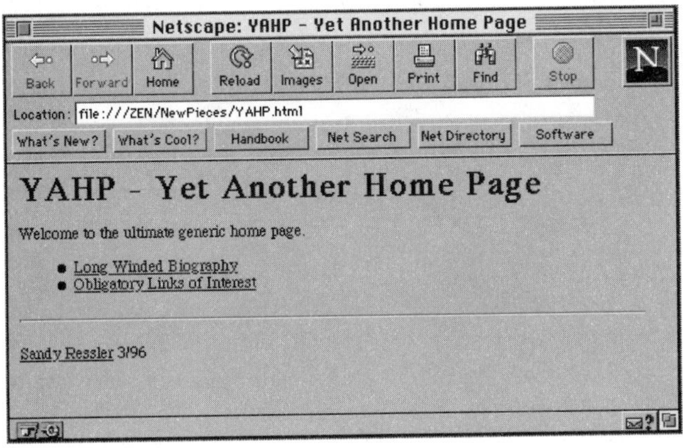


```
<HTML>
<HEAD>
  <TITLE>YAHP - Yet Another Home Page</TITLE>
</HEAD>
<BODY>
  <H1>YAHP - Yet Another Home Page</H1>
  <P>Welcome to the ultimate generic home page.
  <UL>
     <LI> <A HREF="biography.html">
              Long Winded Biography</A>
     <LI> <A HREF="links.html">
              Obligatory Links of Interest</A>
  </UL>
  <HR>
  <P><A HREF= "mailto:sandy@ability.net"> Sandy
Ressler</A> 3/96
</BODY>
</HTML>
```

An HTML fragment

An interesting authoring issue concerns the conformance of HTML files with the HTML DTD. Some authoring packages help force conformance, while others let you get away with sloppy HTML. Most browsers do not bother to check for compliant HTML and simply do the best they can with the dis-

12. http://www.sq.com/products/hotmetal/hm-ftp.htm
13. By Eric Morgan, eric_morgan@ncsu.edu http://www.lib.ncsu.edu/staff/morgan/simple.html.

play. If you are concerned with interoperability and the longevity of your document, it will pay in the long run to be in conformance.

An alternative to native HTML authoring is to write documents using your favorite text-editor, word process or publishing system and then convert to HTML. A large number of conversion programs exist for just this purpose. For example the `rtf2html` program on UNIX platforms will convert documents in the RTF format into HTML. Similarly, there are converters for latex and FrameMaker[14]. All of these conversion mechanisms depend on a properly written original document. For example, documents written in WordPerfect must use the style feature to convert successfully. Conversion mechanisms often require some hand editing to touch up conversion errors.

Following this conversion type of authoring, Microsoft is introducing an add-on module for MS Word which will output HTML. Interleaf is producing Cyberleaf, a higher-end HTML authoring tool that can read in WordPerfect, Word RTF, FrameMaker MIF, Interleaf, and ASCII formats.

Actually Microsoft's Internet Assistant is much more than a simple converter. It is a very credible attempt to take an existing well–known product, MS Word, and extend it to full–fledged Web authoring.

14. In fact, the fm2html conversion suite is on the CD-ROM accompanying this book!

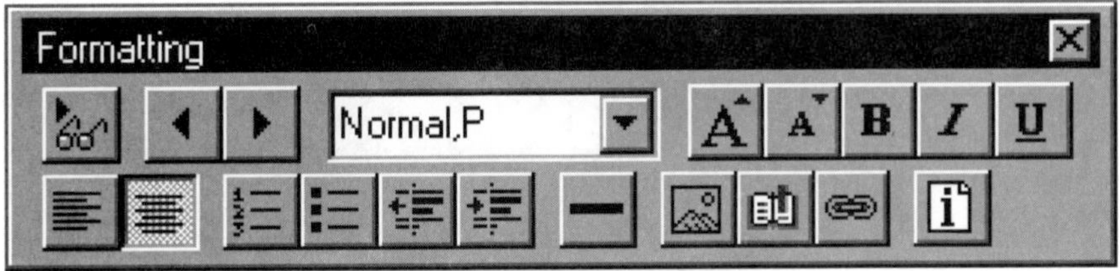

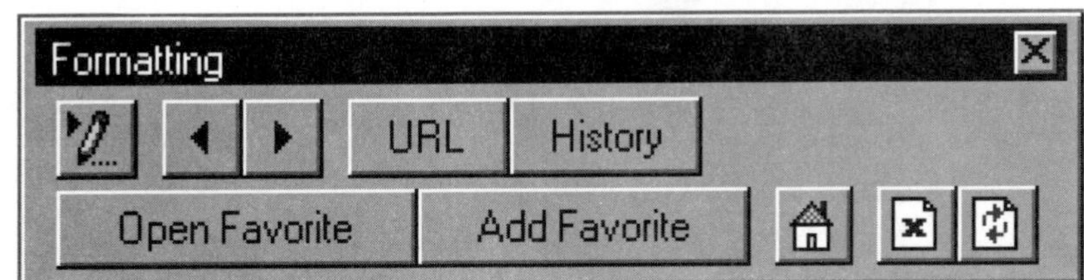

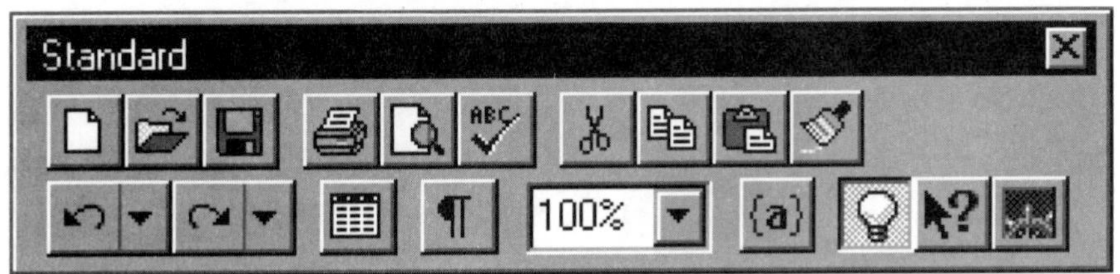

Some control buttons from Netscape's Navigator Gold and HTML authoring package

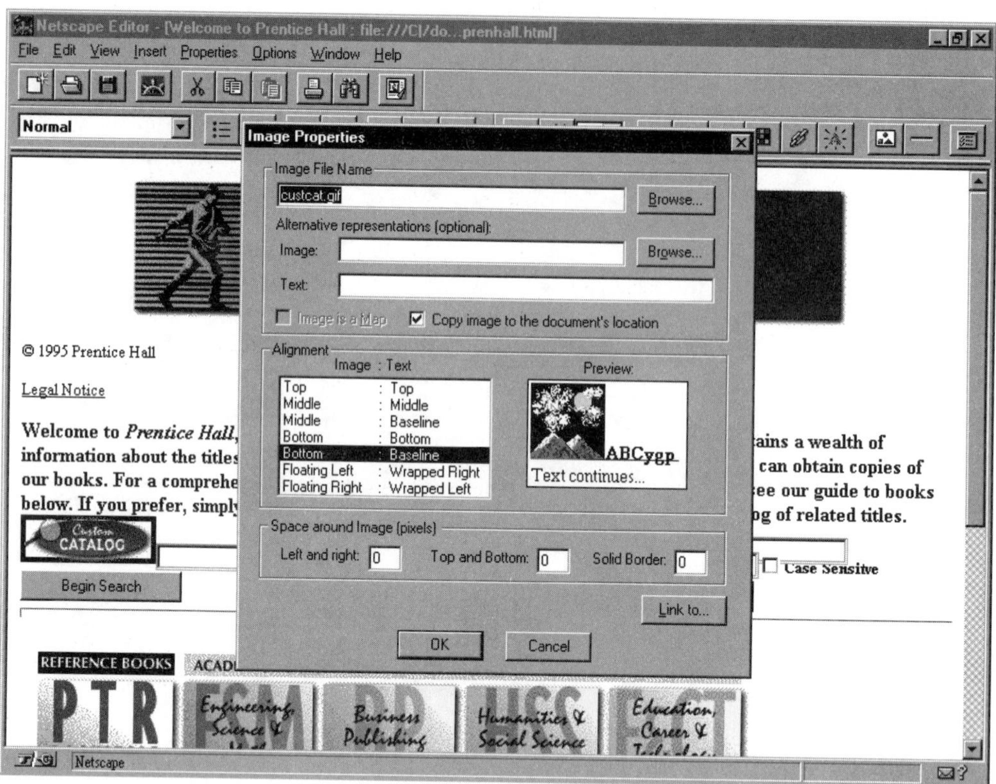

Netscape Navigator Gold WYSIWYG HTML editor has several dialogs to help adjust various tag attributes such as image alignment and manipulation as shown in this figure.

One recent development in Web authoring is the effort to codify Style Sheets. The W3O is leading an effort called Cascading Style Sheets. The idea is to specify a template document in which attributes will cascade down through a hierarchy of styles, to be "inherited" by other style sheets. For example a business letter style sheet would inherit most of its attributes from a generic letter style sheet. As the Feb. 20, 1996 draft proposal on Cascading HTML style sheets by Hakon W Lie and Bert Bos puts it:

> This document specifies level 1 of the Cascading Style Sheet mechanism (CSS1). CSS1 is a simple style sheet mechanism that allows authors and readers to attach style (e.g., fonts, colors and spacing) to

> HTML documents. The CSS1 language is human readable and writable, and expresses style in common desktop publishing terminology.

One of the fundamental features of CSS is that style sheets cascade; authors can attach a preferred style sheet, while the reader may have a personal style sheet to adjust for human or technological limitations. The specification defines rules for resolving conflicts between different style sheets.

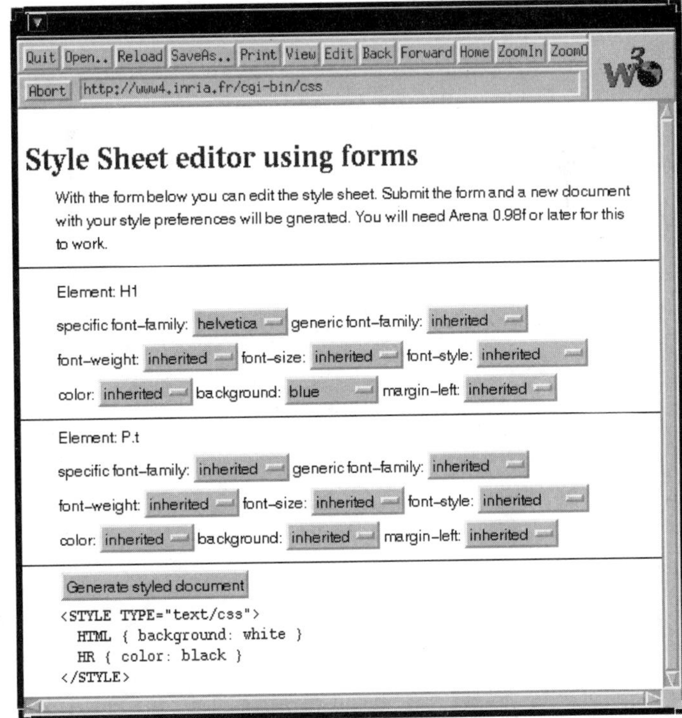

Cascading Style Sheet Editor from W3O

Again from the Cascading Style Sheet level 1 document:

> Designing simple style sheets is easy. One only needs to know a little HTML and some basic desktop publishing terminology. For example, to set the text color of "H1" elements to blue, one can say:
>
> H1 {color: blue}

The example consists of two main parts: selector ('H1') and declaration ('color: blue'). The declaration has two parts: property ('color') and value ('blue'). While the example above only tries to influence one of the properties needed for rendering an HTML document, it qualifies as a style sheet on its own. Combined with other style sheets (one of the fundamental features of CSS is that style sheets are combined) it will determine the final presentation of the document.

The selector is the link between the HTML document and the style, and all HTML tags are possible selectors. HTML tags are defined in the HTML specification [2], and the CSS1 specification defines a syntax for how to address them.

The 'color' property is one of around 40 properties that determine the presentation of an HTML document.

It's always important to keep the user in mind. Different users require different tools. WYSIWYG tools are generally easiest to use and best for beginners. Converters and language oriented authoring tools will help the moderately experienced author cope with conversion headaches and large quantities of text. You might want to keep in mind the following types of Web authors as characterized by Michael Haynes and reprinted with his permission:

The 9 Types of Web Page Creators

Joe/Jane Average College Student

Traits: Owner of a new university-supplied computer account with httpd access. Complete lack of originality. Multiple references to beer/Disney movies. Several photos of Student with college buddies (high school, if freshman Student).

The Good News: They don't know how to get their page linked to the outside world, so only they and their friends download their 16.7-million- color pictures from the last party.

The Bad News: They, their friends and their 16.7-million-color pictures might be on your server.

Mr. "Enhanced For Netscape"

Traits: The second thing you see on his page is a Netscape logo and a link to an ftp site where you can download Netscape <BLINK>NOW!</BLINK>. The first thing you see is about 80 different <TITLE>s scrolling back and forth across your screen.

The Good News: You won't have to look at their pages for long, because there won't be much there to see.

The Bad News: Half of the rest of the people who look at their pages are going to think "Hey, that's cool!" and copy the source.

The Old-Timer

Traits: Pages compatible with HTML 1.0, no graphics and very few attribute tags. Normal-text-size message at top says "This page not enhanced for Netscape. Cope, whipper-snapper."

The Good News: He's likely there because he has something of importance to say.

The Bad News: Whatever it is will likely be boring or far too technical for you.

The 5-Year-Old

Traits: Pictures of their parents, the family pet, etc. More data about the daily life of a kindergartner than you thought possible. Cute "kiddy-talk" dialect to the text. <ADDRESS> contains the note "such-and-such's mother helped her build this page."

The Good News: The first few of these you see give you a warm, fuzzy feeling.

The Bad News: The last few dozen of these you see all look the same.

The Computer Science Major

Traits: Links to the linux FAQ, the Geek Code, Star Wars theme music and DOOM .wad files. Cautious use of Netscape enhancements. Picture of Darth Vader instead of personal pictures. HTML 3.0 (Beta) compliant seal-of-approval at bottom of her page.

The Good News: If you're a geek, you'll find what you're looking for here. Even if you're not, you'll like the page design.

The Bad News: Complete lack of socially redeeming qualities. Unfortunate tendency to upload specs of their home PC.

The Businessman

Traits: Pages without fancy backgrounds and with only one nice, clean, imagemap. Unfortunately, there are no text-links for those using Lynx.

The Good News: You won't go blind staring at his pages.

The Bad News: You might wish you had once you see the prices of the goods/services he's offering.

The Newbie

Traits: Very little created text on their pages, it's almost all links to other people's pages. Missing right brackets in <A HREF>s kill whole lines of information. Several image files are not able to be loaded. <CENTER>.

The Good News: They'll almost have to get better.

The Bad News: They just might not.

The Egotist

Traits: Large image of themself greets you when page is loading. 1/2 Meg .au file of him chatting with his dog. Access counts shown for every page. Several lengthy pages devoted to his compact disk/Magic card/beer bottle collection. More personal details than you'd ever want to know.

The Good News: There isn't any.

The Bad News: Frequently friendly with Mr. "Enhanced for Netscape."

The Maniac

Traits: Last counted 1267 .html files in his public_html directory and 100+ CGI scripts in his cgi-bin directory. Is known as a "Close Personal Friend of Bob [Allison]." Thinks the people at Yahoo! "don't keep up with the Web fast enough." Will be the first on his block to have an ethernet cable hardwired into his brain.

The Good News: You could go through all his pages and never find an error.

The Bad News: You'd never make it through all his pages.

mhaynes@pizza.bgsu.edu

For more information on Web authoring see *Section 5 • 4 HTML* in *Chapter 5 • Document Standards.*

Once you have authored your documents and placed them on a Web site, your attention will often turn to security. If you are trying to sell a product or service, security quickly becomes the major concern.

1 • 6 Web Security

"Relying on the government to protect your privacy is like asking a peeping tom to install your window blinds."— John Perry Barlow

Web servers and browsers present a whole range of security problems. Two of the key security issues are the authentication of requests and privacy. These issues boil down to one — using mechanisms to ensure that I know who you say you are. These mechanisms are more important in some Web interactions than in others.

The more complex Web interactions such as database transactions and shopping require the execution of programs on the server. These programs are most commonly used when you enter and submit data via a form. The data you entered in the form are sent to the server and a program on the server does something with the data; it executes a program and sends a result, if any, back to you.

Security is a major issue here. In fact it is the main reason the creation of the Common Gateway Interface (CGI) protocol was created. This protocol controls how programs communicate with the Web server.

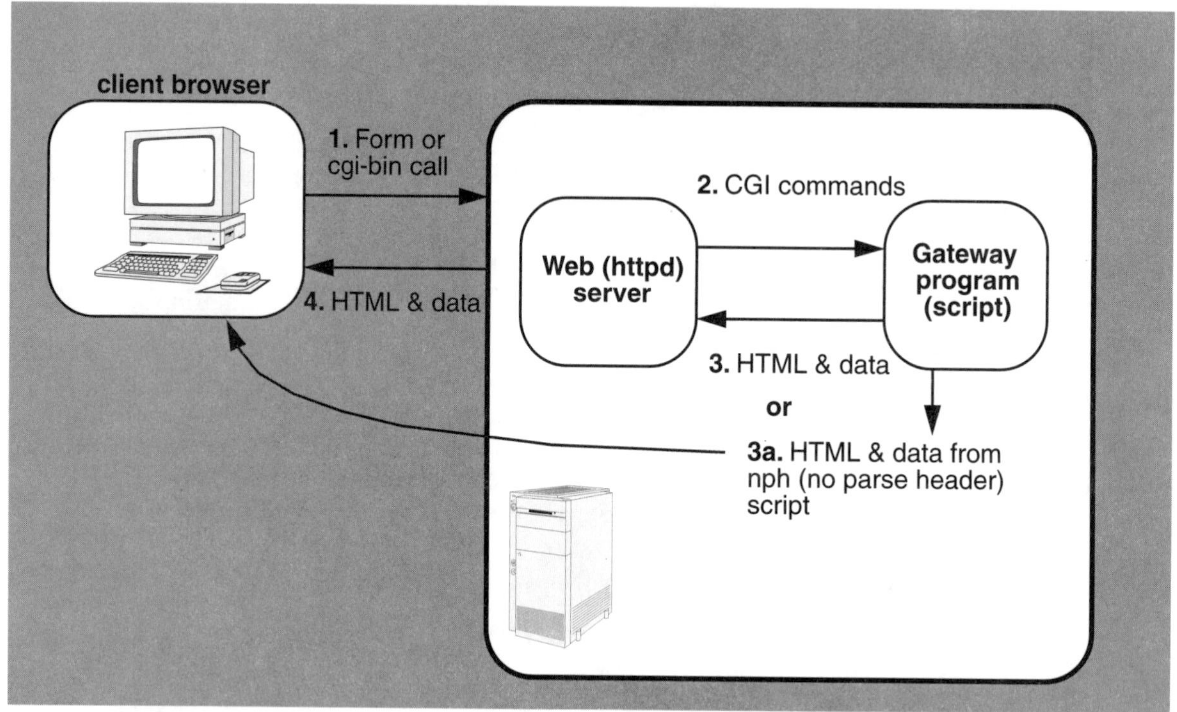

Typical Web Client/Server Interaction using CGI Script.

CGI gateway programs can be written in any language that can execute on the server machine. Typically, UNIX[15] scripts or other scripting languages are used instead of compiled code, because they are easier to debug and maintain. A terrific book by Ian Graham called *"The HTML Sourcebook"* published by John Wiley, described three mechanisms by which data can be passed to the gateway program:

> 1. Command-Line Arguments—The server launches the gateway program with command-line arguments.
>
> 2. Standard Input—The server passes data to the gateway program such that it is read as input (from standard input) by the gateway program client.
>
> 3. Environment Variables—The server puts information in special environment variables before starting the gateway program. The gateway program can then access these variables and obtain their contents.

15. <Blatant Plug>- See "Life with UNIX" by Libes and Ressler, Prentice-Hall, for a wonderful overview of UNIX thinking. </Blatant Plug>

These three mechanisms specify data transfer from the Web server to the gateway program. In addition, a CGI program can pass data back to the Web server by either of two mechanism. As *The HTML Sourcebook* explains, these are:

> 1. Write to standard output—The gateway program passes data back to the server by writing data to standard output. This is the only way that gateway programs can return data to a client.
>
> 2. The name of the gateway program—Gateway programs with names beginning with the string nph- are called nonparsed header programs and are treated specially by the server. In general, the server parses the output of a gateway program looking for headers that it can use to create the HTTP response headers it will send to the client with the returned data. If a gateway program name begins with nph-, the server sends the gateway program directly to the client and does not add any header information.

The behavior and assumptions used by one browser may be different from those used by other browsers, resulting in documents that look different. Similarly, the behavior of secure interfaces must also be scrutinized. Often the implementation of a security algorithm, not the algorithm itself, creates problems. The way a browser interacts and implements security protections is important. Currently vendors vary widely in their approaches.

Perhaps the most far–reaching development towards using secure transactions for true electronic commerce is the recent agreement between VISA and MasterCard. MasterCard issued a press release on February 1, 1996, stating, in part:

> Addressing consumer concerns about making purchases on the Internet, MasterCard International and Visa International joined together today to announce a technical standard for safeguarding payment-card purchases made over open networks such as the Internet. Prior to this effort, Visa and MasterCard were pursuing separate specifications. The new specification, called Secure Electronic Transactions (SET), represents the successful convergence of those individual efforts. A single standard means that consumers and

> merchants will be able to conduct bankcard transactions in cyberspace as securely and easily as they do in retail stores today.
>
> The associations expect to publish SET on their World Wide Web sites in mid-February. Following a comment period, the joint specification is scheduled to be ready for testing in the second quarter 1996. Visa and MasterCard expect that banks will be able to offer secure bankcard services via the Internet to their cardholders in the fourth quarter 1996.

Using the Web to make purchases is currently a little risky. Credit card numbers and other types of confidential information were never intended to be sent through the Internet. The widely distributed, unregulated, open nature of the Internet is the antithesis of a secure system. Of course, thanks to the mathematically obscure field of cryptography, all hope is not lost. The issue is how to make usable the various types and forms of encryption.

1 • 6 • 1 Digital Signatures and Public Key Cryptography

In the real world, we sign all sorts of legal documents, contracts, checks, time slips and other item. A signature is your unique identification; it is your seal of approval that you have read, approved, and agreed with the document. In the electronic world, we must create the equivalent, a digital signature. Unfortunately it is easy to fake an electronic name. What is necessary is to have some magic way to ensure that a signature is legitimate, not a forgery. That magic is what's known as **Public Key Cryptography**.

Think about what a digital signature really is. When you look at a "signed" document you want to be positive that the signature is authentic, that the person, (your boss, for example) really signed the message (especially if he's terminating your employment). You want to be able to pass a magic wand over the signed document to let you read the document and know that your boss actually signed it.

Encrypted messages are unreadable unless you have the secret decoder ring, the key to decrypting the message. Most encryption schemes currently use a single encryption key. For example, the password you use to logon to a computer system is encrypted with a single key. You type the password itself; it tells the computer to let you in. It's simple and still quite secure, but it does not provide a way for the computer system to ensure, authenticate, that you are who you say you are. If someone steals your password, they effectively steal your identity.

The Data Encryption Standard (DES) has been used for many years and is the basis of the UNIX password system.[16] The U.S. government has kept details of the DES algorithm classified, and many variations have been developed because people assume that a secret trapdoor exists for government eavesdropping. Whether or not this is true, recent advances using a technique called differential cryptanalysis can use a statistical method to break the DES. Protections against this attack have been created. The current "state of the art" is a triple DES: three passes of the algorithm using 112 or 168-bit keys.

Public Key Cryptography involves the use of two keys. Each person in a transaction has a public key and a private key. Everyone can see a person's public key, but individuals keep their private keys private. The two keys are intimately related to each other and were generated at the same time by the cryptography program, such as PGP, you are using.

16. "Picking Crypto Locks", by Peter Wayner, *Byte* Oct. 1995.

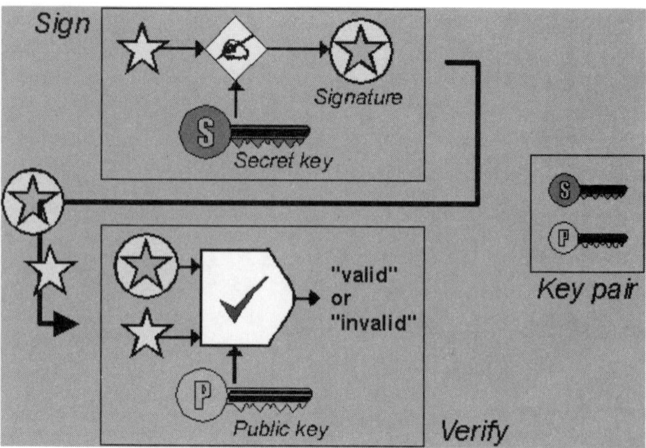

General Public Key Signing Method, the secret key is used for signing and the public key is used for verification.[17]

A message encrypted by one key can be decrypted only by the other. In practice, this means that if my boss wants to send only me a message he encrypts it using my public key. When I receive the message, only I can decode it, using my private key. If my boss wants to send a signed message to a lot of people in the company he encrypts it with his private key and everyone can decrypt it with the boss's public key ensuring that he originated the document.

Pretty Good Privacy (PGP)[18] is a public domain implementation of public key cryptography by Phil Zimmerman of MIT. The program has generated controversy, pitting law enforcement agencies against privacy advocates. No matter what side of the battle you are on, the genie is out of the bottle and is never going back.

In the construction of a secure transaction system, one golden rule is to *never, ever* send clear text through the net. The information must be encrypted on the local client and transmitted in encrypted form. Netscape browsers have a nice user interface feature, a blue bar, which lights up when you are in a secure transaction mode. In addition Netscape and

17. Reproduced from the digicash web page at: http://www.digicash.com/publish/digsig/digbig.html.

18. A FAQ on PGP is located at: http://www.quadralay.com/www/Crypt/PGP/pgp01.html.

other browsers will report that the information you are about to transmit is insecure, when you fill out forms. This is a configurable option.

1 • 6 • 2 Firewalls and Proxies

Many organizations are understandably reluctant to give outsiders access to their internal computer systems. Press stories about computer break-ins and hackers are a staple. The principle technical solution is to create a "firewall." The idea is to leave all of the organization's computing network infrastructure alone, but to have a single point through which outside traffic to and from the Internet, must pass. One particular system is designated as the firewall machine, and additional security measures can be taken on it. Restricted access based, for example, on the domain name can be implemented in the one firewall machine, which checks each request before passing the information on to the destination machine.

Once a firewall is set up, "proxy" servers must also be put into place for the users inside, behind the firewall. Proxy services invisibly look at requests and pass them to the outside world. For example, if I am behind a firewall and I make a request to ftp (File Transfer Protocol) a file from another machine outside, the ftp proxy machine first looks at my request, then passes it on and makes the connection. Proxies must be set up on a per–service basis. HTTP, FTP, Gopher and other services would each be given a designated proxy through which the information passes. Typically, these proxies are specified in a configuration portion of the Web browser.

From a technological point of view, security issues can be addressed in many ways. According to Nicholas Baran in an article "The Greatest Show on Earth,"[19]

> Today there are two basic approaches to secure electronic commerce. The first one focuses on protecting resources by securing individual servers and network sites. This access security is generally addressed by firewalls or other means of 'perimeter' security. The

19. "The Greatest Show on Earth" by Nicholas Baran, *Byte*, July 1995.

> second approach focuses on transaction security. Transaction security addresses unauthorized listening in or eavesdropping on buyer/seller communications; authentication, so both parties are confident they know who they're talking to; message integrity, so the message contents can't be changed or tampered with; and a nonrepudiable record of the transaction in the form of a receipt or signature.

Secure transactions are the critical piece of technology just beginning to be deployed that will enable meaningful electronic commerce. As a result confidential transactions and the use of anonymous digital cash are beginning to appear as realistic purchasing options.[20]

DigiCash has created Ecash, electronic cash with many of the advantages of real cash.

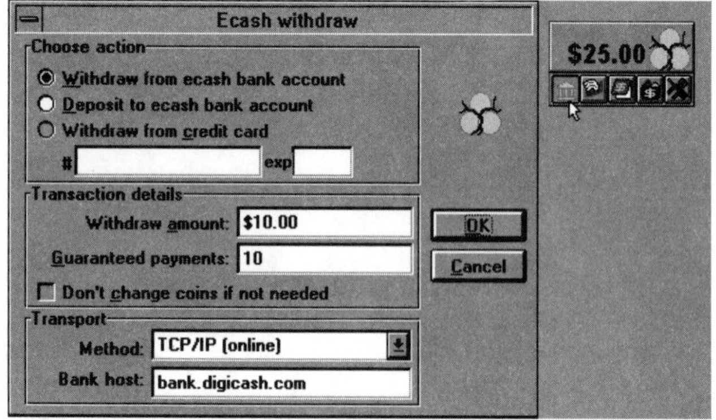

An Ecash withdrawal from a bank

In addition to anonymous cash transactions, secure credit card purchases will probably become even more widespread. The infrastructure for both the client browser and the merchant, is rapidly coming into place. One company trying to put all the pieces together is CyberCash.

20. For a good overview of this rapidly changing domain, check out the book *Frontiers of Electronic Commerce* by Kalakota and Whinston (Addison Wesley), 1996, or the Web site at: http://commerce.ssb.rochester.edu/book.html.

CyberCash's secure financial transaction technology is used by *Virtual Vineyards* to sell on-line wines. Unbeknownst to the buyer, the transaction, goes something like the following:

> Customer clicks on the cybercash icon, to establish a link between the customer, virtual vineyards, and the participating bank, Wells Fargo. The customer fills out credit card information and it is encrypted (using 768 bit encryption) and sent to the CyberCash server, which initiates a standard credit card authorization request to the bank. Once processed, CyberCash sends an electronic receipt and credit card authorization to Virtual Vineyards. The whole process takes several seconds.[21]

1 • 7 Commerce on the Web

The development of real electronic commerce will require the development of a number of business models. These models are currently very much in a state of flux. A few, however, are starting to appear.

An article focusing on real word electronic commerce by John Rhodes"[22] states:

> Several basic models for commerce on the Web have emerged: selling space, selling subscriptions, and selling goods or services.
>
> Space sales on the Web are similar to a conventional advertisement but with the addition of a "link" that lets customers click and go to the advertiser's own site for more information or further interactions....
>
> Subscriptions sales typically offer some "teaser information" to the Web audience while restricting access to the core of the site to users who have already registered and/or subscribed.
>
> Product/services sales are perhaps the most visible and talked-about new Web opportunity. At last count, more than 2,000 major store and nonstore retailers were active on the Web. Active selling sites run the gamut from niche product sales enterprises, such a

21. From "Virtual Vineyards Taps CyberCash's Technology by Shoba Naroyan in Oct 95 V1 No. 6 WebWeek.

22. Web At Work by John Rhodes, Nov 95 Multimedia Producer http://www.kipnet.com/mmp_nov95/web.html

> Royer's Flowers Direct[23], Computer Express[24], Art.Online[25] and Gadget Guru to supermarkets like Internet Shopping Network[26], and purveyors of financial information, such as Dun and Bradstreet.

One of the original organizations explicitly set up to explore the opportunities and problems of electronic commerce is CommerceNet[27]. The CommerceNet Consortium is a nonprofit association of companies engaged in various aspects of electronic commerce. The consortium has six working groups: Connectivity, Network Services, Payment Services, Directories and Catalogs, Internet EDI, and Engineering Data Transfer/Design-to-Manufacturing Integration. Check out the Web site for the details.

In addition to the consortium, CommerceNet has joined forces with Nielsen Media Research, which also does television ratings, to conduct Internet demographics surveys. As businesses try to sell products and services, it is increasingly critical to know who the audience is and what the demographics are. Partial results of the surveys are on-line at the CommerceNet Web site; with the full survey results costing $5000[28].

1 • 8 Customized Profiles

As the quantity of on-line information continues to explode, one of the principal problems users face is finding the information. Even if you happen to have a high speed Internet connection and lots of time to spend surfing from link to link, chances are you will not be able to scour all the relevant information

23. http://go.flowerlink.com/html/flink/pennsylvania/royers/royers.html

24. http://www.cexpress.com

25. http://bighorn.terra.net/artonline

26. http://gnn.com/gnn/bus/isn/index.html

27. http://www.commerce.net

28. Proceeds from sales of the survey are used to fund additional Internet research, conduct new Internet pilots/projects, and educate the public about the Internet.

sources. However Internet searching starting points such as Yahoo and Lycos have made it much easier to find information.

An alternative to spending the time searching yourself is to specify a set of topics or interests and have an automaton wander through the Web locating the information, and compiling it into a tidy summary. These personalized knowledge robots, knowbots, can spend the time locating information and you can review the results at your leisure.

Check out the World Wide Web Robots, Wanderers, and Spiders page for a list of over 70 web wandering programs. (See *Section 1 • 4 Worms, Spiders, and Knowbots* for more information on these.) Most are free. Many include source code. Some wanderers perform validation services, but most are used to generate resource discovery databases that can be searched at later times.

More traditional news clipping services have long been available for busy corporate executives. Although costly, they can prove invaluable.

Individual, Inc. offers a customized news service called First! It sifts through news. Its existing products include BookWire[29] and NewsPage.[30]

Dow Jones, a long–time provider of clipping services, offers a service called Custom Clips. The information can be delivered via email or fax. In addition it has a product called DowVision, which offers real time filtered news feeds from such information sources as *The Wall Street Journal*, Dow Jones News Service, and Press Release Wire services.

1 • 9 Internet Starting Points

"The Internet, of course, is more than just a place to find pictures of people having sex with dogs." — Time Magazine July 3, 1995

One major service that has come into existence since the creation of the Web are the so-called Internet Starting Points. They are also called Jumpstations,

29. Find it at http://www.bookwire.com.

30. Located at: http://www.newspage.com.

net directories, and any number of other names. These sites have turned the diverse information sites on the Web into usable information resources. It cannot be overstated how useful these services have become.

An important thing to keep in mind is that the search engines work and gather their information in different ways. Some index all words in the text of Web pages. Some have a human providing editorial guidance and presentation. Still others try to find information by concepts, not simply by keywords. If one source doesn't lead you to what you're after, try another.

The presentation of the material found also varies. Yahoo's more hand crafted approach is difficult to scale but easy to read. It incorporates the OpenText search engine with their subject categories for more automation. Lycos, AltaVista, eXcite, and InfoSeek are all reachable from the Net Search button on the NetScape button bar. Microsoft's Internet Explorer provides an equally convenient search button. In fact, the position of default Internet Starting Point within a browser is an important selling and marketing issue. Around February of 1996 Netscape changed its default from Yahoo to Infoseek, causing some distress at Yahoo.[31]

Netscape's Net Search button points to a page with over a dozen Internet Starting points. In March 1996 it described the services as follows. They are listed in here in alphabetical order:

ALTA VISTA

> Offering compact or detailed searches through what the company claims is the largest Web index, Digital Equipment Corporation's Alta Vista can help you find your way through 8 billion words filling 16 million Web pages. It also provides a full-text index of more than 13,000 newsgroups.

31. "Netscape Switch Has Chief Yahoo Upset :-(", WebWeek Feb. 1996

DEJANEWS

Search what the company claims is the world's largest publicly searchable Usenet news archive with DejaNews. Versatile search options allow you to find articles by date, author, subject, and newsgroup. Usenet is a powerful Internet resource; DejaNews helps put it to work for you.

THE ELECTRIC LIBRARY

Rather than searching the Web, check out the Electric Library's contents. Launch comprehensive searches across this deep database of more than 1000 full text newspapers, magazines, and academic journals, plus images, reference books, literature, and art.

EXCITE

Excite tracks down information by searching for concepts, not just keywords. Updated weekly, Excite's database contains what the company claims are more than 1.5 million Web pages, 50,000-plus Web page reviews written by journalists, the latest two weeks of Usenet news, and classifieds. Excite also includes City.Net, news from Reuters, and an interactive cartoon.

INFOSEEK GUIDE

This searchable directory provides reviews of popular Internet resources—Web sites, Usenet newsgroups, and FTP and Gopher sites—cross-referenced across multiple topics. Once you've found a relevant site, the "Find Similar" function searches for more of the same. The guide performs precise searches for specific phrases and proper names, and searches are sensitive to case, numbers, and special characters (for example, AT&T or 49ers).

LYCOS

This comprehensive catalog of the Internet finds what you need in seconds, including text, graphics, sounds, and videos. PC World magazine recently rated Lycos best of the top 11 Internet search engines in both quality of information and relevancy of results.

MAGELLAN

Explore Magellan, McKinley's Internet Guide. Magellan provides reviews and ratings for a vast collection of Web, FTP, and Gopher sites, and Usenet newsgroups. Users can browse Magellan topics or search specific keywords or phrases. Magellan's green-light feature indicates content that is deemed appropriate for general viewing.

NET LOCATOR

Jump to and between the results pages of your favorite finding tools. Net Locator from NlightN uses frames to give you quick access to a variety of on-line search services. Try it. You can type a search just once, then get the results pages from many search engines.

OPEN TEXT INDEX

The Open Text Index searches every word of every Web page the company has indexed—some 21 billion words and phrases in all. The company claims it's one of the largest indexes available. Pose queries of virtually any length, or focus in by searching only titles or links.

SEARCH.COM

clnet's search.com combines more than 250 search engines at one site to offer a single gateway to all the information on the Net. search.com, a service of clnet, offers access to all of the major search services, plus hundreds of specialized databases.

SHAREWARE.COM

clnet's shareware.com makes it simple to find software on the Internet. More than 170,000 files are available for easy searching, browsing, and downloading from shareware and corporate archives on the Internet. According to Newsweek, "shareware.com does for software what Yahoo did for finding Web sites."

WHO WHERE?

Fast, easy to use, and free, WhoWhere? is a comprehensive WhitePages service for locating people and organizations on the Net. WhoWhere? intuitively handles misspelled or incomplete names, and it lets you search by initials.

YAHOO!

Arguably the pioneer Internet guide, Yahoo has been accepting submissions since what seems like the beginning of it all. There's an editorial filter at work here—not every college student's home page makes it into the directory—but Yahoo's veteran status has allowed it to build a comprehensive cross-discipline resource base.

Finally, Yahoo is branching out to a service called Yahooligans an Internet starting point for kids. After all, they know how to use this stuff better than we old folks.

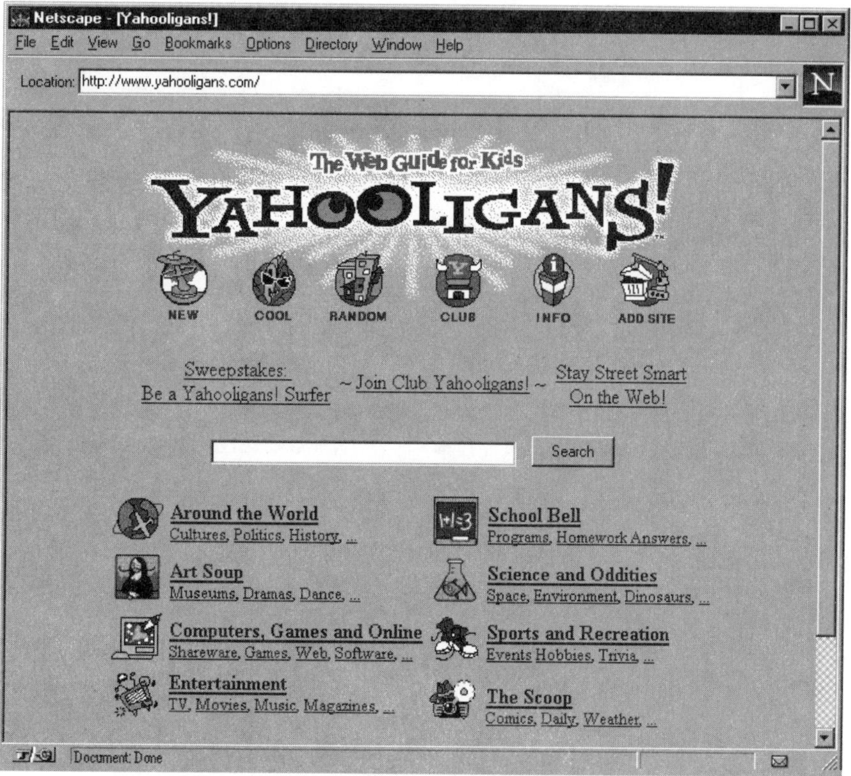

A children's oriented version of Yahoo!

1 • 10 Web Underlying Protocols

One of the Web's great strengths is standards. The following alphabet soup of standards from the formal standards world and the Internet standards world are part of the technical foundations of the Web.

1 • 10 • 1 URI

The URI or Universal Resource Identifier is a generic, all-encompassing term used to identify all Uniform Resource (UR) specifications. Other UR specifications are, by definition, part of the set of URs described by the URI.

In addition, work is ongoing on a Uniform Resource Citation (URC). A URC will be a set of attribute/value pairs describing an object. Some of the attributes include author, publisher, date, and copyright status.

1 • 10 • 2 URL

The Uniform Resource Locator (URL) specification is a way of naming and addressing objects on the Web. Following is the Abstract from the Internet Draft specification of Uniform Resource Locators (URL):

Internet Draft - CERN
Uniform Resource Locators (URL)

A Unifying Syntax for the Expression of Names and Addresses of Objects on the Network

Abstract

Many protocols and systems for document search and retrieval are currently in use, and many more protocols or refinements of existing protocols are to be expected in a field whose expansion is explosive.

These systems are aiming to achieve global search and readership of documents across differing computing platforms, and despite a plethora of protocols and data formats. As protocols evolve, gateways can allow global access to remain possible. As data formats evolve, format conversion programs can preserve global access. There is one area, however, in which it is impractical to make conversions, and that is in the names and addresses used to identify objects. This is because names and addresses of objects are passed on in so many ways, from the backs of envelopes to hypertext objects, and may have a long life.

A common feature of almost all the data models of past and proposed systems is something which can be mapped onto a concept of "object" and some kind of name, address, or identifier for that object. One can therefore define a set of name spaces in which these objects can be said to exist.

Practical systems need to access and mix objects that are part of different existing and proposed systems.

This paper discusses the requirements of a universal syntax that can be used to encapsulate a name in any registered name space. This will allow names in different spaces to be treated in a common way, even though names in different spaces have differing characteristics, as do the objects to which they refer.

The universal syntax applies to objects available using existing protocols, and may be extended with technology. It makes a recommendation for a generic syntax, and for specific forms for "Uniform Resource Locators" (URLs) of objects accessible using existing Internet protocols.

The syntax has been in widespread use by World-Wide Web software since 1990.

1 • 10 • 3 URN

The Uniform Resource Name (URN) associated with an item is meant to be a persistent name that would return a list of current URLs pointing to the item. The URN is assigned by an Internet naming authority, such as the Internet Assigned Number Authority (IANA). To take an example from a recent Open Systems Today article:

the URL of a file

ftp://ftp.uu.net/published/osys-today/urdrafts.tar.Z

The URN for the same file could be:

URNg1

IANA:merit.edu:9283492.

In the URN, the IANA indicates that the following organization (merit.edu) has the authority to assign URN IDs and that the subsequent number is the ID assigned by that organization.

Searching clients such as WAIS that use URN would return a list of URLs, one for each site containing the document. Over time, sites may delete or add the document, but the URN would always return the most recent list of URLs. URNs are still being debated in committees and will eventually emerge as an extremely significant protocol.

1 • 10 • 4 SGML/HTML

The Standard Generalized Markup Language (SGML) has grown in popularity and use corresponding to the growth of the Web. HTML, a specific SGML application, has fueled the growth and awareness of SGML. SGML is a markup language used primarily to define and mark up the structure of a document [SGML].

Logical document structures are the document's components: such as chapters, sections, headings, and paragraphs. Together they comprise the entire document. Instances of these logical document items are the document itself. For example, the name `<CHAP>` might refer to all chapters, a structural item of a document. "Chapter 3 - Web Feet" is a particular chapter.

The entire structure of a document is defined in a Document Type Definition (DTD), which is a kind of metalanguage. DTDs define the structure of documents in a rigorous, formal manner. Once a DTD is defined, authors can write documents that conform to the DTD. In the case of the Web, authors create documents that conform to the HTML DTD. Applications do not necessary enforce conformance. This often causes confusion as one person's document "worked just fine," but has problems when viewed on another browser. Indeed, the HTML DTD did not, keep pace with HTML features for some time.

1 • 10 • 5 Z39.50

Z39.50 is a protocol for search and retrieval tasks usually associated with the library information retrieval community. A glossary entry[32] explaining Z39.50 states that the Z39.50 protocol is the "name of the national standard developed by the National Information Standards Organization (NISO) that defines an applications level protocol by which one computer can query another computer and transfer resulting records, using a canonical format." This protocol provides the framework for On-line Public Access Catalog (OPAC), which people use to search remote catalogs on the Internet using the commands of their local systems. Projects now in development will provide Z39.50 support for catalogs on the Internet. Search and Retrieval (SR), ISO Draft International Standard 10162/10163, is the international version of Z39.50.[33]

1 • 10 • 6 MIME

After years of experiments and non-standard, non-interoperating implementations, multimedia mail has yet to become widespread on the Internet or elsewhere, outside of isolated communities. Multipurpose Internet Mail Extensions (MIME), a standards-track Internet format defined by an Internet Engineering Task Force Working Group, offers a simple standardized way to represent and encode a wide variety of media types, including textual data in non-ASCII character sets, for transmission via Internet mail. MIME extends RFC 822 in a manner that is simple and completely backward-compatible, yet flexible and open to extension. In addition to enhanced functionality for Internet mail, the new mechanism offers the promise of interconnecting X.400 "islands" without the loss of functionality currently found in X.400-to-Internet gateways. This paper describes the general approach and rationale of the new mechanisms for Internet multimedia mail.[34]

32. From the "Internet Terms Glossary" of URLS located at http://www.vtls.com/glossary.html.

33. See http://www.research.att.com/~wald/pe-doc.txt "Z39.50 in plain english" by Clifford Lynch for more information.

34. Nathaniel Borenstein, Internet Multimedia Mail with MIME: Emerging Standards for Interoperability. ULPAA'92 Vancouver, May 1992.

MIME's influence has gone far beyond email. Mosaic and Gopher use the MIME protocol as a mechanism to communicate various data types. Associating applications with data types enables end users to launch special–purpose viewers for special purpose data types. This provides an extensible capability to applications that otherwise would remain closed or difficult to modify.

1 • 10 • 7 HTTP

HTTP—the HyperText Transfer Protocol—is the native network protocol used by Web.

The following comes from the Internet Draft of the IETF[35] HTTP specification:

Abstract[36]

> HTTP is a protocol with the lightness and speed necessary for a distributed collaborative hypermedia information system. It is a generic stateless object-oriented protocol, which may be used for many similar tasks such as name servers, and distributed object-oriented systems, by extending the commands, or "methods", used. A feature of HTTP is the negotiation of data representation, allowing systems to be built independently of the development of new advanced representations.

One recent development is S-HTTP, the Commerce Net Secure HTTP Proposal. According to a draft:[37]

> Secure HTTP has been designed to enable incorporation of various cryptographic message format standards into Web clients and servers, including, but not limited to, PKCS-7, PEM, and PGP. S-HTTP supports interoperation among a variety of implementations, and is backward compatible with HTTP. S-HTTP aware clients can talk to S-HTTP oblivious servers and vice-versa, although such transactions obviously would not use S-HTTP security features.

35. The IETF, Internet Engineering Task Force, is one of the governing bodies of the Internet.

36. See http://info.cern.ch/hypertext/WWW/Protocols/HTTP/HTTP2.html for the nitty gritty on HTTP.

37. See http://www.commerce.net/cgi-bin/textit?/information/standards/drafts/shttp.txt

S-HTTP does not require client-side public key certificates (or public keys), supporting a symmetric session key operation mode. This is significant because it means that spontaneous private transactions can occur without requiring individual users to have an established public key. While S-HTTP will be able to take advantage of ubiquitous certification infrastructures, its deployment does not require it.

S-HTTP supports end-to-end secure transactions, in contrast with the existing de-facto HTTP authorization mechanisms which require the client to attempt access and be denied before the security mechanism is employed. Clients may be "primed" to initiate a secure transaction (typically using information supplied in an HTML anchor); this may be used to support encryption of fill-out forms, for example. With S-HTTP, no sensitive data need ever be sent over the network in the clear.

1 • 11 The Ubiquitous Web

Clearly, the Internet and Web have become ubiquitous. Television commercials show Web addresses. News broadcasts tell you to check their Web weather site. National magazines like *Business Week* and *Information Week* have advertiser indices with URLs. Radio shows tell you to send email and check their Web site for communication and archived shows. Billboards announce advertiser's sites. All this has occurred in just a short couple of years.

With maturation comes ratings. In particular two ratings services, Magellan and Point Communications, rate sites. Those that pass can put icons declaring their success on their home page. Magellan rates sites with one to four stars. Point gives a site the coveted "Top 5% of All Web Sites" award if it is rated sufficiently high.

The Internet is not new. Lots of information has been available *if* you knew how to get it. The Web has changed everything. The vast collection of information is now accessible via the Web browser to the common, non technical, person.

It seems likely that the expansion to the general public which hasn't happened yet, is also just around the corner. A network–capable computer called an Internet Appliance is already being sold. It costs less than $500. Success is not assured but all of the pieces are coming together.

The final infrastructure is the Cable modem. The same cables that bring you Cable TV can also bring you high bandwidth Internet connections at reasonable costs.

All of these converging technologies may provide greater easier and more democratic access to information. They may also cause a greater rift between the haves and have nots or society. Only time will tell. Either way these are exciting times, as these fundamental societal changes take place.

Chapter 2 • World Wide Web—the Next Generation

"I never think of the future. It comes soon enough." —Albert Einstein

On the Web, the next generation is rapidly approaching. It is in fact, constantly evolving. This chapter profiles a few of the exciting developments on the horizon.

2 • 1 Java/HotJava

In the overheated realm of the Web, it is probably accurate to characterize Sun Microsystems' Java as the white hot leader of the pack. Simply put Java, brings action to the Web, which currently consists of inactive, static document elements. First, let's clarify some terms.

Java is a new computer language. **HotJava** is a Web browser implemented in Java.[1] According to Bill Joy, co-founder of Sun, Java is "C++ done right". Java is an interpreted language. Little chunks of Java code are sent through the net to the browser and when appropriate they execute, right there on the user's machine. Those little chunks of code are called applets. In current Web browsers, text, graphics, and sounds just sit there. Applets can make the graphics animate, the sounds play, and the text move.

According to the Sun White Paper on Java, Java is[2]:

> "Java: A simple, object-oriented, distributed, interpreted, robust, secure, architecture neutral, portable, high-performance, multithreaded, and dynamic language."

This is a mouthful any way you slice it. However, the body of the white paper is interestingly written and goes on to explain the relevance of each of the admitted buzz words to Java.

Java's result is the ability to interact with graphics, sounds, and text in new and compelling ways. For example, a cube appearing on the Web document page can be spun around, a button will detect the presence of a cursor, buttons can highlight when a cursor is near, and image maps can show you where those invisible hot spots really are. To take one example: a HotJava page contains a stock market ticker tape with some animated strip charts and a dynamically updated table. [3]

The toolkit you use to develop Java applets is called the Java Development Kit (JDK). The JDK includes a nice utility called the appletviewer. The appletviewer takes an HTML file as its input and runs the Java applet. You don't have to be on-line. It is very convenient.

1. "Software's Other Bill" by Antony Perkins, *The Red Herring*, Oct. 1995,
2. The Java Language: An Overview, located at http://java.sun.com/doc/Overviews/java/java-overview-1.html.
3. Visit the main Sun Java Web site demo pages to look at the ticker tape, at: http://java.sun.com.

The Applet Viewer running a sample applet.

Java also addresses many of the problems of portable code. Because it is an interpreted language you simply port a Java interpreter to a particular hardware platform. Most Java code, and the applications should run on that platform. This technique is not new; UCSD Pascal, Smalltalk, and Lisp have used the same idea in the past. As soon as HotJava browsers appear on different computing platforms, the applet Java code can be executed on those platforms.

The interpreted nature of Java also allows the HotJava Web browser to adapt new data types on the fly. If a new sound or video compression format sweeps the Net, Java–based browsers will be able to adapt rather than being upgraded. The HotJava White Paper describes this capability:[4]

> HotJava's dynamic behavior is also used for understanding different types of objects. For example, most Web browsers can understand a small set of image formats (typically GIF, X11 pixmap, and X11 bitmap). If they see some other type, they have no way to deal with it directly. HotJava, on the other hand, can dynamically link the Java code from the host that has the image, allowing it to display the new format. So, if someone invents a new compression algorithm, the inventor just has to make sure that a copy of the Java code is installed on the server that contains the images the inventor wants to publish. All the other browsers

4. *The HotJava Browser: A White Paper*, located at: http://java.sun.com//doc/overview/hotjava/browser-whitepaper.ps

in the world will have to be upgraded to take advantage of the new algorithm. HotJava upgrades itself on the fly when it sees this new type.

Netscape includes a Java interpreter with its second–generation browser. Microsoft has also licensed Java for use with its Web browser, the Internet Explorer. Sun wisely decided to open up its technology to all rather than put yet another browser out onto the Net.

2 • 2 Netscape 2 and Beyond

Netscape, the Web company to watch, seems to be run by a bunch of kids snatched right out of their college cradles into instant entrepreneurial stardom. Started by Marc Andresson and most of the other original creators of Mosaic, with the able assistance of Jim Clark, who started Silicon Graphics, Netscape has recently announced a flurry of new products packed with new features. Actually Netscape is almost constantly introducing new features as it tries to remain ahead of Microsoft in "The Browser War."

Reportedly, Netscape has captured 70-85% of the Web browser business. It certainly seem to get enough hits on its site: in Feb. 1996 they were claiming to get 40 million hits per day, and by April 1996 50 million hits per day! Netscape 2.0 will solidify that margin if its new features are used. Authors will be able to create compelling new content that will only be viewable on the Netscape browser. Other browsers makers will probably either follow Netscape's lead or start screaming for more adherence to standards. Only time will tell.

Let's look at the technical changes new to Netscape 2.0. The two major items are the incorporation of a Java interpreter and the capability of adding "plug-ins." Plug-ins enable third-party vendors to write code that cooperates with Netscape through a clearly defined Application Program Interface (API). For example Adobe has created an Acrobat API that enables Netscape to display Acrobat PDF files inline; it's called Amber. Other plug-ins under development include Apple's QuickTime for digital video and Macromedia Director Player, called Shockwave, for full multimedia interaction. All these media types are presented to the user in-line on the Web page. The inclusion of a Java interpreter allows for dynamic elements such as animations and live information updating to also appear in-line. (See *Section 2 • 1 Java/HotJava* for more details.) These dynamic elements are possible through the inclusion of Java applets (mini programs) right in the HTML document.

In addition to these major technical and architectural changes described, Netscape 2.0 adds a feature called Frames. Frames are primarily a graphic design and user interaction enhancement. A page can have multiple frames; each frame refers to a separate URL. These multiple rectangular page areas can be scrolled independently and can also independently submit queries and display results.

Static areas for such things as button bars and tables of contents are called Ledges. As you can imagine Frames and Ledges may lead to a lot of "graphic abuse" on the Web. Ledges can also solve an interesting problem faced by Web advertisers. You are probably familiar with those often–annoying rectangular graphic ads on the tops and bottoms of web pages. A Web site can place an ad in a Ledge and it will just sit there, not interfering with the rest of the ever–changing document. Infoseek and Web searching service has begun to do this.

As this book was nearing completion, new versions of Netscape were being beta–tested. The next version, Netscape 3.0, also called the "Atlas" version, continues the frenzied pace of change. Atlas fixes the annoying "Back" behavior introduced by Frames. In version 2, the Back button does not now take you "back" a Frame if only the frame changed; you must use a menu item for that. The previous Back behavior was an annoying user interface change. However, never let it be said that the Netscape folks don't admit to mistakes and learn from them.

The mail facility is more robust and adds some drag and drop capabilities. Continuing the dreadful trend of HTML "enhancements," Netscape 3 now allows individual table cells to have different background colors.

On the plug-in front, a streaming audio plug-in is included with the Live3D (formerly WebFX) VRML browser and an AVI digital movie player. The most interesting software included with the release is CoolTalk.

CoolTalk is a suite of software for collaborative computing. It includes a real–time audio tool to literally talk to other users, much like Internet phone–type products. More significantly it includes a full-featured white board that people can share. While the audio is nice it's unclear how useful it is due to the bandwidth limitations of modems.

However, the white board is clearly a big winner. The first time I tried it I connected to some chap I first thought was in another state. It turned out that he was across the globe in Israel. We shared drawings and chatted (yes, there is also a chat tool), and it really worked! This type of facility used to cost many thousands of dollars and a significant workstation. CoolTalk is by InSoft Inc. You can visit them at: http://ice.insoft.com.

2 • 3 Integrated Chat

"I know a lot of people without brains who do an awful lot of talking."
— The Scarecrow, Wizard of OZ

Chat systems offer users the ability to congregate in "virtual rooms" using only textual interfaces to talk to each other. Internet Relay Chat (IRC), is the protocol used to support this interface. The results can be quite amusing. With the coming of the Web and technologies such as 3D interfaces, via VRML, users are being offered new types of interfaces on top of the traditional chat services.

One approach is to simply offer a "helper" application that is integrated with a Web browser. The Global Chat client by Prospero Systems is just this type of application.[5] Prospero Systems also created Global Chat client and Global Stage server.[6] They offer chat servers in three friendly sizes: the cafe, the theater, and, the stadium.

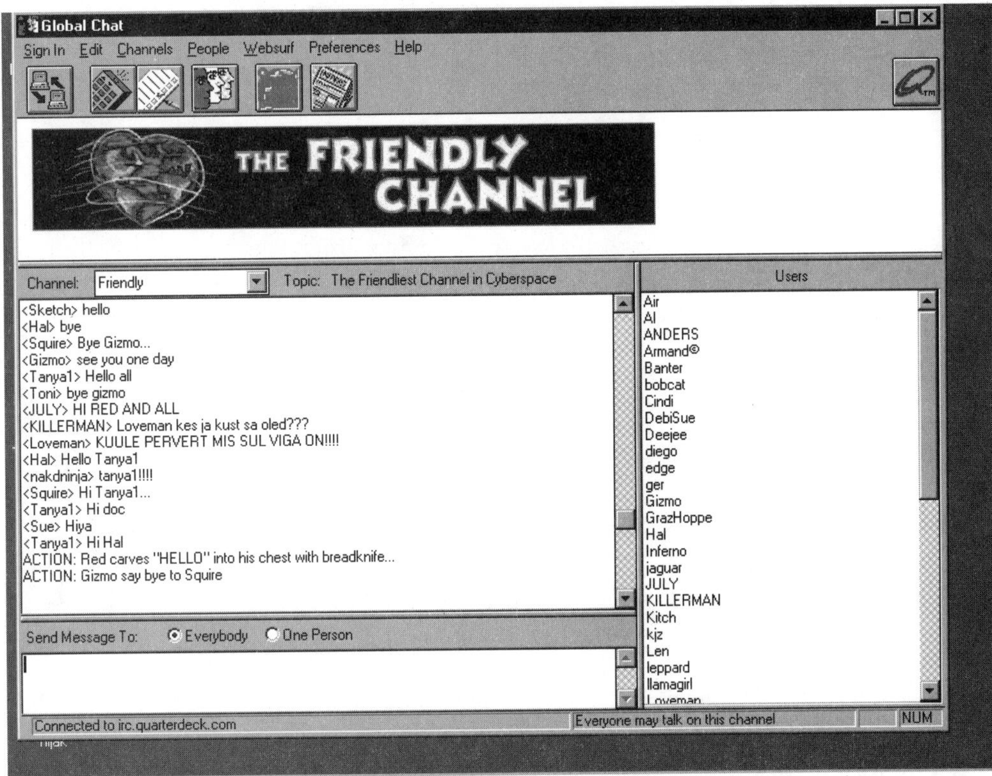

Quarterdeck's Global Chat stand-alone or helper chat application.

2 • 3 • 1 Ubique

One fascinating extension to the Web comes from a company called Ubique Ltd. This Israeli start-up company has created something called Virtual Places. It works either as an extension to existing browsers or with a modified Mosaic browser called Sesame. Ubique was acquired in mid–1995 by AOL.

5. Prospero has been acquired by Quarterdeck, http://www.quarterdeck.com.

6. http://www.prospero.com/globalchat

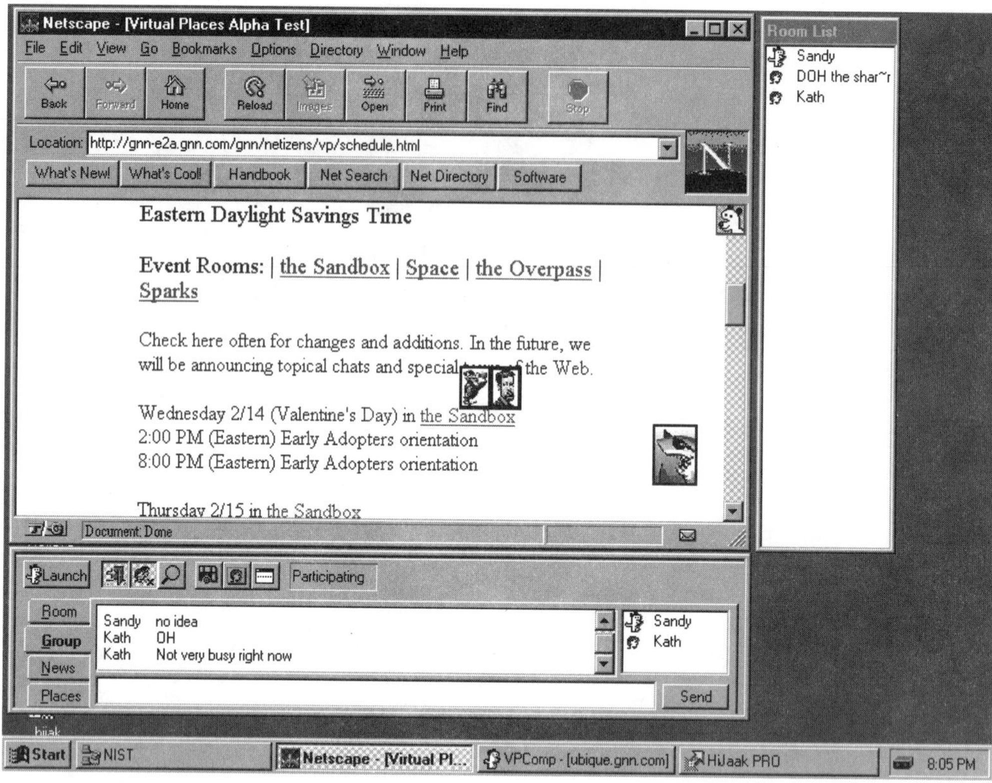

Ubique's Virtual Places running with Netscape and icons on a page for people. The chat log on the bottom window gives a history of the conversation.

Ubique's technology offer three basic capabilities: integrated chat and Web browser; real time audio communications; and guided tours, either automated or with a tour guide. Let's take a brief look at each.

Users are visually represented in a Virtual Place by an icon. You can select from among the variety of existing cartoony icons or design your own, such as a small photo of your face.

When you go to a Web site that is running a Virtual Places server, you can place your icon on the page. This lets other people click on your icon, signaling the desire to start a conversation. If you start a chat, an extra line on the bottom of the Sesame Web browser displays the chat.

If you and the person you are chatting with have a fast enough Internet connection and the right sound hardware, you can start talking. Yep, you can use thousands of dollars of computing hardware and the Internet to replace a telephone. Actually, it is useful for quick conversations, though the sound quality is variable and dependent on the bandwidth of the moment. Furthermore, it's cute as all hell and makes a great demo. (See *Section 2 • 6 Streaming Technologies-Audio/Video* for information on these products.)

The most interesting capability Ubique offers is the guided tour. Basically, you can, offer people a ride on a magic carpet. Up to 10 people can get on the carpet with you. After all are aboard, you can surf the Web, showing people whatever you want. Their Sesame Web browser goes along for the ride. This is a fabulous way of showing people Web sites.

With the purchase of Ubique by AOL, the magic carpet facility has been converted into the AOL Road Trip. AOL itself offers many of its own Road Trips, and users can create their own. After you create a Road Trip, you can enter a chat room and ask others to hop on for a ride.

To top it all off, you can set up a script that acts as a little automaton and takes people on tours. In this way, people can be guided though the wonders of your Web site without your actually being there.

2 • 3 • 2 Web and Real Time Audio

Another interesting capability is the increasing interest in the Internet as a replacement for the telephone. While I don't think AT&T has anything to worry about, the possibilities are intriguing. The potential lies primarily with the integration of live audio with other computing activities.

Some interesting products are just beginning to appear. Two are the Internet Phone from Vocaltec, and PowWow from Tribal Voice. Of the two, PowWow seems geared more towards integration with the Web, and Internet Phone more as a replacement for the telephone.

Real conversations are difficult because of the half–duplex nature of most sound cards and the software. This means that the sound can only go in one direction at a time, rather like 1970's CB radio conversations. You need to say "hello how are you...over" or something like that to indicate that you're finished talking. It is a great way to talk to people overseas and in faraway lands without paying the phone company though.

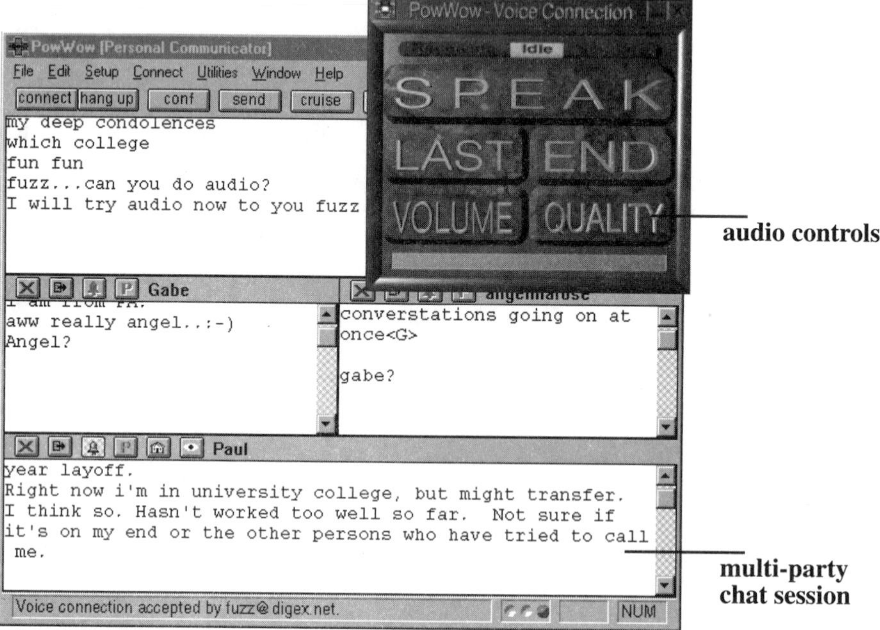

PowWow multi-party chat windows and audio control panel.

In terms of integration, the PowWow people have a leg up. They work with a URL that uses the "powwow" protocol and is integrated more with Web browsers. For example a Web page might have the PowWow icon on it. When selected it executes a URL that looks like: "powwow:sandy@interramp.com." This URL would cause your running PowWow process to try to contact my running PowWow process. With a successful connection we could chat via typing or with audio.

Another nice integration feature of PowWow is its ability to take people on a Web "cruise." Once you establish yourself as cruise leader, you can use your Web browser to surf the Web, and all other members of the Web will "travel" with you, using their Web browsers. This is virtually the same as the Ubique "road trip."

Finally, there is PGPfhone developed by Phil Zimmerman of Pretty Good Privacy (PGP) fame. PGP, is the encryption software that has gotten Zimmerman into hot water with the U.S. government on numerous occasions, and elevated him into a "cause celebre" with the right to privacy advocates. PGPfhone is a free encrypted audio system than enables users to have secure audio conversations. PGPfone is distributed by MIT. Depending on the resolution of various export control laws, PGPfone may be available only for citizens of the United States and Canada.

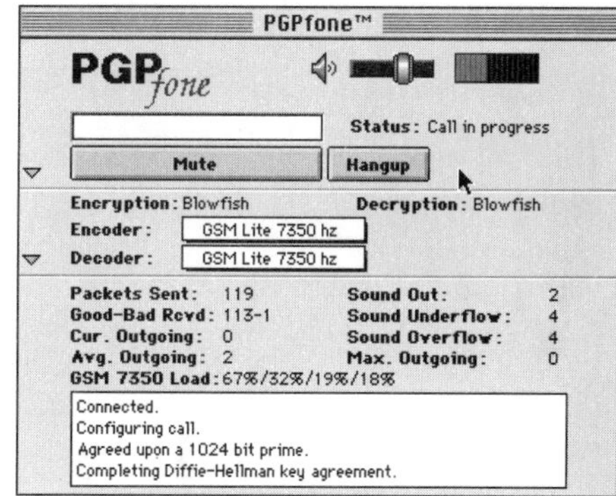

PGPfone, encrypted audio software.

2 • 4 3D Interfaces (VRML)

"Reality is whatever refuses to go away when I stop believing in it." - Philip K. Dick

One of the most compelling ways to look at the Web is through a three–dimensional interface. Virtual Reality Modeling Language (VRML) allows authors to build 3D worlds. Eventually, you will be able to interact with other people, see their avatars, (their visual stand-in), and collaborate on work, or just chat.

2 • 4 • 1 VRML

VRML is the Web's answer to adding 3D user interfaces to your browsing experience. A 3D graphical environment representing a store, shopping mall, house, museum, library, human body, or anything else you can imagine can become a user interface. Through it you can potentially access Webs of information about topics that match the various environments in intuitive spatial ways.

How it all started.

One of the strengths of VRML, and one reason it emerged and became popular so quickly, was the wise decision not to reinvent everything. VRML 1.0 is based on Silicon Graphics Open Inventor. The decision to use a subset of Open Inventor was quite controversial. Ultimately, pragmatics and the willingness of Silicon Graphics to contribute a parser and the specification to the public won the day. In the words of Mark Pesce the principal VRML cheerleader concerning Open Inventor, "it was already debugged." Pesce managed to promulgate compelling visions of a 3D Web, and, quite simply VRML caught fire.[7]

What it is and what it isn't

VRML is really not all that complicated... yet. It is simply another 3D modeling language, but with one crucial difference: it associates URLs with those objects. In some sense, this is not all that major a development. There are probably dozens of ways of representing 3D models. But 3D Web interfaces *are* important. They bring the full potential of complex, realistic computer graphics into an intimate relationship with the Web and the information available there. This stuff isn't just cool (which it is) and fun (which it also is); it's useful and intuitive. A VRML world, of a "museum" through which you could wander and get information, is a simple yet powerful user interface.

7. VRML was and continues to be refined with the participation of many people in a mailing–list discussion www-vrml@wired.com. In addition several Usenet newsgroups such as comp.lang.vrml exist for discussions.

VRML also has clever mechanisms of referring to files via URLs to create worlds, something "normal" 3D modeling languages also lack. The WWWinline statement, part of VRML, is like a C language `#include` statement or macro expansion, and lets you create worlds by referring to other files that are included in the main world. The reference to a file, however, can be a URL pointing to a file on any Web–accessible machine. Therefore, complex worlds created with files distributed all over the globe are realistic.

Another novel use of VRML is to help visualize the statistics of activity on a Web site. The `vrstat` perl program, developed by Denis Leconte, can produce 3D bar charts that can be spun around in real time using a VRML browser such as Live3D. While it's unclear how useful this is yet, it makes a great demo, and extensions will clearly make it useful.

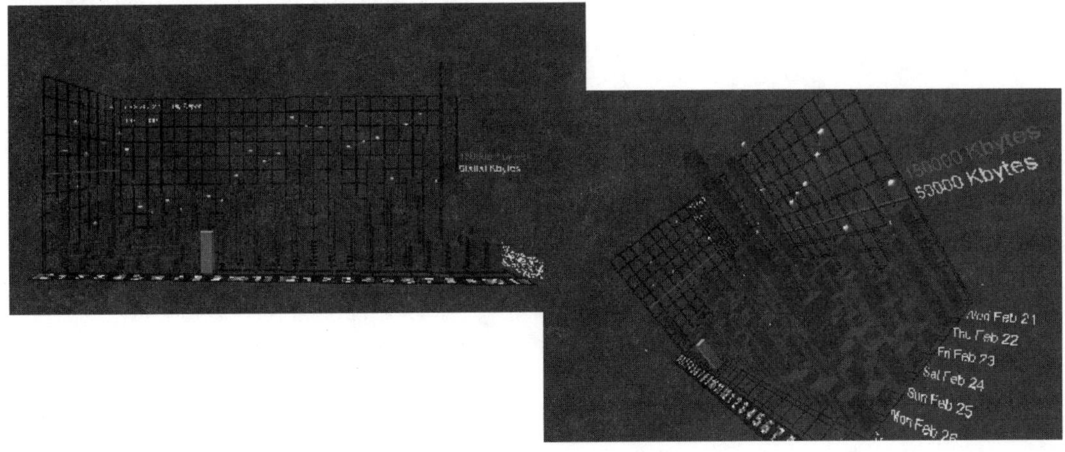

Two views of the VRML output of vrstat, Web site statistics.

2 • 4 • 2 VRML 2.0 – Moving Worlds

Now it's time for VRML The Next Generation, actually called VRML 2.0. After a frenzied year activity, more extreme hyper–frenzy took place because of the VRML community's desire to put behaviors into the models. One proposal the "Moving Worlds" specification, led by Silicon Graphics, Sony and a several others, garnered so much support that Netscape decided to endorse it and buy the leading VRML browser company, Paper Software Inc., makers of WebFX. Politics aside VRML 2.0 is a quantum leap beyond 1.0.

VRML 2.0 has many new features. The most significant change is the addition of behavior. With VRML 1.0 you can travel around in a cyberspace world, but it's a dead world. Nothing moves or reacts to you. With VRML 2.0, objects can execute scripts that cause them or other objects to take some programmed action. The Moving Worlds proposal[8] explains:

> VRML 1.0 provided a means of creating and viewing static 3D worlds; VRML 2.0 will provide much more. The overarching goal of the Moving Worlds proposal for VRML 2.0 is to provide a richer, more exciting, more interactive user experience than is possible within the static boundaries of VRML 1.0. The secondary goals of the proposal are to provide a solid foundation that future VRML expansion can grow out of, and to keep things as simple and as fast as possible — for everyone from browser developers to world designers to end users — given the other goals.
>
> Moving Worlds provides these extensions and enhancements to VRML 1.0:
>
> •*Enhanced static worlds*
>
> •*Interaction*
>
> •*Animation*
>
> •*Prototyping*
>
> **Enhanced Static Worlds**
>
> You can add realism to the static geometry of your world using new features of Moving Worlds:
>
> New nodes allow you to create ground-and-sky backdrops to scenes, add distant mountains and clouds, and dim distant objects with fog. Another new node lets you easily create irregular terrain instead of using flat planes for ground surfaces.

8. The Moving Worlds Proposal can be found at: http://webspace.sgi.com/moving-worlds/MW.full.html.

Moving Worlds provides sound-generating nodes to further enhance realism -- you can put crickets, breaking glass, ringing telephones, or any other sound into a scene.

If you're writing a browser, you'll be happy to see that optimizing and parsing files are easier than in VRML 1.0, thanks to a new simplified scene graph structure.

Interaction

No more moving like a ghost through cold, dead worlds: now you can directly interact with objects and creatures you encounter. New sensor nodes set off events when you move in certain areas of a world and when you click certain objects. They even let you drag objects or controls from one place to another. Another kind of sensor keeps track of the passage of time, providing a basis for everything from alarm clocks to repetitive animations.

And no more walking through walls. Collision detection ensures that solid objects react like solid objects; you bounce off them (or simply stop moving) when you run into them. Terrain following allows you to travel up and down steps or ramps.

Animation

Moving Worlds wouldn't be able to move without the new Script nodes. Using Scripts, you can not only animate creatures and objects in a world, but give them a semblance of intelligence. Animated dogs can fetch newspapers or frisbees; clock hands can move; birds can fly; robots can juggle.

These effects are achieved by means of events; a script takes input from sensors and generates events based on that input which can change other nodes in the world. Events are passed around among nodes by way of special statements called routes.

Prototyping

Have an idea for a new kind of geometry node that you want everyone to be able to use? Got a nifty script that you want to turn into part of the next version of VRML? In Moving Worlds, you can encapsulate a group of nodes together as a new node type, a prototype, and then make that node type available to anyone who wants to use it. You can then create instances of the new type, each with different field values -- for instance, you could create a Robot prototype with a robotColor field, and then create as many individual different-colored Robot nodes as you like.

The scripts associated with Moving World Nodes can be in several languages, particularly Java. Also note that Paper Software Inc., now owned by Netscape, is the developer of Live3D, the Netscape VRML plug-in, which will follow the Moving Worlds proposal.

Finally one area being delayed a little for standardization is that of multi-user interaction. Everyone in the VRML community wants to be able to create worlds in which people can meet and share an environment. This is being left for further addendums to VRML 2.0 but the possibilities are wide open such as networked games. This is one area to watch closely.

2 • 4 • 3 Authoring VRML

Creating a VRML world is not as simple as creating a Web page. You need an authoring tool. Although readable, VRML files, are generally pretty nasty, filled with lots of polygons and lighting definitions. Modifying VRML with a text editor is doable but it is not a pleasant experience.

VRML authoring tools are popping up all over. World–building systems such as Virtus Walkthrough and Caligari, have been around for a few years and are adding VRML as a file format they can create.

If you happen to have a Silicon Graphics workstation you can use WebSpaceAuthor. This tool is as close as you can get to WYSIWYG VRML authoring. It has controls for specialized VRML constructs such as levels of detail (LOD), links, and inlines.

Using these tools, you create the world visually and associate the URLs easily. As these tools mature they will provide more support for VRML features, such as file references via URL and the definition of predefined viewpoints. The result will undoubtedly be more creative integration of VRML worlds with the Web.

2 • 4 • 4 Integration with other Net Technologies

The integration of chat services and VRML worlds offers another host of possibilities. Imagine the touring capability of Ubique taking you along on a VRML ride. You will talk to store clerks, in cyber malls. Tour guides will show you around their cyber museum.

Worlds Chat from Worlds Inc. is a fascinating social 3D environment. It offers users the ability to pick a persona, an avatar, and wander around, chatting with other people in the environment. The environment has numerous clever dimensions and designs, plus sounds effects to complete the ambiance. Worlds Inc. also offer another more complex environment called AlphaWorld, where you can claim land and build structures. As time goes by, more and more complex architectures and spaces are being created.

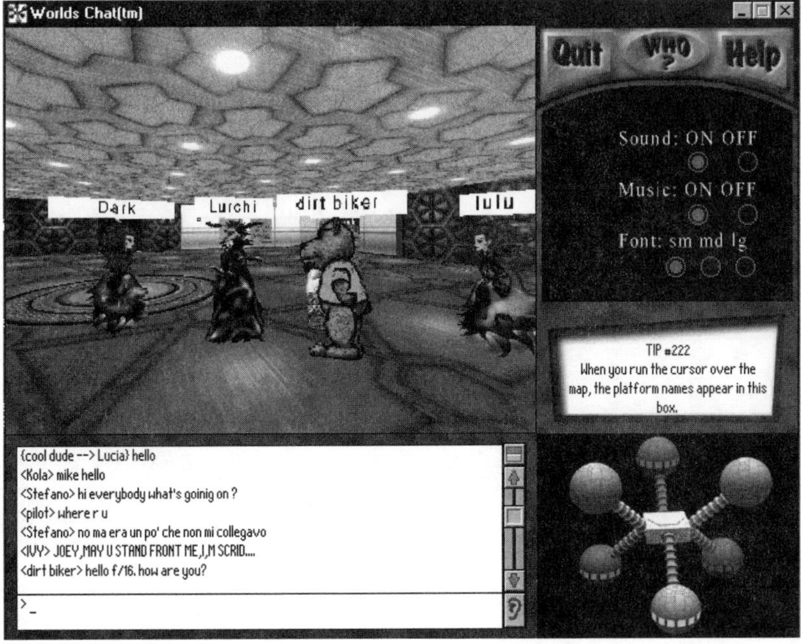

A scene from Worlds Chat, a VRML based, social chat environment.

One of the most robust, new environments, is CyberGate from Black Sun Interactive. The folks at Black Sun have teamed with Point Communications, which rates Web sites to create an environment with lots of useful links.

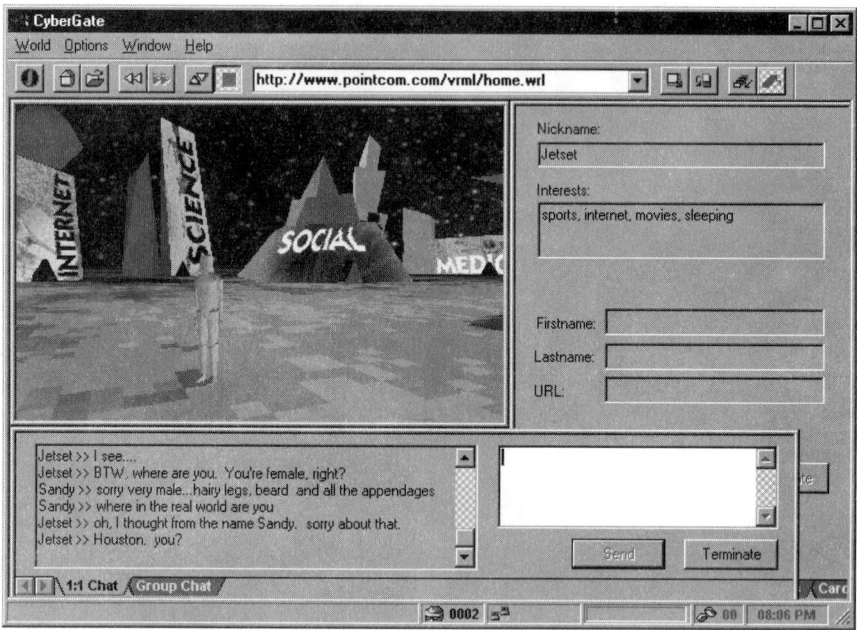

CyberGate a VRML based information space with hundreds of URL links

As this book went to press, VRML was undergoing major changes. In a one–year period, VRML went from an interesting but pie-in-the-sky Web format to a mainstream application. Sun, Silicon Graphics, and Microsoft are all putting significant investments and marketing resources into the concept of 3D graphics for the Web. All these players, quite naturally, have different perspectives on the direction of the specification. Only time will tell how it will all play out. Several things are clear, however. First and foremost, VRML will become not merely another 3D graphics specification, but one which allows networked interaction. Objects can be imbued with behavior and users can interact with these objects which often will be stand–ins, or avatars, for their human counterparts.

One example of the true potential of these integrated technologies comes from Starbright World. The Starbright Pediatric Network is an experiment at connecting seriously ill children, in hospitals, with an avatar–based virtual world. In this world the children can talk to other seriously ill children and play games with each other in the virtual world. These types of distractions and interactions can lessen the boredom and isolation felt by children experiencing long hospital stays.

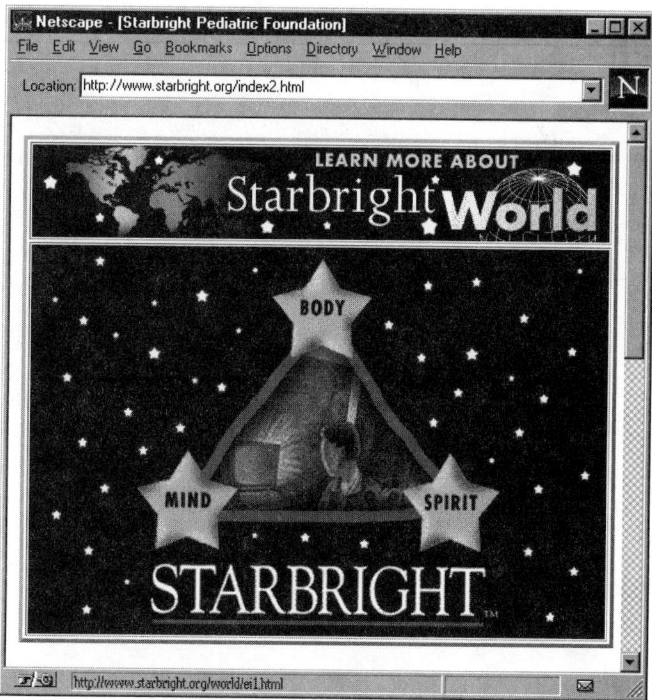

The Starbright World home page, a pediatric network for sick children.

The two major approaches to adding behavior are epitomized by the SGI-Sun approach and the Microsoft approach. SGI, Sun and Netscape have all agreed to use Sun's Java as a language to program behaviors and embed them in 3D objects. Microsoft has come up with its own proposal, known as ActiveVRML, based on a functional programming language called ML. All these parties will battle it out in the marketplace.

With Netscape's release of Live3D integrated applications are starting to appear. One demo shows the lunar lander on the moon. Clicking on the astronaut of the lander causes a connection, via RealAudio to play back, out of NASA archives, actual audio from Apollo 11.

2 • 4 • 5 Microsoft's ActiveVRML

Microsoft's entry into the 3D Web world comes via a technology called ActiveVRML. ActiveVRML is part of a suite of "Active" Internet technologies called ActiveX. It appears that ActiveX is really Microsoft's answer to Java, but we'll have to wait and see who wins that battle.

ActiveVRML is based on a functional programming language. It is elegant, but not the successor to VRML 1.0. Another proposal, "Moving Worlds," was selected as the one upon which to "standardize". From the Microsoft document "A Brief Introduction to ActiveVRML":[9]

> To allow the creation of interactive animations to be as natural as possible, ActiveVRML is based on a simple and intuitively familiar view of the world; that is, as a hybrid of continuous variations and discrete events. For example, the behavior of a bouncing ball consists of continuous trajectories and discrete collisions. Trajectories cause collision events, and collision events cause new trajectories.
>
> Using ActiveVRML, one can create simple or sophisticated animations without programming in the usual sense of the word. For example:

- *Although many frames are generated in presenting an animation, the author is freed from any notion of sampling or frame generation, but rather describes how various animation parameters vary continuously with time, user input, and other parameters.*
- *An author describes events influencing an animation and the effects of these events on the animation. The*

9. You can find the ActiveVRML document at: http://www.microsoft.com/intdev/avr/avrml001.htm.

author is freed from the programming mechanics of checking for events and causing the effects to happen.

- *Although animations involve an extremely high degree of simultaneity (concurrency), the author is freed from such programming issues as multi-threading.*
- *Linguistically, there are no statements (commands) that are executed for their effect, but rather expressions that are analyzed for their value. ActiveVRML uses this approach to make specifying animations as natural as possible, while simultaneously retaining maximal opportunities for optimization.*[10]

Here's a sample fragment of ActiveVRML code:[11]

> So in AVRML we will create a transformation that changes with time, and attach that transformation to a new copy of the ball. The result is a new ball with the inherent property (just like color or texture) that it has a position at all times specified by the transformation applied to it, which is itself dependent on time. Here's the code fragment...:

```
// read in a ball from disk

Ball = readGeometry("sphere.wrl");

// create something that moves objects

Motion = translate(time, 0, 9 - (time - 3)^2);

// make a new ball that moves over time

FlyingBall = transformGeometry(Motion, Ball);
```

> The second line creates a thing called Motion. You can think of this as a property, as yet unattached to anything, that describes a 3D path in space; it can be sampled at any time. The value of Motion is some thing that can translate 3D geometry. The three arguments specify how that geometry should be moved along the X, Y, and Z axes respectively. In AVRML, time is a special system-supplied value — it's the current time of the simulation (we'll say more about this later). So Motion is now a free-running little entity, which is constantly changing as the moments pass. The third line connects Motion together with Ball,

10. Also from the Microsoft document "In programming language terms, ActiveVRML is a declarative, rather than imperative, language."

11. From the Microsoft document "The ActiveVRML Approach to Interactive Animation," at http://www.microsoft.com/intdev/avr/avrml000.htm.

creating a new, composite 3D thing called FlyingBall. Thus, FlyingBall inherits the dynamic quality of Motion, so FlyingBall is itself a thing that is moving as time progresses, with no further help from us.

The concept of time is built into ActiveVRML. It also provides an elegant functional programming language framework. Given that Microsoft now employs many of the greatest computer graphics minds, I doubt that ActiveVRML will fade into the sunset.

2 • 4 • 6 Apple's QuickTime VR

QuickTime VR (QTVR) is Apple's technology for creating an image–based virtual environment. Instead of using polygons to construct a space geometrically you use images. The image appearing on the computer screen is that of a photo, but you can look anywhere you want. Imagine that your head is on top of a tripod and you could spin it around with complete freedom. That's the type of view you get with QTVR. Actually, you can hop from one tripod position to another, but you can't walk smoothly. You can integrate this environment with your Web pages as yet another data type, used with a helper application.

To create this type of environment, you take photographs using an ordinary 35mm camera. The easiest thing to do (and the authoring software expects this) is to have the pictures processed and placed onto a Kodak PhotoCD. The photos are taken by placing the camera on a tripod and rotating the camera 360 degrees, taking each picture when there is approximately 50% overlap with the previous image. Depending on the lens, it takes anywhere from 12 to 18 images to complete the 360 degrees. The images, from the PhotoCD are stitched together seamlessly by a magical tool called the "stitcher," which is part of Apple's QTVR authoring kit.

The resulting panorama image is processed further into a QuickTime VR movie, which is a single QTVR "node." You can allow the user to move from one node to another by repeating the same photography and processing steps with the tripods in different locations. The closer together the tripod positions are

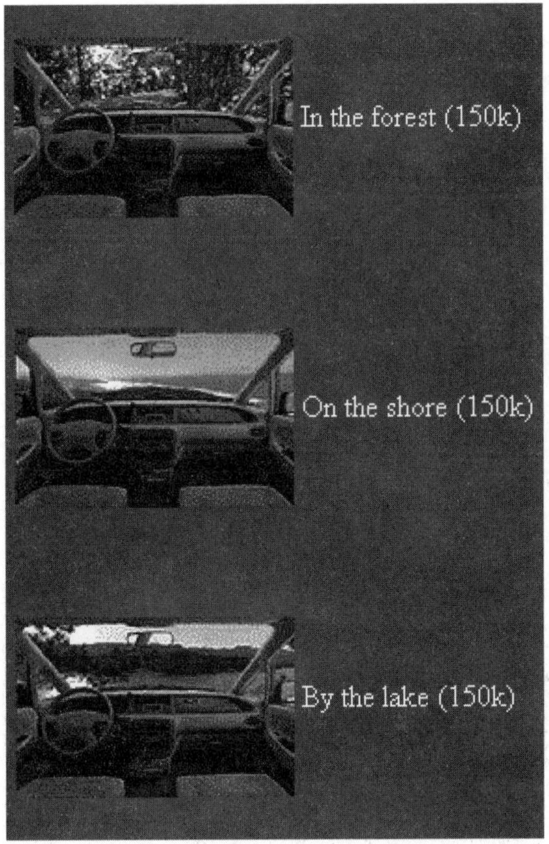

the smoother the travel appears. In addition the user can zoom in on any section of the image, giving a reasonably effective illusion of moving closer to parts of the scene.

One novel use of QTVR was created by Honda. On their Web site (http://www.honda.com) they let you virtually sit inside their new Odyssey minivan. You can see what the view looks like if you were on top of a hill, in a forest, by the sea shore, or by a lake!

OK I'm a computer geek; I admit it. During a vacation in Israel, I shot several QTVR nodes. I photographed them using a hand–held camera (no tripod). This caused a number of anomalies. The QTVR authoring allows adjustments for some problems; using the stitcher program in an "interactive" mode, I was able to get reasonable QTVR nodes. Check 'em out on the CD that comes with this book.

The "stitched" panoramic 360–degree image.

Normalized QTVR view in which you can "turn your head".

The other type of image QTVR can present is a "navigable object." In this method the object is photographed from all points of a sphere surrounding the object. The object is placed on a turntable and photographed every 10 degrees or so, the camera is moved 10 degrees and so on. When the separation is 10 degrees, the result is 36 x 36 photos. The images are processed through the QTVR authoring kit, and another type of QTVR movie, a navigable movie, is created. The user can interact with the object by spinning it around or up and down. It's an extremely intuitive and effective user interface for examining objects. Usually a video camera is used to grab still frames for this technique since image quality is not as critical as it is in the panoramas.

Currently, QTVR is used on the Web as just another type of data. Clearly, it could be used in ways similar to VRML, where clicking on a particular portion of the image would link you to another part of the Web. We'll just have to wait and see.

If fact just before this book went to print Apple announced the features for QTVR Version 2.0. The new version will allow direct embedding of URLs as the hot spots in QTVR nodes, opening up a clear path to highly integrated image based virtual environments and the Web. A much anticipated programmers API will allow simpler applications to use this technology. Sounds can also be associated with particular locations. QTVR nodes embedded in Web pages, via Apple's QuickTime plug-ins can dramatically present "real" spaces such as museums, malls, cities and so on with compelling and intuitive interfaces. This is a major development, keep an eye open for this truly exciting stuff!

2 • 5 Macromedia Director — Shockwave

Macromedia Director is one of the most successful multimedia authoring and delivery programs around. It has been used for a wide variety of "real world" products. Originally a Macintosh–only system it has migrated and become a first class PC application. Director multimedia content can be authored on one platform, either the Mac or PC, and played back on either.

As multimedia vendors start to wake up to the reality of the Web, both multimedia and Web developers are starting to cooperate in joint development and delivery systems. Netscape has announced a deal with Macromedia to allow "Director Player" documents to play in a Web page. It will accomplish this using Netscape's new plug-in architecture. Director Player documents do not have to be simply one–way playback windows, they can be fully interactive multimedia experiences.

First, a little background on Director. Back in the stone ages (you know, around 7 years ago), if you wanted to do complex animation on a Macintosh you had to use something called VideoWorks. VideoWorks eventually grew up to be called Director, and was ported to the PC platform. Today, if you want to create multimedia content playable on both the Mac and PC platforms, you would be wise to check out Macromedia's Director.

Its roots as an animation system are still quite evident. It lets you set up animations on a frame by frame basis; the frame is its unit of time. The items that move and make sounds in your multimedia presentation are called "cast members." You arrange the cast members in a "script," and the actions, you specify take place over time. Using a computing language called Lingo, similar in style to HyperTalk, you can program in an object oriented way, the actions and interactions of objects and the user. Director is not simple to use and has a big learning curve. It's been called the Swiss Army Knife of multimedia authoring packages. You can do almost anything with it. In the worst case, there are mechanisms to link with native C code. There is also a large user community; thousands of experienced people are using the system.

Shockwave is Macromedia's attempt to merge the capabilities of Director with the Web. Director version 5 includes Shockwave authoring capabilities. To view a Shockwave file, you first get the Shockwave (Netscape) plug-in. When you go to a page with a shockwave animation, it gets loaded and plays inline on the Web page. Director animations can have synchronized sounds and interactions, which should enhance a Web site when used judiciously. So far the main drawback is the amount of time it takes to load the Shockwave animation. Although it is often lengthy, it can be a valuable attention–getter.

2 • 6 Streaming Technologies-Audio/Video

One of the most interesting and useful technologies starting to crawl through the Web is **data streaming**. Data streaming is the connection of a large set of data on the server to the client, through a constantly flowing stream of data. For example a collection of audio that might be ten minutes long may be tens of Mb large. Ordinarily, you would have to wait for all the audio to be downloaded to your client browser machine before you started hearing it, with data streaming, a small portion is sent and you start hearing it almost instantaneously. While you are listening the steaming software simultaneously brings in new data...multitasking...hey what a concept!

2 • 6 • 1 Real Audio

Surfing by Voice

An interesting application of speech recognition is being pursued by Texas Instruments. In "Surfing the Web by Voice," in the Proceedings of Multimedia 95, Charles Hemphill and Philip Thrift, introduce some novel concepts. First is the idea of a speakable hotlist, which the user can use with relatively natural language. Next is the concept of speakable links to navigate. The third concept consists of smart pages to add intelligence to the documents.

The practicality of this streaming audio is hard to overstate. In fact, a company called RealAudio will be happy to sell you an audio server that dishes out audio streams that can be played back using free client software. Unlike much of the new whiz-bang-cool software out on the Net this software is truly useful. The RealAudio Web site serves National Public Radio. I enjoy listening to the news on NPR but I rarely get to listen to all of it. So, once in a while, I simply dial up NPR on the RealAudio site and listen to one of the many archived. It's like phone mail for radio; it just sits and waits there for you.

2 • 6 • 2 Video

Usable video conferencing is one of the major goals of Internet technology development. CU-See Me developed at Cornell University's Information Technology organization (CIT) has moved us closer to this goal. It initially was a Macintosh–only 4-bit gray-scale window of conversing people. Since those days, it has moved towards color and the Windows platform. White Pine Software is commercializing the software for Windows and Win 95.

Another approach to desktop video is the Mbone. The Mbone uses a technology called multicasting, a tricky extension of the TCP/IP protocol. The Mbone is used primarily on higher-end workstation equipment with 56K or greater Internet connection. Its principal advantage is that it runs on many hardware platforms. The MBONE Information Web is a good place to find information on this technology.

A few companies are trying to marry streaming video to Web browsers. XING, a company with a significant track record in MPEG players, offers StreamWorks. The StreamWorks client is installed as a helper application for your Web browser. When you click on a video segment offered by a Web site, the StreamWorks client launches. On a 28K baud modem, the video quality is poor. However these are still pioneering days. It's amazing it works at all.

Another streaming video technology is offered by VDOLive. VDOlive is now being used by CBS News and Paramount in some novel streaming video experiments. The VDOLive system can function as a Netscape plug-in; the video appears inline, right on the Web page. They are touting concept of "desktop video broadcasting."

A VDOLive video stream playing inline on the Netscape Web browser.

Finally, Netscape, continuing its hyper-paced introduction of product enhancements, has a technology called LiveLinks for streaming data.

2 • 7 Microsoft

Although Microsoft was slow to warm up to the Internet, it's clear that this 800–pound gorilla has woken up. Microsoft is now running through the jungle, shaking all the trees in it's effort to make the Internet another conquered territory. Simply put, the collection of technologies Microsoft is either buying or creating for the Internet is extremely impressive.

On the authoring front is, the Internet Assistant (IA) for Word, IA for PowerPoint, and IA for Excel. These extensions to already popular products make these tools capable of content creation for the Web. There is also Microsoft FrontPage (formerly Vermeer FrontPage), a highly regarded full–featured authoring tool.

On the browser side, Internet Explorer is gaining on Netscape's Navigator. Microsoft is adding features nearly as fast as Netscape. For Web servers Microsoft is bundling its Web server with every copy of Windows NT.

To bring more active programs to the Web, Microsoft has licensed Sun's Java and is developing its own strategy called ActiveX. Microsoft's goal is to integrate Java with Microsoft's component object model (COM). No stone is being left un-turned; the gorilla is running hard.

2 • 7 • 1 Internet Explorer 3.0

Version 3.0 of the Internet Explorer introduces a host of new features. Frames, and VBScripts (Visual Basic Scripts) are part of the new suite of technologies. Significantly, Internet Explorer 3.0 will also support the W3Os Style Sheet Specification, the Cascading Style Sheet.

VBScript is Microsoft's version of Visual Basic for Web programming. VBScript programs can be embedded in HTML. In addition, and the Web browser, such as Microsoft's Internet Explorer (version 3 or later), can interpret the VBScript.

This following illustration shows a demonstration page of an order form for Pizza. It was created using VBScript embedded in an HTML page. The form calculates the bill and illustrates some of the capabilities of VBScript–enhanced HTML as interpreted by MS Internet Explorer 3.0. The image and file are part of the sample provided by Microsoft with their InternetSDK (System Development Kit) and ActiveX(TM) Development Kit

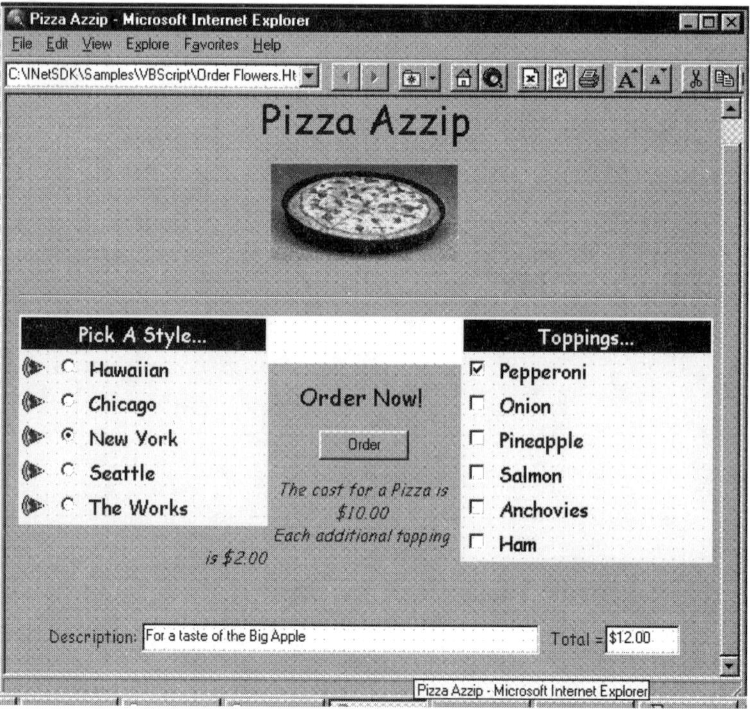

Web page with VBScript forms in Microsoft's Internet Explorer version 3.

2 • 7 • 2 ActiveX

ActiveX Technologies are a new set of technologies being touted by Microsoft as the way to create "active" Web documents. ActiveX Controls will enable developers to create Web pages with actions such as games, multimedia, animation and video.

On March 12, 1996, Microsoft issued a press release describing these technologies.

> ActiveX Technologies form a robust framework for creating interactive content using software components, scripts and existing applications. Specifically, ActiveX Technologies enable developers to build Web content easily using ActiveX Control (formerly OLE Controls), active scripts and active documents.
>
> A key benefit of using ActiveX TEchnologies is the ability to integrate applications into Web browsers so data managed by those applications becomes accessible as Web pages. This technology, called ActiveX Documents, lets a user navigate a corporate intranet to view a department's Web page, examine the department's budget spreadsheet, query the database for sales data or write a memo—all from within the Web browser and without undergoing the expensive and unnecessary process of converting that content into HTML format.
>
> ActiveX Server Scripts can be written using a host of popular scripting languages including Visual Basic Script, PERL, and JavaScript. Together, these ActiveX controls and scripts allow Web developers, using familiar tools, to build smart, interactive server applications with little or no programming knowledge.
>
> In addition, Microsoft has co-developed an ActiveX plug-in for Netscape Navigator with nCompass Labs Inc., enabling NetScape Navigator browsers to view active content.

2 • 8 Bandwidth

"If God wanted us to fly, He would have given us tickets." - Mel Brooks

Surfing the web is great over a high–speed line at work but that 28.8K line at home can be frustrating. For all practical purposes, the best way to increase your bandwidth at home now is to use ISDN. Approximately 80% of U.S. customers can opt for this approach. It will get you a 128K line installed for around $500 to $700. Monthly fees average about $60 to $100 for moderate use with an internet provider. It's far from cheap but it's not the thousands of dollars per month required for a T1 line.

Perhaps the most promising breakthrough is the push to develop the Cable modem. If we look at the time it takes to download a 10Mb file (say a video clip), it would take 46 minutes with a 28.8K line, 10 minutes with ISDN (128K/sec), 52 seconds on a T1 (1.5Mb/sec) line, and 20 seconds with a cable modem (4Mb/sec)[12]. @Home, the leading developer service of Cable modems, will use a 10Mb/sec connection. The 4Mb figure is the lowest speed. People are talking about speeds of 27-40Mb already.

12. From *Business Week*, Jan 29, 1996, "The Big Daddy of Data Haulers?"

Prototype @Home Web page

The biggest effort to promote this technology is coming from Tele-Communications Inc. (TCI), the nations largest cable TV operator. It is creating @Home, jointly developed with the Kleiner Perkins Caufield & Byers venture capital firm. A web site is accessible now, but it's not that interesting...yet. It is preparing to have video hosts that guide you through the site, as well as other high-bandwidth features including real time delivery and updating of content like the weather, news and other broadcasts. The @Home people have strategic relationships with both Netscape and Macromedia, which will provide a specialized browser and multimedia content.

According to information at the @Home site, the charges will be $30 to $50 per month for basic services.

TCI is not the only player in this game. Jones Intercable, a company based in an Englewood, Colorado, is deploying Cable modem service on a test basis in Alexandria Virginia. According to a *Washington Post* article of February 19, 1996, Jones is providing the 10Mbit service for about $30 a month. You also have to use and subscribe to Jones for your regular cable television service. According to one user of the service, "I heard that someone was moving to Alexandria just to get this service...He was a free-lance writer and really uses the Internet – so he's been asking if there are any free apartments in my building."

Stay tuned for this one.

2 • 9 Crystal Balls and the Web

No doubt, by the time you read this, the Web technologies will have changed, further dramatically. New products are introduced daily. Where all the frenzy will lead is anyone's guess; only a fool would pretend to know.

A few aspects, however, are becoming clear. The Web has changed everything. Commerce, publishing, entertainment, academic research, broadcasting, politics, and someday soon, governments, are all affected by this monumental change.

The specific browser features of the day or the gadget of the hour are unimportant. The key is the ubiquitous communication of information among a wide and diverse set of people. Today ideas are expressed and broadcast instantly to millions of people. Web publishing is leading us toward an ultimate democracy in which everyone—good, bad, and ugly—has a voice. Although it will present many challenges, increased dialogue and access to information will be good for all.

Chapter 3 • Points of View

Each thing we see hides something else we want to see.—René Magritte

Whether you are preparing a ten-page pamphlet or a 300-page book, the process of creating and producing an electronic document can be viewed in many different ways. Each software tool presents a particular conceptual model of the publishing process. This *philosophical* point of view greatly influences the functionality and usability of the software. The better you understand the many points of view, the more effective you will be in choosing and using the available software tools.

Some systems are *page-oriented.* Others focus on the entire document. Some are WYSIWYG (what you see is what you get). Others are *language-oriented* and still others are oriented toward *on-line display and interaction.* Learning and using the publishing tools are easier if you are aware of the philosophy—the point of view—that a system supports.

One way to understand the value of new technologies is to create a metaphor or catchy phrase for a concept. The iconic user interface of the Macintosh is known as a **desktop**. The use of printing software and hardware on this metaphorical desktop is known as **desktop publishing**. This usage brings to mind miniature Gutenberg presses right at your fingertips. Many varieties of desktop metaphors have been created: desktop machining, desktop forgery, desktop prepress, desktop broadcasting, and so on.

The newer technologies of electronic publishing also need new metaphors to cover the issues of document processing, electronic distribution, archival storage, and so on. [1]

Where is that catchy phrase?

Aldus Magazine, a magazine about desktop publishing, graphic design, and other document-oriented issues, had a contest and asked its readers to "create one or more terms that express the essence of where we are going with computers and communications." In the end, the magazine did not choose any one phrase as a winner. Instead, it listed many of the interesting phrases suggested. The entire attempt illustrates the difficulties of creating new metaphors.

AutoPublishing
Cinematic Publishing
Communication Design
Communication Network
CompCom
Computer Aided Publishing
Computer Aided Thinking
Computer Expression
Concept Communication
Creative Interlink
Creative Resourcing
Design Interchange
Design Link
Design Transmit
Device Independent Publishing
Digital Communications Management
Digital Design
Digital Extensions
Digital Media
Electronic Expressionism
Electronic Multidimensional Interlink
Expressions Enhancement
Fingertip Communication
Human Creations Technology
Human Techniscreening
Idea Translation
Instant Design Communication
Instant Link
Intermedia Transmutation
Media Talk
Media Toolkit
Multipublish
Multitechnical
Neocommunication
Neoscribe
Network Design
Network Talk
Perspective Composition
Publications Processing
Sensory Perception
Universal Media Link
Varimedia Translation Nexus

1. From "What's in a Name?" in *Aldus Magazine*, Vol. 2, No. 3, March/April 1991.

The multifaceted world of electronic publishing needs a catchy phrase to describe it. The many points of view used to examine electronic publishing are necessary because there is no single satisfying metaphor.

The term **electronic publishing** means different things to different people. Many of the standards discussed in this book suggest other possibilities such as hypertext, on-line information browsers, and so on. These applications—as well as databases, CD-ROMs, and other electronic repositories—are all part of the domain of electronic publishing. At its core, electronic documents start as text organized into chunks of information, paragraphs, pages, and so on.

In this chapter, we examine many approaches to looking at electronic documents. The views we examine are (1) Visual and Logical Views, (2) The Design Point of View, (3) Communications Views, (4) The Engineered View, (5) The Database View, (6) Specialized Views, and (7) On-line Views. We examine how the creation of electronic documents is influenced by each point of view.

3 • 1 Visual and Logical Views

"It's a small world, but I wouldn't want to paint it." - Steven Wright

Documents have many components—characters, words, paragraphs, chapter headings, sections, and subsections. We can examine each component in two complementary ways, the visual and the logical.

The **logical** aspect of a component refers to its semantically meaningful part, such as the fact that a collection of characters is a word that can be checked for spelling or that a chapter is divided into sections. The **visual** aspect of a document component refers to the size, position, and fonts used to form its physical appearance.The visual components of document elements will be discussed further in *section 3 • 2 The Design Point of View.*

In this section, we examine document components of increasing complexity, starting with the character and progressing through to an entire enterprise. Each document component has a visual aspect and logical aspect; some lean more toward one than the other.

Putting these document components on a scale, from the simplest to the most complex, provides us with a useful frame of reference in which to discuss these issues.

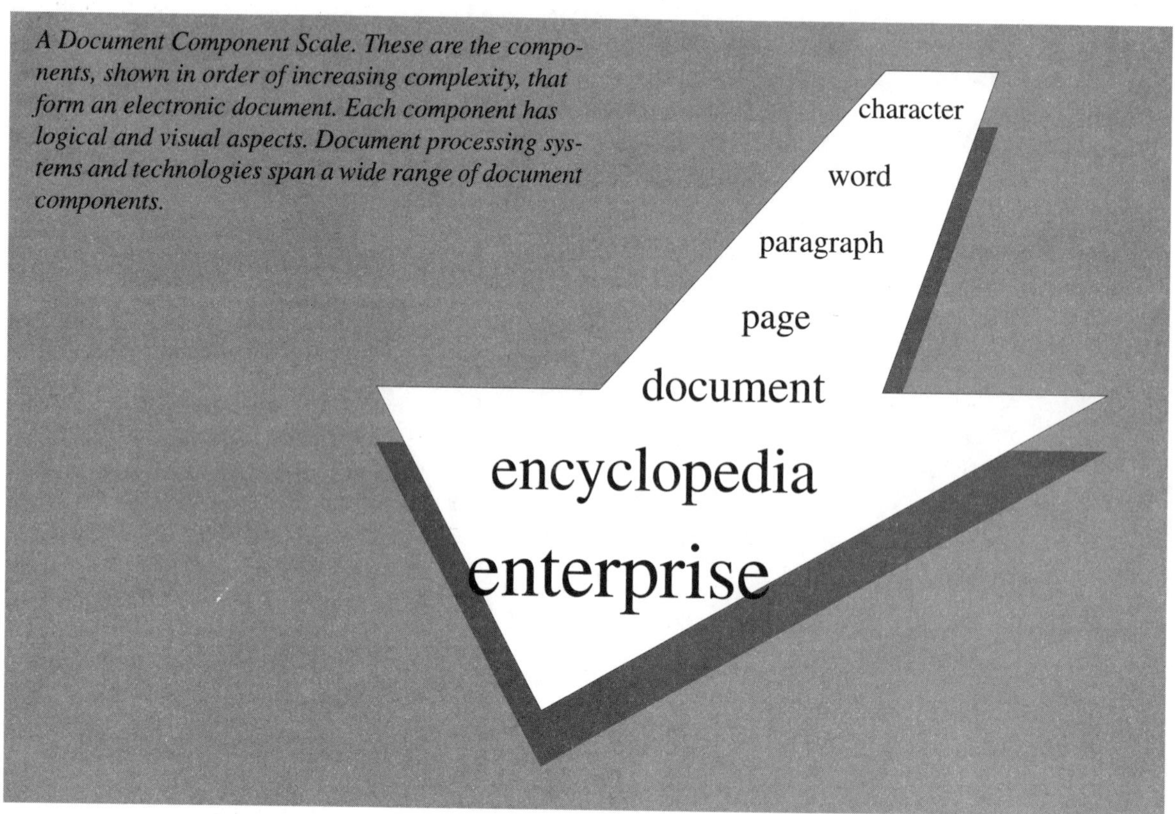

A Document Component Scale. These are the components, shown in order of increasing complexity, that form an electronic document. Each component has logical and visual aspects. Document processing systems and technologies span a wide range of document components.

You can manipulate each item on this scale using software tools. Of course, some tools cover several items on the scale. The orientation of a particular tool—the point of view it supports—will probably be centered around one particular item. In the following sections, we go through the scale by examining each document component individually.

3 • 1 • 1 Character

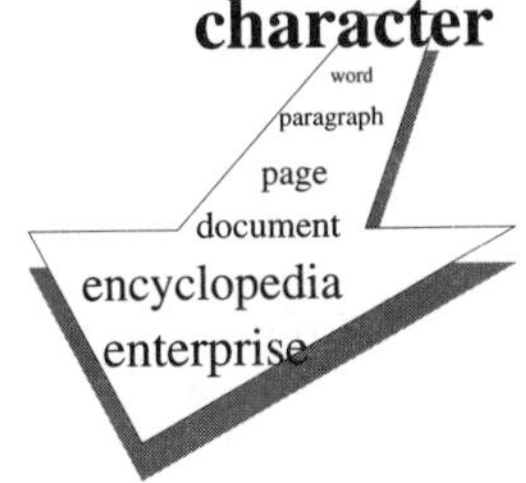

The first level of our document scale is the **character** and its manipulation. Characters, as logical meaningful entities, have values that are represented in the computer according to well–known and established character codes. Character codes are the fundamental representation of text. ASCII is the best known and established character encoding.

Normally you don't have to be concerned about the character code used in your particular system. However, when you want to interchange to other systems, the character code may become a problem. In particular, interchange with systems in countries that use other character codes must pay attention to these codes. Many Asian languages require other character codes, that are necessary to support hundreds or even thousands of characters (for example, Japanese). *Localization* is the process of taking software written for one system and porting it to another system that uses another language and possibly another character code.

Also on the logical (as opposed to visual) side of the discussion is the ability to associate attributes or **tags** with individual characters. Essentially, tags are names you can associate with characters for whatever purpose you like. For example, the FrameMaker publishing system allows the definition of character tags. Each tag defines a particular font family, size, weight, and other properties, which can be applied to any character. These *tagged* characters may then be manipulated as a group if necessary.

Named attributes or tags such as these provide a convenient mechanism for manipulating the visual appearance of characters throughout a document. You can also use them for semantic purposes. For example, you could associate the name "placeHolder" with particular characters you wish to use temporarily. You can search for the tag "placeHolder" to locate the particular text. You can even print a report listing all occurrences of the "placeHolder" tag and where they occur in the document, creating an automated list of work to be done.

Is ASCII Dead?

The need to print clear multilingual text in today's global computing community has made ASCII obsolete. The characters defined by ASCII are 7 bits wide, allowing only 128 characters. Many languages have extra characters with umlauts, accents, and so on. This has given rise to the new ASCII called ISO Latin 1 (ISO standard 8859:1), a clear text encoding for characters with 8 bits per character.

There is also Unicode, a 16-bit character representation created by a consortium of computer vendors. It is an attempt at representing all characters, including those from China, Japan, and Korea, where the languages have several thousand characters. This is a truly global attempt at character representation.[a]

a. Get the whole story on UNICODE at their Web site at http://www.stonehand.com/unicode.html.

For the visual side of characters, many font manipulation tools are available that could be considered part of font definition software. If you want to change the appearance of the character T, for example, you would use a font definition tool.

There are many more issues concerning the visual aspects of characters and fonts. Please see *Section 3 • 2 • 1 Fonts and Typography* later in this chapter for a discussion of these issues.

3 • 1 • 2 Words

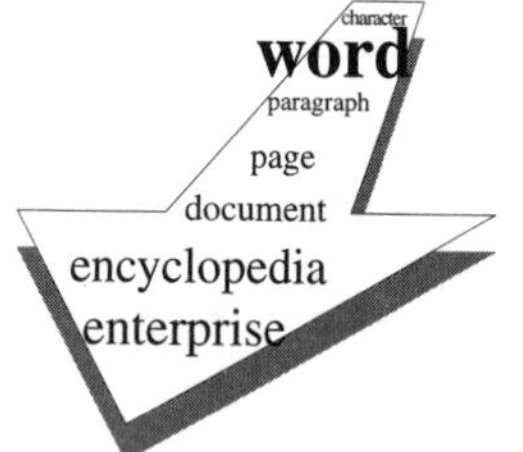

The act of writing takes place at the word level of the document component scale. Most of the discussion about writing is in *Section 3 • 3 Communications Views,* later in this chapter. Spelling checkers and grammatical aid systems are some of the electronic publishing tools that help with writing. The growing popularity of computer-assisted writing aids attests to their growing sophistication.

Another manipulation of words is automatic hyphenation. This is a manipulation of the logical or semantically meaningful aspects of words. Often, publishing systems allow the user to modify some variables to control the precise way automatic hyphenation is performed. For example, these could be variables to control the minimum and maximum number of characters before and after the hyphen. In addition, electronic publishing systems that support several languages must also have hyphenation dictionaries appropriate for each language. Hyphenation algorithms differ among publishing systems.[2] The same document in two systems may not appear exactly the same, even if the fonts and page margins are identical, because the hyphens will break the words at different places. Hyphenation is part of the process of formatting and can hinder efforts to interchange documents with perfect fidelity. It's amazing how complicated these little details can be!

2. Donald Knuth's book *The TeXbook*, Volume A of the Computers & Typesetting series published by Addison–Wesley, Reading, MA, 1984, contains an appendix with a good treatment of hyphenation issues.

3 • 1 • 3 Paragraphs with Tags and Styles

Moving up the complexity scale, we now come to the paragraph. One of the most powerful document processing tools is the ability to attach attributes, tags, or styles to paragraphs. I use the terms **tags** to refer to the logical aspect of paragraphs and **styles** to refer to the visual aspect of paragraphs.When writing, we generally treat the content and appearance of paragraphs uniformly. Individual paragraphs have the same margins and typefaces (they should *also* contain a coherent idea). Many software products treat the paragraph as an entity that can be manipulated as a unit.

When manipulating a paragraph, it is important to distinguish the logical aspects from the visual. The logical use of a paragraph tag might be to identify all chapter headings. The publishing system may support the intent of a document structure and not allow the creation of a chapter heading in the middle of a table. Identification of the logical structure of a document is one of the major features of formal document standards and is discussed in detail in the Document Standards chapter. (See *Section 5 • 3 SGML* in *Chapter 5 • Document Standards* for a discussion of document structure.)

Style Names from PageMaker

Another logical use of tag names is the actual name itself. The name "Body text" conveys the meaning that the body copy in a document will be associated with the tag "Body text." It is important to select meaningful tag names. Cryptic, "cutesy" names obscure the intent of the tag or style. Spend the painful time creating good names that will be meaningful to others in your organization.

The development and use of a consistent set of paragraph tags can be of tremendous value. This task should be done at the start of any significant project. Visual consistency can be achieved by using the same tags in the same places. Just as important, changes can be applied to specific tags or styles in one place and then applied to the entire document. The concept of a style sheet is intended specifically to allow changes in one place to migrate to the rest of the document. Changes made to a style sheet can also be applied to other documents, helping to automate and keep consistent all documents of a particular project or organization. Coherent tag names allow the logical aspects of the document to guide the visual appearance. Style sheets are just starting to appear for Web page authoring. (See *Section 1 • 5 Authoring* in *Chapter 1 • World Wide Web* for more info on Web style sheets.)

3 • 1 • 4 Page

Contrary to the other document components, the page is purely visual and has no meaningful logical aspects. Indeed, we could also have this discussion for a "screen" of information. Pages and screens are convenient well understood units of information content. Pages are the physical spaces in which textual content appears. Page sizes can be altered and documents can be reprinted in different sizes and formats for on-line browsing and so on, with no effect on the content. Pages do not have any logical aspects other than their very existence. They represent a canvas upon which the content is painted.

From a visual point of view, the page provides a place for a number of items. Headers, footers, body text, and page numbers are some of these items. They are placed on a page, in a consistent position throughout the document. The positioning of these items is primarily a matter of design; but there are also computational factors. Some of the page-specific items, such as the page numbers, running headers, and running footers, can be computed or extracted from the text. The content of these items can be changed, based on the specifics of the page.

Although a page has a specific size that is rarely changed, paying attention to the size is sometimes crucial. Many systems support specific page sizes implicitly. This implicit assumption can cause a nasty problem if you need to interchange documents with an organization that uses a different standard page size. This might happen when a U.S. organization exchanges documents with an organization based in Europe as U.S. standard page sizes (8.5 x 11 inches) are different than the ISO A4 (8.25 x 11.75 inches) size used in Europe. The document will probably not print correctly unless you adjust for page size. Online documents formatted for a VGA PC screen or a large screen workstation encounter visual problems more and more as Web browsers dynamically reformat content.

The layout and overall design of components such as text, graphics, and illustration are best manipulated in a **page layout program**. The quintessential example of this type of software is Adobe PageMaker (formerly Aldus). One of the keys to PageMaker's success is that this software speaks the language of designers. It presents the user with a simulation of a pasteboard (an underlying grid for creating the proportions and overall structure of the document), a commonly used graphic design tool.

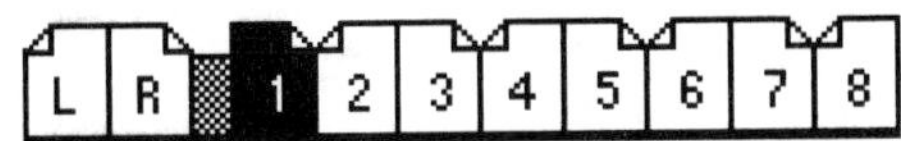

An iconic view of left and right handedness from PageMaker.

One distinction that must be applied only to the page is *handedness*—whether the content of a page is to appear on the right- or left-hand side of the printed document. Margins, columns, headers, footers, and page number positions are sometimes shifted on the page, depending on whether they are to appear on a left or right-hand page. The more powerful electronic publishing systems provide tools to control handedness of particular parts. One example is the ability to force the start of each document (for example, chapters) on a right hand page.

Text flow is yet another term that really crosses the boundary from a page to a document. Newspaper articles leave pointers to the connecting text, such as *"see Bozos column 5, page 22"*. These pointers tell the reader where the text is continued. The visual shape of this flow is either rectangular or follows the shape of graphic elements. Page layout or page makeup programs such as QuarkXPress and Aldus Pagemaker provide tools that allow text flows to travel automatically around graphic elements.

Flowing and Wrapping Text

Text flow is a technique used in many page makeup and publishing systems. Virtually all page layout programs allow the text to flow from one column to another. Some systems have facilities that automatically wrap text around graphic illustrations.

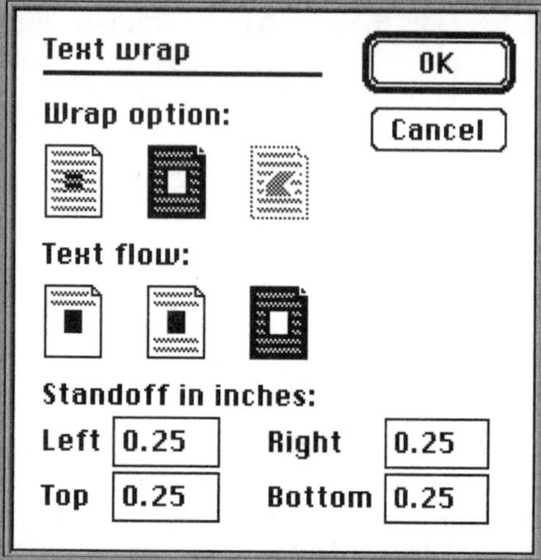

Text wrap

OK

Cancel

Wrap option:

Text flow:

Standoff in inches:

Left 0.25 Right 0.25

Top 0.25 Bottom 0.25

PageMaker 4.0 dialog box for the control of text wrapping.

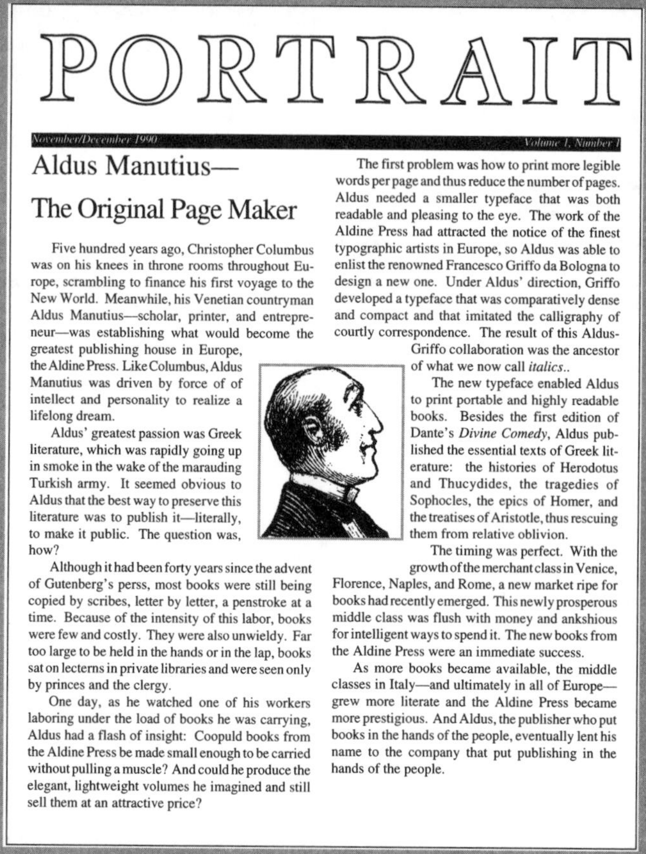

PORTRAIT

November/December 1990 — Volume 1, Number 1

Aldus Manutius—

The Original Page Maker

Five hundred years ago, Christopher Columbus was on his knees in throne rooms throughout Europe, scrambling to finance his first voyage to the New World. Meanwhile, his Venetian countryman Aldus Manutius—scholar, printer, and entrepreneur—was establishing what would become the greatest publishing house in Europe, the Aldine Press. Like Columbus, Aldus Manutius was driven by force of of intellect and personality to realize a lifelong dream.

Aldus' greatest passion was Greek literature, which was rapidly going up in smoke in the wake of the marauding Turkish army. It seemed obvious to Aldus that the best way to preserve this literature was to publish it—literally, to make it public. The question was, how?

Although it had been forty years since the advent of Gutenberg's perss, most books were still being copied by scribes, letter by letter, a penstroke at a time. Because of the intensity of this labor, books were few and costly. They were also unwieldy. Far too large to be held in the hands or in the lap, books sat on lecterns in private libraries and were seen only by princes and the clergy.

One day, as he watched one of his workers laboring under the load of books he was carrying, Aldus had a flash of insight: Coopuld books from the Aldine Press be made small enough to be carried without pulling a muscle? And could he produce the elegant, lightweight volumes he imagined and still sell them at an attractive price?

The first problem was how to print more legible words per page and thus reduce the number of pages. Aldus needed a smaller typeface that was both readable and pleasing to the eye. The work of the Aldine Press had attracted the notice of the finest typographic artists in Europe, so Aldus was able to enlist the renowned Francesco Griffo da Bologna to design a new one. Under Aldus' direction, Griffo developed a typeface that was comparatively dense and compact and that imitated the calligraphy of courtly correspondence. The result of this Aldus-Griffo collaboration was the ancestor of what we now call *italics*..

The new typeface enabled Aldus to print portable and highly readable books. Besides the first edition of Dante's *Divine Comedy*, Aldus published the essential texts of Greek literature: the histories of Herodotus and Thucydides, the tragedies of Sophocles, the epics of Homer, and the treatises of Aristotle, thus rescuing them from relative oblivion.

The timing was perfect. With the growth of the merchant class in Venice, Florence, Naples, and Rome, a new market ripe for books had recently emerged. This newly prosperous middle class was flush with money and ankshious for intelligent ways to spend it. The new books from the Aldine Press were an immediate success.

As more books became available, the middle classes in Italy—and ultimately in all of Europe—grew more literate and the Aldine Press became more prestigious. And Aldus, the publisher who put books in the hands of the people, eventually lent his name to the company that put publishing in the hands of the people.

Page with text flow wrapping around a graphic.

Frames are another frequently encountered term with a strong relationship to the page. In a sense, a frame is a subdivision of a page. It is an invisible boundary in which content appears, just like a page. Frames, however, are not physical things; they are areas that can be manipulated while using the publishing system. Text can flow automatically from one particular frame to another. Corel Ventura (formerly called Ventura Publisher) and FrameMaker (now from Adobe) both use this concept. The Netscape 2.0 Web browser has an on-line frames capability that allows for more flexible Web page layouts and interactions.

Last, but not least, Interleaf generalizes many of the aspects of a page in a feature known as a microdocument. Microdocuments are "little" documents, inserts embedded in the pages of other documents, that can independently retain stylistic characteristics. All the styles associated with a particular document can be retained intact with microdocuments, but the microdocument can be no larger than a page.

3 • 1 • 5 Document

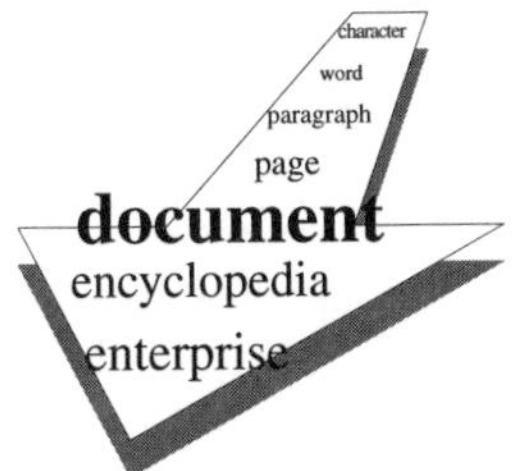

The document in its entirety is the next stop in our analysis of document components. From a visual point of view, the document is a physical object with a particular design. From a logical point of view, the document is composed of a certain structure. The visual design and construction of documents[3] is a topic beyond the scope of this book. However, electronic publishing systems can play an essential role in the manipulation of the logical aspects of a document.

The logical structure of a document is an important characteristic of the document. We can use that structure as a framework to evaluate document processing tools. Some questions to ask in determining the suitability of a particular publishing system are:

3. For an excellent look at the construction of books, see *Bookmaking* by Marshall Lee, R.R. Bowker Company, New York, 1979.

Can the system automatically generate a table of contents?

Can the system generate lists of various elements such as tables and figures?

What kind of graphics can be integrated easily with the text?

How robust are the indexing capabilities, if any?

Is there good bibliographic and cross-referencing support?

Technical publications, in particular, need robust document-oriented tools. The more automated the tools, the better. It is essential that the publishing system provide support for automatic section numbering, running headers and footers, styles or tags, and change control. In addition, support for global changes—changes to many files that are part of a larger document—is a major time saver.

Several publishing systems present the user with the idea of a book[4] as an organizational tool. Books are made up of collections of files. If a change is made to the book, then the change is actually made to all the files that make up the book. If your publishing projects routinely deal with hundreds of files, this type of support will be an important requirement for any publishing system. An on-line equivalent of a book is a Web site with its web of interconnected pages.

As the sheer size of the document grows, we start to see a significant distinction between WYSIWYG (what you see is what you get) and batch language oriented systems. Often you don't want to see extensive, repetitive, massive changes. If you are forced into too many hand manipulations, the publishing system may be unwieldy for the particular publishing application. The higher-end publishing systems try to balance WYSIWYG capabilities with the often awkward and complicated commands of a batch–oriented system. (See *Section 4 • 1 Types of Document*

4. Interleaf Publisher, FrameMaker, and PageMaker all use this concept of a book as an organizational tool. Corel Ventura Publisher uses the concept of a publication for the same purpose. Of course, they all treat this concept somewhat differently.

Processors in *Chapter 4 • Form and Function of Document Processors* for a more through discussion of WYSIWYG versus batch document processing.)

3 • 1 • 6 Encyclopedia

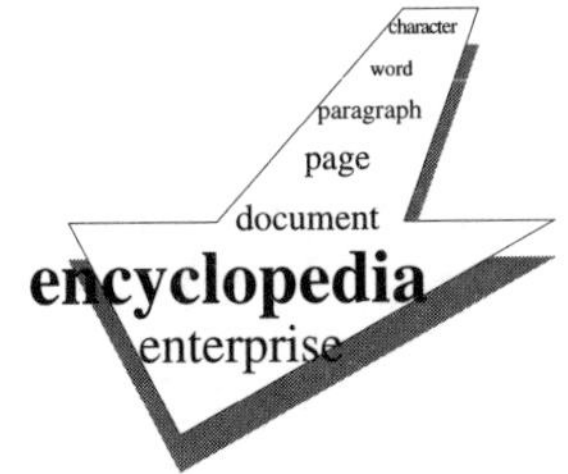

When we discuss the multivolume or encyclopedic scale of documents, our focus shifts from document manipulation to the concept of a data repository. Manipulation of large quantities of related material is one of the strengths of batch–oriented document processing systems. Off–line automated processing is a virtual requirement for this scale of manipulation.

This level, in our document component scale, also represents the highest point at which a collection of documents is part of a coherent whole. Representative examples of documents at this level are the many manuals of an operating system, the volumes of an encyclopedia, and the maintenance manuals for a jet engine. Interleaf is a good example of a system with capabilities at this level. It uses the concept of a cabinet that contains collections of other documents.

Only when a publishing system supports the manipulation of multiple volumes as a unit is the multivolume category qualitatively different from the previous category. The large volume of data and high capacities required for such manipulations are supported only by the high–end publishing systems.

Again, Interleaf is an example of a publishing system that supports different types of style sheets; one that can be applied to individual documents and a master style sheet that is used to modify other style sheets called the master style sheet. Master style sheets are an important feature when massive and consistent changes are required. The language-oriented document processing systems such as `troff` and `TeX` (See *Section 4 • 1 • 2 Language Characteristics* in *Chapter 4 • Form and Function of Document Processors*) are also effective at working with massive amounts of material. Automated scripts can be created and documents processed without human intervention. In general, however, skilled technical users must create these scripts as they require a different type of staff than the turnkey, but more expensive, systems.

3 • 1 • 7 Enterprise

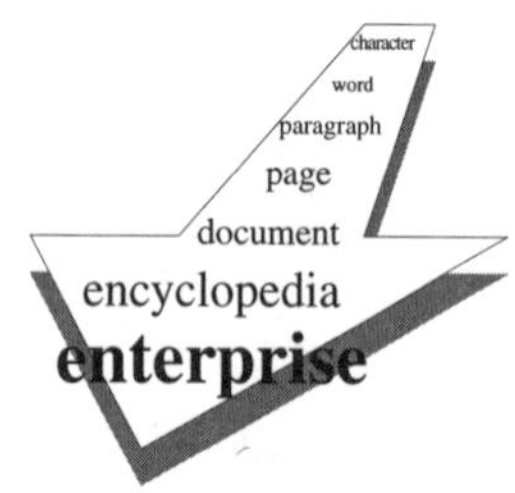

An enterprise (no, I'm not talking about Star Trek), the final level in our document component scale, is discussed here because it relates to the topic of text retrieval. When maintaining or creating a library of documents or other large archival collections of documents, the technical issues are primarily ones of access. Finding information quickly and easily is the primary issue.

The most important area in which to address these issues is that of **classification**. Classification and searching systems are integral parts of library science. A good classification system enables users to locate the information they desire and aids in the management of the documents. After all, if you can't find the information you need, when you need it, you may as well not have it at all. One area where document processing and searching systems intersect is that of **full–text searching**.

Everything Old Is New Again

The Dewey Decimal System is a classification system widely used in libraries. It has the interesting property of infinite expansion. Similarly, Ted Nelson, the man who coined the term hypertext and one of the pioneers of hypertext systems, has taken the idea of variable precision addressing for his Xanadu system. He calls this address scheme *tumblers*, in which any place can be expanded. It's sort of like an outline processor for computer addresses. "The tumbler space is an accordion-like master address space..." [a]

a. See the article "Managing Immense Storage," by Ted Nelson in *Byte* magazine, Jan. 1988, for an in–depth discussion of tumblers and the Xanadu system, Some now say Nelson's dream of a universal hypertext system is being realized with the Web (but he of course disagrees).

Full–text searching is the ability to search for any word in an entire collection of documents. The searching is usually accomplished through the use of a **document browser**. The emphasis in full–text searching is on speed at the sacrifice of space. It is not unusual for the indexes used to locate the text to take up as much space as the text itself. The combination of a good document browser and full–text searching really makes the entire field of electronic books a useful practical commodity, rather than just an interesting toy.

Full–text retrieval engines are widely used in the creation of systems that manage large quantities of text. These retrieval engines are becoming quite prevalent in the CD-ROM and Web site industry[5] and are a key technology to enable access to a library full of information. The large capacity of CD-ROMs is an ideal complement to the large space requirements of full–text retrieval systems.

5. Please see *Section Text Retrieval* in the Appendix Resources for vendors of text retrieval engines.

Text retrieval is a complex field that is growing in importance as the world gets interconnected ever more tightly with networks.[6] Internet Starting Points used with Web browsers all have one form or another of a text retrieval engine. The possibility of indexing the Web challenges the computer science of text retrieval.

The increased capacity of low–cost storage devices like CD-ROMs is also a major factor in text retrieval, because entire databases can be put on-line right at your very own PC. (For more information on text retrieval, see *Section 8 • 5 • 2 Text Retrieval* in *Chapter 8 • Document Management*.)

The enterprise document level is the largest in scope of the seven levels. A collection of documents and tools for the management of an entire organizations documents is covered by this level. Some vendors even offer tools that help manage an enterprise's information resources.

Open Text, a company with a long history of text retrieval software, now offers a Web server that can index an internal Web, an "intranet". In fact, internal enterprise Webs are an increasingly popular use of the Web for project management, status reports, meeting scheduling, meeting minutes, and so on.

In "The Web and its Many Uses" an article in Advanced Systems Magazine, May 95 by Chuck Musciano (chuck.musciano@advanced.com), he argues for the use of the Web for a variety of organization wide functions: e-mail archives (via `mail2html`), meeting minutes, and reports. Concerning he Web as a front end to SCCS, he says "From simple things like on-line mail archives and team document collections to fancy tools that track customer queries and project status, the Web has a place at every level of your development organization."

In addition to increasing collaborations within an organization, internal Webs can be used to test out new technologies. As reported in Web Week,[7] AT&T is using its internal Web to shake out digital payment

6. See "Developments in Automatic Text Retrieval, " by Gerald Salton, in the Aug. 30, Vol. 253, issue of *Science* for a look at where the field of text retrieval is going.

technologies. Primarily geared toward internal purchasing, the trial is also functioning as a testbed for the various types of digital payment technologies.

Another product, AnchorPage, will index your internal Web and allow visitors to search the content. As the scope of your Web grows, finding information becomes even more critical than simply adding information to the Web. Interleaf has a high end product from a long time electronic publishing software vendor. Their Web publishing product, Cyberleaf, addresses, in a comprehensive manner, not only the composition and Web page creation issues, but also organizational workflow issues.

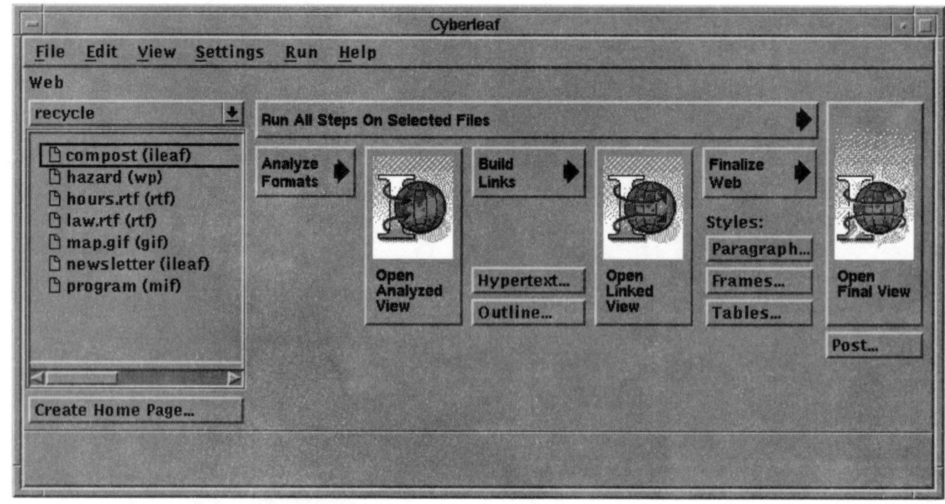

Cyberleaf is a powerful, comprehensive Internet publishing application that allows you to create and maintain high-quality text and graphic Internet document webs, using standard authoring tools including, Word, WordPerfect, Interleaf and FrameMaker.

Cyberleaf combines HTML and GIF data conversion and hyperlinking with complete web production and management capabilities in one easy-to-use, push-button application.

Lotus, InterNotes Web publisher converts Notes databases into Web publishable documents. Notes is probably the preeminent "groupware" product. It enables groups of people to collaborate, by placing and updating information in a Notes server. (For more information of groupware See *Section 8 • 3 Groupware* in *Chapter 8 • Document Management*.) The contents of the Notes server are a valuable resource

7. Vol 1, #8, 1995 and also at http://www.iworld.com.

for an organization. The InterNotes Web publisher enables users of Notes to publish their Notes databases on the Web, widening the availability and utility of the database.

That about wraps up our analysis of document components. The Web is forming new information structures creating a collection of **global networked information**. The rapidly solidifying collection of information, accessible via networks, may quite realistically form a global library. The technical barriers to such a fantasy are quickly disappearing. Only the legal concerns (which are not minor) of intellectual property rights, copyrights, and patent law remain as murky unknowns. (For a more through discussion of the possibilities of networks See *Section 7 • 4 Electronic Distribution* in *Chapter 7 • Applying Standards.*)

3 • 2 The Design Point of View

Design is another point of view that must be considered as we examine ways of approaching the document-creation process. The way a document is visually presented—how it grabs the audience visually—is a critical factor in the overall perception of a document. After all, the end product is an object to be viewed. The aesthetic components that make up the pages, fonts, layout, and color all contribute to the overall goal of producing a document that communicates ideas clearly. (A thorough treatment of document and Web design[8] is beyond the scope of this book, but for a list of good books see *section Publications* in the *appendix Resources.*) The remainder of this section will introduce some of the basics of document design and other topics that have strong relationships to document processing.[9]

8. For excellent guidance on Web design, check out Sun's "Guide to Web Style" at: http://www.sun.com/styleguide/.

9. See *Section 6 • 3 Color* in *Chapter 6 • Media and Document Integration* for some information on color.

3 • 2 • 1 Fonts and Typography

Typography is to writing what a soundtrack is to a motion picture.
—Jonathan Hoefler

Open any computer magazine about desktop publishing and you will see many ads for fonts and font-manipulation software. It may seem that the world has gone a little font crazy. Fonts, specifically, and typography, in general, are extremely important.

In some sense, typography is something that is so obvious, so visible, and so all-encompassing that most people simply don't notice it. However, it is precisely because typography is so pervasive that it is so important.[10] Fonts are not simply the shape of letters for creating words; they are letterforms with carefully designed shapes and subtle differences that relate to each other and that combine to make a pure visual statement.

Some software tools pay more attention than others to the role of fonts and typography. Depending on your specific needs, these tools may or may not be important. However an awareness of the crucial factors can only help when judging the capabilities of a particular tool. In general, page makeup and page layout programs have much more flexible typographic features than their batch–oriented counterparts. The WYSIWYG nature of page makeup systems is more suitable to adhoc design and experimentation.

10. For a good overview of typography filled with practical rules of thumb, see *Using Type Right,* by Philip Brady, Northern Lights Books, Cincinnati, OH, 1988.

Appropriate Fonts

Some fonts are simply more appropriate than others for particular uses. The figures below illustrate inappropriate and appropriate font usage. You decide.

The Declaration of Independence

When in the course of human events, it becomes necessary for one people to dissolve the political bands which have connected them with another, and to assume among the powers of the earth, the separate and equal station to which the laws of Nature and of Nature's God entitle them, a decent respect to the opinions of mankind requires that they should declare the causes which impel them to the separation.

We hold these truths to be self-evident, that all men are created equal, that they are endowed by their Creator with certain unalienable rights, that among these are life, liberty and the pursuit of happiness. That to secure these rights, governments are instituted among men, deriving their just powers from consent of the governed,—That whenever any form of government becomes destructive of these ends, it is the right of the peo-

The Declaration of Independence

When in the course of human events, it becomes necessary for one people to dissolve the political bands which have connected them with another, and to assume among the powers of the earth, the separate and equal station to which the laws of Nature and of Nature's God entitle them, a decent respect to the opinions of mankind requires that they should declare the causes which impel them to the separation.

We hold these truths to be self-evident, that all men are created equal, that they are endowed by their Creator with certain unalienable rights, that among these are life, liberty and the pursuit of happiness. That to secure these rights, governments are instituted among men, deriving their just powers from consent of the governed,—That whenever any form of government becomes destructive of these ends, it is the right of the people to alter or to abolish it, and to institute new government, laying its foundation on such principles and organizing its powers in

If you are faced with selecting a font, it is important to consider the number of variations available in a font family. Some font families have more than a dozen variations. This within-family flexibility can only make the designer's job easier. Using several variations within a single font family is almost always aesthetically safer than mixing arbitrary fonts.

Serif vs. Sans Serif Fonts

There are two broad categories of fonts: serif and sans serif. Serif fonts are fonts with finishing strokes at the ends of the main strokes of the letters. Many serif fonts exhibit calligraphic qualities in their main strokes. Sans serif fonts do not have the finishing strokes (serifs) and are often considered more modern. Overall, serif fonts are easier to read. As a general (albeit very oversimplified) rule, sans serif fonts are better for headings but not for main body text.

Serif examples

Originally letters were adaptations of natural forms employed in picture writing, but by a process of evolution [actually degradation] they have become arbitrary signs with little *resemblance to the symbols from which they are derived. These arbitrary shapes* have passed through their periods of uncertainty and change; they have a long history and manifold associations; they are classics, and should not be tampered with, except within limits which a just discretions may allow.
— Fredrick Goudy
The Alphabet and Elements of Lettering

Sans serif examples

The test which a well-formed letter must meet is, that nothing in it shall present the appearance of being an afterthought—that every detail shall at least seem to have been foreseen from the start; and, when letters are used in combinations to form words and sentences, that no one of them shall stand out from its fellows or draw attention to itself at the expense of those with which it is associated.
— Fredrick Goudy
The Alphabet and Elements of Lettering

Many tools are available for font manipulation. These tools allow precise adjustments of kerning tables (the spacing between letters), the creation of new letterforms, the extraction of outlines, distortions, and so on. One important reason that such a variety of detailed tools exists is that font design has such an important impact on the document as a whole. Letterforms are a key ingredient in a document, and designers use them as the raw material to be manipulated by their designing tools.

Of course, it's important not to get too carried away with these tools.

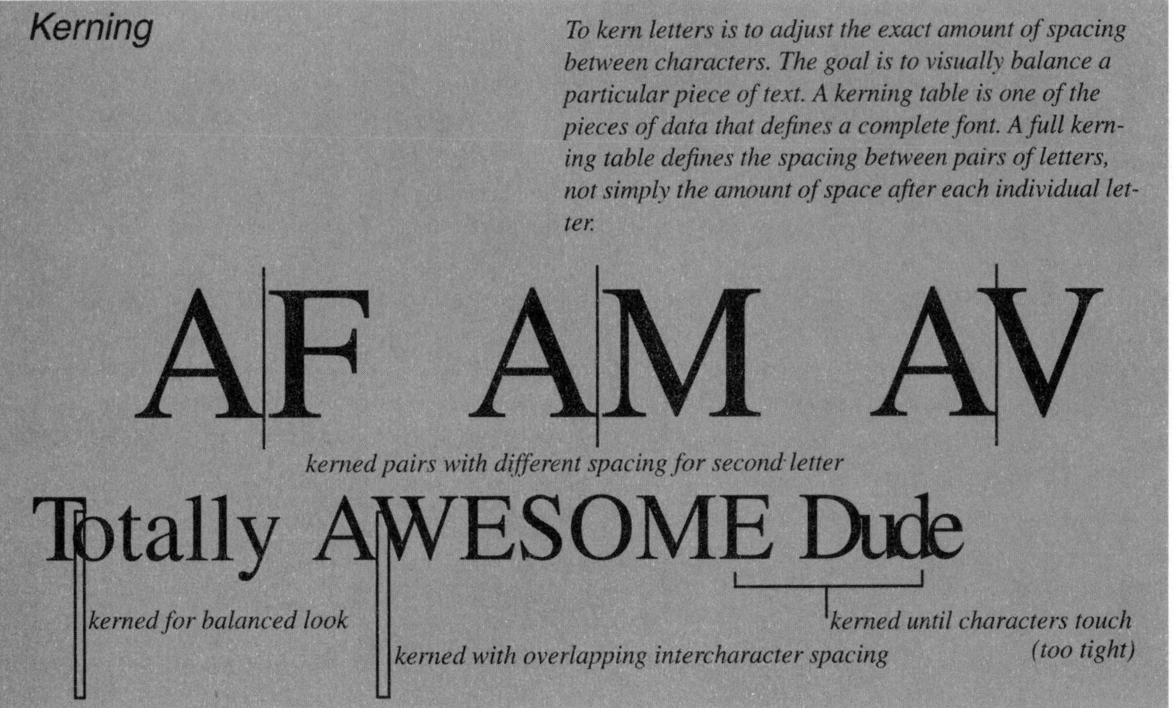

Kerning
To kern letters is to adjust the exact amount of spacing between characters. The goal is to visually balance a particular piece of text. A kerning table is one of the pieces of data that defines a complete font. A full kerning table defines the spacing between pairs of letters, not simply the amount of space after each individual letter.
AF AM AV
kerned pairs with different spacing for second letter
Totally AWESOME Dude
kerned for balanced look
kerned with overlapping intercharacter spacing
kerned until characters touch (too tight)

Individual characters may also be used as graphic components. The line between font manipulation and graphic illustration can blur quite easily.

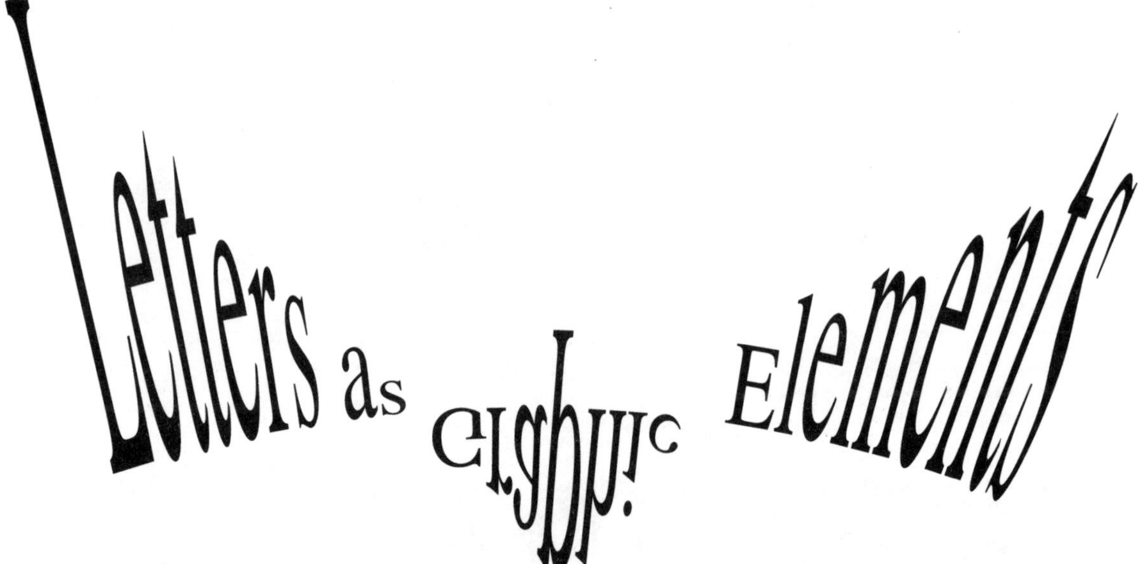

The many software tools available for font manipulation allow such a wide variety of choices that the traditional letterform is no longer sacred. Characters used as illustrative elements bring us back to the age of illustrated manuscripts filled with carefully crafted characters. There is of course the added danger of "font junk," the use and abuse of font manipulation tools by the amateur.

Fonts are also one of the more problematic aspects of document interchange. A font used in one document may or may not exist as a "system" resource on another computer system. Sometimes, if a document depends on the system to provide the font, and it's not there, an available font is substituted and the look of the document changes. Adobe's Multiple Master font technology addresses some of these problems and is a key component of their Acrobat line of products. Multiple Master fonts are able to parameterize more of the font that other font technologies. (For more information on Acrobat, see *Section 7 • 4 • 2 Electronic Page Delivery* in *Chapter 7 • Applying Standards*.)

Another somewhat obtuse but powerful character manipulation system is the METAFONT language.[11] METAFONT is a precise mathematical description of fonts; in many ways, it models the way ink is placed on paper by a pen. METAFONT is the creation of Donald Knuth—the same man who brought you TeX (see *Section 4 • 1 Types of Document Processors*). METAFONT is a language for describing characters in excruciatingly precise terms. After creating or modifying a description, the system chews away on the "code" and spits out a new font. These fonts can then be used by TeX, turning this interesting academic exercise into a practical and useful tool.

11. The complete description of METAFONT can be found in *The METAFONT book* by Donald Knuth, Addison Wesley, Reading, MA, 1986.

Some METAFONT Parameters

These are some of the over 60 parameters manipulable in the Computer Modern typeface, created with METAFONT.

vertical parameters for height and depth manipulation

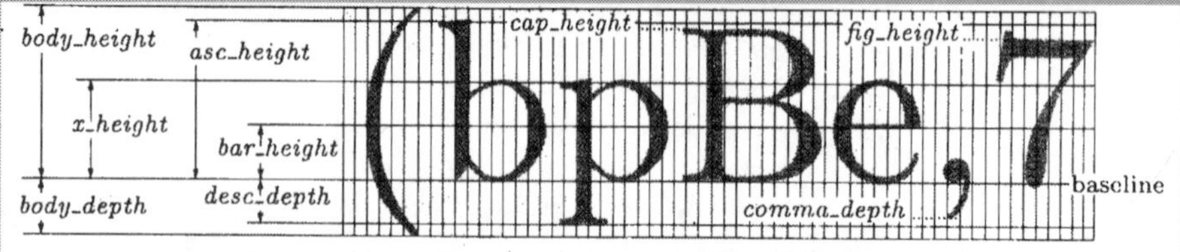

darkness or weight manipulation parameters

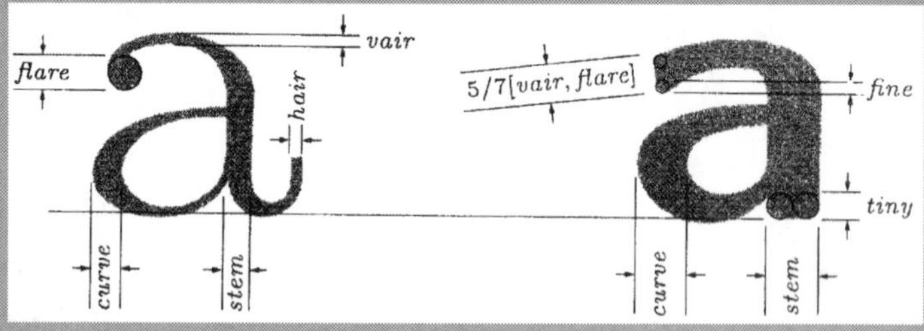

parameters for controlling serifs and arms

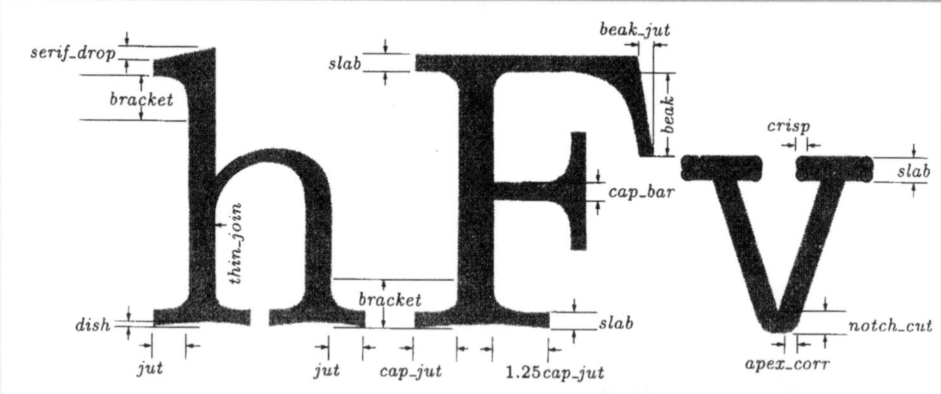

3 • 2 • 2 Layout and Composition

The placement of the various components of a document on a page is the **layout**. Document layout and composition are critical pieces of the design puzzle. Unfortunately, the only help electronic publishing tools have to offer is assistance through the use of templates. Some tools, like Microsoft's Wizards in MS Word, lend you a helping hand to fill in templates. Tools that aid in the overall layout and structural composition of documents exist only in research laboratories. Automated aids for global design features such as overall balance, proper use of white space, and so on, do not exist as product features.

Typical document processing systems have **style sheets** or **master pages**, that define a particular visual layout. The visual layout of document elements on the style sheets can be applied to the entire document. The number of master pages and the flexibility in working with them are important capabilities of a document processing system. Often, global changes to a document are accomplished using these types of pages or styles. Careful use of master pages and style sheets is a significant help in the management of overall document consistency. (For a more through discussion of document management issues, please see *Chapter 8 • Document Management*.)

In the future, it may be possible to have design "helpers" in much the same way that grammar checkers now help. Such suggestions are not pure fantasy. We are already starting to see the application of image-recognition systems in the pen-based portable computer field. Users can create rough sketches, and the system cleans up the drawing on PDAs (Portable Digital Assistant) like Apple's Newton. Image recognition is being taken a step farther with the concepts of **shape grammars**.[12] In the architecture and computer graphics domains, shape grammars have been used to create simulated buildings in the style of Frank Lloyd Wright[13] and paintings by Kandinsky.[14] The concept is to create a grammar, a lan-

12. For a good explanation of shape grammars, from its principle proponent, see "Introduction to Shape and Shape Grammars, " by G. Stiny in *Environment and Planning* B, 7, 1980.

guage, from a set of shapes as well as the allowable operations upon those shapes. Many interesting grammars have been created to describe the styles of architects and artists.

3 • 3 Communications Views

When the writer becomes the center of his attention, he becomes a nudnik. And a nudnik who believes he's profound is even worse than just a plain nudnik.
—Isaac Bashevis Singer

First and foremost, a document is a tool to communicate information. The type of information will affect the type of communications. Different information types are entertainment, reference, scanning, mandatory versus optional, sales, friendly, and formal. Each information type has customary visual conventions. Used poorly or too often, they will cause your document to look like just more pieces of paper. Used judiciously and with imagination, they can be a valuable aid.

But ultimately, the content expressed in the document is what really matters. If the reader understands the content, your communication was successful.

13. See "The Language of the Prairie: Frank Lloyd Wright's Prairie Houses," by H. Koning and J. Eizenburg in *Environment and Planning* B: Planning and Design 8, 1981.

14. See "A Rule System for Aesthetic Research in the Visual Arts," by R.G. Lauzzana and L. Pocock-Williams in *Leonardo* 21, No. 4, 1988. Also see "Storing Art Images in Intelligent Computers" by Joan L. Kirsch and Russel A.Kirsch, in *Leonardo* 1988 for a good overview on the use of shape grammars and art images.

Often the main trick to successful communication is getting the reader to pay attention. Look at some of your junk mail; innumerable attention–getting devices will come into view. Colored stamps, fake telegrams, pop-ups, personalized names, metallized envelopes, and more are all attention grabbers.

In the domain of electronic documents, clip art collections of all sorts can help you draw attention to your documents. Clip art collections with all sorts of specialty images (see *section Clip Art* in the *appendix Resources*) from military symbols to biological parts to cartoons, can convey a message to the reader. Clip art and unimaginative attention–getting devices can cut both ways, however.

HOW TO USE COMPUTER-GENERATED PIE CHARTS AND BAR GRAPHS TO MAKE ABSTRACT CONCEPTS UNDERSTANDABLE TO MORONS LIKE YOUR BOSS

Let's say you have to write a Safety Report. The old-fashioned, pre-computer way to do this would be something like this:

```
In March, we had two people who got
sick because they forgot and drank
coffee from the vending machine.
Also, Ed Sparge set fire to his desk
again. Ed has promised that from
now on he will put his cigar out
before he dozes off.
```

But now using the graphics capability on your computer, you can produce a visually arresting and easy-to-understand report like this:

SAFETY REPORT FOR MARCH
TOTAL NUMBER OF INCIDENTS

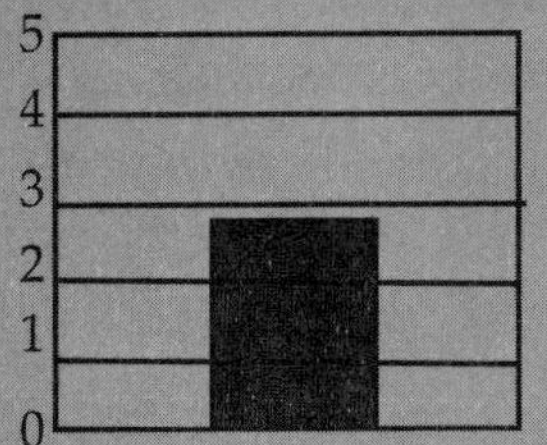

BREAKDOWN BY CAUSE

Looks Aren't Everything

If you owned stock in these companies, which Annual Report would you rather receive?

The Big Bad Beautiful Corporation A N N U A L R E P O R T

Earnings throughout 1997 were slow due to the progressive erosion of market share. The downsizing effort will continue until quarterly cash flow improves.

	Year ending October 31	
	1996	1997
	(in thousands)	
Net dividends to shareholders from:		
Investment income	$ 40,111	$ 5,432
Realized gain on investment transactions	$ 12,555	$ -1,045
Total dividends	$ 43,111	$ 0
Net Income (LOSS):		
Beginning of year	$644,972	$(200,369)
End of year	$120,804	$(576,972)

The Bigger Baddest Inc. Annual Report

This was it! The year we finally broke even and started to make a profit! The R&D finally paid off. Market share is growing. Happy dividends.

	Year ending, October 31	
	1996	1997
Net dividends to shareholders from:		
Investment income	2,000	12,342
Realized gain on investment transactions	1,322	6,578
Total dividends	1,778	4,223
Net income:		
Beginning of year	-31,000	1,332
End of year	-2,221	31,233

Customizing the content of an article for a particular audience is a good way of improving communication. Of course, doing this is extremely difficult for large–volume publications, such as newspapers and magazines. One interesting technique used by the *Washington Post* (and others) is called **zoning**. The *Post* has a column called Dr. Gridlock that describes the trials and tribulations of travel in the Washington, D.C. area. The content of this column is modified for specific areas by the use of readers' addresses via delivery zones.

SCIENCE, POLITICS, and FOOD PYRAMID GRAPHICS

Although design doesn't mean everything, it can have important and even political impact. For instance, take the case of the food pyramid.

In April 1991, the U.S. Department of Agriculture (USDA) was going to publish a replacement of the basic four food groups wheel, a staple of classrooms since the 1950s. The idea was to increase the importance of grains, fruits, and vegetables and to reduce the importance of meat and dairy products, following more recently discovered good nutritional practices. As you might imagine, the beef and dairy lobbyists were not too happy about this turn of events. After a great deal of criticism, publication of the pyramid was halted. According to one nutritionist angered by the USDA reversal, "It was the visual that made the impact. That's what upset people; it clearly showed you should not have as much meats and dairy products as you should grains, fruits, and vegetables—which is the truth."[15]

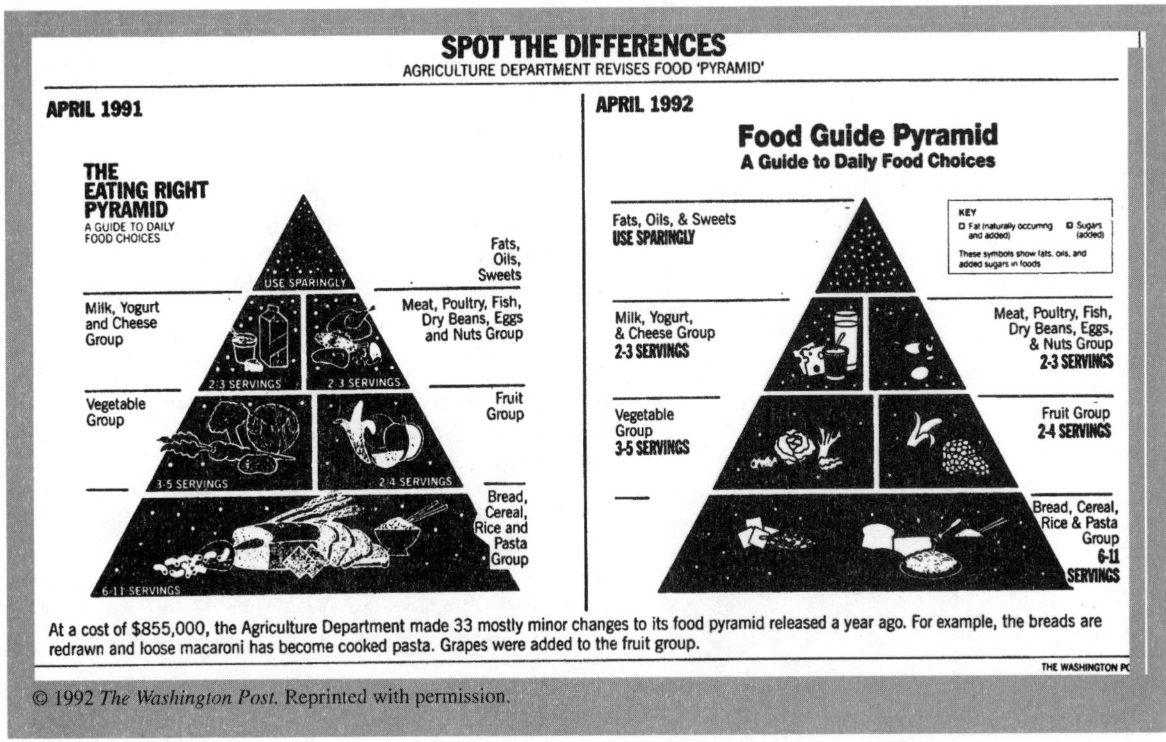

SPOT THE DIFFERENCES

AGRICULTURE DEPARTMENT REVISES FOOD 'PYRAMID'

At a cost of $855,000, the Agriculture Department made 33 mostly minor changes to its food pyramid released a year ago. For example, the breads are redrawn and loose macaroni has become cooked pasta. Grapes were added to the fruit group.

THE WASHINGTON P

15. From the article "U.S. Drops New Food Chart," by Carole Sugerman and Malcolm Gladwell, in the *Washington Post*, April, 1991.

One year later (and $855,000 more), the USDA unveiled a refined pyramid and had more data supporting its case. In the end, good science won out, and the lobbyists had to live with the design of the food pyramid.[16] Now the Food Pyramid is a classroom staple and also appears on the packaging of many products in your supermarket.

3 • 3 • 1 Aid for Grammarless Writers

A man's grammar, like Caesar's wife, must not only be pure, but above suspicion of impurity.— Edgar Allan Poe

As we examine ways in which technology can help in the communication of ideas, publishing systems can provide a number of tools to aid grammar. At times the technology of word processing and desktop publishing systems is more fun than writing. Integrated graphics with text, WYSIWYG displays, and font manipulations can divert the writer from the communications task at hand. In a Washington Post article titled *"Does Technology Contribute to Bad Writing? Perhaps It Might Probably Could—Or NOT,"* Michael Schrage, a columnist for the *Los Angeles Times,* commented:

> Indeed, some people argue that word processing technology makes the physical task of writing so much easier that some people toss self-discipline to the electrons and hedonistically indulge themselves by larding their prose with everything but the kitchen sink. Conversely, the "perfectionists" turn into digital Flauberts, writhing in agony over which comma should go where and if that semicolon is really the best way to go.

Some products, used judiciously, aid the process of writing correctly and with good grammar, but nothing can stop the rambling author from rambling with run-ons and going on and on and on.

Products such as RightWriter (Cue Software), Grammatik (Reference Software) and Correct Grammar (Lifetree Software) rate documents for readability. Grammar checker systems can generate reports about average sentence and paragraph length, the

16. From "The $855,000 Pyramid," by Carole Sugarman, in the *Washington Post*, April 28, 1992.

use of passive voice, the use of jargon, and other writing aspects. They also provide suggested changes. These packages use readability scores to rate the document as appropriate for a particular reading grade level.

A few readability indexes are widely recognized. Chief among these are the Flesch-Kincaid Score and the Fog Index. According to the RightWriter (a grammar checker) manual: [17]

> The Flesch-Kincaid formula is the United States Government Department of Defense standard (DOD MIL-M-38784B). The government requires its use by contractors producing manuals for the armed services. The Readability Index is equivalent to the Overall Reading Grade Level (OGL) for the document.
>
> Grade Level = (.39 x ASL) + (11.8 x ASW) - 15.59.
>
> ASL = average sentence length (# of words /# of sentences).
>
> ASW = average # of syllables/word (# of syllables /# of words).
>
> A good range is 6-10.

17. From the MacUser's Manual of RightWriter, version 3.1, 1990, Readability Index section.

RIGHTwriter® Options

The following illustrations show some of the stylistic analysis options available using RIGHTwriter® 3.1 on the Macintosh.

Writing Style

Education Level	Type of Writing
○ General Public	○ Fiction
○ High School	○ General Business
○ College	○ Technical Report or Article
	○ Manual
	○ Proposal

[Save Changes] [Cancel]

Style Rules

☐ Passive Voice	☐ Conjunction Start	☐ Consider Omitting
☐ Split Infinitive	☐ Weak Sentence Start	☐ Ambiguous Wording
☐ Difficult Sentence	☐ End With Preposition	☐ Cliche
☐ Use Verb Form	☐ Negative Sentence	☐ Weak Wording
☐ Long Paragraph	☐ Use Simpler Terms	☐ Overused Phrases
☐ Start With But	☐ Use Simpler Word	☐ Single Word Quote
☐ Long Sentence	Sentence Length [ ]	☐ Contraction

[OK] [Save Changes] [Cancel]

AT&T sells a writing tool called WWB, the Writer's Workbench software, that runs under the UNIX operating system. It is an interesting collection of utilities that help analyze writing style and suggests changes to fix grammatical problems. It can look for problems with punctuation, sentence length, readability, split infinitives, and overall organization. WWB even has a utility to compare your language style with that of another document, facilitating consistency over large numbers of documents.

3 • 3 • 2 Random Writing Tools

Aside from the various grammatical aids previously mentioned, spelling checkers are certainly the most frequently used writing tool. Spell checkers vary from ones that simply list the words not found in a dictionary to ones that make suggested corrections. The better spell checkers can work with several dictionaries and may be able to use a general dictionary, a site-wide (organization) dictionary, one for a user, and one for the particular document.

Most of the widely used word processing packages provide or work with a built-in thesaurus. These are always useful when searching for that hard–to–think–of–word, utterance, expression, maxim, term, slogan, verbiage, declaration, idiom, phrase, remark, statement, comment, and so on.

One innovative writing tool introduced back in 1987 is the Microsoft Bookshelf. It was one of the first serious mass market CD-ROMs and was aimed at writers. The storage capacity of the CD-ROM enabled Bookshelf to contain 11 reference books and information data sets. Among these were *The American Heritage Dictionary, Roget's II: Electronic Thesaurus, Bartlett's Familiar Quotations, The Chicago Manual of Style,* and the *U.S. ZIP Code Directory.* The combination of these reference materials in the context of a PC and a word processor is a powerful tool.

Budding poets can also be computerized. The "Rhymer" from WordPerfect Corporation is a rhyming dictionary available for use with WordPerfect on PCs. You can search for words by a number of phonetic characteristics. Act like a bloodhound and search for a sound; it will simply astound, not confound. Just imagine the possibilities of rhyming for searched quotes with words found in the thesaurus! Onward writers—now you have as many tools to abuse as graphic designers do!

A Little Spelling Checker Humor

Some spelling checkers not only find spelling errors but also suggest replacements. On an electronic mailing list that discusses FrameMaker issues, there was even a series of messages about amusing word replacements. Some of the suggested replacements were bomb for IBM, salivation for Xyvision, masochist for Massachusetts, and—the hands–down winner—replacing Interleaf (a prime competitor) with FrameMaker.

On-line Quotes

Writing with the capability of searching for quotes can be amusing. Let's say you're preparing a presentation about writing books. A search for quotes containing the words "write" and "book" using Microsoft Bookshelf yields:

"A bad *book* is as much of a labor to *write* as a good one; it comes as sincerely from the author's soul." — Aldus Huxley

NIFTY TOOL!!

3 • 4 The Engineered View

Documents are complex objects. Let's now examine the document as an object composed of a variety of pieces that must be "engineered" together.

Often, the only time all pieces of a project come together is when the final report is due. All the information gathered from a variety of sources must be assembled into a coherent, deliverable product. Most likely, many people contribute to the final report. Their individual idiosyncratic uses of publishing tools must be integrated into a consistent product.

Data created by spreadsheets or images from drawing tools are also often included in completed documents. The assembly of all these components brings us to the topic of the compound document.

3 • 4 • 1 Compound Document

The compound document, as its name suggests, is a document composed of many parts. These parts may originate from vastly different systems and exist in many different formats. From a technical standpoint, the integration of these pieces into a coherent whole is a formidable task. Each part must be integrated seamlessly into what appears to be a single consistent document. Even more difficult is the often necessary requirement to go back to the original system that created the data, such as a spreadsheet, to edit the data.

Electronically created compound documents resemble information quilts patched together from a variety of information sources. You may use information created for one purpose in one particular system in several systems. You may also use the information for a different purpose than was intended. Documents created with such information can quickly become impossible to maintain and update.

The original data sources become an integral part of the creation process, and great care must be exercised to maintain those data sources for future versions of the document. Text, graphics, and scanned photos may be assembled for one purpose and later reassembled for another (i.e., a Web site). You may reuse document content. If proper care is taken of all the various data sources, you can reuse the information. Reusing the content allows an organization to profit from the publication of the content again and again.

Before we get into some more detail, let's take a look at the forest before starting a hike through the trees. Many technologies created in the last several years impact compound documents. The concept, however, is simple and elegant. The user should be allowed to read, or write a document. Inside the document are all sorts of media types that the user may want to mess around with as part of the editing process.

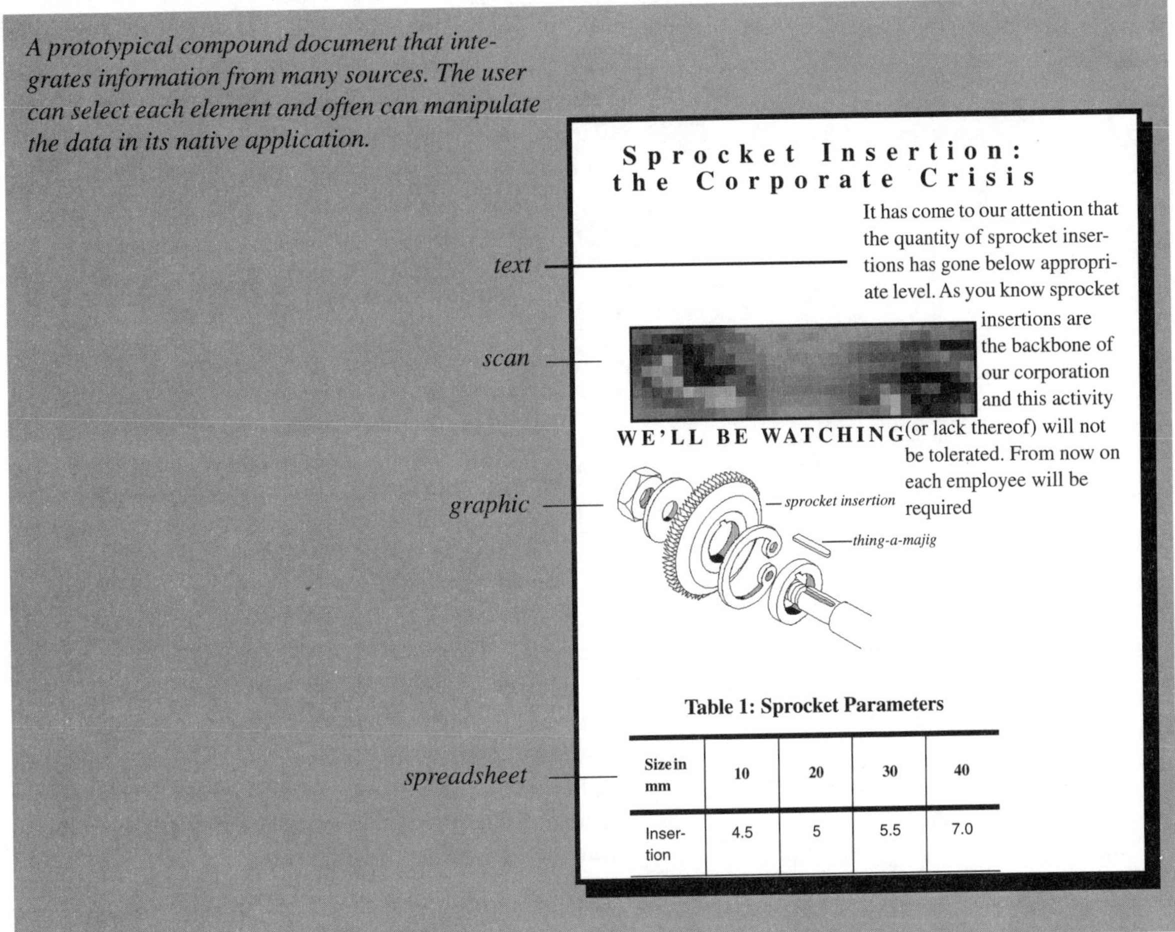

A prototypical compound document that integrates information from many sources. The user can select each element and often can manipulate the data in its native application.

The world starts getting complicated when vendors, of necessity, address issues concerning the storage and interoperability of these complex compound documents. For example, if a document contains a variety of spreadsheets embedded in the document, it is comforting for the user to know that the spreadsheet will be updatable. The document itself becomes the focus of a user's attention and becomes the principal vehicle for system-wide data integration. One trend has been to represent the various media types as "objects." Then you can use and reuse the objects and the software which operates on them. A wide variety of object storage mechanisms have appeared with no clear winner on the horizon. Expect confusion to be the norm for several more years, at least.

Two major integration strategies are Microsoft's OLE 2.0 and Apple's OpenDoc. OpenDoc is a collaboration between Apple and IBM and was designed for multi-platform operations. A somewhat dated, but still valuable comparison of OpenDoc to OLE is available from IBM at: http://www.austin.ibm.com/pspinfo/odoc-ole.html.

From the OpenDoc FAQ:

> *What is OpenDoc?* OpenDoc is a multi-platform, component software architecture that enables developers to evolve current applications into component software or to create new component software applications. OpenDoc software will run on Apple Macintosh personal computers, as well as Windows, Windows NT, OS/2, and AIX systems. With software enabled by OpenDoc, users will be able to mix and match software to fit their needs, combining text, graphics, video, spreadsheets, and many other types of data into a single document.

Individual elements, called components, may be edited by "component editors." A component editor is a "independent program that manipulates and displays a particular kind of content."

The object representation for OpenDoc is called the System Object Model (SOM) and is from IBM. Again from the OpenDoc FAQ it is a "platform-independent framework for allowing component software to exchange data and instructions. It is a highly efficient dynamic linking mechanism for objects, which supports multiple languages and provides a gateway to distributed object servers."

Another element of the OpenDoc Architecture is Bento, a portable compound document and multimedia storage library and format. Finally there is also "Component Glue," an acknowledgment that Microsoft exists. Component Glue "enables interoperability with Microsoft Corporation's Object Linking and Embedding (OLE) technology for inter-application communication. OpenDoc's significantly simpler API allows developers to program Microsoft OLE much easier via OpenDoc." (See the OpenDoc Web site for more gory details at: http://www.opendoc.apple.com.)

OLE 2.0 from Microsoft is based on yet another object storage model called the Common Object Model (COM). It is more appropriate to compare COM to CORBA (Common Object Request Broker Architecture) rather than to OpenDoc. COM and CORBA are also not attacking the exact same problems, so a comparison here is also flawed. In an excellent article, *"OLE and COM vs. CORBA"* by Michael Foody in the April 1996 issue of UNIX Review, Foody points out that, "In general terms, COM...is used in desktop applications to provide a binary standard for software component interoperability and ORBs are used as the infrastructure to construct larger-scale distributed systems. Of course, Microsoft is working on a distributed version of COM, designed for use in enterprise-class distributed systems, while IBM is busy working with Apple to use SOM as the basis for a desktop component model called OpenDoc."

Both IBM and DEC have had other software projects that address the challenge of compound documents. IBM's MO:DCA (Mixed Object Document Content Architecture) is a combination compound document and object architecture. DEC's CDA (Compound Document Architecture) is a system resembling the philosophical approach of ODA. (For more information on the Office Document Architecture standard, (See *Section 5 • 5 ODA* in *Chapter 5 • Document Standards*.)

As we've just seen, the concepts of compound documents have been around for quite some time. The coming of the Web, however, makes the creation and use of compound documents a common place occurrence. With all the advantages the Web has brought, it has also magnified some of the problems of conformance, performance, and standardization. Vendors are trying to differentiate themselves by introducing hot new technologies. Content creators are placed in a bind because the use of these new technologies, although compelling, limits the audience and distribution possibilities. There are no simple answers; just be aware of what's going on so you can make educated choices.

3 • 4 • 2 Active Documents

The various architectural approaches discussed in the previous section permit the creation of new types of document processing. One new type is the **active document**. A number of publishing systems already tout this capability, but may call it different things. For example, a pie chart of data from a spreadsheet, included in a document, may update itself when the spreadsheet changes. In another case, a paragraph just rewritten may initiate an electronic mail message to a manager, informing the manager of the change and requesting approval. The document is no longer a passive object; it is doing things. The notion of a document with active components is another step in the direction of a totally integrated information environment.

Several technologies are available for inter-process and inter-application communication. Publishing systems approach the problem of application communications in several ways. Ultimately, the publishing system depends on the services provided by the operating system. Most operating systems provide some mechanism for interapplication communications, and these mechanisms are exploited by some of the publishing systems. For example, on MS-DOS platforms running MS Windows, a facility called OLE (Object Linking and Embedding) is used by MS Word for Windows to include "live" EXCEL spreadsheets. The Macintosh's System 7 operating system has a "Publish and Subscribe" facility for inter-application communication. Interleaf and FrameMaker on UNIX platforms use RPC (Remote Procedure Calls) to allow an AutoCad drawing in a document to be linked to the AutoCad application.

Interleaf's **active document technology** is one of the more ambitious implementations of the active document approach. Document sections can behave in certain ways and take various actions. For example, a document can be directed to send e-mail to various managers for approval before permission is granted for the public to view the document. In fact, one of Lotus Notes, strengths is to allow the organization of this type of work flow procedures with various types of documents. (See *Section 8 • 3 Groupware* in *Chapter 8 • Document Management* for more information on work flow issues.)

This feature could prove invaluable to organizations that require complex configuration management of documents, because documents are just one portion of an engineering effort. For example, the production of an airplane must correspond accurately to the various designs and tests of the airplane. The ability to embed "intelligence" into documents is an interesting approach to the configuration management problem. (For more discussion on this topic, See *Section 8 • 2 Configuration Management* in *Chapter 8 • Document Management*.)

Here again, the Web provides ample examples of the ability to take older concepts and apply them to newer implementations. Active document technology is perhaps best exemplified in the Web with the emergence of Java. The ability to transmit little programs called applets has taken the Web by storm. The enthusiasm with which the Net has embraced Java is both a credit to Sun's technology and their ability to market it in a Net-friendly manner. Java applets allow authors to wake up their documents. No longer passive reading material, a Java-cized document can shout, sing, and interact with the reader. Active documents have hit the mainstream.

3 • 5 The Database View

Let's move now to an examination of the relationship of documents to databases. Documents can relate directly to databases in two main ways. First, as the report or simple printout of a database. This is known as database publishing. Second, and more interesting, is the use of a database to hold the document content. The various components that comprise a document can be placed into a database. The database can be queried by the publishing system and out pops the printed pages (if only it were that simple). These types of systems are possible today; however, there are no hard and fast rules for accomplishing such implementations. Each organization's needs and requirements must be carefully analyzed, and no one solution will fits everyone's needs.

Reusing a document's components is becoming increasingly possible. Reuse is possible only if you can identify and reassemble pieces of content. Mechanisms to break apart the original document into meaningful component parts can be developed using standards and well-defined recommended practices. Reuse is also another potential benefit for the use of a document structuring standard like SGML.

Sometimes the seemingly simple task of finding the relevant material may, in fact, be the most difficult aspect of reusing content material. Document repositories must be created with appropriate key words or embedded tagging mechanisms that enable meaningful retrieval. Electronic imaging systems, which scan reams of documents and store the images on optical disks as a replacement for microfilm, are a growing industry. Without sufficient tagging, these systems are a small step forward from microfilm technology. An image of a page without the means of asking for information about what is on the page is no better than a picture. About the only savings is in physical storage space (which may, in fact, be significant for an organization).

3 • 5 • 1 Database Publishing

> ***The Vietnam Memorial***
>
> One of the most interesting database publishing efforts to date was the "printing" of the names on the Vietnam Memorial in Washington, D.C. The memorial contains the names of all the U.S. citizens killed in the Vietnam war. The names are etched in stone in chronological order, but within any particular day, the names are in alphabetical order. Data Development, Inc., of Palm City, Florida, was responsible for this painstaking work. This project also teaches a lesson about the quest for total accuracy. Obviously, accurate spelling of the names was of utmost importance. All 50,000 names were proofread six times yet six errors still escaped notice.

An extension of report–generation capabilities, which has been around for many years, database publishing adds a level of integration between the database and the publishing system. A report is one visual representation of a database. Slick publications produced by pouring data into visual templates might be another representation of the same database.

Database publishing tools allow you to choose particular fields in a database for printing. Particular styles can be applied to these fields and selectively printed. Such tools are invaluable for catalogs with thousands or hundreds of thousands of entries, such as a yellow–pages directory and parts catalogs, which must be updated regularly. Information from inside the database is extracted and combined with the publishing system to produce good–looking documents, not simply printouts.

The most common form of database publishing involves **merge** facilities. A merge facility combines regularly structured information with a template document. For example, a list of names and addresses, one per line with tab separators, might be combined with a form letter that contains special codes that indicate, to the document processor, when to insert data from the data file.

Merging Data

Most word processor systems provide the ability to merge data with template documents. Typically, this is called mail merge or simply a merge facility.

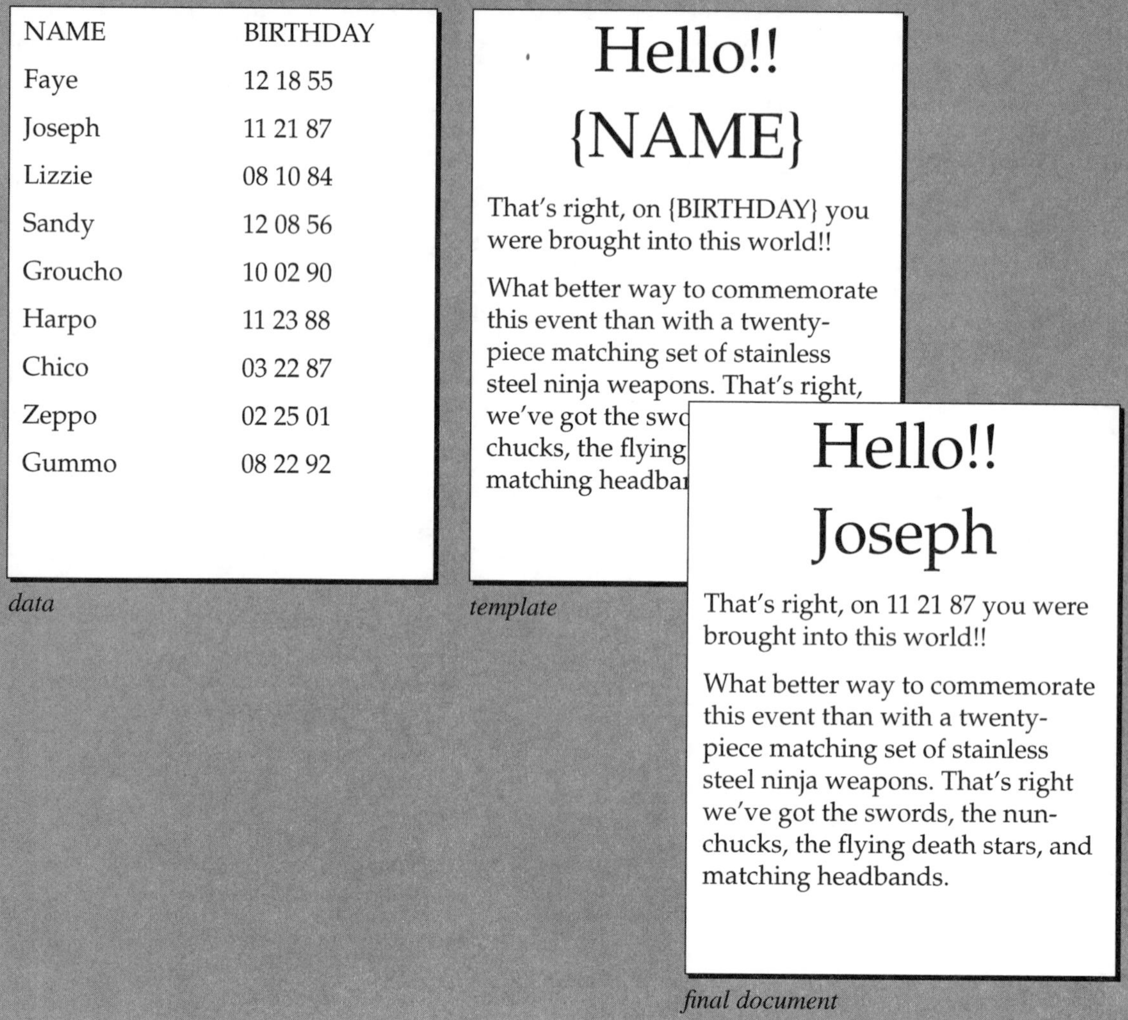

NAME	BIRTHDAY
Faye	12 18 55
Joseph	11 21 87
Lizzie	08 10 84
Sandy	12 08 56
Groucho	10 02 90
Harpo	11 23 88
Chico	03 22 87
Zeppo	02 25 01
Gummo	08 22 92

data

Hello!!

{NAME}

That's right, on {BIRTHDAY} you were brought into this world!!

What better way to commemorate this event than with a twenty-piece matching set of stainless steel ninja weapons. That's right, we've got the swo
chucks, the flying
matching headbai

template

Hello!!

Joseph

That's right, on 11 21 87 you were brought into this world!!

What better way to commemorate this event than with a twenty-piece matching set of stainless steel ninja weapons. That's right we've got the swords, the nun-chucks, the flying death stars, and matching headbands.

final document

A tighter link between the database (information source) and the document (information sink) aids the communication process in several ways. Information in a database will eventually need to be explained, summarized, and otherwise communicated to someone. With a link the information can reach the document faster and with fewer potential errors. Translations and transcriptions of database information to documents are error–prone tasks; the more direct this process can be, the better.

If you take the concepts of database publishing one step farther, you arrive at the concept of a document that functions as a *front end* to a database. The information in a document that came from a database can serve as the interface to a database. Database queries via the document and automatic updates bring the database/document connection full circle. Live link and active documents provide the technological foundations for a tight linkage.

3 • 5 • 2 Customized Publishing

If a collection of information—the content of a document—is kept in the proper type of database, publishers can reuse the content and create customized texts. Hardware and software advances are both contributing to a new publishing technology, that enables documents to be custom made for particular audiences.

In 1990, a partnership between McGraw-Hill and the University of Southern California was described as follows:

> Textbook publishers are offering new computer and printing systems that allow professors to custom-design textbooks by handpicking course materials from electronic databases stocked with traditional textbooks, magazine articles, and other published information.
>
> These customized books can be printed in limited quantities by the campus bookstore and distributed to students, sometimes within hours—not weeks or months—after ordering.[18]

One enterprising Washington, D.C., based company is taking another direction in custom printing. You might call it "just-in-time" printing. It produces an

18. See "Customizing: A Textbook Case" by Carla Lazzareschi, in the *Washington Post*, Sept. 22, 1990, and "Professors Customize Textbooks, Blurring Roles of Publisher, Seller and Copy Shop," by Michael Miller, in the *Wall Street Journal*, Aug. 19, 1990.

hourly newspaper, called "The Latest News," for people who travel the Washington to New York air shuttle.[19] Information from wire services is fed into document processing systems and formatted right away. This approach blurs the line between printed media and radio.

The ultimate in customized publishing is represented by some of the research at MIT's Media Lab. One interesting project unites information from wire services and television news. Using a computer screen with a touch screen interface, the reader can interact with this "newspaper." Fingering topics brings articles into view, touching a color picture can bring it to life as video. This work and other projects at the Media Lab are pointing the way to personalized interactive information sources beyond the newspaper...but I'd still like to read it in bed.[20]

Finally, to no one's surprise, the Web, the great technology integrator, provides ample example of interactions with and publications of databases. The most common use of database publishing on the Web are the Internet Searching starting points, (see *section 1 • 9 Internet Starting Points*) that allow users to query the database. The result is an instant database publication of the search results.

A great example of customized publications is the ability to customize your own starting page when using Microsoft's Web browser, the Internet Explorer. The Internet Explorer lets you pick a set of favorite links—national or world news, weather, comics and television listings—and have them displayed on your starting page. Of course, you must have the Microsoft Network set as the "home" page for this to work, but it's a compelling feature.

19. The newspaper called "The Latest News" is published by States News Service, 1333 F Street, NW, Washington, DC 20004. Tel: (202) 628-3100.

20. For a more comprehensive look at the media lab, see the book *The Media Lab*, by Stewart Brand, published by Penguin Books, New York, 1988 or their Web site at: http://www.media.mit.edu.

3 • 6 Specialized Views

Full–featured document processing systems often include specialized areas that have their own mini-processors. For example, mathematical equations, tables, and flow charts are all elements that can make up a document. Specialized document processors are available for each element.

Specialized document processing tools support many of the semantics needed to edit these particular elements. Embedding such knowledge in the programs allows manipulations that are more natural for the particular type of document element. For example, movement of a box in a flow chart could cause all connected lines to remain attached to the box. A table editor may allow for the insertion of rows of data with a simple command. (For a more through explanation of these systems, please See *Section 4 • 1 Types of Document Processors* in *Chapter 4 • Form and Function of Document Processors*.)

FrameMaker's Equation Editor

Within FrameMaker's publishing system is an equation editor, that actually does mathematical manipulations on the equations! While not as powerful as TeX's equation typesetting abilities, it is WYSIWYG in nature.

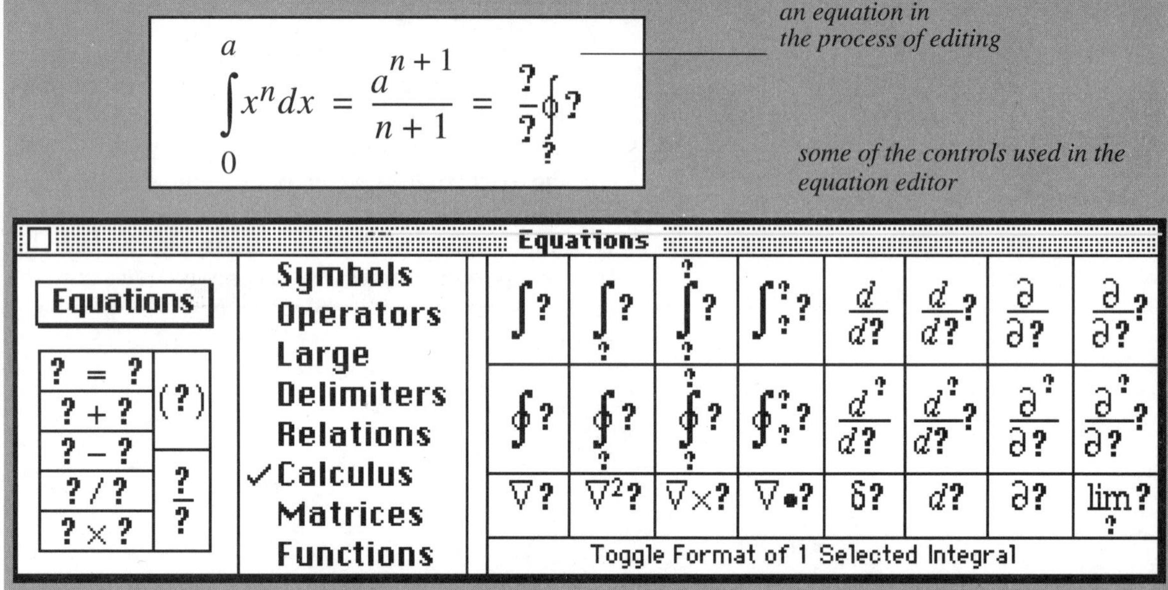

$$\int_0^a x^n dx = \frac{a^{n+1}}{n+1} = \frac{?}{?}\oint_?^? ?$$

an equation in the process of editing

some of the controls used in the equation editor

Equations

Symbols
Operators
Large
Delimiters
Relations
✓Calculus
Matrices
Functions

Toggle Format of 1 Selected Integral

Tables represent a particularly common document element that many systems support. Table editors exist in all kinds of electronic publishing systems, ranging from the low–end word processors (such as MS Word), through page layout systems (such as PageMaker), to the higher–end systems (such as Interleaf).

PageMaker's Table Editor

PageMaker comes complete with a separate utility for creating and editing tables. The following describes some of the types of manipulations possible with this table editor.

Resize rows and columns simply by dragging a boundary (table recomposes automatically)

Group cells to create a heading spanning many columns, or to create a cell of any size

Apply lines and shades to enhance and clarify

Import text and data from spreadsheets and word-processing programs

Combine vertical and horizontal alignment within cells

Financial Highlights

(in thousands, except per-share data)

		1988	1987	1986	1985	1984
Income Statement	Net sales	$ 79,054	$ 39,542	$ 11,136	$ 2,234	$ —
	Income (loss) before extraordinary credit	$ 14,608	7,806	2,362	438	(217)
	Extraordinary credit	—	—	—	80	—
	Net income (loss)	$ 14,608	$ 7,806	$ 2,362	$ 518	$ (217)
Per Share	Income (loss) before extraordinary credit	$ 1.15	$ .66	$ .21	$ .04	$ (.02)
	Extraordinary credit	—	—	—	.01	—
	Net income (loss)	$ 1.15	$ .66	$ .21	$ .04	$ (.02)
	Weighted average shares outstanding	12,740	11,842	11,281	11,281	11,281
Balance Sheet	Working capital	$ 52,878	$ 38,738	$ 2,590	$ 1,084	$ 685
	Total assets	72,798	48,987	6,381	1,674	793
	Lease obligations	118	219	—	—	—
	Shareholders' equity	62,418	43,336	3,616	1,253	735

Use the "Number format..." command to insert percent signs, decimal points, currency symbols, and so on

Add and subtract figures automatically with the "Sum" command

Another interesting and growing specialized document processing field is **legal document assembly**. The high-end document assembly packages, such as CAPS by CAPSoft or WorkForm by Analytic Legal Programs, allow Joe Lawyer to produce document templates that can be used by others on the staff. The templates are produced by answering a series of questions to direct the software to assemble the document by pulling in the correct text from its textual database. Accuracy is of the utmost importance in legal documents. One misplaced word can be the source of litigation or of numerous other complexities.[21]

Maintenance manuals used by the military raise another legal issue. These manuals usually contain lots of "WARNING" boxes indicating some important message. For example, "applying more that 10 fps torque will cause death and destruction." It is legally mandated that the WARNING be placed before the text of the section covering that topic.

The placement of mandatory items has some interesting ramifications for on-line reading, exemplified by hypertext browsers and the Web.[22] An on-line document browsing system must be designed to display the WARNING before allowing the display of the associated text. Random browsing through the document must factor in this requirement. The trick, of course, is to do this without interfering with the flexibility of browsing and searching, which is desirable in the on-line document viewers.

Another interesting specialized writing category are **programs for children**. As the cost of compute power has dropped, a market for children has developed. Microsoft has a particularly appealing program called Creative Writer. Taking a cue from KidPix by Broderbund, a kids-oriented paint program, Creative Writer uses sound for all types of feedback. When you drag an object, a scratching

Details Count, Oh Those Quote Marks

Even the seemingly tiniest detail can have major implications. For example, a *Washington Post* article titled "U.S. Appeals Court Finds Error Curbs Insurance Sales by Banks"[a] reported:

> A federal appeals court yesterday threw bankers, insurance agents and their lawyers into a tizzy by ruling that back in 1918, Congress misplaced a pair of quotation marks and accidently repealed the law that allows national banks in small towns to sell insurance....
>
> OCC (Office of the Comptroller of the Currency) attorneys argued that Congress didn't mean to take away the power, but that claim "runs up against the stubborn fact that the troublesome quotation marks are located where they are, not where the parties argue that the 64th Congress intended them to be," said Judge James L. Buckley.

Two techniques to manage complexity and avoid errors are configuration management and clear project organization.

a. Article by Jerry Knight, Washington Post Feb. 8, 1992.

21. For a survey of legal document-assembly software see, "Legal Documents," by Craig Sherod in *Computer Publishing Magazine*, Feb. 1991.

22. Hypertext systems allow the user to jump from one related topic to another by following links through a web of information. Of course, the Web is now the classic hypertext system. For a good overview of this important topic see the book *Hypertext & Hypermedia* by Jakob Nielsen, Academic Press, New York, 1990.

sound plays; when you erase with the vacuum cleaner; it sounds like one. Button and lever selections have colorful play like visual feedback as well.

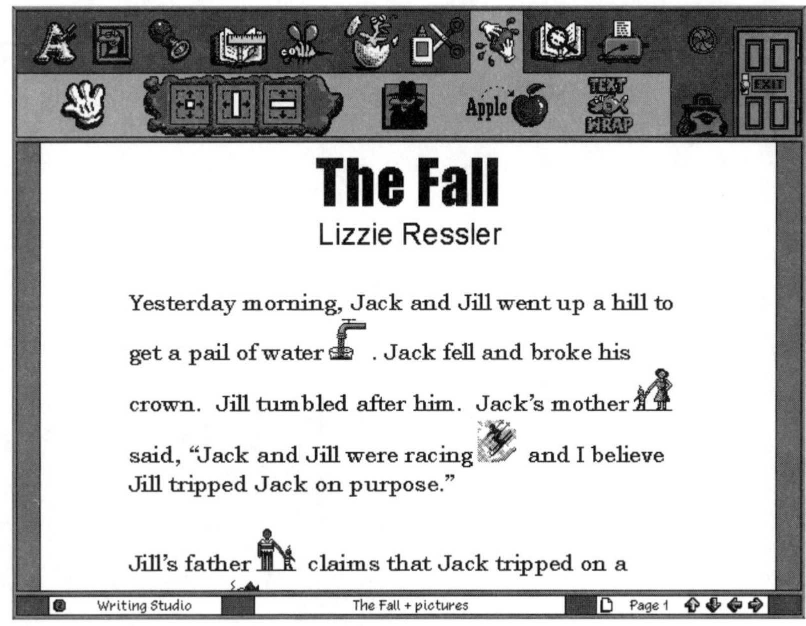

Microsoft's Creative Writer - word processing for kids.

For beginning users, a character, called McVee, pops up in a manner similar to Apple's balloon help, but more kid-oriented, and leads you through various procedures. One novel feature is in a "magic apple." After you write a story you can select the apple and many words are recognized, and little pictures are placed beside them. The look is like an old children's story book. It is very effective.

Budding movie and television authors can get **script writing software**. These packages format the document according to industry norms. They also help in the process of character and scene development.

ScriptRighter screenplay formatting software is a Windows based product.

Some of the control button in ScriptRighter

Scriptware and MovieMaster are two more word processing tools specifically set up to aid the development of scripts.

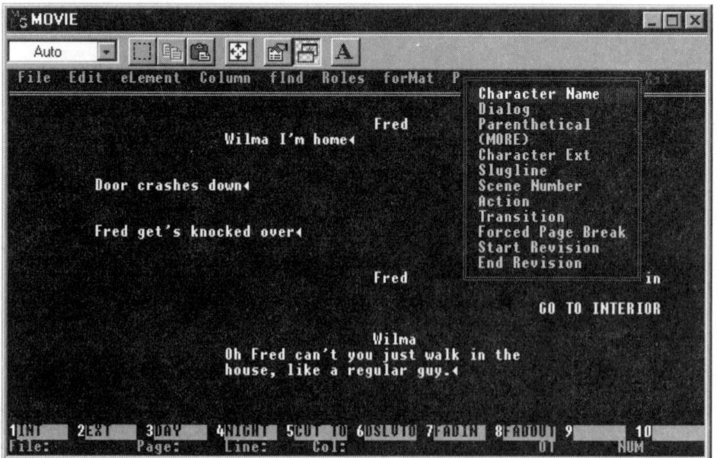

MovieMaker script writing software

All of these writing tools understand the semantics of scriptwriting. Characters, dialogue, action, and scenes are all meaningful document processing terms to these programs. Of course, you still have to have the imagination to write something interesting in the first place.

Finally there is a Web site called "The Writers Computer Store" at http://www.hollywoodnetwork.com/hn/shopping/kiosk/index.html. It contains good pointers for locating these types of specialized writing software products.

3 • 7 On-line View

The increasing use of the Web has moved the once highly specialized field of on-line documents into ordinary computing practice. The design of a document and its delivery are becoming more intertwined with the use of the Web as a principal medium for information dissemination.

In the design of a document for print, information is often constructed and organized around reasonable chunks of information, chapters, sections, subsections, and pages. The on-line form of a document also has these types of units, but the organization must take into account factors such as the bandwidth of communications and the speed of displays. In general, one could say it is "better" to break a large document into a bunch of little ones for on-line viewing. It's very annoying to come upon 20-30 page documents that have been moved onto the Web as a single file. The browser spends costly time sucking up the whole document, and programs tend to crash even more than usual under the load.

The key difference between on-line and paper documents is the issue of interaction, the user interface. A Web browser used often provides a well understood interface. The documents, however, must also be organized to take advantage of the interactivity without distracting the user.

The Web is in some sense in the same evolutionary state that WYSIWYG document systems were 10 years ago. The Mac provided a nice user interface with lots of nice fonts; and it encouraged "by God if I've got those fonts I'm going to use 'em" attitudes. The features offered by Web browser vendors are compelling and cry to be used. But they tempt, like the Sirens, and lead to clutter, obfuscation, and poor usability.

The problem is that most people are clueless about graphic design, layout, and typography, and it shows. A document with 15 different fonts, all on one page, is cluttered, noisy, and distracting, and the surface finish overpowers the message intended by the author.

In early 1996, Netscape changed its clean home page to one which used a series of "Frames" and Java generated activity. These frames forced the user to change from the familiar "back" button to use the mouse "back frame" selection. In addition, the performance was significantly worse, partially due to Java, but mostly due to the drawing and redrawing of the content in the frames. The graphic and user interface design was very good and cleanly laid out, however, the other problems overwhelmed the benefits (in this author's opinion). It was clearly a case of feature-driven design. Netscape was going to show off the capabilities and damn the consequences. After less than a month of the new frame-based design, they reverted to the older non-frame based design as the default, and let the user turn on the new design if selected, a much better migration path.

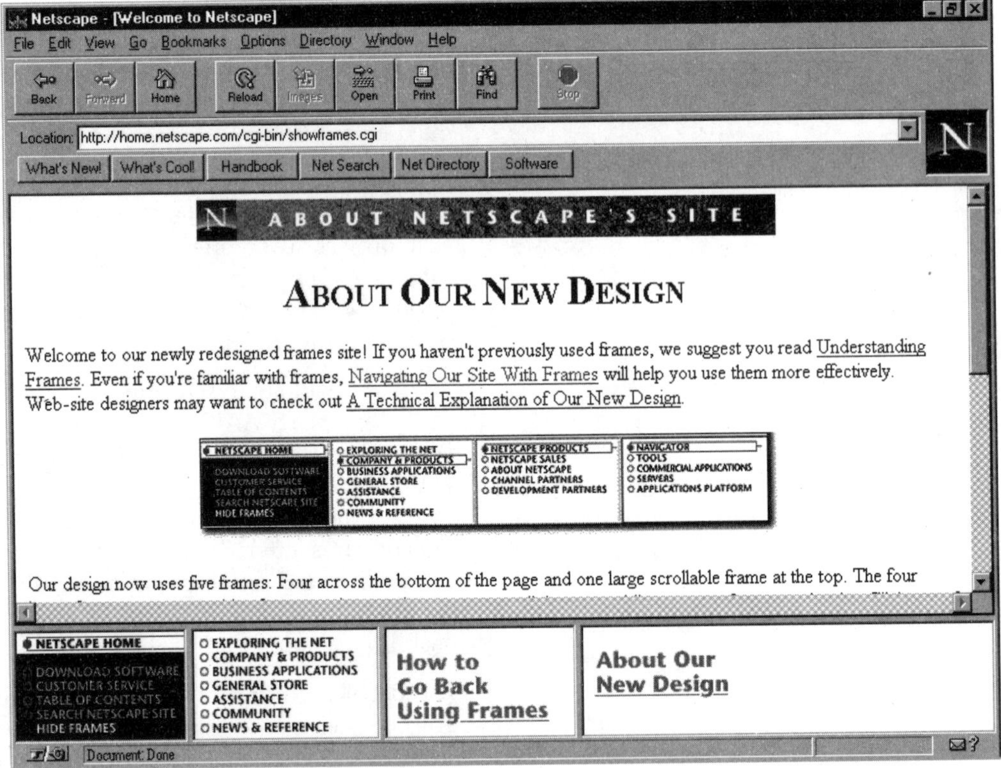

Netscape's frame-based home page design

Web authors are currently intoxicated with the growing list of features. Tables, frames, Java, and VRML are all useful technologies when used in moderation and used for a purpose. The use of technological features for the sake of using features has led to many ugly Web pages. Restraint is the best rule of thumb.

3 • 8 Summary

There is no single correct way to look at document processing issues. Each project has unique constraints and circumstances. However, it is important to appreciate that different points of view exist and are useful.

For one project, design may be paramount; for another, the logical structure may be critical. In the end, any evaluation of a publishing system depends on what you need for a particular project.

In any evaluation of a system, half the battle is to ask good questions. The various points of view discussed in this chapter provide a useful frame of reference that will help you to ask good questions.

Chapter 4 • Form and Function of Document Processors

Form ever follows function. —Louis Henry Sullivan

Document processors take a number of forms and perform a variety of functions.

What does the term **document processing** mean? After all, a document is something to be written and then read. Talking about "processing" a document can seem out of place.

When we use a computer to write or edit, we use a publishing tool such as a **word processor** or a **page layout system** to place our thoughts onto paper or display. The concept of **processing** is central to this task.

As we think about document processing we can view a document in two ways. First, a document functions as **data**, which are entered by the author and processed by the document processor. Second, the document functions as a piece of **software**, which directs the function of the document processor. Each document processing system tends to lean toward one approach or the other.

We now ask, when is a document data, and when is it software?

Documents function like software when they direct a document processor to perform according to procedures that are embedded in the document. Such documents are usually created with a simple text editor with a variety of special commands embedded in the text.

In contrast, documents that function more like data are created using a word processor or a WYSIWYG (What You See Is What You Get) editor. The user is not given the opportunity to enter data that will corrupt the document or stop the formatting abruptly. Thus, the **user interface** prevents most basic errors and bad data. Of course, this is an oversimplification of real life. Users can and will do all sorts of nasty things that can break documents; however, they must try hard.

Let's examine a few ways in which writing a document with a document processor is like writing software. The content (source code) of a document must be put into a form that can be processed (compiled). The actual printing (execution) or display of the document is the final step. The document processing program interprets the content and produces a printable form. All the various codes in a document—sometimes hidden, sometime visible—must be syntactically correct, or the document will not process correctly. Rigorous syntactic checking is possible when documents are created using certain international standards such as SGML or HTML (see *Chapter 5 • Document Standards*).

Another important similarity between document processing and writing software is in the area of **debugging**. Sometimes, when a document is printed, it looks crazy. It is not unusual to produce a document with very large errors, such as margins off by a couple of inches, illustrations that don't appear, and fonts of the wrong size. Often this is due to a "bug" in the document. For example, a table of contents might be generated by looking for all paragraphs tagged with the name SUBSECTION. If a particular subsection was not tagged correctly (i.e., with the tag SUBSECTION), then it would not appear in the table of contents. These types of problems can become insidious. Usually, they are not easy to spot and can be very difficult to track down. Wouldn't it be nice if document processing systems included debugging tools as part of the system?

The two major differences between document processing systems are how the user enters the information and how that information is interpreted. Therefore, writing with one system is different from writing with another system. The internal capabilities of the system will affect writing, design, and production. For example, many technically–oriented publishing systems do not support a feature such as the automatic flowing of text around a graphic. (See *Section 3 • 1 • 4 Page* in *Chapter 3 • Points of View* for an illustration of flowing text.) It is unwise to design a layout that needs this feature if the publishing system doesn't permit that type of text flow.

Let's turn now to a discussion of the various types of document processing systems.

4 • 1 Types of Document Processors

Build a system that even a fool can use, and only a fool will want to use it.
—George Bernard Shaw

There are many different types of document processors. A useful way to analyze them is to put them along a line that goes from simple text editing to WYSIWYG.

Classification of Electronic Publishing Systems

The continuum of publishing system types starts with text editors and goes through the language-oriented document processors to full WYSIWYG systems.

TEXT EDITOR	STRUCTURE EDITOR	LANGUAGE	WORD PROCESSOR & PREVIEWER	WYSIWYG
Simple entry of text: *emacs* *vi* *ed* *WordStar*	*Text entry within language framework:* *Author/Editor* *emacs modes*	*Descriptive markup embedded within text:* *troff* *TeX* *Scribe*	*Semi-WYSIWYG with hidden markup and fast previewing:* *WordPerfect* *MS Word*	*Full page images in real time:* *FrameMaker* *IslandWrite* *Interleaf* *MacWrite* *V. Publisher* *PageMaker* *Quark*

The path from text editors to WYSIWYG systems is *not* a path representing systems of increasing functionality. WYSIWYG systems do not have all the functionality of language–oriented systems; similarly, language–oriented systems do not have the functionality of structure editors. Specific products such as WordPerfect and MS Word blur the line between traditional word processors and WYSIWYG systems with new versions running under a Graphical User Interface (GUI), such as Windows 3.1 or the Macintosh.

4 • 1 • 1 WYSIWYG Features

As the name implies, the main characteristic of a WYSIWYG (What You See Is What You Get) system is not only that you can *see* the document before you print it, but also that you can edit it while you are looking at it. The display happens in real time, without any significant delay.

This Book in Progress

FrameMaker, a WYSIWYG document processing system, was used to create this book. Here's an illustration of the book in progress. It was possible to get reasonable views of the pages on the screen while writing.

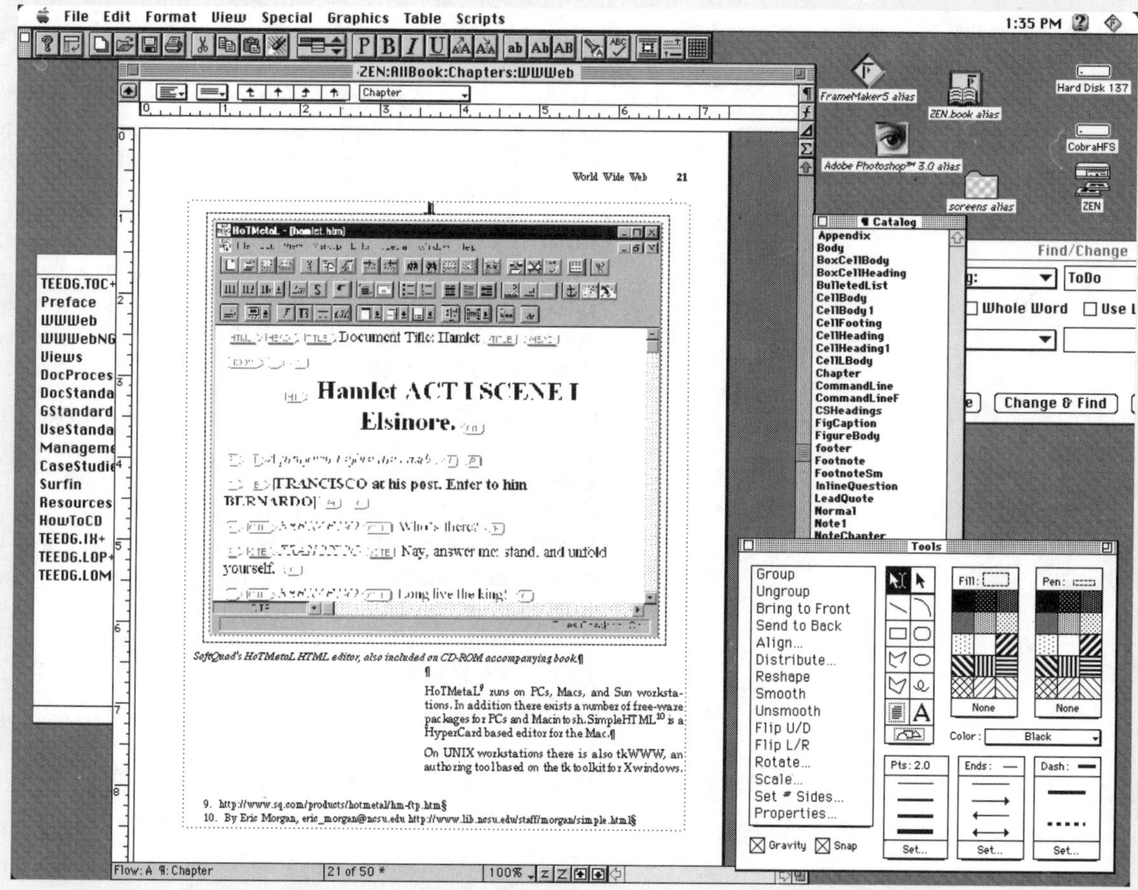

Most WYSIWYG systems use one of two approaches to editing specialized document types, such as tables, equations, and graphics. Some systems try to provide everything by having graphics and equation editors always available. Others automatically pop-up specialized editors when the document type is selected. From a user's perspective, either approach can be implemented smoothly. A smooth, consistent user interface is particularly important in a WYSIWYG system.

Another way to handle a variety of document types is to actually launch other applications that are external to the publishing system. For example, if a spreadsheet included in a document is selected for editing, the spreadsheet program might be started when the figure is selected. (See *Section 3 • 4 The Engineered View* in *Chapter 3 • Points of View* for a discussion of these issues.) Web browsers use the concept of "helper" applications to accomplish the viewing of data types not explicitly understood by the Web browser.

Most WYSIWYG systems provide tools to associate visual styles to document elements. For example, a paragraph tag called `CODE` may be used to visually set off the computer source code, in a set of software documentation, with a particular font.

One of the more significant challenges for WYSIWYG systems is to create visual systems for global processes. The management of large numbers of files is not something you really want to do in a WYSIWYG form. When handling large volumes of documents, you certainly don't want to be forced into more input interaction than is absolutely necessary. Changing the layout of several thousand documents needs to be an automatic process.

WYSIWYG systems tend to be more closed than their language–oriented cousins. To have real–time WYSIWYG editing, publishing systems use their own proprietary formats for the sake of efficiency.

However, WYSIWYG systems are not necessarily closed. Some systems provide interfaces to programmatically get at the internal representations. More commonly, systems sometimes define and use published interchange formats (see *Section 5 • 1 • 3 Lots 'O Formats* in *Chapter 5 • Document Standards*) , which can be used as the basis of translators.

Now that we've seen WYSIWYG, let's turn our attention to the more complex language–oriented publishing systems.

4 • 1 • 2 Language Characteristics

Language–oriented document processing systems are much better than their WYSIWYG relatives at performing global or bulk actions. Manuals with thousands of pages of reference material do not necessarily have to be seen to be formatted. In fact, *"What WYSIWYG advocates forget is: sometimes you don't want to see it at all."*[1]

Some documents span many thousands of pages. Typical among these are technical documents such as maintenance manuals and software documentation. Two major classes of tools can handle these documents. One is the older (some would say more mature) markup, command–driven, language–oriented document processors typified by programs such as troff and TeX. The other class are WYSIWYG publishing packages, typically running on workstations, exemplified by Arbortext's The Publisher, FrameMaker, and Interleaf.

Comparing troff and TeX

troff and TeX are the two most widely used language–oriented document processing systems. Originally developed for UNIX platforms, they have been moved to several other operating systems. TeX, in particular, is available for PCs. Each system has a number of associated preprocessors and/or macro packages to enhance their functionality.

	STYLE FILES	MACRO PACKAGES	BIBLIOGRAPHIES	FIGURES	TABLES	EQUATIONS
TeX	LaTeX	LaTeX	bibtex	pictex	\TBL	\EQ
Troff	monk	-mm -ms	refer	pic	tbl	eqn

1. From a 1991 USENET network posting by John Hevelin.

Perhaps the best argument in favor of language–oriented document processing systems, according to Brian Kernighan, is that, *"Once a task is well understood, it should be relegated to batch processing."* [2] Nothing is quite so frustrating as being forced into repeated cumbersome interactions with a system to accomplish routine tasks. The ability to automate your routine tasks, which may, in fact, not be routine to anyone else, is critical. The specification of these tasks may take some time and be difficult. However, once they are specified, they are easily used again and again.

The features provided by a publishing system vary according to the scale of documents it was designed to handle. A system intended for simple reports will not be able to manage multi–author documents with thousands of pages. Large–scale systems must support more rigorous forms of change control and the ability to make global changes across entire sets of documents.

4 • 1 • 3 Specialized Languages

Various document types such as tables, equations, and graphs have their own special properties. Several specialized languages describe and create these document elements. In the Web world, a good example is the extensive set of markup tags to define tables that have already been developed and implemented.

Specialized document processing systems are a microcosm of the general case of document processing. For example, there are WYSIWYG flow charting systems and language–oriented flow charting systems. The same is true for equation processors and tables. (See *Section 3 • 6 Specialized Views* in *Chapter 3 • Points of View* for a discussion and illustrations of these specialized processors.) These specialized languages, sometimes called "little languages,"[3] are used to perform very specific functions.[4]

2. For an excellent overview of document processing systems, see "Issues and Tradeoffs in Document Preparation Systems," by Brian Kernighan in EP90 *Proceedings of the International Conference on Electronic Publishing, Document Manipulation & Typography*, Sept. 1990, Cambridge University Press, New York.

3. Jon Bently originated this term in his column "Programming Pearls" in *Communications of the ACM.*

Flow Charting

These illustrations from the paper "flo—A Language for Typesetting Flowcharts" are from an experimental flow charting language. flo is a preprocessor to pic (a graphics language for typesetting), which, in turn, is a preprocessor to troff.

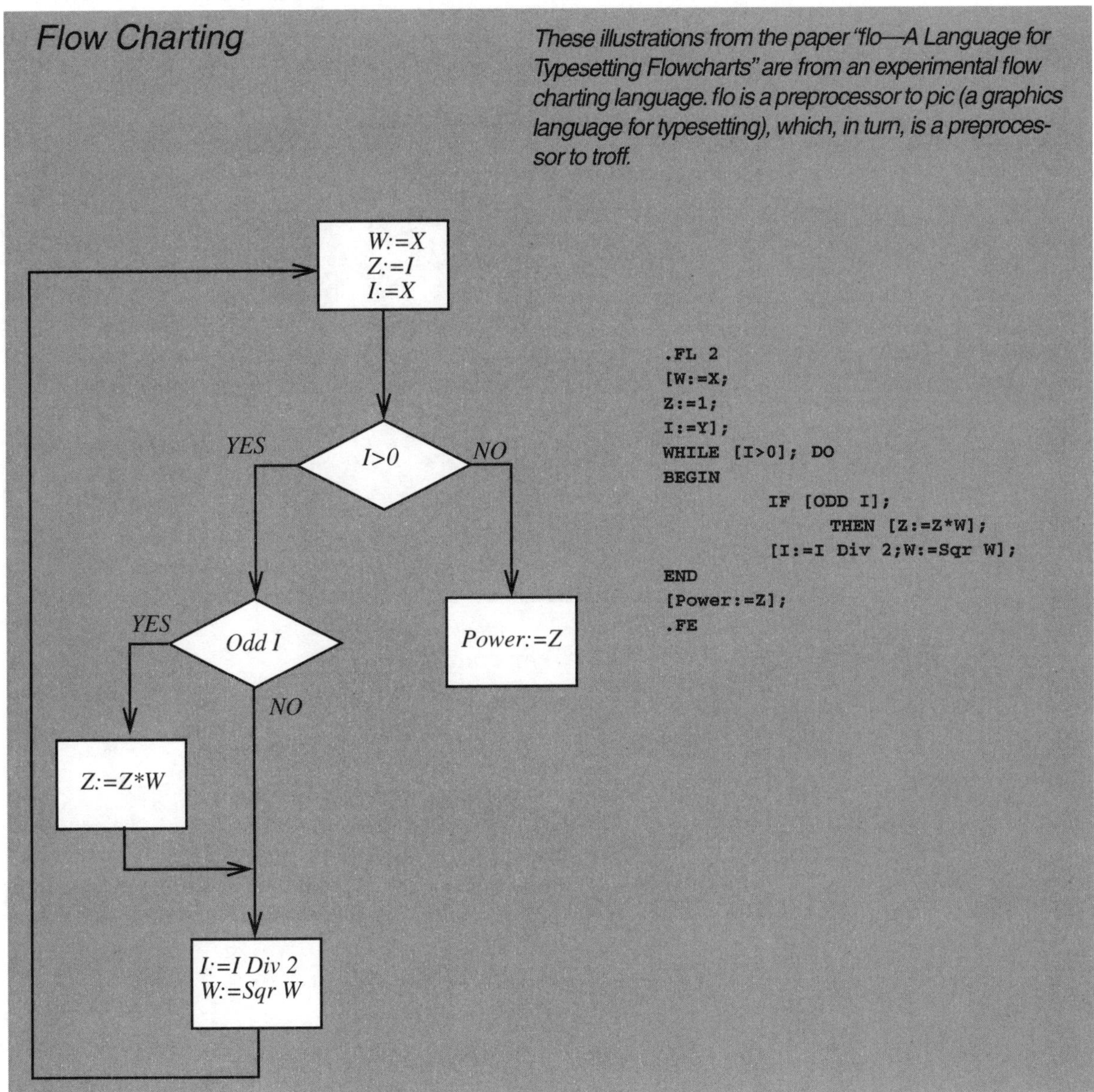


```
.FL 2
[W:=X;
Z:=1;
I:=Y];
WHILE [I>0]; DO
BEGIN
          IF [ODD I];
                THEN [Z:=Z*W];
          [I:=I Div 2;W:=Sqr W];
END
[Power:=Z];
.FE
```

4. From *"flo—A Language for Typesetting Flowcharts"* by A. P. Wolfman and D. M. Berry in EP90 *Proceedings of the International Conference on Electronic Publishing, Document Manipulation & Typography*, Sept. 1990, Cambridge University Press, New York.

Graphs, an important part of business and scientific publishing, deserve their own document processing language. The little language, `grap`, serves this need. Grap is a troff preprocessor language for the specification of graphs.

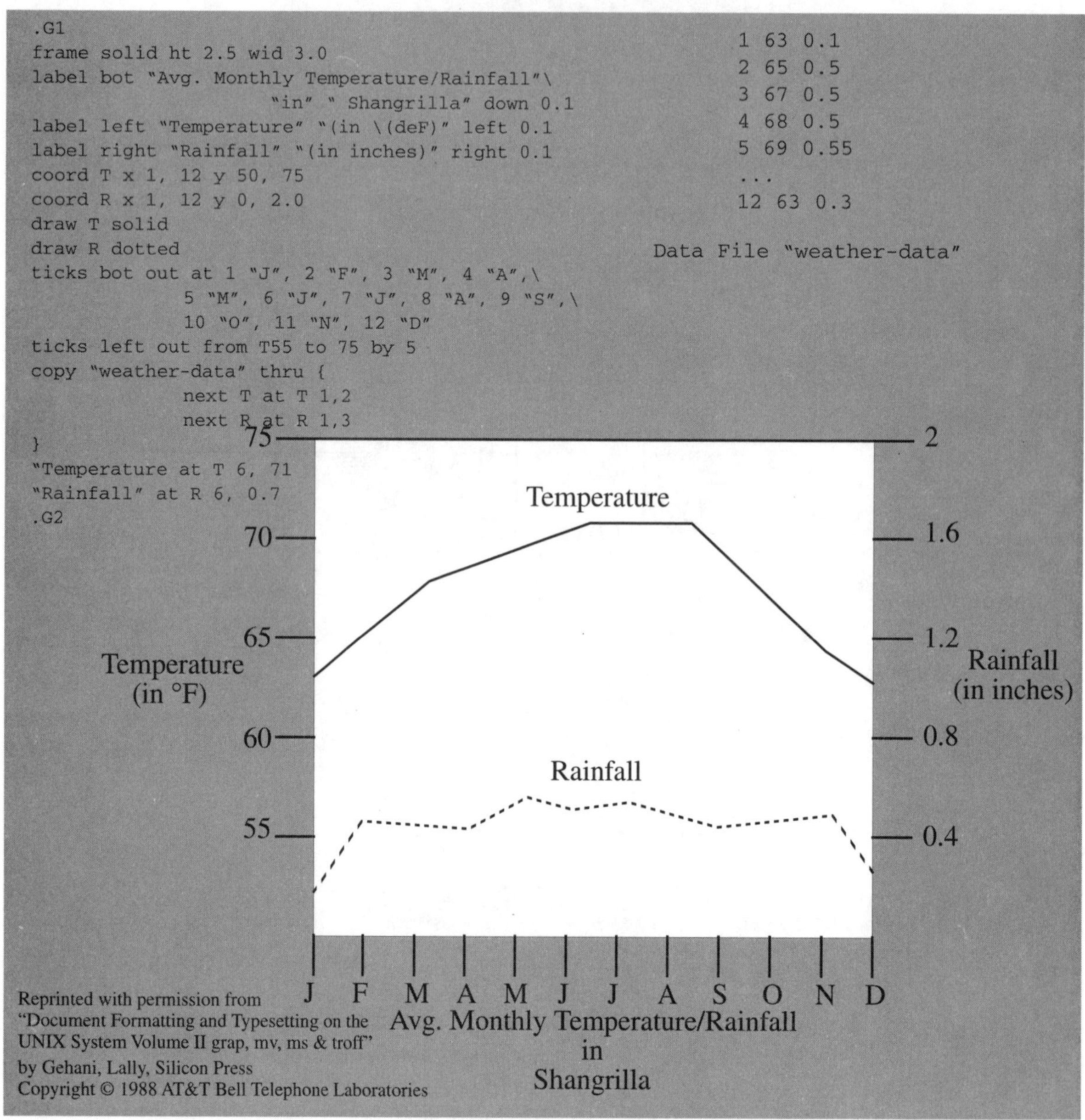
.G1
frame solid ht 2.5 wid 3.0
label bot "Avg. Monthly Temperature/Rainfall"\
"in" " Shangrilla" down 0.1
label left "Temperature" "(in \(deF)" left 0.1
label right "Rainfall" "(in inches)" right 0.1
coord T x 1, 12 y 50, 75
coord R x 1, 12 y 0, 2.0
draw T solid
draw R dotted
ticks bot out at 1 "J", 2 "F", 3 "M", 4 "A",\
5 "M", 6 "J", 7 "J", 8 "A", 9 "S",\
10 "O", 11 "N", 12 "D"
ticks left out from T55 to 75 by 5
copy "weather-data" thru {
next T at T 1,2
next R at R 1,3
}
"Temperature at T 6, 71
"Rainfall" at R 6, 0.7
.G2
1 63 0.1
2 65 0.5
3 67 0.5
4 68 0.5
5 69 0.55
...
12 63 0.3
Data File "weather-data"
75
70
65
60
55
2
1.6
1.2
0.8
0.4
Temperature
Rainfall
Temperature
(in °F)
Rainfall
(in inches)
J F M A M J J A S O N D
Avg. Monthly Temperature/Rainfall
in
Shangrilla
Reprinted with permission from
"Document Formatting and Typesetting on the UNIX System Volume II grap, mv, ms & troff"
by Gehani, Lally, Silicon Press
Copyright © 1988 AT&T Bell Telephone Laboratories

"grap–ing around" - A sample grap specification and the resulting graph.

> ### *UNIX, troff, and groff*
>
> Troff and the associated preprocessors are a wonderful example of the UNIX tool–building philosophy: develop powerful tools that do a specific function very well. The UNIX environment allows these tools to be glued together to function as one.
>
> The GNU project, an effort to create high quality software available with source code, has created their own version of troff called groff, keeping the spirit of tool building alive.

For the sake of completing the major UNIX troff preprocessor languages, `eqn` (to specify equations) and `tbl` (to specify tables) must be mentioned. Eqn and tbl are the "elder statesmen" of troff preprocessors and have been used for almost 20 years. They are robust, industrial–strength languages and are part of the standard UNIX document processing tools.

Bibliographies represent another document type for which specialized languages ease the processing. The management of bibliographies is an area where language–oriented systems are far superior to the WYSIWYG folks. TeX users have a set of macros called BibTeX, and troff users can use `refer` to manage references and bibliographies. The appearance of a reference in the text can be modified by the author. These packages can also work with relational databases or other filing mechanisms to store bibliographies used by an entire organization. WYSIWYG publishing systems are still playing catch–up in this domain.

Many language–oriented document processing systems can be used with previewing software. This software lets you look at the document on the screen before printing, saving some trees in the process. Previewers represent a midway point on the line between language–oriented and WYSIWYG document processing systems, discussed earlier in this section. Previewing systems allow you to look at the printed form of the document on the screen, just as you do in a WYSIWYG system; however, you cannot modify the image, and the display may take a while. Ghostscript, the GNU project's free version of PostScript, will let you preview PostScript files and is available on many computer platforms including PCs.

Typically, you use a previewing system by observing approximate views of the page, making some edits, observing again, making more edits, observing the page, and so on, finally printing the page. Switching back and forth between the previewing mode and the editing mode can be time–consuming. However, it is faster and more flexible than printing each page. TeX and troff previewers are widely available. Previewers are great aids, especially if the speed and availability of printers in an organization are poor. More importantly, previewers help to balance the often rigid complexities of language–oriented document processing systems with the adhoc nature of WYSIWYG systems. A relatively new system, Adobe's Acrobat (see *7 • 4 • 2 Applying Standards*) can also be used this way.

4 • 1 • 4 WYSIWYG versus Languages

Each class of programs has its advantages and disadvantages. The features you need depend on what you are trying to do.

The WYSIWYG class of document processors is more appropriate for seat-of-the-pants design and for rapid changes with less rigidity. However, the language–oriented document processors have a significant advantage when it comes to global changes. This is a desirable characteristic if you are concerned with uniformity over many thousands of pages.

Free Doesn't Mean Simplistic

TeX was created by Donald Knuth of Stanford and has been put into the public domain. Both free and proprietary implementations of TeX are available. Books, large reports, and many other full–featured documents have been written with TeX. It's basically free, but it's definitely not a toy. It rivals and often surpasses commercial proprietary systems.

Language–oriented document processors are awkward to use and are anything but intuitive. The publishing department's staff will need a significant amount of time and experience to become familiar with the idiosyncrasies of the software. Writing a document with such a package is remarkably similar to programming and requires as much attention to detail. However, the payoff on the investment in time and training is significant. In particular, if your organization must repeatedly accomplish the same complicated tasks, you may be able to automate much of the process using language–oriented document processors. You can create style sheets with specialized commands for your own needs. These commands will not only be relatively simple to use but will also ensure conformance to your organizations requirements. The open nature of the language–oriented document processors is also extremely important for those exceptions to the rule—which seem to happen every other day.

Numerous WYSIWYG software packages address the needs of the technical documentation ("techdoc") market.[5] Interleaf, FrameMaker, and Arbortext's The Publisher are three of the more significant ones, each with interesting characteristics.

Interleaf is oriented toward the dedicated publishing department. It has robust facilities for sharing documents and handling publication series with large collections of documents. If you use Interleaf on any number of computing platforms, the user interface will be virtually the same and familiar to the user.[6]

FrameMaker takes the good-neighbor approach to user interfacing. It is integrated with the normal working environment and window system's look-and-feel for any particular host machine. For example, if you use FrameMaker on a DECstation under a Motif look-and-feel window system, then FrameMaker behaves as a normal Motif application. On the Macintosh, FrameMaker looks and feels like a normal Macintosh application.

Arbortext's ADEPT*Publisher is a good example of a system that balances the closed nature of turnkey systems with the complexity of open systems. It provides a number of specialized WYSIWYG editors such as table and equations editors. Using the SGML version of the product, the entire document can be output as a validated SGML document. Validation is done in an interactive manner, not as an after–the–fact process. In addition, ArborText offers a feature called the ADEPT Command Language (ACL) for language–oriented capabilities, such as the automated editing of large documents.

All these systems walk the tightrope between WYSIWYG and languages. Too much emphasis on the language side, and the user interface suffers; too little, and global automation is difficult.

5. These are by no means the only, or even the best, publishing systems for your needs and are mentioned here only as examples.

6. In 1992, Interleaf changed its approach to user interfaces. They now support native look-and-feel interfaces. This means that users will not get exactly the same interface on the different platforms, but Interleaf will look and behave more like other applications on the same platform.

Let's turn our attention now to a comparison of the functionality that WYSIWYG and language–oriented systems offer.

4 • 1 • 5 Comparative Functionality

How do document processing systems compare with respect to functionality? In particular, how does the WYSIWYG versus language orientation affect the functionality? As in *Chapter 3 • Points of View*, it is useful to examine functionality in terms of the various points of view, such as design, communications, engineered, and specialized.

Most often, the primary function of any document processor is to format a document. The inherently visual nature of a WYSIWYG system allows for a more interactive, adhoc design of a document. More often than not, it also gets in the way of routine repetitive tasks. Language–oriented systems provide more opportunities for automation.

DESIGN

The fonts used by a system can profoundly affect the look and portability of the document. WYSIWYG systems have an inherently more difficult time dealing with fonts because they must have versions that can be displayed on the screen as well as printed. Adobe Type Manager solves this problem for the Adobe PostScript fonts, and TrueType from Microsoft and Apple uses the same font description both for printing and display.

The selection and adjustments of fonts and the overall typography of a document are easier with WYSIWYG systems than with language–oriented systems. The tedious trial and error of document editing, printing, and document editing, again and again and are very time consuming.

Many implementations of both major types of document processing systems—language–oriented and WYSIWYG—allow the creation and use of document **templates**. The terminology for templates varies. Sometimes they are called styles; other times, macros. However, they usually have the same function. A template is a particular document format that can be used over and over again. Some systems refine the concept of templates, categorizing them by types. Fonts, paragraphs, and page layouts can be categorized with individually named styles for particular use. These named styles can be used for many documents.

COMMUNICATIONS

When considering the communications point of view, WYSIWYG systems provide most of the tools. Spell checkers and a thesaurus usually require interaction. Language–oriented grammar checkers can also provide useful reports, which you can use later to help edit the document.

The ability to search the text and replace it with another piece of text is one of the more basic of all functions that an editing system should provide. However, search and replace functionality can become much more sophisticated once we remove the limitation of text–only search and replace. Some systems allow the searching of tags and styles. The searching itself can use flexible "wild cards" or regular expressions to match patterns of text. (See *Section 3 • 1 • 7 Enterprise* in *Chapter 3 • Points of View* for an explanation of regular expressions.) The ability to search for an item, such as a cross reference, is also useful.

ENGINEERED

From an engineering functionality point of view, WYSIWYG and language–oriented systems provide similar capabilities. We are all familiar with the ability of even simple document processing systems to generate page numbers. Tools for large documents are often able to generate much more, including tables of contents, lists of figures, and lists of tables. The careful, consistent use of tags or styles enables these systems to determine the textual items to include in the various lists.

The ability to create running headers and footers, such as those used in this book, is a valuable feature for larger documents. They give the reader an instant context for the page being read, as well as an overall professional appearance. Document processing systems can automate this entire task by using particular tags or styles to identify the header and footer text. Language–oriented systems are much easier to automate.

A flexible autonumbering mechanism is a must for technical documentation. (How else could we reliably refer to Section 1.3A.4.2.9a?) A range of choices for numbering is important. For example, you may want some sections to be numbered in roman numerals *(I,II,XI,VI,L)*, other with letters *(a, b, c, aa, ab, ac)*, and still other with digits *(1, 2, 2.1, 2.2, 3)*.

Another extremely important feature is index generation. The system should support several different indexing schemes. Critical among these is the ability to sort the index on a variety of criteria. In more extensive indexes, the ability to highlight the primary entry makes the index even more useful.

For example, the following index entries show how terms may appear under several headings.

baseball scandals	scandals	baseball
drugs 13	baseball 10-30	drugs 11,**13**,55
gambling 14-17	football 54-67	gambling 14-17
sex 20-25	political 75-275	sex **20-23**,24,25
		see also books- Baseball Babylon

In addition, one particular entry may be the major one. If so, it is often highlighted.

The ability to put cross references in the index is also useful. A good index is vital to any large reference document. The more flexible the document processing system is, the better.

From a functional point of view, index generation is virtually identical for WYSIWYG and language–oriented systems; you must always mark the item to appear in the index by hand. If, however, you do want to develop a semi–automated scheme, it would be easier with language–oriented systems because of their inherently more open nature.

Cross referencing is another area where larger document processing systems excel. Traditionally, cross references have been a prime source of errors. This problem seems quite natural; the section you referred to in one part of the document moves or is even eliminated over the course of editing. To ensure accurate cross references, document processing systems are almost essential. (Of course, nothing can replace a good copy editor.) WYSIWYG and the language–oriented systems are virtually the same here, although selecting a target reference is somewhat easier with the WYSIWYG system.

One final aspect of the engineering point of view is *structural validation*. Structure editors, which use standards–based markup, can let you know if the document is structurally valid. They can tell you if a document has all the right pieces and if they are in the right order. In the case of Web documents that use HTML, there are HTML validation programs (and services) that can tell you if the structure of your document is correct.[7]

SPECIALIZED

Documents are rarely composed of text only. A good document processing system must be able to handle images, graphics, tables, and equations. The degree to which a system allows manipulation of these specialized items may prove significant for your particular application.

Most systems allow the exact position of the graphic or table to *float*. This means that the system will move the position of the item—sometimes to the next page—to avoid large areas of white space.

Some WYSIWYG publishing systems provide the usual sort of drawing manipulation tools. These include cutting and pasting, along with rotating, stretching, and scaling. The system may also support positioning functions such as alignment and distri-

7. A particularly popular validation service is run by Webtechs (formerly called HaLsoft) at: http://www.webtechs.com/html-val-svc/.

bution of many items. You should also look for the capability to manipulate images with respect to brightness, contrast, and other factors. These capabilities, however, are not easily translated to the language–oriented systems, so a strict comparison is not appropriate. If you are using a language–oriented system and need these functions, the best solution is to process the items in an auxiliary system and import them into the publishing system.

4 • 2 Stages of Document Processing

What are the stages a document passes through as it moves toward completion? What happens in each stage and what role does a document processing system play? We will now examine these questions, as well as some other useful practices.

4 • 2 • 1 The Phases of the Process

Let's examine the six phases in the document creation process. These phases are design, writing, illustration, editing, production, and distribution.

DESIGN

Using a document processing system to design a publication invites many possibilities. The document has both a visual appearance and a logical design. The order of the items, such as the cover page, the table of contents, the chapters, the appendixes, and the index, makes up the logical structure of a document.

Style sheets and project-wide templates define the document's visual appearance. They must work within the framework of a document's logical structure. Properly used styles can help make a document conform to a specified document structure. This structure may be mandated by corporate standards or other factors.

WRITING

Writing with a document processing system is different from writing without one. The supplementary tools such as grammar and spelling checkers, thesaurus, and reference guides aid the process of writing.

Sometimes these tools are part of the system. At other times, they are utilities that can be used with many word processors that are not directly tied to a particular system. However, you can invent system–specific personal tricks to take advantage of system capabilities. For example, some systems allow text to be hidden based on some condition, such as a comment or other user–defined property.

To take another example, while writing this book, I created a paragraph tag called *editorial*, which I used to keep temporary comments to myself. Sometimes I would print out all paragraphs with the tag *editorial*, effectively producing a "to do" list of tasks left on the book.

You can use this trick, in one form or another, on many systems. This and other capabilities were created for other purposes, but as you become more experienced with a particular system, you learn tricks and use them as you write.

ILLUSTRATION

Integrating graphic illustrations or photographic images with the text of a document is one of the more troublesome and complex areas of electronic publishing. The publishing system must be able to include graphics, but it must not necessarily be able to display the graphics on the screen.

As for clip art, you can't simply buy a collection blindly. You must know whether it will work with your publishing system and what kinds of manipulations you will be able to accomplish. (See the *Clip Art* section in the *Resources* appendix for more information.)

EDITING

Electronic publishing systems don't really provide much help in the editing phase. Instead, someone must review the text and check the content. However, on some systems, you can mark up the text electronically using underlines, strikeouts, and color.

For electronic markup to work, everyone on the project must agree on its meaning. When several people are involved with the same document, one important consideration is access. Permissions for access to the files must be properly set up. It's also important to have some sort of versioning or lockout system so that people don't accidentally write on each other's files.

Another problem that occurs when many people work on a document stems from font usage. The WYSIWYG systems can display only the fonts that are available on the computer. Everyone on the project must have the same set of fonts so that the document will print and appear correctly on the screen.

PRODUCTION

The usual way of preparing a document for printing is to create a series of PostScript files. (Yes, it's true that not everyone must create PostScript, but it's as close to a universal standard as the world has.) If your publication will be printed at a service bureau you must be sure that the bureau has all the fonts you need. The high quality printers of 1200 dpi (dots per inch) or more will also print patterned areas very differently that standard laser printers do. A 50% gray pattern will appear much darker on a standard 300–dpi laser printer than on a 1200–dpi printer. Halftone images will also have a very different overall lightness. Color printing is a totally specialized art; if you're using color printing, don't try it yourself, get a trained professional.[8]

8. For an excellent book on color and electronic publishing, see *Color for the Electronic Age*, by Jan V. White, Watson-Guptill Publications, New York, 1990.

DISTRIBUTION

You can distribute electronically produced documents in two ways: through traditional paper distribution channels and through electronic distribution. The Web and Internet have become the medium of choice for the electronic distribution of documents. CD-ROMs still provide a good mechanism for mass distribution without the network hassle.[9] If you are writing a document that will be electronically browsed, you will probably want to arrange the visual appearance appropriately.

Electronic distribution also brings up the problem of run-time software. To broaden your potential market, the electronic document you want to distribute must run on as many systems as possible. Web documents that take advantage of specific vendor "enhancements" will not be viewable with all browsers. (See *Section 9 • 11 The Internal Revenue Service (IRS)* in *Chapter 9 • Case Studies* for an example of a Web site which take account of different browser capabilities.) You may want to explore the possibility of converting the document to several formats.

4 • 2 • 2 Recommended Practices

Just as software engineering practices provide a method for controlling and managing the software–creation process, **document engineering** provides a method for controlling and managing the document– creation process. Document engineering is not a genuine field of study...yet.[10] But let's discuss what may be the key elements of this new field.

Good conventions for naming the document elements, such as paragraph tags and styles, are as important as good naming conventions in software development. Although a strict comparison to

9. The Voyager Company of Santa Monica, CA http://www.voyagerco.com, publishes a series of books called *Expanded Books*. They have republished books such as *Jurassic Park* by Michael Crichton *and The Complete Hitch Hiker's Guide to the Galaxy*, by Douglas Adams. These were, and still are, some of the few mass–market electronic books.

10. See "Towards Document Engineering," by V. Quint, M. Nanard and J.André in EP90 *Proceedings of the International Conference on Electronic Publishing, Document Manipulation & Typography*, Sept. 1990, Cambridge University Press, New York.

software engineering quickly falls apart, keep in mind that the document you are creating must be processed before it can be printed or displayed.

Concurrent engineering (CE)[11] is another field of study from which you can draw a number of parallels to electronic publishing. Design for manufacturing, one aspect of CE, is an approach in which a designer of an electronic circuit board, for example, selects component parts, based not only on functionality but also on availability. An amusing story from the book *A Whack on the Side of the Head* illustrates this point:

> One of my manufacturing clients has a "single-sourced" capacitor designed into a circuit-board his company was producing. Manufacturing people typically go out of their way to avoid single-sourced parts, i.e., those produced by only one outside vendor. They reason that if only one vendor is producing a particular sub-component, then an entire manufacturing group can be idled if anything happens to the vendor's capability to produce.
>
> Things were fine until the vendor had production problems and could no longer meet demand. My client spent a lot of time attempting to track down more capacitors, but was unsuccessful. Finally, he went back through five layers of management to the design department to see how critical this capacitor was, and if it would be possible to use a replacement. When the design engineer was asked why this particular capacitor had been chosen, he replied, "I chose it because it's blue, and it looks good on the circuit board." The designer had never bothered to consider what impact such a choice would actually have on getting the product out the door. His tunnel vision had prevented him from even looking for such a problem.[12]

Similar problems occur in electronic publishing. A graphic arts department may design a page layout without any consideration of the fonts available for printing. A complicated multicolumn layout may be virtually impossible for the system used by other

11. For a good general text on concurrent engineering, see *Concurrent Design of Products and Processes* by James L. Nevins and Daniel E. Whitney, McGraw-Hill, New York, 1989.

12. From *A Whack on the Side of the Head*, revised edition, by Roger von Oech, Warner Books, New York, 1990.

staff, but simple with the system used by the designer. Similarly, design for a home repair manual may be fine for paper printing, but on-line viewing may require a larger screen and different layout.

Concurrent document engineering makes a great deal of sense. In practical terms, this means that you should find out if the people or service bureaus that will be involved with the document have all the necessary resources, such as fonts and software. If the document is intended for electronic distribution, you should check things like run-time software and platform portability. Early on, bring in the people involved in the later stages of the process. Printers may have advice on color separations, and this advice may affect the way you input images into the document. Internet service and Web site providers may have recommended Web browsers and display conventions.

Good document management is another practice you should follow. (See *Chapter 8 • Document Management* for a more through discussion of these issues.) Simply put, the most important aspect of document management is to have a clear understanding of exactly what you need to manage. Fonts, collections of styles, template documents, and so on, must be clearly identified and should be placed under a central configuration control system.

Now that we've discussed the various types of document processing systems and some of their functions, let's turn to the issue of markup. Markup is the basis for the major document standards and is a fundamental concept used in virtually all document processing.

4 • 3 Markup

Markup is information that is embedded in the text of a document that is not intended for printing or display. It may consist of instructions to a printing device, commands for a word processor, or even comments to a coauthor. All language–oriented document processing systems require some sort of markup. WYSIWYG systems often have markup that is hidden from the user. Otherwise, all you have is text with no information for the document processor.

4 • 3 • 1 Types of Markup

The three main classifications of markup discussed in the following sections has inspired the creation of a number of standards. It is also possible to create the markup itself in a number of ways, which are discussed at the end of this section.

SPECIFIC MARKUP

Specific markup, sometimes called procedural markup, is often found in word processors and older (yet still used) typesetting systems. The function of specific markup is to tell the system how the text should look when printed. Typically, these are instructions to format a section of text bold or centered and of a particular size.

Specific markup can also be used to tell the system to perform some processing function on the text or on other items (for example, to count the number of figures). Sometimes the markup is hidden from the user; this is the case in a WYSIWYG system. TeX and troff commands embedded in a document are a form of specific markup. In effect, the markup consists of procedural commands that direct the document processing system to perform certain functions.

GENERALIZED MARKUP

Specific markup tells the system what to do with a document. In contrast, **generalized markup** describes the document to the system. Also called descriptive markup, generalized markup tells the system about the document elements. It does not tell the system what to do with that information. **SGML** is a standard for placing descriptive generalized markup in a document.

The act of placing markup into a document is time consuming and unwieldy. However, several good tools make this process reasonable. (See *Appendix A • Resources* for some tools.) Ideally, you would like to automate the markup process to the point of invisibility.

What is Markup? One of the editors of the Text Encoding Initiative (TEI) (see *Section 9 • 2 Text Encoding Initiative* in *Chapter 9 • Case Studies*), a project developing markup specifications for humanities scholars, says this about markup:

> Why does the TEI encoding scheme matter?... It is a tool for scholars, but it has many applications, some of them commercial as when it helps to reduce the documentation for a fighter plane from three tons of printed information to a disc of easily retrievable, cross-referenced electronic data. Markup, if one needs a fancy word, is a branch of hermeneutics, a system of explication. Markup makes explicit what was not so clearly arranged before. It allows huge amounts of data to become parsed character data, that is meaningfully arranged data with tags that can help collect or arrange the data according to the needs of the retrieving user.[13]

13. The TEI is a scholarly activity seeking to create a standard way of marking up text for humanities research. The quote is from remarks by Lou Burnard and Michael Sperberg-McQueen, editors of the TEI, at a July 1991 TEI workshop. The text was posted to the Internet by A. Flannagen. The TEI Web site is at: http://www-tei.uic.edu/orgs/tei/.

Specific Markup: An Example

Specific markup is the kind of markup typically found in word processing systems. The markup, usually inserted as invisible codes, directs the document system to perform functions usually associated with formatting.

```
The Constitution of the United States of America PREAMBLE We the people of the United
States, in order to form a more perfect Union, establish justice, insure domestic
tranquility, provide for the common defense, promote the general welfare, and secure
the blessings of liberty to ourselves and our posterity, do ordain and establish this
Constitution for the United States of America.
```

raw text

```
[fontSize+2][fontBoldItalics][center]Th
e Constitution of the[hardReturn]
United States
America[fontRegular][fontSize-
2]PREAMBLE [leftJustify][allCaps] We
the people [notAllCaps] of the United
States, in order to form a more perfect
[fontItalics]Union [fontRegular],
establish justice, insure domestic
tranquility, provide for the common
defense, promote the general welfare,
and secure the blessings of liberty to
ourselves and our posterity, do ordain
and establish this Constitution for the
United States of America.
```

specific markup

The Constitution of the
United States America

PREAMBLE

WE THE PEOPLE of the United States, in order to form a more perfect *Union*, establish justice, insure domestic tranquility, provide for the common defense, promote the general welfare, and secure the blessings of liberty to ourselves and our posterity, do ordain and establish this Constitution for the United States of America.

formatted text

CONTENT MARKUP

Content markup is the use of generalized markup to describe the semantic elements of a document. Strictly speaking, this is an application of generalized markup and, indeed, of SGML.

For example, you might have a recipe marked up with tags such as <INGREDIENTS>, <TEMPERATURE>, and <SERVINGS>. These tags describe the content, not the structure. You can imagine having hundreds of recipes in this form and integrating the information with a database. You could ask questions of this data base to produce, for example, a shopping list for a particular set of recipes.

This type of markup is the subject of a great deal of research. It gets very complicated very quickly. Often, it is difficult to clearly and unambiguously identify actions and objects in the real world.

Take the issue of naming an item. In a description of a new porch you're about to build, you could refer to a joist as (1) the 10th support from the left end, (2) the joist 150 inches from the left end, (3) the 3rd loadbearing support, (4) the corner support, or (5) the pink joist. Descriptions of objects often mix naming conventions; as a result, the markup of content is very difficult unless the text is highly structured and almost legalistic in nature. To deal with this issue, you must try to anticipate the way the document and content markup will be used. Alternatively, you must be willing to highly restrict the markup to do meaningful content markup. These issues are also part of the work of the Text Encoding Initiative. (See *Section 9 • 2 Text Encoding Initiative* in *Chapter 9 • Case Studies*.)

4 • 3 • 2 Markup Creation

As you can easily imagine, the act of marking up text can be arduous. There are a number of ways to attack the problem. Tools to aid the markup process range from no automation to fully automated.

The first markup method is brute force. You simply use a text editor to embed the markup at appropriate places in the text. In the next method, markup is entered by hand, but by an editing tool that knows about allowable markup. In the case of SGML generalized markup, there are a number of structure editors. (See *section Document Processors* in the *appendix Resources* for a list of these editors.) These editors "know" what kind of markup is allowed at any particular place in the text. The user is allowed only to enter legal types of markup entities. This approach has several benefits. The mental overhead is greatly reduced, and you're assured of producing legally marked–up documents. Sometimes, however, having an electronic checker looking over your shoulder can be overly intrusive. Inevitably, you need to turn off the checking. From a user interface point of view, the better systems balance markup validation with ease of use.

A semi–automated approach is another way to enter markup. A document already in one publishing system's format is used as the input to an automatic markup process. For example, a FrameMaker document could be translated into HTML by using a converter to translate FrameMaker (MIF) markup into HTML tags.[14]

Although useful, this conversion approach has limits. You must start with a highly structured document. More problematic is the reality that document structure is often implicit in specific markup systems. The fact that a sentence is bold and all capitalized may *imply* that it is the start of a section, but it does not state so explicitly. The structure must be inferred based on the particular style used to format the document, rather than on an explicit command that says: `<THIS IS THE START OF A SECTION>`. If a figure or caption also contains a sentence that is bold and all capitalized, the markup system would misinterpret it as the start of a section.

Generalized markup using SGML defines the structure of a document. Troff documents use a form of specific markup. Often you must use implicit assumptions about troff documents to complete the translation to SGML. The same is true for documents in TeX or MS Word.

14. The suite of scripts called fm2html does just this and is included on the CD-ROM accompanying this book.

Finally, you can use automated markup systems that use document images from scanners as input. The software is told what to expect and creates the markup based on those expectations. As in the previous FrameMaker example, highly structured documents can be successfully translated, but poorly structured documents are much more difficult.[15] A newsletter cannot be fed into the scanner when the software is expecting a particular kind of technical report, at least not if you expect meaningful results.

15. Avalanche Development Company, an Interleaf subsidiary, in Boulder, Colorado, has a product called FastTAG that automatically marks up documents accord to rules you specify.

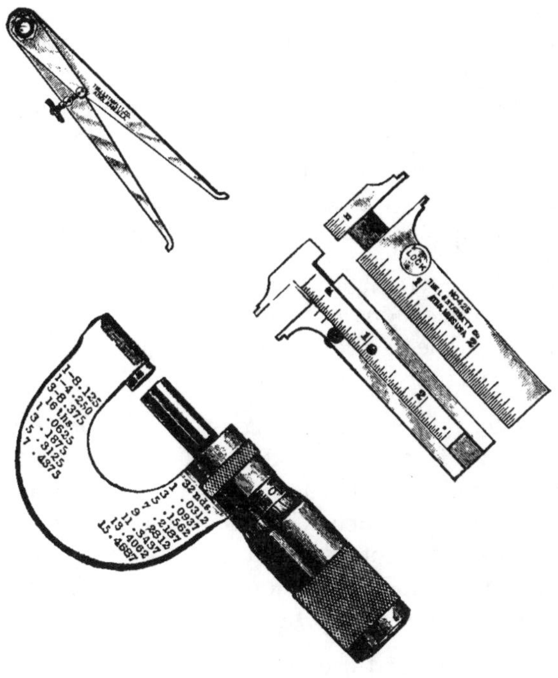

Chapter 5 • Document Standards

A committee is a group that keeps the minutes and loses hours. —Milton Berle

Standards for electronic publishing can profoundly affect the publishing process. All aspects of the process, from design to authoring through production, can be influenced by the use or misuse of standards.

First, let's define the key terms. A **standard** is a set of agreed–upon procedures or data formats that you use to accomplish a task. Standards become part of the software tools you use to get your work done. This chapter will examine both de facto (informal) and formal publishing standards. It will also explore document exchange, the motivation behind a great deal of document standards work. Document interchange seeks to answer the question: How can I give you my electronic document and *know* that you can use it?

Publishing is evolving into one of many forms of information dissemination. On-line reading and browsing, also known as Web surfing, hypertext, hypermedia, and CD-ROM based delivery mechanisms are realities when the proper standards are implemented. Thus, the standards themselves should be viewed as enabling technologies. They lower the risk of trying a new technology. If everyone uses a particular standard, you take less risk publishing a document that uses that standard.

One long–term goal of publishers is to create customized publications from repositories of textual information. The content, stored in a database, is the raw material that is refined into information products.

The term *information refineries,* used to describe this process, is an apt analogy. Raw "crude" text is poured in the top of a processing chain and out flow numerous products. CD-ROMs, on-line information services, Web sites, customized textbooks, personalized newspapers, and more are all potential products of these repositories of information.

The widespread use of formal publishing standards may permit the establishment of such information refineries. However, it is also clear that not all types of text are suited to be sliced, diced, mixed, and tossed to produce an arbitrary salad bowl of products. While it is tempting to use the refinery paradigm, we must not be seduced into inappropriate applications. Sometimes, the author intended a book to be read as a whole. Similarly, sometimes the content must be read in context.

It is useful to consider two types of standards: document standards and the graphics standards commonly used to represent the graphics included as part of a document. Often, standards refer to existing standards rather than to the reinvention of an area already covered by a standard. Combinations of appropriately chosen document and graphics standards can provide powerful solutions to the many complex problems of electronic publishing.

5 • 1 De Facto Standards

"There is no monument dedicated to the memory of a committee." - Lester J. Pourciau

Sometimes, when a product becomes very popular and widespread, the data formats for text or graphics used by that product become a de facto standard. When appropriate for your particular application, a de facto standard format is an easy and convenient way to exchange information. For example, in the Computer Aided Design (CAD) world, AutoCAD's format DXF is the de facto standard for CAD data on PC's. Adobe's PostScript is another de facto standard.

These specifications should not be confused with formal, official standards. True standards—formal standards—are generally developed over periods of 2 to 10 years by committees of technical experts. The committees work under the sponsorship of national or international standards–making bodies such as American National Standards Institute (ANSI), International Telegraph and Telephone Consultative Committee or Comité Consultatif International Télégraphique et Téléphonique (CCITT), European Computer Manufacturers Association (ECMA), or International Organization for Standardization (ISO). The formal standards–making process is excruciatingly painstaking and slow, but it's the best way to address all concerns. (For more discussion about formal standards, see *Section 5 • 2 Formal Standards* later in this chapter.)

One significant difference between de facto and formal standards is that de facto standards are often proprietary. The exact structure of a data format— a de facto standard—may well be a trade secret. PostScript Type 1 fonts were a tightly held secret until 1990. In that year, Apple and Microsoft announced the TrueType font format, a shot across the bow at Adobe's PostScript monopoly.[1] Subsequently, the Type 1 font specification was made public. (Seems as though a little competition is useful.) Yet, keep in mind that PostScript would never have

1. For some candid and amusing thoughts on the standards process check out the chapter "The Politics of Open Systems" in *The Open Book* by Marshall T. Rose, Prentice Hall, Englewood Cliffs, NJ 1990.

come into existence through the formal standards–making process with the political and technical compromises that so often are a reality.

5 • 1 • 1 Document Processors

The classic document processing systems, some of which are still quite popular, are batch–language oriented. The intuitive appeal of WYSIWYG systems must sometimes give way to the sheer volume of processing necessary for documents consisting of thousands of pages. In fact, sometimes documents are so mundane and routine that you don't want to look at them (for example, documentation for hundreds of similarly structured subroutines). Let's briefly examine three systems: Scribe, troff, and TeX.

Scribe was a ground–breaking document processor, the creation of Brian Reid formerly of Carnegie–Mellon University. He single–handedly revolutionized the field of document processing with his doctoral dissertation, Scribe.[2] Along with the overall ability to format text according to markup instructions, Scribe introduced the notion of styles. A Scribe document does not contain detailed formatting instructions. Documents can be created and printed according to a particular format such as "Thesis," "Report," and "Letter."

From an early Scribe manual:

> To use Scribe, you prepare a *manuscript file* using a text editor. You process this manuscript file through Scribe to generate a *document file*, which you then print on some convenient printing machine to get paper copy.
>
> Scribe controls the words, lines, pages, spacing, headings, footings, footnotes, numbering, tables of contents, indexes and more. It has a data base full of *document format definitions*, which tell it the rules for formatting a document in a particular style. Under normal circumstances, writers need not concern themselves with the details of formatting, because Scribe does it for them.

2. See Brian K. Reid, "Scribe: A Document Specification Language and its Compiler," Ph.D. Dissertation, Carnegie–Mellon University, Pittsburgh, PA, Oct. 1980.

The *manuscript document* an author creates has markup statements throughout. These statements describe the various components of the document to the Scribe processor. The descriptive markup the author places in the document is interpreted and formatted by the Scribe document processor. Scribe has generally been superseded by TeX and troff. Nevertheless, it remains an important document processing system.

In the UNIX world of document processing, troff is king. Actually, document processing applications were one of the first serious UNIX applications and one of the motivations behind its creation.[3] Created by Joseph Ossana, troff is first and foremost a typesetting system. Troff processes the markup that an author must embed into a document as formatting instructions. The modular nature of UNIX, coupled with the power of troff, has led to a number of troff preprocessors: *Eqn* for typesetting equations, *tbl* for tables, and *pic* for line drawings. *Grap*, a little language to specify graphs, is actually a *pic* preprocessor. Each of these preprocessors is a little language in and of itself. (See *Section 4 • 1 • 3 Specialized Languages* in *Chapter 4 • Form and Function of Document Processors* for illustrations and a discussion of these preprocessors.)

It is common to see a command line such as

```
cat doc.txt | pic | tbl | eqn | troff -mm
```

to produce the printed copy of a paper. (In UNIX, the | symbol is a "pipe," which directs the output of the commands to its left to the input of the commands on its right.) `cat doc.txt` sends the file (`doc.txt`) as input to `pic`, which interprets drawing commands; to `tbl`, which interprets table making commands; and to `eqn`, which interprets equations. The output of all three of these preprocessors is input to `troff`, which does the actual typesetting according to the `mm` macro package.

TeX is one of the premier document processing systems in existence. It is arguably the most popular batch–language oriented document processing sys-

3. For an excellant overview of UNIX document processing tools, see "The Unix System Document Preparation Tools: A Retrospective, " by Brian Kernighan, in the *AT&T Technical Journal*, Vol. 68, No. 4, July/Aug. 1989.

tems. It is available on virtually any computing platform and can be legally obtained for free. An extensive series of books by Donald Knuth (the author of TeX) documents the source code and functionality of TeX.[4] Commercially supported implementations can also be purchased for platforms such as the IBM PC.

LaTeX, a macro preprocessing system used with TeX, is the primary way documents are authored[5]. LaTeX uses the concept of style files to encapsulate commands and for processing instructions to format particular document elements.

Troff and TeX are used as the basis for internal publishing standards by a number of large organizations. AT&T's UNIX and OSF's (Open Software Foundation) software documentation originates as troff documents. TeX is used by the American Mathematical Society for a number of publications, and the electronic publishing magazine *EP-ODD* uses TeX and troff as the principal means for electronic submissions.

5 • 1 • 2 PostScript

PostScript is *THE* de facto standard page description language because of its extremely wide market penetration. It has evolved into more than simply a way of describing marks on a page. The thorough way in which it handles graphics and fonts, along with the consistency and quality of its implementations, has led PostScript into many areas. Document exchange and on-line document displays are two of the more prominent ones. PostScript, in combination with Apple's LaserWriter, effectively started the desktop publishing phenomenon.

For several years, PostScript was available only as a language that ran inside a printer. The printer's manufacturer had to license PostScript from Adobe. Close conformance to the PostScript specifications

4. A 5-volume series of books on computers and typesetting published by Addison–Wesley, Reading, MA, all authored by Donald Knuth, represents some of the finest computer software documentation ever produced. They are (A) *The TEXbook,* (B) *TEX: The Program,* (C) *The METAFONT Book,* (D) *METAFONT: The Program,* and (E) *Computer Modern Typefaces.*

5. See *LaTeX: A Document Preparation System* by Leslie Lamport, Addison–Wesley, Reading, MA, 1986.

was guaranteed, because Adobe made sure that a particular implementation of PostScript worked correctly for a particular printer. This proprietary conformance testing is one way to ensure consistent implementations of software. However, it depends on the honor of a particular vendor (not that I'm implying that any vendor would lead us astray, of course).

As more and more PostScript printers became available, PostScript became a reasonable medium for document exchange. For example, if I send you a PostScript document, I have a high degree of confidence that the document you print will be correct. However, a PostScript document is not generally considered a revisable form of the document and is difficult to edit. (For a more through discussion of the issues involved with document exchange, see *Section 7 • 2 Document Exchange* in *Chapter 7 • Applying Standards*.)

Like any commercial product, PostScript is evolving to meet new requirements and fix old problems. PostScript Level 2 addresses many past complaints, such as poor memory management and limited color support. PostScript Level 2 also offers several other interesting features. One of its significant improvements over its predecessor is in the area of color manipulation.[6] Full support for the CMYK (4-color printing) color model should make life easier for color printing.

The fundamental change of PostScript Level 2 is the incorporation of the CIE color mode (see *Section 6 • 3 • 1 Pure Color Models* in *Chapter 6 • Media and Document Integration*). The CIE color space specifies a mathematical relationship of color to human perception and is, therefore, independent of any output device. PostScript Level 2 provides a mechanism (called CIE based ABC) that enables developers to map the CIE color space to a particular output device.

6. A good introduction to PostScript Level 2 is presented in "Moving Up to Level 2 " by Bruce Fraser, in *Publish*, Nov. 1991, Better yet, check the Web for the PostScript FAQ archived at http://www.cis.ohio-state.edu/hypertext/faq/usenet/postscript-faq.

The extensions needed for Display PostScript have been included in PostScript Level 2, allowing the same PostScript interpreter to be used for either printing or display applications. True WYSIWYG displays are all the more likely if the same software is used both to display a document on the screen and to print it on paper.

In the area of data compression, PostScript Level 2 also offers significant improvements. Level 2 includes a new operation that accepts a compression algorithm. This includes the JPEG (Joint Photographic Experts Group) and LZW (Lempel-Ziv-Welch) compressions algorithms.

A second generation PostScript is called PDF (Portable Document Format) and is the core of the Acrobat product line from Adobe. Its principal difference is optimization for display, as its primary function is the on-line display of documents. One key to this technology is the use of a new font technology called "Multiple Master." The new fonts work with Adobe Type Manager (ATM) to "mimic the style, weight, and spacing of the document's original faces automatically." PDF also stores a document as a series of randomly accessible pages, facilitating hypertext links. The overall product line that uses this technology is called Acrobat. (See *section 7 • 4 • 2 Electronic Page Delivery* in the *chapter Applying Standards* for more information on Acrobat.)

5 • 1 • 3 Lots 'O Formats

Software vendors have defined many document and graphics formats. They have made many, but not all, of the specifications public. Vendors of open specifications correctly reason that publicizing their formats will encourage the creation of new software products that use their formats and more of their products. A few of the more popular formats are discussed next.

DCA/RFT

DCA/RFT, the Document Content Architecture/ Revisable Form Text, commonly referred to simply as DCA, is the format used by IBM's DisplayWrite. It is capable of representing a document with one or two master formats.

Graphics are possible inside a DCA document via a special Inserted Escaped Graphic identifier. This identifier lets a document treat a graphic as a block located in the text.

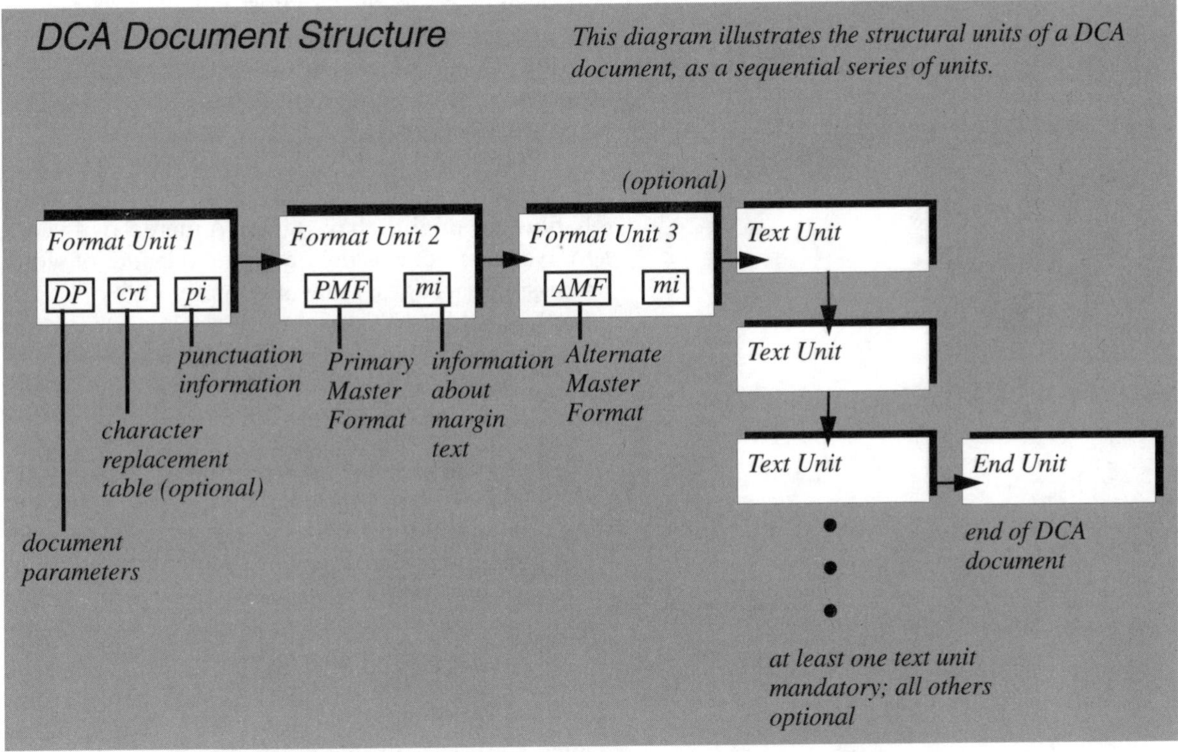

DCA has an automatic numbering scheme that can be used to specify the numbering style of footnotes. It is possible, using this feature, to allow the user to define custom numbering sequences.

RTF

Microsoft has defined the RTF, Rich Text Format, for use by its principal publishing product MS Word. On the Macintosh, it is the most commonly used document exchange format. Many products include import filters to allow input of text in this format.

MS Word has grown up to be the king of the hill of word processors. As such, RTF is a widely used interchange format. However, many word processors and document publishing systems seem to have trouble reading and writing proper RTF files. MS Word, not surprisingly, is clearly the most reliable program to read and write RTF files. There are also a number of RTF to HTML converters around. For example check out rtftohtml at http://www.sunpack.com/RTF/rtftohtml_overview.html.

WORDPERFECT

Oh, how the mightly have fallen. A mere 3 or 4 years ago, WordPerfect was the undisputed leader of word processing packages. Now after a buyout by Novell, who then sold it to Corel, WordPerfect is struggling to keep market share and is playing catchup with the formidible marketing clout of Microsoft and its MS Word.

One particularly effective aspect of WordPerfect's design is the use of multiple views. A user can view the document in three ways. The *normal* view shows mainly the textual content with minor highlighting, color changes for font variations, and a few other visual cues. The *show-codes* view lets you see and edit all the hidden control codes used by the system. In this view, users can get into the nitty–gritty when required. The third view is the *print-preview* mode, which is most useful for displaying the relationship of inset graphics to the text. Of course, a fourth view is implicit: the printed document itself.

5 • 1 • 4 Dealing with Formats

Can I get document X into system Y? Will my WordPerfect system accept this vital MSWord document?

The answers to these questions depend on a variety of factors. The specific document processor may or may not support the import or export of a number of formats. Even if a format is reportedly supported, the import/export function often does not do a complete translation. The result of a successful translation will almost always produce a document that must undergo extensive editing. Style and paragraph tags are usually lost, even if the overall formatting was translated successfully. Unfortunately, it is necessary to understand more than you might care to know when transferring a document from one format into another.

ASCII is the most interchangeable format for documents. Unfortunately, the one lowest common denominator of document interchange, the text–only option, has some problems. The difficulties are not with ASCII but with the different ways in which computing platforms treat lines of text. There is no standard for the end-of-line (EOL) character. For example, UNIX computers use a line feed as the EOL. PCs use a carriage return (CR) and line feed (LF) in that order. Macintoshes use a CR while VMS systems use a character count rather than a particular character.

These different EOL characters are usually not that much trouble; however, in this age of networked distributed computing, with disks on server machines shared across many computing platforms, things can get ugly. Text on one platform will often not display correctly when the text file came from another platform. The networking software often takes care of these disparities, but not always. This issue becomes more significant when dealing with "write once" media or CD-ROMs, which are intended to provide data to many platforms.

When dealing with formats, it is crucial to be conscious of certain basic categories of information. Graphics (vector and bitmapped), font usage, style usage, global information, and properties are some of the basic functional categories of information that must be converted by a translator. Also, keep in mind that document fidelity is a difficult goal to attain.

5 • 2 Formal Standards

"The only thing that saves us from the bureaucracy is its inefficiency." - Eugene McCarthy

There are two major formal electronic publishing standards, Standard Generalized Markup Language (**SGML**) and Office Document Architecture (**ODA**). There is a world of misunderstanding about both. This section reduces that misunderstanding. With the arrival of the Web, SGML has relegated ODA to another bit player. HTML, the language of the Web, is an application of SGML.

Along with these major standards are a number of associated supporting standards for fonts and character encodings. Consider SGML and HTML to be the leading actor and actress in an electronic publishing play. The character bits are played by ISO 646 (7-bit coded character set).[7]

Formal standards are open and not under the control of one company or, for international standards, one country. Reaching international consensus takes time. The intent is to give all participating parties a fair say in the technical results. Individual companies and countries all jockey to shape the standards in the mold of their own products and interests. This would give them an advantage when bringing products to market.

The process of making a standard is long and incredibly painstaking. The time and difficulty are the prices for a truly open process. De facto standards are often technologically more sophisticated and come to market faster than formal standards. Unfortunately, everyone pays a price for the monopoly sometimes gained by the holder of the de facto standard.

Hey! FIPS You!

A FIPS (Federal Information Processing Standard) is a standard used by the U.S. government for procurement purposes. If a FIPS exists in a particular domain and a major procurement is to be made, the procurement must conform to the FIPS. Usually, but not always, a FIPS simply points to an existing national or international standard. The prime motivation behind FIPS is to provide technical guidance to government agencies. The National Institute of Standards and Technology (NIST) is mandated by Congress to produce FIPS.

7. Forgive me, I couldn't help myself :-)

One other important difference between de facto and formal standards is in the area of conformance testing. Conformance testing[8] is the way to ensure that a particular vendor's claim for a product that meets the functionality of a standard is indeed valid. The conformance tests themselves are performed by an accredited neutral party. True interoperability can happen only when conforming implementations of a standard exist. De facto graphic standards such as TIFF and PICT exist in dozens of slightly different variations. My TIFF file won't necessarily be usable by your software that supposedly reads TIFF files. Formal standards implemented by conforming systems are the best way to guarantee interoperable functionality.

Aside from its inherently open nature, the real clout of a formal standard comes from its use in procurement specifications. By itself, a standard is not legally binding, However, when a procurement specification states that standard XYZ *must* be used, lots of people start paying attention to standard XYZ. Of course, de facto standards could be used for a procurement specification, but formal standards provide a more competitive open basis for the procurement.

8. In the United States, the National Voluntary Laboratory Accreditation Program (NVLAP) accredits laboratories for just this purpose.

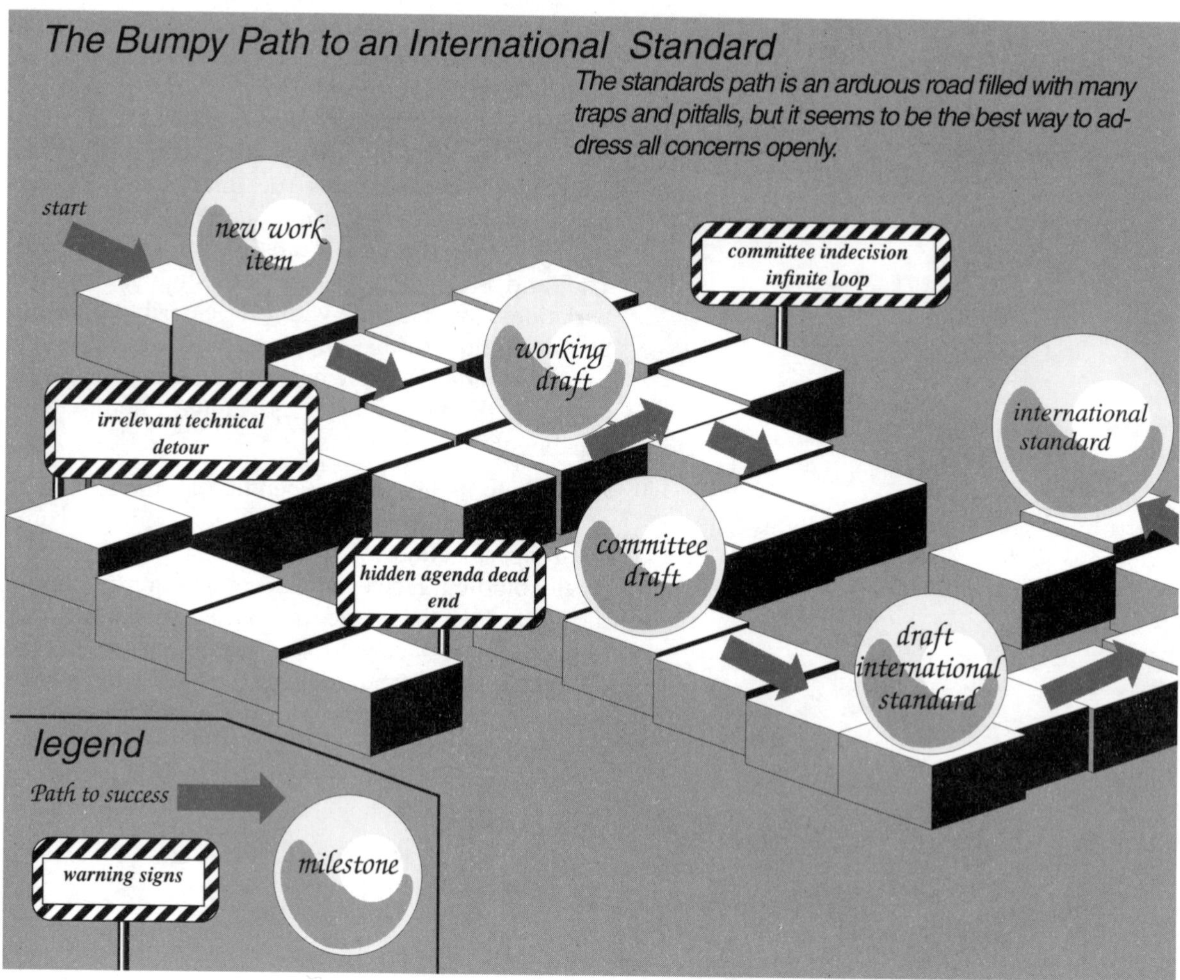

Considering the enormous difficulty of creating a formal standard, you might think that they would be far and few between. Nothing could be further from the truth, however.

Alphabet Soup

As the old saying goes, "The nice thing about standards is...there are so many to choose from!" Here are a few standards in the document processing domain related to or part of SGML and ODA.

Standard Name	Description
DAP	Document Application Profile — usage specifications for ODA
DSSSL	[ISO 10179] Document Style Semantics and Specification Language — the style sheet standard primarily intended to work with SGML
FOSI	FormattedOutput Specification Instance — style specifications for CALS compliant electronic documents
HTML	HyperText Markup Language [IETF] —application of SGML
HyTime	[ISO 10744] HyperMedia and Time based document — the hypertext standard based on SGML
IETM	Interactive Electronic Technical Manual — a hypertext standard from the CALS community
ODA	[ISO 8613] Office Document Architecture — one of the two principal formal document standards, encompasses document layout and structure
ODIF	Office Document Interchange Format — an ASN.1–based specification for document interchange, is Part 5 of ODA
SDIF	[ISO 9069] Standard Document Interchange Format — an ASN.1–based specification for document interchange, works with SGML
SGML	[ISO 8879] Standard Generalized Markup Language — one of the two principal formal document standards, an extensible language for the description of document structure

Another ISO Standard is the so-called Font Standard, ISO 9541. It was greatly influenced by Adobe. Publishing of the Adobe Type 1 specification has enabled it to become a prime technical contributor to the formal standard.

5 • 3 SGML

The most important formal standard in electronic publishing is the Standard Generalized Markup Language (SGML). For years, people invented different mechanisms for marking up text with such things as typesetter control commands, printer codes, structural hints, and probably anything else you can imagine. SGML is a standard way of embedding *tags* within the body of a document to create all sorts of markup.

SGML is also one of the more misunderstood standards. It allows the creation of a set of tags with which you can clearly and unambiguously define the structure of a document. It does not, however, address the issues of document layout—how it looks. Let's examine this notion of document structure, because it is fundamental to understanding SGML.

Take this book—please! It consists of three major elements: the *front matter*, the *main body*, and the *back matter*. The *front matter* contains the title page, the preface, and the table of contents. The *main body* contains the chapters. The *back matter* contains the appendixes, and index. Chapters consist of sections, and many sections consist of subsections. Most books have this familiar structure. This structure and the many variations can be precisely described by SGML.

Structure and style are different aspects of a document. SGML addresses the structure only. This is one of its great strengths and, some say, its great weakness. SGML does a wonderful job of capturing the content of a document and enabling that content to be manipulated at a later time. However, the information a document carries due to its visual design and layout is essentially lost unless careful, additional steps are taken. Additional style standards and specifications exist and are being implemented to address this issue. (See *Section 5 • 3 • 3 DSSSL* for a discussion of the major style standard.) One particular document structure can be visually represented in many different styles.

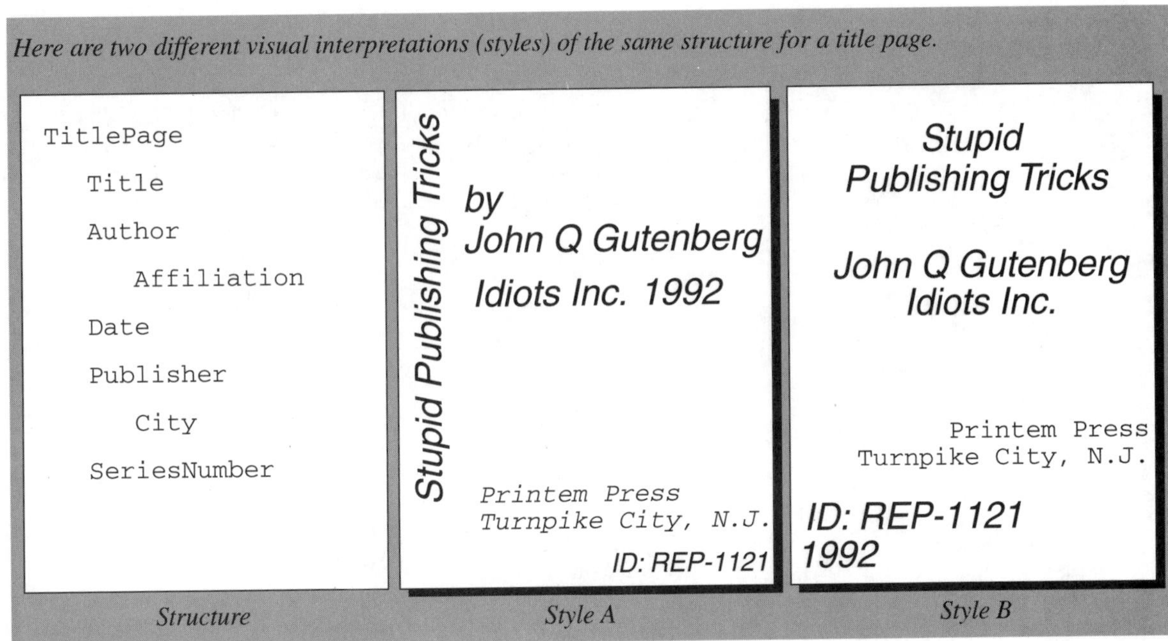

Let's take a look at how the structure of a typical office letter might appear. The names associated with each item in the letter are tags.

A Letter's Structure

The structure of all letters for a particular organization may be defined as illustrated here. The labels are equivalent to SGML tags. The structure can be represented as a hierarchical collection of elements. The arrangement of the elements is the structure, and the information associated with each element (the instance) is the document content.

Letter
IntroMaterial
Date
Name
Company
Street Address
ZipCode
Name
Paragraph(s)
Signed
Salutation
Name
Title

The structure of a letter

WYSIWYG SERVICES

"We look at it so you don't have to."

1825 Clover Ave.
Brooklyn N.Y. 02133
(212) 764-5352

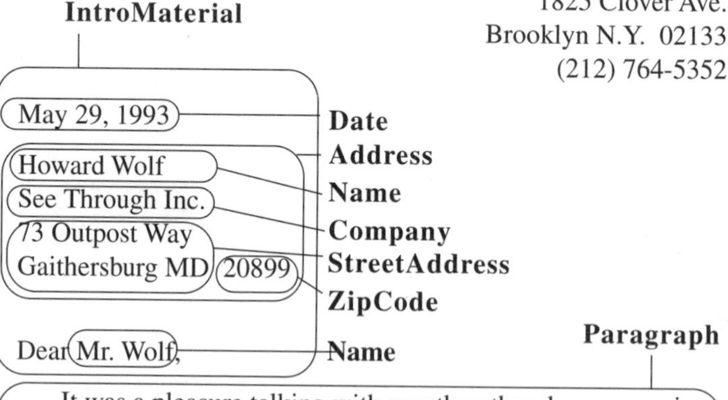

It was a pleasure talking with you the other day concerning our document scanning services. As you know, we provide complete input, throughput, and output facilities.

I have taken the liberty of enclosing pricing information and a brochure describing our services. I hope things go well with your building plans and that we can assist in any way. Please feel free to call if you have any questions.

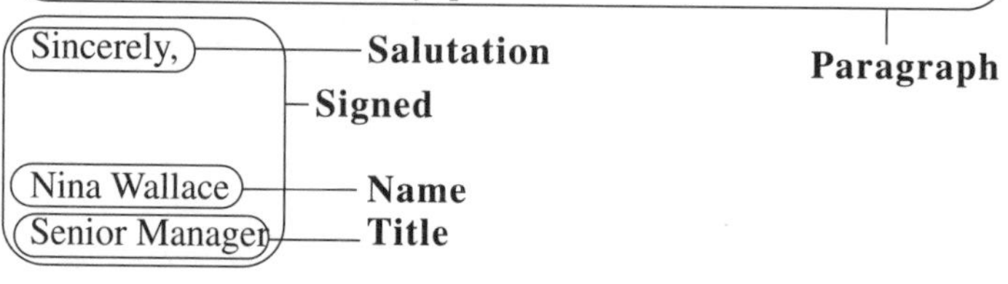

One specific letter—a document instance

SGML is many things to many people. In the preface to *The SGML Handbook*, Charles F. Goldfarb,[9] the "father" of SGML, states that:

> — It is a tagging language.
>
> — It handles logical structures.
>
> — It is a file linking and addressing scheme.
>
> — It is a data base language for text.
>
> — It is a foundation for multimedia and hypertext.
>
> — It is a syntax for text processing style sheets.
>
> — It allows coded text to be reused in ways not anticipated by the coder.
>
> — It is a document representation language for any architecture.
>
> — It is a notation for any kind of structure.
>
> — It is a metalanguage for defining document types.
>
> — It represents hierarchies.
>
> — It is an extensible document description language.
>
> — It is a standard for communicating among different hardware platforms and software applications.
>
> SGML is and does all of these things, but the whole is much more than the sum of the parts. Moreover, it is only by understanding the whole that one can make the best use of SGML.
>
> Reprinted by permission of Oxford University Press © 1990.

SGML is an important standard, and one worth understanding. Most important a moderate understanding of the basic concepts will lead you to appropriate uses of SGML.

The Congressional Record

The U.S. Government Printing Office (GPO) is using SGML to help produce the *Congressional Record* in the various required formats. According to an article in *Government Computer News*,[a] the GPO is investigating SGML as a potential replacement for its current tagging system. John Chapman, Chief of the Electronic Dissemination Task Force of the GPO, states that the *Congressional Record* averages 1.2Mb per day. A bill must first be printed for discussion on the floor of the Congress (format 1). Next, it is entered into the *Congressional Record* (format 2). If the bill goes through committee reconciliation, a conference report between the House and Senate is printed (format 3). The report may then be reprinted in the *Congressional Record* with yet another format (format 4). Finally the text must be printed as an approved bill to be signed by the speaker of the house and the president (format 5). SGML would allow the text in a database to be printed in these formats without touching the content of the database.

a. From "Electronic publishing will help put record straight" by Karen Schwartz, in *Government Computer News*, Sept. 3, 1990.

5 • 3 • 1 Speaking of Metalanguages

Now it's time for a little jargon. **Metalanguages**: what are they and why should you care? First, as the name implies, a metalanguage is a language. Languages are used to describe all sorts of things. A

9. Absolutely everything you ever wanted to know (and more) about SGML is in *The SGML Handbook* by Charles Goldfarb, edited and with a forward by Yuri Rubinsky, Oxford University Press, New York, 1990. Not only is the information clear, through, and readable, but this book serves as a model for the presentation of an ISO standards.

Integrated Chameleon Architecture

A collection of free data translation tools created by researchers at Ohio State is being made available to the public. The Integrated Chameleon Architecture (ICA) is a result of the Chameleon Research Project led by Sandra Mamrak. Translators from LaTeX to SGML and Scribe have been created using these tools.

What IS a Parser Anyway?

In any discussion about SGML, the words "SGML parser" are inevitably spoken. A parser is a computer program that is used to interpret text or data. The interpretation is accomplished because the parser follows specific rules. These rules allow the parser to interpret a language. Usually, that language is a computer language such as C or FORTRAN. Natural language parsers (for example, a program to interpret English) are much more difficult to create, because a natural language is not as limited and strictly defined as a computer language.

Parsing interprets only the syntax of a language. It is up to someone or something else to assign meaning to the recognized pieces of a language. An SGML parser follows the rules specified by the SGML standard. The tricky thing about SGML is that the DTD defines the rules for how to interpret the rest of the document. That's equivalent to allowing a C programmer to extend the language at the beginning of the program!

meta-language describes another language. SGML has the ability to describe languages that describe document structures. A complete SGML file contains not only the marked–up text, but also the definition of that markup. This markup definition, or language, is called a document type definition or DTD. Another very powerful aspect of metalanguages in the computing world is the fact that programs can be *automatically* constructed using metalanguages.

An analogous, real–world example is the universal remote–control device that can be taught to control any VCR. You teach it the language of your particular VCR so that it can speak your VCR's language. The act of teaching the universal remote to speak one particular VCR's language is analogous to creating a program from a metalanguage. The result is a specialized language that performs the required functions. It's compact and exactly what you need. Most importantly, metalanguages (and universal remote controls) are flexible. Change your VCR, and you simply reteach the remote. Change the markup language, and regenerate your markup processor.

Back in computer land, let's say that I want to write a new computer language. Let's also say that this new language could be expressed using a metalanguage. It might then be possible to use a metalanguage tool to create interpreters or compilers for my new language. This type of language technology exists and is widely used. The metalanguage is called BNF (Backus-Nauer Form), and the tools to generate new interpreters are called parser generators or compiler-compilers. One common tool in this domain is called YACC (Yet Another Compiler Compiler).

At this point you may rightly ask, "So what? Who cares?" Well, in the SGML domain, some clever people have written a computer tool called the Amsterdam SGML Parser (ASP-SGML).[10] It is analogous to YACC, but it creates an SGML parser for a specific type of document, the one described by the SGML metalanguage. The motivation for all this work is flexibility. The easier it is to modify a parser, the easier it is for end users to tailor the language to their particular needs. In addition, this approach opens up the creation of inexpensive specialized SGML parsers for specific applications.

5 • 3 • 2 Document Type Definition (DTD)

There are two parts to an SGML representation of a document. The first is called a **document type definition** (DTD). The second is the content of the document itself, with all the markup tags defined in the DTD. A key and elegant feature of SGML is that it is extensible. A DTD can define new tags and tags based on other tags.

10. You can find the ASP-SGML parser, plus other public domain SGML software at: http://www.sil.org/sgml/publicSW.html.

DTDs and Documents

*A DTD represents the structure for a certain type of document, for example, a booklet. A document instance is a particular booklet (or memo, or report, or book) such as **The SGML Primer**.*

DTD

```
<!--  Comment declarations can help clarify a DTD. This DTD,
      for example, strings together some of the declarations
      that describe this booklet. -->

<!DOCTYPE booklet
[<!ELEMENT booklet --  (title, (text|dtd|instance|diagram)*) >
 <!ELEMENT  tsp "The SGML Primer"  -- the title we'll use  -->
 <!ENTITY   % declars "element|attlist|entity|notation"    -->
 <!NOTATION pict SYSTEM "use for declaration diagrams"      >
 <!ELEMENT  dtd (%declars;) -- parameter entity shorthand  -->
 <!ATTLIST  dtd    type   (silly|serious)  serious          >
 <!ELEMENT  (title|instance|%declars;) (#PCDATA)            >
 <!ELEMENT  diagram  EMPTY >
 <!ATTLIST  diagram graphic NOTATION (pict) #REQUIRED>
 <!ELEMENT  text           (para)* >
 <!ELEMENT  para           (#PCDATA|quote|emph)*>
 <!ELEMENT  (quote|emph)   (#PCDATA)>
]>
```

Document Instance

<BOOKLET><TITLE>The Document Instance</TITLE>
<TEXT><PARA>The sample document instance that follows contains the text of the document incorporating the markup as specified in the Booklet DTD.**</PARA>**
<PARA>Why the term **<QUOTE>**document instance**</QUOTE>**?
Because we are referring to a particular document that is one instance of the many possible documents that could be created in accordance with the Booklet DTD. **</PARA>**
<PARA>Markup within the document instance is called
<EMPH>descriptive markup</EMPH>. Descriptive markup identifies the elements within the document instance that make up its logical structure.**</PARA>**
<PARA>Note the tag names for elements in the document instance below are, naturally, the names declared as markup in the DTD.**</PARA></TEXT>**
</BOOKLET>

Modified from Illustrations in *The SGML Primer*. © 1991, by SoftQuad Inc. Reprinted with permission of the publisher.

The DTD defines elements, and the document content provides specific instances of those elements. Put another way, the DTD is like a mold, and the text is like the metal poured into that mold. An element is a thing, a placeholder, a name. An instance of an element is the object itself. For example, a DTD may define "chap" as the element for a chapter. In this book, *World Wide Web* is a particular instance of a "chap."

DTDs themselves are becoming standardized. Standard DTDs are the key to meaningful document interchange. SGML without a DTD is like listening to someone speaking a foreign language. When you listen, you can recognize that a language is being spoken and that words, phrases, and sentences are in the speech, but you just can't understand anything. The DTD enables SGML parser to understand the stream of text being processed. Of course, this analogy shouldn't be taken to far. The parser doesn't "understand" anything, and the only "meaning" that can be extracted is a valid document structure.

Standard DTDs

The Standard for Electronic Manuscript Preparation and Markup was the first formally standardized collection of DTDs for a particular application. Developed by the Association of American Publishers (AAP), it contains three DTDs (Book, Article, Serial). In 1988, it was approved as an ANSI (American National Standards Institute) standard: ANSI/NISO Z39.59-1988. The standard also describes the exact keyboarding required to mark up a book, article, or serial document.

An SGML Structure Editor

Author/Editor, an SGML editor by SoftQuad of Toronto, is a structure editor for the creation and validation of SGML marked-up text. The editing tool will allow only correct tags to be entered in the correct context.

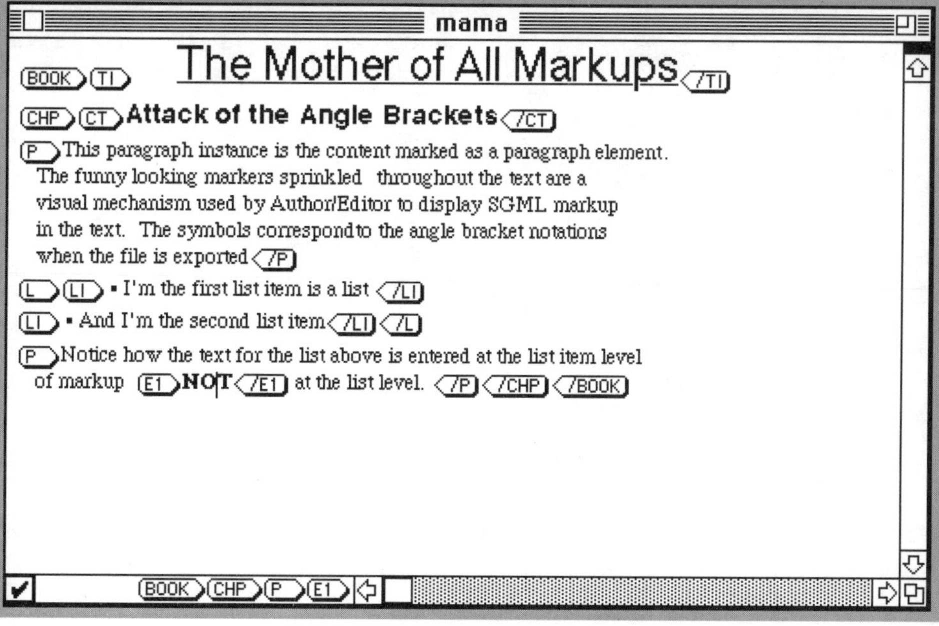

mama

BOOK TI The Mother of All Markups /TI

CHP CT **Attack of the Angle Brackets** /CT

P This paragraph instance is the content marked as a paragraph element. The funny looking markers sprinkled throughout the text are a visual mechanism used by Author/Editor to display SGML markup in the text. The symbols correspond to the angle bracket notations when the file is exported /P

L LI • I'm the first list item is a list /LI

LI • And I'm the second list item /LI /L

P Notice how the text for the list above is entered at the list item level of markup E1 **NOT** /E1 at the list level. /P /CHP /BOOK

BOOK CHP P E1

This discussion should make one thing clear: putting all this markup in a document is a lot of work. Techniques and commercial products are available for converting documents into SGML marked–up documents. SGML conversion is also THE area in which a clear understanding of what SGML is and is not is vital.

"SGML-Like"—And We Could Get "Sort of Married" Too..., an article[11] by Bill Zoellick of Avalanche Development Company, now Interleaf, aptly points out the dangers of systems and consultants who ignore the fundamentals of SGML markup. He states that SGML markup without a DTD, as some systems attempt, is not really valid markup. The DTD "is the coin of the realm. If you do not have a DTD, you cannot play the SGML game." The DTD imposes a set of rules and a structure that a document must follow. It will also allow another SGML system to interpret (parse) your document according to valid SGML rules. Marking up a document without following the rules specified by a DTD is problematic and should not be called SGML. SGML parser/verifiers can analyze a document and its markup for conformance to a DTD. Of course, fixing the document may be no simple task; that's all the more reason to do it the right way from the start.

11. See " *'SGML-Like'—And We Could Get 'Sort of Married' Too....* " by Bill Zoellick, in *DISC Magazine*, Fall 1990.

Grammar Checking and SGML

Avalanche Development Company has a grammar checking product called "Proof Positive" that uses the SGML markup of a document in a variety of useful ways.

Readability level

<DOC> *cannot exceed a readability level of Grade 8*
but <HELP> *must have a readability level of Grade 5*
but <APPENDIX> *can have a readability level up to 11*

Tagged structure to define acceptable (and different) readability levels.

User–defined grammar rules

Items in a step list must start with a verb — *Rule definition*

	results
<STEP> *About that outer cylinder assembly, she's got that special bolt that a lot of guys might want to remove. And I suppose it wouldn't hurt any to retract that actuator pin while you're at it.*</STEP>	***FAIL***
<STEP> *Outer cylinder assembly: special bolt removed, actuator pin retracted.*</STEP>	***FAIL***
<STEP> *Remove special bolt and retract actuator pin from outer assembly.*</STEP>	***PASS***

Modified from "Grammar Checking and SGML" a presentation by Severson and Van Vooren at SGML '91
The system does not function exactly as shown. Text above is for illustrative purposes only.

5 • 3 • 3 DSSSL

The Document Style Semantics and Specification Language (DSSSL, pronounced dissel) is the style sheet standard. The formal DSSSL standard is known as ISO/IEC 10179:1995. DSSSL is intended to work with SGML or other document formats "for which a property set can be defined according to the Property Set Definition Requirements of ISO/IEC 10744."[12] DSSSL consists primarily of two mini-languages: a transformation language and a style language.

DSSSL's main function is to associate formatting information with document elements. DSSSL includes a transformation language used to describe

12. From the Web page "DSSSL Online Application Profile" compiled by Jon Bosak, of Novell at http://occam.sjf.novell.com:8080/docs/dsssl-o/do951212.htm.

the association of formatting information to the logical elements of a hierarchically structured document, such as an SGML–tagged document. It has a general mechanism for mapping the tree structure represented by an SGML DTD into another tree structure representing the visual composition of a document.

Like any other computer language, DSSSL is a language with a specific syntax and a collection of keywords. It will allow a designer to associate visual style descriptions with SGML elements. For example, using DSSSL, you can instruct a formatting processor to print all elements with the tag <SECTION> using Futura oblique bold with a 14-point size. The logical element <SECTION> would be associated, via a DSSSL specification, with the formatting information of the font Futura oblique bold 14 point.

DSSSL's second principal part is the style language. It will allow you to associate visual styles with collections of elements that are not specifically identified as logical elements. For example, the first paragraphs of a chapter may require different typography from all the other paragraphs. You could format such a paragraph with a larger font size and with a large initial cap. The knowledge that such a paragraph is still a paragraph can be maintained, however. At a later time, when you insert a new first paragraph, DSSSL takes care of the formatting.

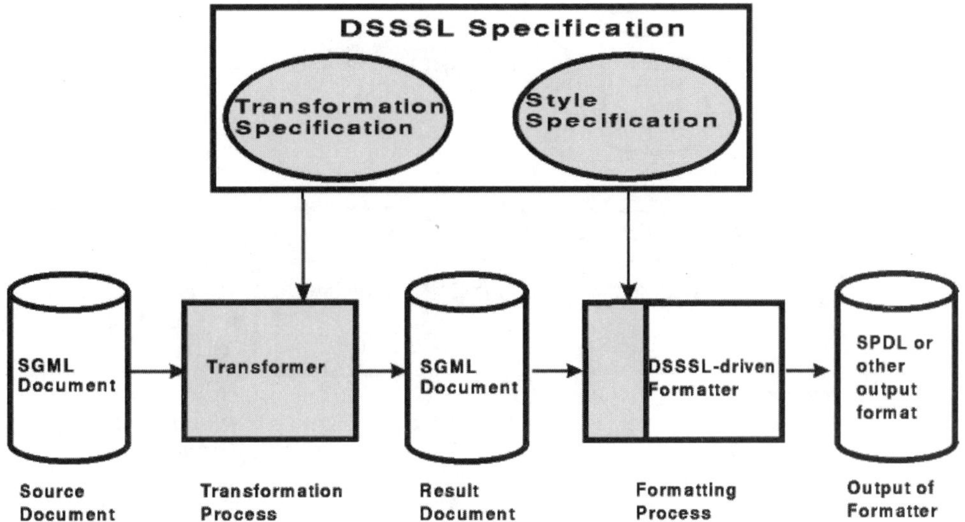

DSSSL Conceptual Model[13]

DSSSL's complexity and generality make implementations difficult. In recognition of this complexity, a new effort called DSSSL Online is beginning to reach fruition. DSSSL is being used as the basis of a Web style sheet. The complexity of DSSSL will also make complete implementations difficult and scarce. However, the future standards team of SGML and DSSSL should prove immensely powerful.

13. From DSSSL document at http://occam.sjf.novell.com:8080/dsssl/dsssl96/586#X.

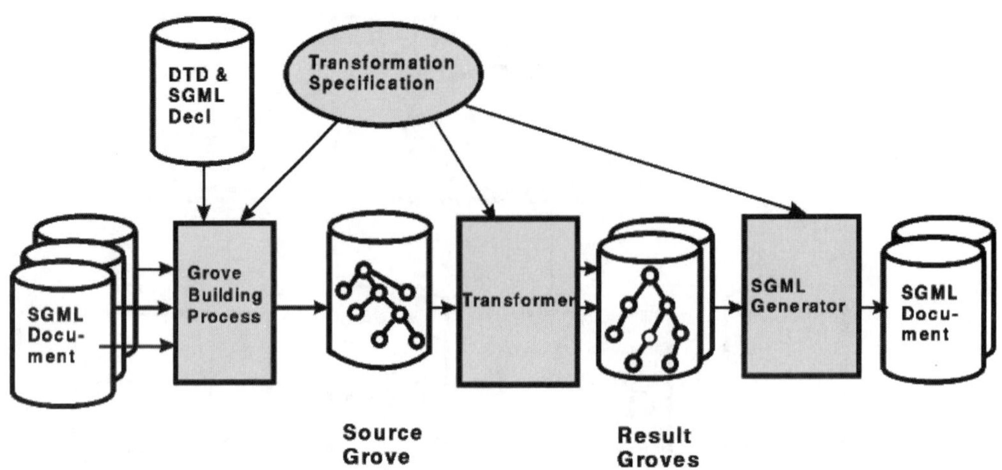

The DSSSL Transformation Process[14]

One method being used to create usable forms of DSSSL is to implement a subset known as DSSSL Online. DSSSL Online is being proposed as the basis of a common style sheet language for the Web.

5 • 3 • 4 HyTime

If computers are the wave of the future, then hypertext is the surfboard.
—Ted Nelson

HyTime, ISO/IEC standard 10744, is the international standard to represent linked and time-based information. It is the hypertext standard and is an extension of SGML.

Hypertext is a maturing technology that allows you to jump from one piece of text to another using an on-line reading system.[15] For a good overview of this field check out *Hypertext & Hypermedia* by Jakob Nielsen (Academic Press 1990). Formally, HyTime is called Hypermedia/Time-based Structuring Language (HyTime).

14. From DSSSL document at http://occam.sjf.novell.com:8080/dsssl/dsssl96/586#X.

15. The classic survey of hypertext systems is J. Conklin's "Hypertext: An introduction and survey," *IEEE Computer* 20,9, Sept. 1987. It may be a little dated, but is still quite valuable; the Web didn't spring up out of a vacuum.

The HyTime standard is an application of SGML. It uses the capabilities of SGML to formalize the representation of a linking capability, music, and time.

If this sounds like an odd combination, you're right. The initial HyTime work was motivated by an interest in representing music; therefore, time was very important. Musical events led to a connection with hypermedia, and now both a music description and hypermedia standards are being developed by closely related groups. Eventually, the work was split into HyTime and SMDL (Standard Music Description Language). HyTime is an application of SGML, and SMDL is an application of HyTime—you got that clear now? [16]

Gestural Style Sheets

The model of time specified in HyTime allows for the creation of gestural style sheets. This concept, developed by Donald Sloan of the State University of New York at Binghamton, is exactly analogous to the concept of style sheets as used in document processing. The separation of music time from real time would allow the virtual time unit (VTU) to be defined for one gestural style sheet as "Allegro" and for another as "fast as Horowitz used to play it." The mapping of the VTU to real time permits such tempo changes.

Some of the objectives of HyTime are to support music publishing, business presentations, and computer-assisted instruction with music and sound effects. HyTime has three key concepts— Events, Links, and Time. An **event** is some action, possibly external to the application; that is, a user. A **link** is a connection between one or more "anchors" in the information. **Time** is represented as durations of various sorts within a very flexible framework.

One key conceptual contribution of HyTime is its model of time. Time can be represented in two ways, musical and real. Musical time is abstract and analogous to the logical structure of a document. Real time is concrete and analogous to the physical formatted document. These two time representations can be synchronized using HyTime.

HyTime's model of time is intended for nonmusical as well as musical applications. It uses the concept of a unit of music time called a virtual time unit (VTU). A VTU is not inherently equivalent to any real number of seconds or any other concrete measure of time. For example, if an application were video-based, the VTU might be defined as the time for one video frame. For a musical application, the unit might be an eighth note.

16. For a thorough description of HyTime see *"Making Hypermedia Work: A User's Guide to HyTime"* by Steve J. DeRose and David G. Durand, Kluwer Academic Publishers, 1994.

Keep in mind that these concepts are nothing revolutionary. However, HyTime formalizes the representation of these concepts using SGML. It should be possible to represent and interchange the information represented in HyTime with systems that interpret HyTime information. Hypermedia is desperate for such an interchange standard. The Web has somewhat hijacked this more rigorous hypertext model, and it remains for the future to see if HyTime will have a significant impact on the Web.

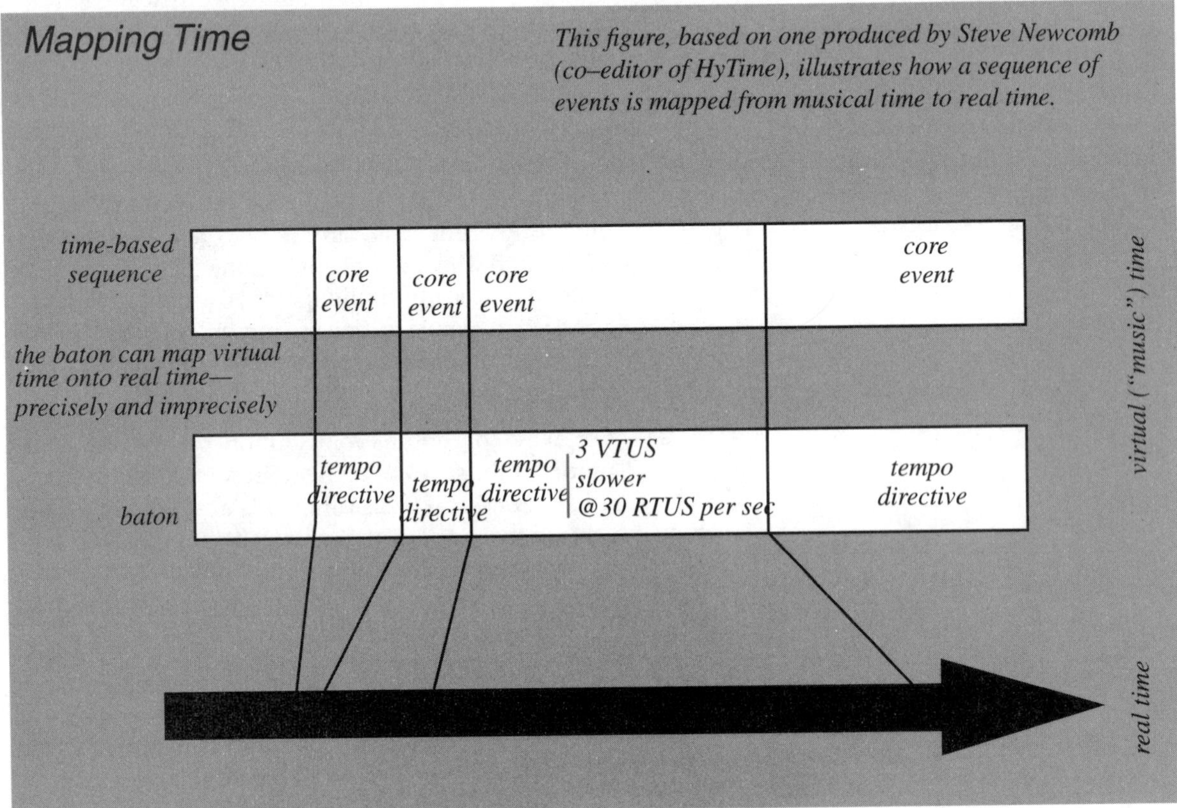

HyTime is a standard for the representaion of hypermedia. Hypermedia includes documents with audio, video, and other types of data, as well as the ability to link from one element to another. HyTime provides a robust formal mechanism to describe these links and is effectivly a superset of the type of documents we see on the Web. The relationship of one link to another can have more meaning than the simply "go to" of a Web document. A link can be the "parent" or "owner" of another link, and these relationships can be exploited by intelligent applications.

In reality, SGML is a necessary foundation to HyTime, but HyTime goes far beyond the capabilities of SGML and introduces new concepts.

HyTime introduces the concept of an architectural form. The HyTime standard itself consists of a collection of six sets of architectural forms. An architectural form is a formal mechanism, using SGML syntax, of defining extensible templates. In SGML, the Document Type Definition is the way to define, formally, the structure of the document. In HyTime, the architectural form is also a formal definition not merely of a document structure but of an extensable template, sort of a meta-DTD. It is a way of introducing object oriented concepts into the semantics of SGML. An architectural form is similar to the definition of a class (in Smalltalk terms), from which subclasses can be created.

These are structures that can be extended into additional structures.

"Readme.1st SGML for Writers and Editors"[17] contains the following consise description of the six HyTime collections of architectural forms:

1. *Base: Element and attribute architectural forms common to the other five modules and also usable independently (e.g., attributes for controlling the location and type of referenced elements).*
2. *Measurement: Expression of size and position of objects using application-chosen measurement units (e.g., seconds, inches, words, virtual units).*
3. *Location address: Assignment of Ids to non-SGML objects and to elements in other SGML documents (useful for hyperlink anchors).*
4. *Hyperlinks: Relationships among information objects, in the same or multiple documents.*
5. *Scheduling: Description of "finite coordinate spaces" and scheduling events to occur within those spaces.*

17. Written by R Turner, T Douglass, and A. Turner, Prentice Hall, 1996.

6. *Rendition: Presentation of objects in finite coordinate spaces.*

For an application system to take advantage of HyTime encoded document, it must use a HyTime engine. Even though HyTime is an application of SGML that uses constructs from SGML, it really requires a different kind of processor. An SGML parser can successfully parse a HyTime document, but the results will essentially be meaningless for any of the HyTime constructs. The HyTime engine will take the results of the SGML parse and interpret the HyTime constructs meaningfully. Visit the HyTime Web page at UMass-Lowell maintained by Lloyd Rutledge at: http://dmsl.cs.uml.edu/standards/hytime.html for a list of companies, products and other information about HyTime.

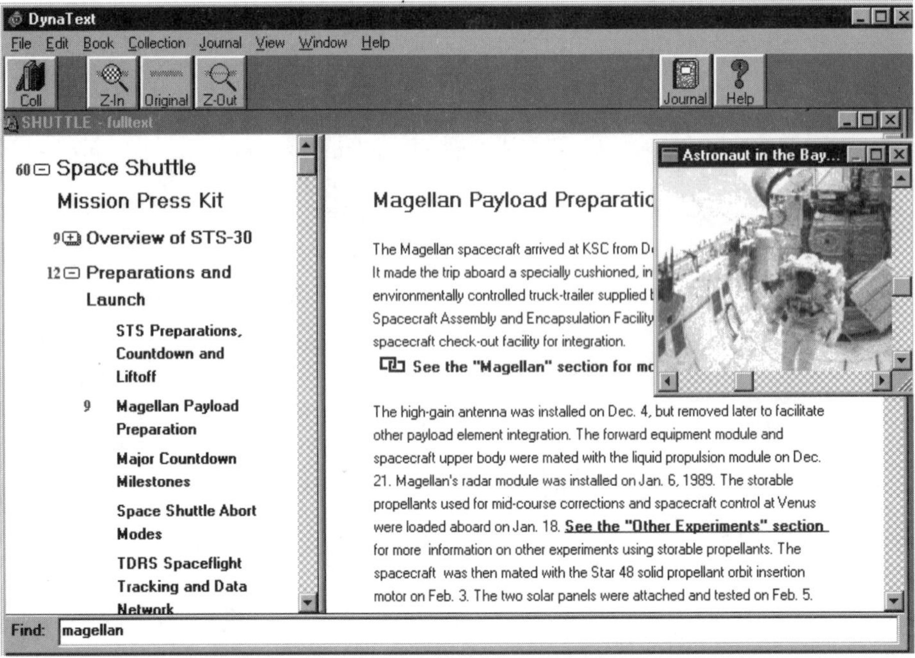

DynaText hypermedia (HyTime) browser from Electronic Book Technologies

The value of using HyTime is the same as for using SGML. Standard accepted representations of document content will ultimatly last longer and depend less on quirky, fashionable specifications subject to the whims of the leading vendor of the day.

5 • 4 HTML

HTML, the proverbial coin of the realm for the Web, started out life (in CERN) as a convienent way of creating hypertext documents viewable with World Wide Web browsers. Tim Berners-Lee, father of the Web, at CERN, knew nothing about SGML; however, some other people did[18] and eventually made a case for paying more attention to "proper" SGML. Primarily, this involved the creation and distribution of an SGML DTD for HTML. This means you can take an HTML document, run it through an SGML parser, and determine if your document is structurally correct. This is important stuff! If you ever hope to use your content in several ways, you must ensure that your documents are well–structured.

Much of the Web community and vendors responsible for Web browsers do seem to be willing to keep the SGML flame burning or at least to tolerate it. Vendors who add new features and tags to HTML, at least seem willing to give SGML good lip service. Ultimately, however, vendors must be willing to include true SGML parsers as part of their products.

So the question really becomes: if HTML and the Web work, why bother with all this SGML stuff? Mostly, it boils down to two issues. First, a desire to keep your electronic documents functioning and readable in perpetuity. Secondly, a desire to use and deliver content in a variety of ways.

Electronic documents—digital documents—will never degrade; they will never turn yellow and corrode. However, the software and operating systems necessary to read the documents will become inoperable and render the electronic documents useless. How many have had the experience of not being able to read old Apple II diskettes or even older punch

18. Notably Dan Connoly and Elliot Kimber who created the first HTML DTD and critiqued it, respectivly.

cards? The only hope is a strict adherence to a well defined standard. The Federal Aviation Administration (FAA) requires that the schematics for airplanes be archived for at least 20 years. They mandate that the drawings must be kept in the IGES graphics standard.

OK, let's now assume everyone agrees that real HTML that conforms to SGML is the accepted Web language. Now there turns out to be an explosion of HTML versions. Many companies, notably Netscape and Microsoft, introduce new HTML tags to improve the functionality of their browsers. Companies try to distinguish themselves from one another by introducing new tags and browsers that interpret those tags. Netscape is the classic example, introducing the concepts of Frames and inline Plug-ins that allow multi-paned windowed interfaces and multimedia content. It's great for the user but rough on standardization. In a competitive market, this behavior is to be expected; however documents that use these tags will be truly readable only with one vendor's browser. If that vendor ultimately establishes the de facto standard, then all is well. If not, content will eventually be lost and rendered unreadable.

The only way to ensure uniform adoption of standards is to apply conformance tests to the use of the standard and browsers. Conformance tests are where the rubber meets the road in the world of standards. It is only by passing a conformance test that a document or browser can truly claim to comply with a standard. This type of branding is well known in the commercial world also, for proprietary specifications. A recent example is Microsoft's branding of products as "Windows 95" compliant and allowing only those products to bear the Windows 95 logo. Someday we may see the moniker "HTML Compliant" stamped on products by an authoritative organization; until then, chaos rules.

Using content in multiple ways is done reasonably only when the content itself is "authored" in a highly structured way. This is one of the principal strengths of SGML. Multimedia databases, books for the blind, talking books, printed text, and so on can be created from a single content source if that content is well–

structured. Remember that using your content in many ways makes your project more profitable and efficient.

Of course, that does not mean that SGML is the only way to structure documents. However, it is a formal internationally–accepted standard. It functions as well as any other structuring specification, so why not use it?

5 • 4 • 1 Steve Tibbett's HTML Cheat Sheet

The collection of HTML flavors is growing. Hopefully, this trend will stop, and all vendors will agree on a "standard" HTML. But for now that's life in the HTML fast lane. What follows is the "HTML Cheat Sheet," created by Steve Tibbett and reproduced here with his kind permission :[19]

HTML Cheat Sheet

This page is a quick reference to all the HTML tags that are supported in the most popular World Wide Web browsers. This page requires that your browser support tables, or it will look terrible. I will try to indicate which browsers support which tags, where possible. Please send me coments on missing tags, incorrect documentation, etc. This page created by Steve Tibbett. You are visitor #9755 since 17-Oct-95.

Quick Reference (Links don't work in some browsers)					
<a>	<address>	<area>	<b>	<base>	<bgsound>
<big>	<body>	<cite>	<code>	<dd>	<dl>
<dfn>	<dir>	<dt>	<em>	<form>	<head>
<html>	<hr>	<i>	<img>	<input>	<isindex>
<kbd>	<li>	<lt>	<map>	<marquee>	<menu>
<ol>	<option>	<p>	<samp>	<select>	<small>
<strong>	<sub>	<sup>	<table>	<td>	<textarea>
<th>	<title>	<tr>	<tt>	<u>	<ul>
<var>	<frame>	<frameset>	<noframes>	<h1>	<blockquote>

19. Check for Steve's updates at: http://letterman.corel.ca:1782/cheat.html. Some headings have been modified for printing.

Quick Reference (Links don't work in some browsers)					
<center>	**<!-->**	**<blink>**	**<embed>**	**<basefont>**	**<font>**
<caption>	**<object>**				

Tag	Description	Example	Output	Level
<html>	Surrounds the entire HTML document. Browsers don't always require this.	`<html> ... </html>`	None	1
<!-->	Inserts a comment into an HTML document. Not displayed.	`<!-- Steve Was Here -->`	None	1

Header Elements				
<head>	Surrounds docu-ment.header section.	`<head> ... </head>`	None	1
<title>	Specifies the document title. Typically displayed in the browser window title bar..	`<title> ... </title>`	None	1
<isindex>	Specifies that the current document is a search-able index. The browser will use a mechanism of its choice to let the user start a search.	`<isindex>`	None	1
<base>	Specifies the URL of the current document, for relative links.	`<base href="basename">`	None	1
<body>	Contains the body of the page. One per page.	`<body> ... </body>`	None	1

Text Elements				

<a>	Begins text anchor or hypertext link.	`<a href="cheat.html">`
		`Cheat`
		`</a>`
			Cheat	1

Text Elements				
<p>	Begins a new paragraph. Contains a paragraph in HTML 3.0 (i.e, you should include </p>)	`One<p>Two`	One Two	1
<center>	Centers text horizontally.This is a Netscape tag; see `<pallign=>`	`<center>Test</center>`	Test	NS
** **	Inserts a line break. This may or may not be less space than inserted by the <p> tag.	`One Two`	One Two	1
<hr>	Inserts a horizontal line across the browser window.	`One<hr>Two`	One ——— Two	1
<img>	Inserts a graphic image or the alternate text if the browser can't show the graphic.	`<img src=badurl alt="Text">`	Text	1

Logical Text Styles				
<h1>	Header. Sizes range from 1 through 6 Use for headers, not just for big text.	`<h1>Big</h1>` `<h6>Small</h6>`	Big Small	1

<blockquote>	Block quote. Quoted text from some source. Usually indented.	`<blockquote>`
		`Now is the time.`
		`</blockquote>`
			Now
			is
			the
			time
				1

<em>	Emphasize text. Most browsers use italics.	`<em>Hello</em>`	*Hello*	1
<strong>	Strong text emphasis. Typically boldface.	`<strong>Hello</strong>`	**Hello**	1
<code>	Code sample - uses monospaced font	`<code>Hello</code>`	`Hello`	1
<kbd>	Keyboard key - for indicating that a user should press a specific key	`<kbd>Hello</kbd>`	`Hello`	1
<samp>	Sample program output.	`<samp>Hello</samp>`	`Hello`	1

Logical Text Styles				
<var>	Program variable	`<var>Hello</var`	*Hello*	1
<dfn>	Definition	`<dfn>Hello</dfn>`	Hello	1
<cite>	Citation	`<cite>Hello</cite>`	*Hello*	1
<address>	Address - typically a mailing address.	`<address>Hello</address>`	*Hello*	1

Physical Text Styles				
<b>	Bold face text.	`<b>Hello</b>`	Hello	1
<i>	Italicize the text.	`<i>Hello</i>`	*Hello*	1
<u>	Underline the text.	`<u>Hello</u>`	Hello	1
<big>	Makes text big, relative to the current font.	`<big>Hello</big>`	Hello	3
<small>	Makes text small relative to the current font.	`<small>Hello</small>`	Hello	3
<sup>	Displays superscript (small, raised) text.	`<sup>Hello</sup>`	Hello	3
<sub>	Displays superscript (small, lowered) text.	`<sub>Hello</sub>`	Hello	3
<tt>	Use a typewriter-style monospaced font, typically Courier if available.	`<tt>Hello</tt>`	`Hello`	1
<blink>	Makes text flash. Hated by all. See URL about:mozilla if using Netscape.	`<blink>Yikes!</blink>`	Yikes!	NS
<address>	Address - typically a mailing address.	`<address>Hello</address>`	*Hello*	1

Definition Lists				

<dl>	Begin a definition list. A definition list is a list of header/body pairs. The header is left-aligned, the body text is indented and word wrapped.	`<dl>`
		`<dt>Header`
		`<dd>Body`
		`<dt>Header`
		`<dd>Body`
		`</dl>`
			Example	1

<dt>	Definition term. Left-aligned text - doesn't need to be terminated.	See <dl>	See <dl>	1
<dd>	Definition body. Indented text displayed below the definition term. Doesn't need to be terminated.	See <dl>	See <dl>	1

Other Lists				

<ul>	Begin an unordered list. An unordered list is just a list of items with bullets.	`<ul>`
		`<li>First`
		`<li>Second`
		`<li>Third`
		`</ul>`
			Example	1

<ol>	Begin an ordered list. An ordered list is a list of items, with a counter of some sort.	`<ol>`
		`<li>First`
		`<li>Second`
		`<li>Third`
		`</ol>`
			Example	1

<menu>	Begins an "interactive menu". Most browsers display this the same as an unordered list.	`<menu>`
		`<li>First`
		`<li>Second`
		`<li>Third`
		`</menu>`
			Example	1

<dir>	Begins an "directory". Most browsers display this the same as an unordered list.	`<dir>`
		`<li>First`
		`<li>Second`
		`<li>Third`
		`</dir>`
			Example	1

Other Lists				
<li>	List Item. This is an item in an ordered or unordered list. Doesn't need to be terminated.	`See <ul> or <ol>`	`See <ul> or <ol>`	1

Forms				
<form>	This tag contains a form.	`<uform [action=URL] [method= (post|get)]>... </form>`	Example	2
<input>	This tag marks a *text* box, *password* box, *checkbox*, *radio* button, *submit* or *reset* button on a form. Type type field can be any of these.	`<input name="name" type=text value="default" size=32 malength=64>...</input>`	Example	2
<textarea>	This marks a rectangular text input area on the form.	`<textarea name="name" [rows=1] [cols=1] Default Text </textarea>`	Example	2
<select>	Lets the user select an item from a list. The list items follow this tag prefaced by <option> tags.	`<select name="name" size=2 multiple> <option>Cheese <option>Beans </select>`	Example	2
<option>	This tag is an option on a <select> menu.	`See <select>`	Example	2

Tables				
<table>	This tag contains a table.	`<table> ... </table>`	Example	3
<tr>	Table row. Each row of a table is contained in this tag.	`<tr> ... </tr>`	Example	3
<td>	Table data.	`<td>Data</td>`	Example	3
<th>	Table header. Generally like the <td> tag but centers the text.	`<th>Header</th>`	Example	3

Tables				
<caption>	Creates a caption outside the table (at the top or bottom). Align and valign options work as usual.	<table border=1> <caption valign=bottom> Caption! </caption> <tr><td>Table Body</td>/tr>/table>	Caption! TableBody	3

Client Side Image Maps				
<map>	Client side image map.	<map> name="map"> <area shape=rect coords="0,0,64,64" href="_URL_"> </map> <img usemap="map" src="some.bmp">	Example	3
<area>	Client side image map area.	See <map>	See <map>	3

Frames				
<frameset>	This tag **replaces** the <body> tag for pages using frames.	<frameset rows=*,*> <frame src="this.html"> <frame src="that.html"> </frameset>	Example	NS,MS
<frame>	Specifies the source for one of the cells in a frame.	<frame src="this.html>	Example	NS,MS
<noframes>	Browsers with frames hide this text; others show it. Used to tell users to get a better browser.	<noframes> Ha ha ha </noframes>	Example	NS,MS

Microsoft-Specifig Tags				
<marquee>	This tag creates an animated piece of text sliding across your browser window.	<marquee>Helo</marquee>	Example	MS

Microsoft-Specifig Tags				
<bgsound>	Loads up and plays a sound when the user enters the page.	<bgsound src="start.wav">	None	MS

Miscellaneous Tags				
<embed>	Embeds foreign content in an HTML document.	<embed src=cmx.cmx>> Only visible if you have the Corel CMX Plugin for Netscape installed.		NS
<object>	Embeds an "object" in an HTML document.			3

Presentation Tags				
<font>	Lets you change the font name or size.	Hello<font size=+2>Hello</font>	Hello Hello	NS,MS
<basefont>	Sets the base font size. Relative font size changes are based on this size.	Hello<basefont size=4>Hello<basefont size=3>	HelloHello	NS.MS

<body> tag options				
back-ground=	Specifies an image to tile as the page's back-ground.	<body background=mar-ble.gif>.	(marble.gif in background)	2
bgcolor=	Sets the page's back-ground colour.	<body bgcolor=#ff0000>	(Bright red back-ground)	2
bgproperties=	Lets you fix the page's background like a "watermark".	<body bgproper-ties=fixed>.	Non-scrolling background bitmap	MS
text=	Specifies the colour for text on this page.	<body text=#000000>	Black text.	2
link=	Specifies the colour for hypertext links on this page.	<body link=#ffff00>	Bright yellow links.	2
alink=	Specifies the colour for anchor hypertext links on this page.	<body link=#808080>.	Middle grey links	2

<body> tag options				
`vlink=`	Specifies the colour for seen hypertext links on this page.	`<body link=#0080ff>.`	Bright blue links.	2

<img> tag options				
`src=`	Specifies which image to show.	`<img src=bullet.gif>`		1
`alt=`	Text to show if the image can't be shown.	`<img src=bullet.gif alt="Text">`		1
`align=`	Image alignment: left, center, right, top, middle, bottom, texttop, absmiddle, baseline, absbottom.	`--<img src=bullet.gif align=top> --<img src=bullet.gif align=bottom> --`	-- -- --	2
`hspace=`	Horizontal space to leave for the image.	`L<img src=bullet.gif hspace=30>R`	L R	2
`vspace=`	Vertical space to leave for the image.	Left `<img src=bullet.gif vspace=20>` Right	Left Right	2
`border=`	Draws an optional border around the graphic.	`<img src=bullet.gif border=2>`		2
`dynsrc=`	Specifies an animation to play; uses *src* if can't play animation.	`<img dynsrc=test.avi` start=mouseover loop=infinite src=bullet.gif>		MS
`start=`	Specifies when to start a *dynsrc* animation.	See *dynsrc*.	See *dynsrc*.	MS
`loop=`	In a *dynsrc* animation, specifies how many times to play it (or "infinite").	See *dynsrc*.	See *dynsrc*.	MS
`width=`	Tells the browser how wide the image is.	`<img width=32 height=32>`	No visual effect.	2

<img> tag options				
height=	Tells the browser how high the image is.	<img width=32 height=32>	No visual effect.	2

<td,tr,th> tag options				
bgcolor=	Sets the background colour for a single cell in a table.	<td bgcolor=#00ff00>	This cell has a green background.	MS
colspan=	Makes a wide cell in a table.	<td colspan=5> (this cell is 2 cells wide)		3
rowspan=	Makes a tall cell in a table.	<td rowspan=2>>.	This cell is 2 rows high (the next row is empty)	3
align=	Controls horizontal text alignment; values are left, center, and right.	<td align=right> At The Right.	At The Right	3
valign=	Controls vertical alignment; values are top, middle, and bottom.	<td valign=bottom> Bottom.	Bottom	3
width=	Cell size specifier- can be in pixels or percent.	<td width=20>	A 20 pixel wide cell	3
height=	Cell size specifier - can be in pixels or percent.	<td height=20>	A 20 pixel high cell	3

<frameset> tag options				
rows=	Specifies vertical sections and sizes, asterisk means remaining space.	<frameset rows=20%, *,10%>	Example	NS
cols=	Like rows= but for horizontal sections.	<frameset cols="*,*">	Example	NS

<frame> tag options				
src=	URL to place in frame cell.	<frame src=test.html>	Example	NS
name=	Window name to use for this frame. _blank,_self, _parent, _top are special names	<frameset name=fred>	Example	NS

<frame> tag options				
`marginwidth=`	Set the blank space in pixels around the content.	`<frame marginwidth=4>`	Example	NS
`marginheight=`	Sets the blank space in pixels around the content.	`<frame marginheight=4>`	Example	NS
`scrolling=`	Set to yes, no, or auto. Controls scrollbar presence.	`<frame src=fred.html scrolling=no>`	Example	NS
`noresize=`	Disables frame edge dragging so users can't resize them.	`<frame src=fred.html noresize>`	Example	NS

<ht> tag options				
`width=`	Specify ruler width in pixels or percent.	`<ht width=50%`	Example	NS, MS
`align=`	Align ruler:left, right, or center.	`<hr width=50% align=right>` `<hr width=50% align=left>`	Example	NS, MS
`size=`	Specifies ruler height in pixels.	`<hr size=10>`	Example	NS, MS
`noshade`	Turns off the "shadow" under the line.	`<hr><hr noshade>`	Example	NS, M

Unordered List example	

`<ul>`
`<li>This is the first list item in an unordered list.`
`<li>This is the second list item in an unordered list.`
`<li>And this here is the third item.`
`</ul>`
	This is the first list item in an unordered list.
	This is the second list item in an unordered list.
	And this here is the third item.

Ordered List example

```
<ol>
<li>This is the first list item
in an unordered list.
<li>This is the second list item
in an unordered list.
<li>And this here is the third
item.
</ol>
```

This is the first list item in an unordered list.
This is the second list item in an unordered list.
And this here is the third item.

Menu example

```
<menu>
<li>This is the first list item in an
unordered list.
<li>This is the second list item in
an unordered list.
<li>And this here is the third item.
</menu>
```

This is the first list item in an unordered list.
This is the second list item in an unordered list.
And this here is the third item.

Directory example

```
<dir>
<li>This is the first list item in an
unordered list.
<li>This is the second list item in
an unordered list.
<li>And this here is the third item.
</dir>
```

This is the first list item in an unordered list.
This is the second list item in an unordered list.
And this here is the third item.

Definition List example

`<dl>`
`<dt>Chair`
`<dd>A piece of furniture often found with four legs and a high back, which people sit on.`
`<dt>Table`
`<dd>A table is another piece of furniture, also with four legs, but with no back.`
`</dl>`
	Chair
	A piece of furniture often found with four legs and a high back, which people sit on.
	Table
	A table is anothe piece of furniture, also with four legs, but with no back.

Form example

```
<form action="dummy.html" method=get>
<input name=first type=text
value="Default"> <br>
Password:
<input name=secind type=password
size=8 maxlength=8><br>
<input name=third
type=checkbox checked>Checkbox<br>
<input name=fourth
type=radio>Radio <br>
<hr>
<textarea rows=2 cols=16>
This is the default text.
</textarea>
<ht>
<select size=2 multiple>
<option>First
<option>Second
<option>Third
</select>
<hr>
<input value="Send" type=submit>
<input type=reset><br>
</form>
```

Default

Password:

Checkbox

Radio

This is the default text.

First
Second
Third

Send Reset

Table example

```
<table border=3 width=100%>
<tr>
<th>Left</th>
<th>Right</th>
</tr>
<tr>
<td>Left Data</td>
<td>Right Data</td>
</tr>
</table>
```

Left	Right
Left Data	Right Data

Client Side Image Map example

```
<map name="map>
<area shape=rect
coords="4,5,86,113"
href=cheat.html>
<area shape=rect
coords="45,45,149,173"
href=cheat.html>
</map>
<img usemap="#map" src="map.gif">
```

The official keeper of the HTML specification is the World Wide Web Organization (W3O). The W3O is an organization jointly sponsored by INRAI (Institut National de Recherche en Informatique et en Qutomatique...The French National Institute for Research in Computer Science and Control) and MIT. It was founded by Tim Berners-Lee, creator of the Web, when he moved from CERN (European Laboratory for Particle Physics) to MIT. The W3O is shephearding a number of specifications through the standards process.[20] In collaboration with the W3O, an HTML working Group of the IETF, was created in or around May 1994 . The W3O is coordinating testing efforts of HTML.

20. Find the W3O at: http://www.w3.org.

5 • 4 • 2 Link Validation

An SGML parser can check that an HTML document is syntactically valid. It can't check if the link in the document actually points to valid places but there are tools to help accomplish this. For example, one tool called "`linkcheck`", a perl script, is available at ftp://ftp.math.psu.edu/pub/sibley.

Another useful Web management helper is a tool that aids in the relocation of Web pages. If you have a Web site or page that's popular, it becomes a problem when you have to move the page (for whatever reason). It would be nice to be able to tell other sites, that refer to your pages about the new location. The reference log file keeps track of where your visitors are coming from. (See *Section 1 • 3 Web Maintenance* in *Chapter 1 • World Wide Web* for more information about these type of tools.)

Some of the new Web site management products, like Interleaf's Cyberleaf and Adobe's SiteMill, help with this arduous task. Link maintanence is nasty and sites will unquestionably degrade over time. It is an important issue that must be addressed if you hope to create a Web site that remains current.

5 • 4 • 3 A Gentle Introduction to HTML Syntax

Let's take a brief, very brief look at HTML itself. Rather than going through HTML in an overly simplistic way, let's examine the syntax and principles of HTML. Go to any book store or read the many online information resources for the details on HTML.[21] Look here for some syntactic and structural principles.

Keep in mind that HTML is an application of SGML. Because of this, the syntactic conventions are all derived from SGML. For example, the unbelievably baroque syntax for a comment `<!-- stuff to be commented out -->` derives from the nature of SGML. According to the SGML standard, a comment

21. See http://sunsite.unc.edu/boutell/faq/index.html or news:comp.infosystems.www.authoring.html, or http://www.ncsa.uiuc.edu/General/Internet/WWW/HtmlPrimer.html, to name a few.

is defined as:

```
comment declaration =
mdo,     (markup declaration open)
( comment,
( s |
comment )* )?,
mdc      (markup declaration close)

comment =
com,   (comment delimeter)
SGML character*,
com     (comment delimeter)
```

These "production rules" are used by people who build parsers, the programs that interpret a language.

The strange look of SGML comments derives from the generality possible with SGML. One can redefine almost everything. The trick with comments is that you want to be sure that the parser does *not* interpret anything inbetween the start and end comment delimiters. Keep in mind that the HTML document is "parsed, " it is interpreted by a program, the browser. This is very much akin to the batch–language oriented document processors (see *Section 4 • 1 • 2 Language Characteristics* in *Chapter 4 • Form and Function of Document Processors*). In effect, the HTML document itself is a program, that drives the HTML browser, your Web browser.

Markup tags generally have a start and an end. In between the start and end tags is the content.

Start tags generally consist of a tag name surrounded by angle brackets, like `<THIS>`, and end tags have the same tag name preceeded by a slash and also surrounded by angle brackets, like `</THIS>`.

Many HTML tags require parameters. These parameters are sometimes interpreted by the browser and sometimes by the server. Let's dissect the tag for a link:

```
<A  HREF="http://www.ability.net">Access Ability</A>
```

The <A> is the start of an Anchor tag.

The HREF or hypertext reference is an attribute of the Anchor tag.

The value of the HREF is either a URL or a file accessible from the point of view of the server.

The text "Access Ability" is what the browser should display to the user as a link.

Finally, the </A>, like most tags, ends with a forward slash and the tag name "A".

In general, the syntax of much HTML markup, like SGML, is as follows:

```
<TagName Attrib="Value1"
Attrib="Value2"
Attrib3="value3> content text </TagName>
```

where the existence of attributes is optional, and the number of attributes is variable.

Sometimes the values for an attribute are fixed, from a list; in these cases, the value does not appear within quotes. For example, the IMG tag, used to define where and how to place an image in a page, has attibutes values for the ALIGN attribute of BOTTOM, MIDDLE and TOP.

```
<IMG SRC="filename.gif" ALIGN=BOTTOM>
```

(For the geeks among us, these are the elements of an enumerated list.)

5 • 5 ODA

"Never eat more than you can lift." - Miss Piggy

And in this corner, off to a slow start, weighing in with both an architecture and interchange format, is the Office Document Architecture (ODA) standard.

ODA was the other major player in the electronic document standards game, and European users will argue that it is still relevant, so some background is useful. Not limited to the structure of a document, it addresses the complete range of visual presentation issues—how a document looks. It is important to recognize the word "architecture" in the ODA name. It is an entire framework for representing, in a complete manner, both the structure and the visual presentation of the various elements that make up the structure.

If a document is encoded using ODA, and you give it to another ODA site, you can expect it to look exactly the same when printed at the other site. Clearly, ODA is a much more ambitious standard than SGML. Just as clearly, that is the reason why the standard itself ,and the implementations of ODA, have been slower to come into existence.

ODA describes a document as a hierarchical collection of objects—a tree-structured relationship—just like SGML. But the terminology ODA uses is, of course, different from the terminology used by SGML.

ODA refers to document structure in two fundamental ways. Documents have a logical structure and a layout structure. The logical structure of a document is very similar to the SGML document structure defined in a DTD. The layout structure, however, refers to the positioning of elements as objects to be placed on paper. This layout structure divides a document into page sets, pages, frames, and blocks to describe the way information is to be placed on paper. The connection between the logical and layout structures is made via a layout directive.

ODA Basics

These two figures show a sample document—a simple business letter—and the layout structure used to represent the letter with ODA.

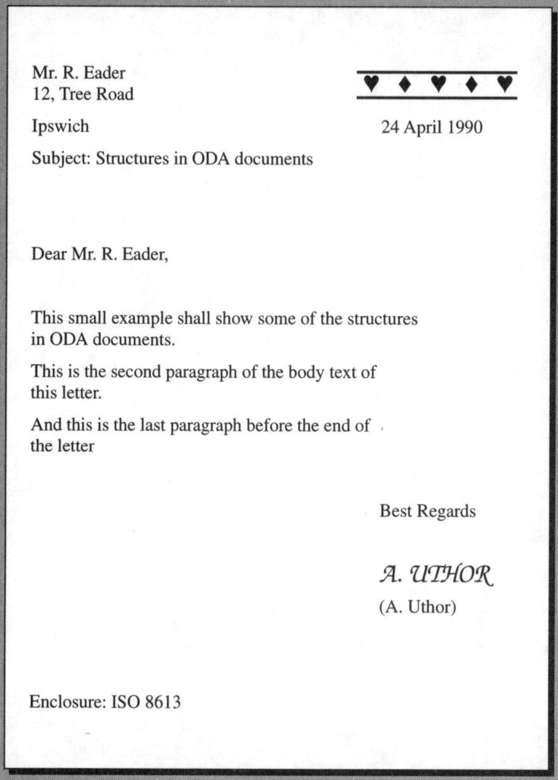

Mr. R. Eader
12, Tree Road
Ipswich
Subject: Structures in ODA documents

♥ ♦ ♥ ♦ ♥

24 April 1990

Dear Mr. R. Eader,

This small example shall show some of the structures in ODA documents.

This is the second paragraph of the body text of this letter.

And this is the last paragraph before the end of the letter

Best Regards

A. UTHOR
(A. Uthor)

Enclosure: ISO 8613

Example of a business letter

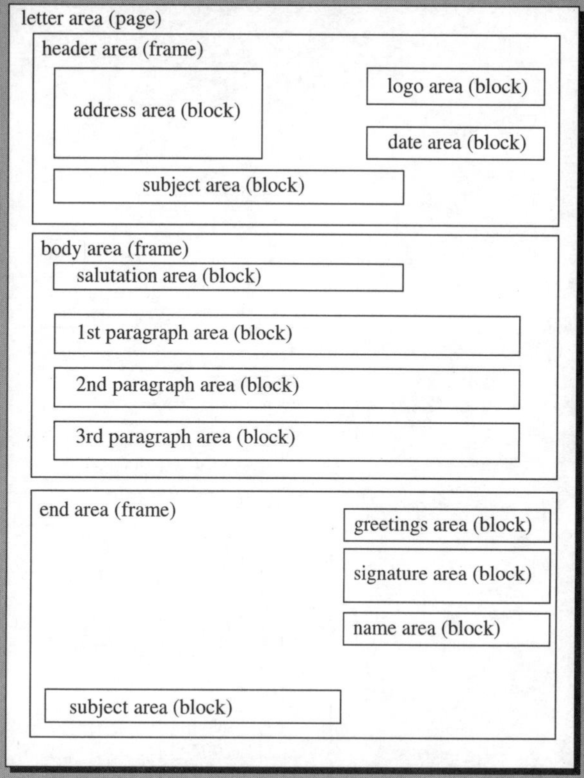

letter area (page)
header area (frame)
address area (block)
logo area (block)
date area (block)
subject area (block)
body area (frame)
salutation area (block)
1st paragraph area (block)
2nd paragraph area (block)
3rd paragraph area (block)
end area (frame)
greetings area (block)
signature area (block)
name area (block)
subject area (block)

Layout structure of the business letter

Next the relationship of the logical and layout structures for this simple business letter are illustrated. Note one important property: each content object is directly associated with the lowest, most basic logical and layout objects. This makes a good deal of intuitive sense. Some small (logically indivisible) piece of content must be associated with a layout object to be visible. The content itself forms a sort of interface between the logical and layout trees of an ODA document.

Layout and Logical Structures

Content forms the interface between the logical structure and layout structure trees in an ODA representation.

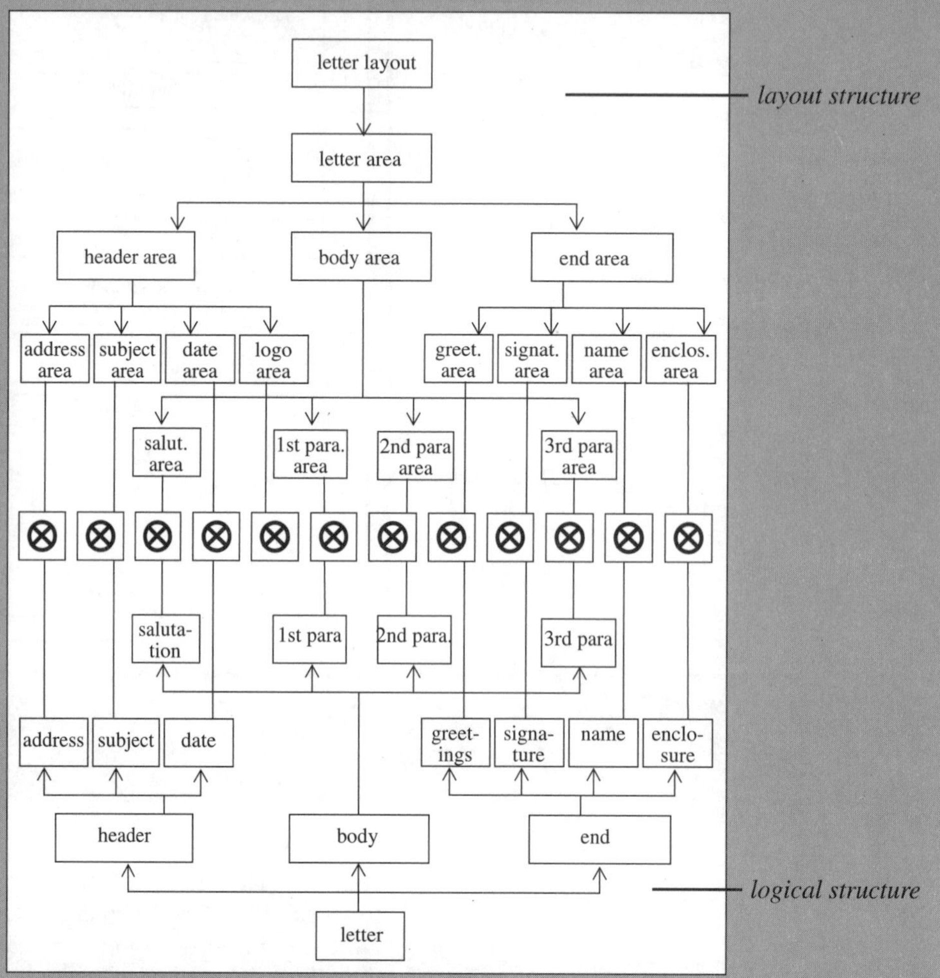

Wolfgang Appelt, *Document Architecture in Open Systems The ODA Standard*, © 1991, by Springer-Verlag. Reprinted with permission of the publisher.

It is important to clearly understand that ODA is an interchange standard. To ensure, for example, that my page will appear correctly on your printer, ODA addresses the appearance of the document's many component parts. These components can include such things as fonts, raster, and geometric graphics. (Raster graphics are bitmapped objects. See *Section 6 • 1 Bitmaps and Objects* in *Chapter 6 • Media and Document Integration* for a discussion of graphics issues.) If one systems's idea of a curved line is not the same as another's, interchange will suffer. ODA attacks this difficult problem by standardizing the representation for the component parts.

We can trace the processing of an image for a particular content object as follows. Let's consider a line. The line is represented according to the Geometric Content Architecture portion of ODA as a CGM (Computer Graphics Metafile) object. It is imaged according to a presentation attribute. The presentation attribute (from the layout structure of the overall representation) is associated with a semantic logical object (from the logical structure) via a layout directive.

OSI Reference Model

At the beginning of the OSI effort, the committees developed a reference model. This model is used as the conceptual framework for the development of more standards. The seven-layer reference model is most often seen in the networking world. End users, generally only use the top layer—the Application—unless, of course, the network cable becomes unplugged, in which case, the physical layer demands your attention.

Application services are provided by the upper layers	**Application**	*Ultimately responsible for managing the communications between applications*
	Presentation	*Responsible for adding structure to the units of data that are exchanged*
	Session	*Responsible for adding control mechanisms to the data exchange*
End-to-end services are provided by the lower layers	**Transport**	*Responsible for reliability and multiplexing of data transfer across the network (over and above that provided by the network layer) to the level required by the application*
	Network	*Responsible for data transfer across the network, independent of both the media comprising the underlying subnetworks and the topology of those subnetworks*
	Data Link	*Responsible for transmission, framing, and error control over a single communications link*
	Physical	*Responsible for the electromechanical interface to the communications media*

For a much more "snappy" description of OSI (from which these descriptions are taken) see:
"The Open Book: A Practical Perspective on OSI" by Marshall T. Rose, Prentice-Hall 1990.

ODA and SGML take fundamentally different approaches to electronic document standardization. One—SGML—is a robust extensible language that focuses on document structure and does not address document layout. The other—ODA—provides an architectural framework that addresses both document structure and layout.

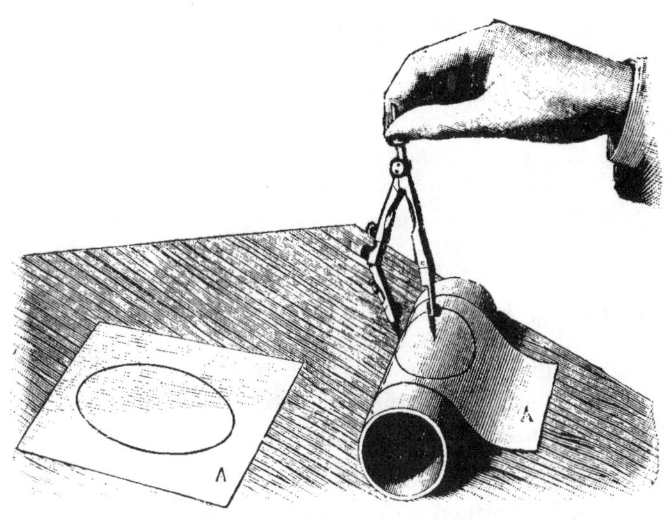

Chapter 6 • Media and Document Integration

The union of the mathematician with the poet, fervor with measure, passion with correctness, this surely is the ideal. —William James

The relationship between different media types such as graphics, video, and sounds with text in a document processing system is finicky. The integration of graphics, audio, and video with text into a complete electronic document is the source of many problems. This chapter examines these problems. In addition, we examine media formats and standards commonly used in electronic publishing. The decision about what media format to use has ramifications all along the document processing path, and we will also examine these. (The broader topic of compound documents is also discussed in *Section 3 • 4 The Engineered View.*)

As the increasing availability of high performance systems and Web browsers becomes ubiquitous, documents with many different types of media sometimes have problems. Media players, such as video or sound and graphics, are dependent on the execution of helper applications or more robust Web browsers. One terrific service by the folks at Lawrence Livermore Labs is a WWW Viewer Test Page.[1] On this page, they have compiled all the data types with a test button. When the test is selected, the Web server sends back data of the selected type. This is extremely useful for checking the functionality of a Web browser and its operating environment.

6 • 1 Bitmaps and Objects

Before we dive into text and graphics integration issues, let's examine some computer graphics fundamentals. There are two broad categories for representing graphic images—bitmap and object–based.

A **bitmapped** representation is the classic form used by "paint" systems. Each dot on the display screen corresponds to a bit of information in computer memory (hence the term bit, mapped). In contrast, object–based systems (sometimes called geometric) are usually referred to as "draw" systems. Object–based graphics use a geometric description to represent objects, such as lines, circles, and curves. These objects can be meaningfully manipulated as objects, not simply as dots on the screen. For example, to move a line, you can grab the end point and drag it to another place on the screen while the line stays intact; this is called rubber banding. The "paint" and "draw" distinctions originated with the success of MacPaint and MacDraw on the Macintosh, which use bitmap and object–based representations, respectively.

Each approach has advantages and disadvantages. Using the bitmapped approach, you cannot select end points of lines or reshape curves. However, you can feather the edge of a shape into a soft blur or smoothly transition from one pastel shade to another. Painterly visuals such as soft edges and blurring are not practical when a system uses an object–based approach. Image manipulations with

1. Located at http://www-dsed.llnl.gov/documents/WWWtest.html

functions such as edge detection and contrast enhancement also require a bitmap representation. Some graphics systems attempt to combine these two paradigms; however, the bitmap and object paradigms are the two fundamental representations of images.

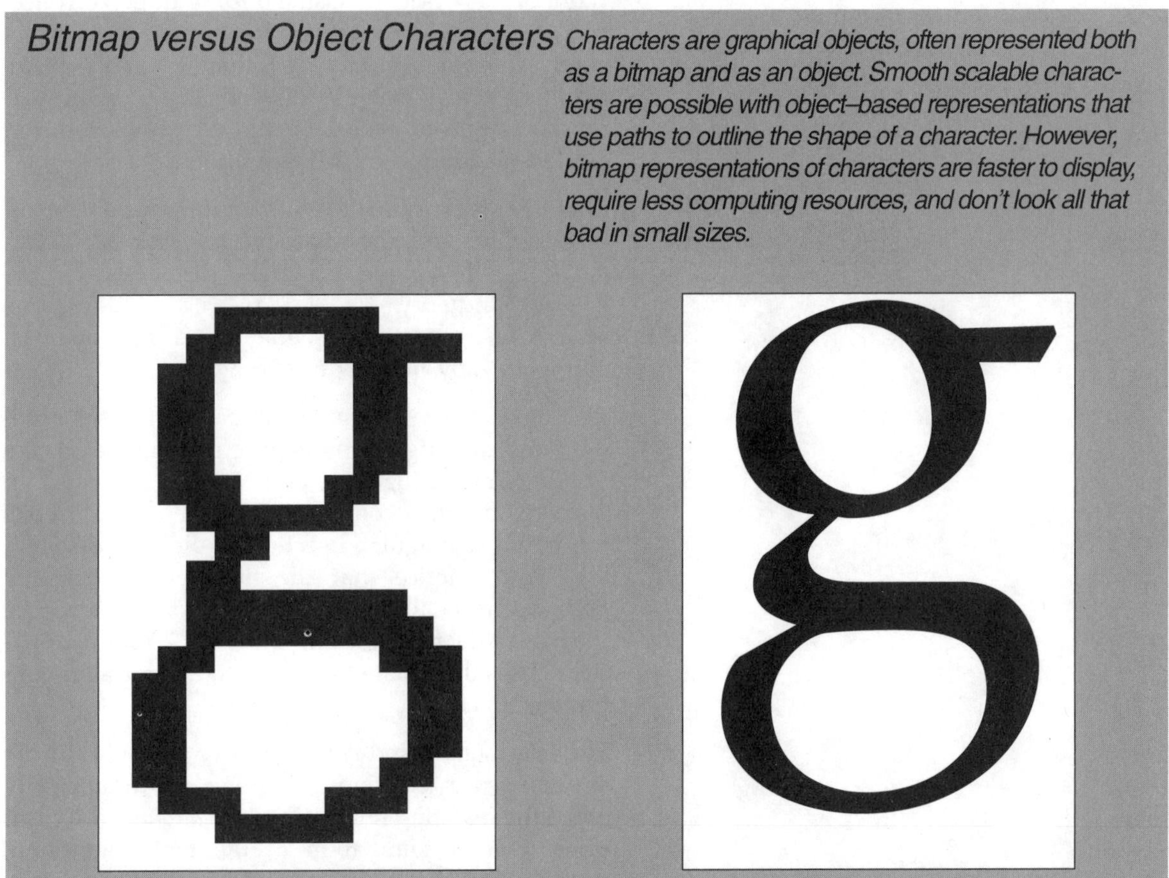

Bitmap versus Object Characters *Characters are graphical objects, often represented both as a bitmap and as an object. Smooth scalable characters are possible with object–based representations that use paths to outline the shape of a character. However, bitmap representations of characters are faster to display, require less computing resources, and don't look all that bad in small sizes.*

The implementation and use of an object–based representation for fonts was a key element in the desktop publishing revolution. Adobe's Type 1 font format allowed users virtually unlimited scaling of characters, while retaining the quality of the letterform. The object representation of the letterform is what produces this capability, along with the "hints" to maintain the quality of the strokes.[2] Jagged, blocky–looking letters are the result of scaling the bitmap representation of a character.

6 • 2 Dots and Pictures

A dot or mark is some visual blip, smudge, or collection of pixels that appears on the printed page or display. Certain kinds of images and image manipulation techniques depend on the manipulation of tiny dots, especially the images reproduced with the technique known as halftoning.

Photographs are images with continuous shades of black, white, and gray. These shades are *tones*. *Halftoning* is a technique, originally developed for the printing industry, to reproduce continuous–tone images using printing techniques capable of black and white only, not shades of gray.

In halftoning, a *dot pattern* is created by rephotographing the original photograph through a screen. The dots blend together, both on the paper and in our eye, to give a convincing illusion of continuous tones. In the magnified section of the following figure, you'll notice that the brighter an intensity desired, the smaller the size of the dots. In addition, the darker the tone, the larger the dots. Your eye spatially fuses the small dots so that they appear as continuous tones.

The size, shape, and orientation of the holes in the screen used in creating a halftone can dramatically affect the resulting image. *Digital halftoning* is a computer graphic simulation of the rephotographing process. PostScript, a page description language, uses the same terminology (that is, with the `setscreen` command) to allow the precise manipulation of halftone screens.[3] The resolution, orientation, and shape of the dot may all be manipulated. (See *Section 5 • 1 • 2 PostScript* in *Chapter 5 • Document Standards*.)

2. For more information on Type 1 fonts, see http://www.adobe.com/Type/Type.html at the Adobe Web site.

3. See *PostScript: Language Reference Manual* (also known as the Red book) by Adobe Systems, Incorporated, Addison-Wesley, Reading, MA, 1985, for all the gory PostScript detail.

A new form of halftoning, called stochastic halftoning, uses a semi-random arrangement of dots to create gray levels and color. The results offer smoother gradations of color.

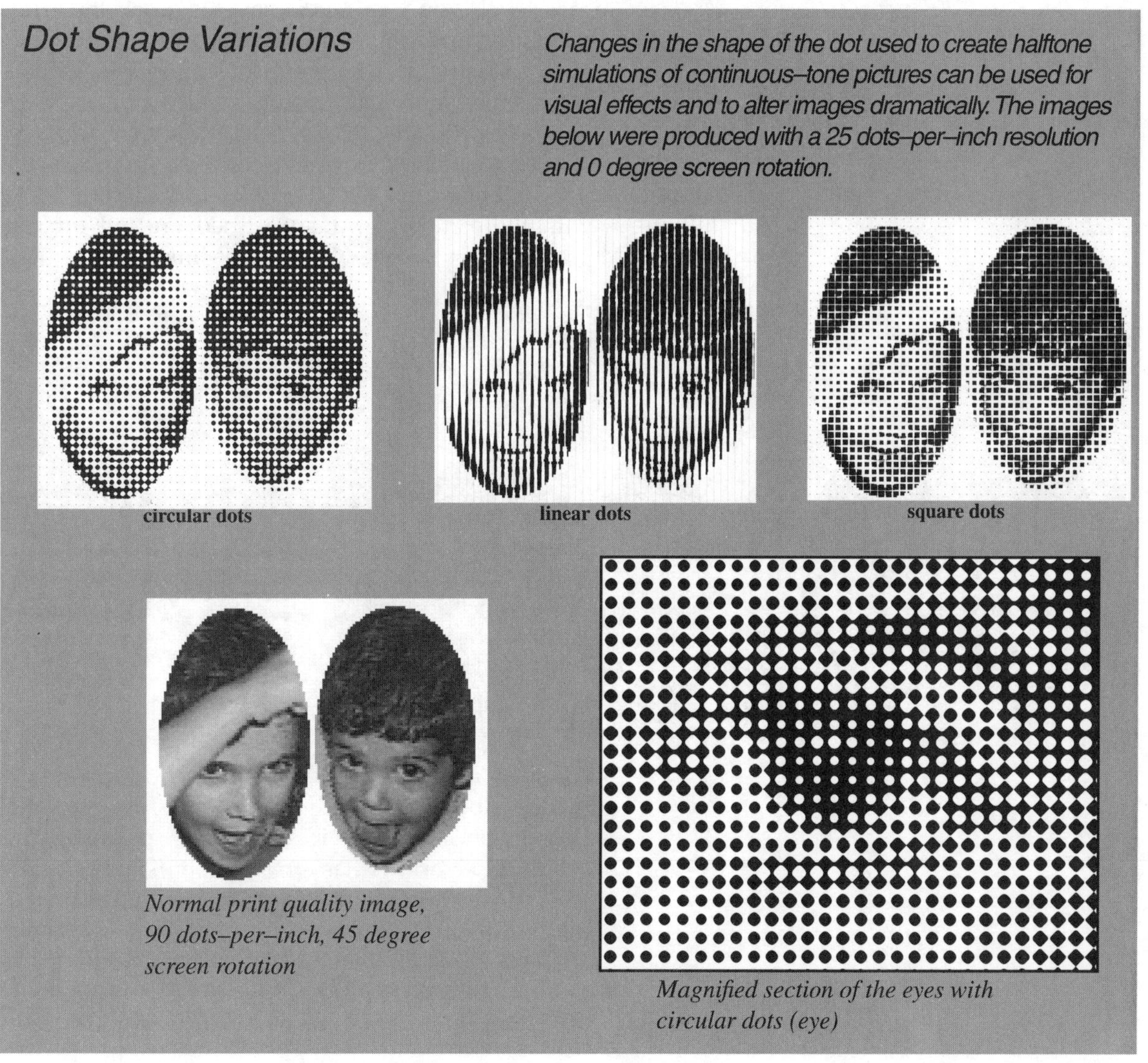

Dot Shape Variations
Changes in the shape of the dot used to create halftone simulations of continuous–tone pictures can be used for visual effects and to alter images dramatically. The images below were produced with a 25 dots–per–inch resolution and 0 degree screen rotation.
circular dots
linear dots
square dots
Normal print quality image, 90 dots–per–inch, 45 degree screen rotation
Magnified section of the eyes with circular dots (eye)

Another technique used to create the simulation of continuous–tone images is *dithering*. Dithering is sometimes considered a type of halftone. Unlike halftones, which vary the *size* of the dot, dithering varies the *number* or *density* of the dots within a fixed array. For example, a dither pattern that uses a three-by-three array of dots can represent 10 different intensity levels by displaying more, less, or no dots in the grid area. The trade-off is resolution: the more gray levels you wish to display, the larger the array necessary, and, therefore, the less resolution available. Each grid area represents a single pixel. Dithering results in much poorer quality images than halftoning. But for devices such as screen displays, which cannot vary the dot size with sufficient resolution, it is very useful.[4] The way in which the dots within the dither grid are turned on and off can greatly affect the overall image, as illustrated below.

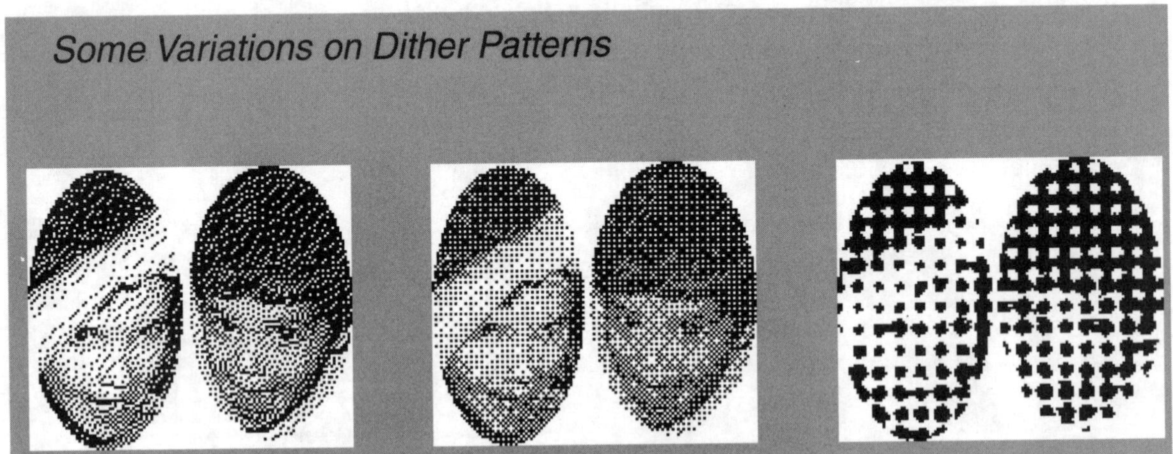

Another interesting consequence of simple mark manipulations is the advent of inexpensive resolution–enhancement devices for laser printers. The typical laser printer has a resolution of 300 dots per inch (dpi). Resolution–enhancing computer boards that plug into the controller section of a laser printer are now available. They can enhance the printing resolution from 300 to 600 or 1000 dpi by manipulations of the dot shape and some other tricks with the laser.

Resolution enhancement has spawned a small cadre of new products. They fall into two general categories: edge smoothing and gray-scale enhancement. *Edge smoothing* is used by Apple's FinePrint, DP-

4. For a good introduction to halftones and dithering see the classic text on computer graphics, *Computer Graphics: principles and practice—2nd edition,* by J. Foley, A. van Dam, S. Feiner, and J. Hughes, Addison-Wesley, 1990.

Tek's Super Smoothing Technology (SST), HP's Resolution Enhancement Technology (RET), and LaserMaster's TurboRes. *Gray-scale enhancement* products use various forms of halftoning to improve photographic imagery. Some of the products using this approach are Apple's PhotoGrade, DP-Tek's LaserPort Grayscale controller, and XLI's Super LGA. Simply put, both categories use very fine control of the laser's energy level (for vertical resolution) combined with a true resolution increase (horizontal) to improve the print quality.[5]

6 • 3 Color

We believe in color. Blood, guts, and color.
—Dr. Steve Erde (developer of a hypertext system for pathology)

Color can be used in an almost infinite number of ways to enhance a document. While this topic is largely beyond the scope of this book, a brief overview of commonly used color concepts is useful. The addition of color to a document can significantly increase the production costs as well, so it really does pay to be careful with color.[6]

The specification of color to a printer is a difficult issue. The statement "Oh...make it a little redder and put just a touch of blue in it" is not going to suffice as a color specification. The color you see on a display screen will probably not be the color printed, unless you pay careful attention to the particular representation of color—the color model—used both by the display system and the printer. Of course, the printing industry has developed a number of useful models, and you don't need a degree in color science to print color. However, as a little background, let's examine some of the fundamental color models.

A **color model** is a particular representation of color, that is useful for at least one particular application. The spectrum of light that we call color can be characterized in may ways. Wavelengths, photons, and

5. For an excellent in-depth article on resolution enhancement, see "Enhancing Laser-Printer Resolution" by Bradley Dyck Kliewer, in the March 1992 issue of *Byte* magazine.

6. Color for the on-line world is covered in the excellent book *Interactivity by design*, by Ray Kristof and Amy Satran, Adobe Press, 1995.

obscure mathematical equations can characterize the physics of light. Several color models permit the precise specification of color. Each model is a different way of representing, characterizing, and categorizing color.

6 • 3 • 1 Pure Color Models

The Munsell and CIE models described in this section were invented independent of a particular application, such as printing or lighting. These models describe color for color's sake. They provide a useful language in which to specify color, independent of the application.

MUNSELL

Created by Albert Munsell, the Munsell color system is accepted by many standards and professional organizations concerned with color. (See color plate 1a.) The system describes color using three variables: hue, saturation, and value. Value is sometimes called brightness. In the three–dimensional space defined by this system, the central axis represents value, hues are organized around the axis, and saturation increases away from the axis. Color can be precisely specified with a notation such as `10R 6/4`, where `10R` designates the hue (`R` is the abbreviation for red), `6` is the lightness, and `4` is the saturation. The numbers all range in a scale from 1 to 10.

One computer–based utility that uses a variation of the Munsell color space is Apple's Macintosh Color Picker. It presents the user with a two–dimensional slice through this color space from which to pick a color.

In contrast to Apple's Color Picker is Adobe's Color Picker used in PhotoShop. It is oriented for fine control of saturation and brightness within a constant hue. In addition, it allows the entry of exact percentages of CMYK (Cyan Magenta Yellow blacK) colors.

CIE

In 1931, an international group of experts called the Commission Internationale d'Eclairage (CIE) developed a mathematical color model. The premise used by the CIE is that color is the combination of three things: a light source, an object, and an observer. The CIE tightly controlled each of these variables in an experiment that produced the measurements for the system. "This system is based on the fact that three colored lights (primaries) can be mixed to match any given color. In 1931 the color matching data obtained for the visible spectrum from a set of observers under rigorously controlled conditions were averaged and adopted as the color matching functions of the normal human eye by the CIE."[7] This diagram and the associated systems that use it mathematically plot a color's wavelength and purity. An x,y coordinate system is overlaid with the diagram to provide a precise means of specifying a color. For example, 0.5x, 0.35y is tomato red.

Kodak's PhotoYCC

PhotoYCC is a color specification created by Kodak. It is an integral part of Kodak's entry into the consumer electronic imaging market called PhotoCD. Coupled with the Color Management System, PhotoYCC provides a significant amount of device independence. Simply put, the color printed or displayed on one device usually doesn't match when printed or displayed on another device. Color is device dependent. PhotoYCC includes a calibration to correct for device idiosyncrasies. Adobe supports this color specification in PostScript Level 2 along with Aldus and NeXT. [a]

a. See the Kodak Web site at http://www.kodak.com/productInfo/technicalInfo/photoCDPapers.shtml

Some electronic publishing systems, such as Adobe's PhotoShop, allow the user to specify exact x,y coordinates corresponding to a color in the CIE system. In the book *Color for the Electronic Age*, Watson-Guptill, 1990, Jan White aptly sums up the importance of the CIE system:

> The value of the CIE system lies in its permanence. Color samples, no matter how carefully produced and preserved, tend to fade over time. The precise CIE numbers, however, can be used as controls in the preparation of replacement swatches.

While the pure color models provide an application–independent view of color, they are not particularly convenient for computer displays and printing. Let's examine some of the more application–oriented color models.

6 • 3 • 2 Computer Graphic Models

In the computer graphics world, the most common color representation is called RGB (red, green, blue). Images are represented in terms of their red, green, and blue components. In addition, display screens (the video tubes) have active areas (phosphors) that emit red, green, and blue light. Combinations of red, green, and blue dots can produce simulations of continuous–tone color images. The red, green, and blue

7. From Belinda Collins, "Evaluation of Colors for Use on Traffic Control Devices," NISTIR 88-3894 National Institute of Standards and Technology, Gaithersburg, MD, Nov. 1988.

dots are so small that the eye and brain blend these discrete dots into a continuous tone. A particular mix of the red, green, and blue components of a screen area corresponds directly to the perceived color of that area.

Another color representation often used in computer graphics is the hue, saturation, and brightness (HSB) model. Because brightness is often called value, the term HSV is also used. Colloquially speaking, hue is the kind of color. For example, red as opposed to blue or yellow. Saturation is the depth or intensity of color—light red as opposed to dark red. Brightness is the overall amount or lightness of a color.

According to the *ASTM Standards on Color and Appearance Measurement, 2nd Ed., 1987,* the definitions of these variable are:

> Hue - The attribute of color perception by means of which a color is judged to be red, orange, yellow, green, blue, purple, or intermediate between adjacent pairs of these considered in a closed ring (red–purple being an adjacent pair).
>
> Saturation - Attribute of a visual sensation according to which an area appears to exhibit more or less chromatic color, judged in proportion to its lightness or brightness.
>
> Lightness - (1) The attribute of color perception by which a nonself-luminous body is judged to reflect more or less light. (2) The attribute by which a perceived color is judged to be equivalent to one of a series of grays ranging from black to white.

Another method used to display color in computer graphics is **dithering**. Dithering is not a color model but a particular way of using color. Dither patterns are used to increase the perceived amount of colors on a screen at one time. While a display may be capable of displaying only 256 distinct colors, dithering can be used to raise the perceived number of colors into the thousands. A good example of the use of color dithering is in Apple's Dither Picker. Documentation accompanying the Dither Picker states:

In order to avoid highlighting problems and other unpleasant color look-up table conflicts, Apple recommends strongly that developers create icons from a palette of 34 colors. The DitherPicker was developed to aid icon designers by displaying a range of dithered patterns created from two solids you choose from the recommended palette of 34 colors. By using these dithered patterns, the perceived number of colors that is available to icon designers is immensely expanded.

One of the most difficult issues in computer–based publishing is color accuracy. The color models discussed in the previous section, RGB and HSB, are directly tied to the display device. These models are strongly device–dependent.

Many color models are inherently device dependent. Output devices such as display screens have different responses to the same color levels. Go into any store with a wall full of televisions for sale, all tuned to the same station, and you'll observe the differences. This color dependency is what makes WYSIWYG color control so difficult. A number of efforts at accurate, device–independent color display and control are impressive. These include PostScript Level 2 and Kodak's PhotoYCC. However, the quest for accurate color display and printing is not yet over.

6 • 3 • 3 Printing Color Models

Several color models have evolved for use in printing. Printing in color is the act of putting inks on paper. This action reverses the additive nature of color produced with light into a subtractive process. A red, green, and blue light source will appear white when combined. Red, green, and blue inks on paper will create a black area.

CMYK

The printing industry and many color computer printers use the CMYK (Cyan Magenta Yellow blacK) color model to create full–color printed images. This model is also know as process color. Four inks with the colors cyan, magenta, yellow, and black are combined using halftoning techniques to create the illusion of continuous–tone color images. (See *Section 6 • 2 Dots and Pictures* in *Chapter 6 •*

Media and Document Integration for a discussion of halftoning.) The perceived subtle nature of color created by the small dots of CMYK colors are a side effect of our perception. Take a look at a color magazine photo with a magnifying glass. The color of a person's skin is not really there! The color mixing is in our brains.

SPOT COLOR

Spot color printing refers to the use of one, two, three, or more single distinct colors within the document. Common uses are to color all section headings a unique color or to color arrows that point out information.[8]

You must use a color system to specify a color and hope that what is actually printed represents what you specified. The most common system is the Pantone Color Matching system. Some of the more complete electronic publishing systems provide software support for the use of particular spot color systems.

WYSIWIP, or *What You Select Is What Is Printed*, can become problematic in the case of spot color. Color matching systems, as these things are known, exist as swatch books from which you select a color. These expensive books contain all the colors for a particular color system; for example, PANTONE or COLORCURVE. Note that the names of the various spot color systems are *not* generic color terms; instead, they are registered trademarks of their respective holders. The inks used to print these swatch books are specially mixed solid colors. If a print job uses a single spot color and the printer indeed uses the special ink, everything should be fine. If, however, the spot color will be produced using process (CMYK) colors, you may be in for a surprise. The use of CMYK process colors will be only a simulation of the selected swatch color. The Trumatch Swatching System is an exception to this rule and is based on CMYK process color. Its swatch book is indeed printed with process colors.[9]

8. For a terrific overview of the possibilities and uses of spot color, see "See Spot Color" by Eda Warren in*Aldus Magazine*, Vol. 3, No. 2, Jan./Feb. 1992.

Cost is another significant issue with color printing. For example, if you intend to produce color PostScript files, you typically must give the printer one file for each spot color. This can quickly raise your production costs. However, spot color is less expensive than full–process color printing. In fact, spot color printing is a cost–effective means of using color. Typically, "you can expect to pay 25-35 percent above the cost of a one-color page for each additional press color."[10] However, only your printer knows for sure.

PANTONE SYSTEM

The Pantone Matching System is a widely used color specification system. The actual colors are a set of more than 533 colors, each with a name or number. You can purchase sample books with the colors printed on coated or uncoated stock. The color of an ink appears more saturated on coated stock because the coating prevents the ink from getting into the fabric of the paper.

The Pantone system is widely used largely because of the variety of swatch books available. These include small books, books with tear–out chips, two–color comparisons, tint selectors, and process color simulations, all on coated or uncoated stock.

Although the Pantone Matching System originated for the printing industry, it is also widely used in the computer–based, graphic arts industry. Programs such as FrameMaker and Adobe Illustrator allow you to select Pantone colors. These can produce reasonable facsimiles of the printed output right on the display screen. However, as discussed in the earlier section on Color Models, the display screen will not be an accurate rendition of the printed color. You will need a proof print to be sure.

9. See "Sampling the Color Matching Spectrum," by Jan V. White, in *Computer Publishing Magazine*, Jan. 1991, for a wonderful description of color–matching systems.

10. From "Big Ideas on Small Budgets" by Ronnie Shushan and Don Wright, *Publish* magazine, Feb.,1992.

6 • 4 Standards and Formats

The variety and different capabilities of graphics formats present users with a number of problems. Which one to use? Making matters worse, often each format has many variations. Specifications change over time, and implementations don't necessarily keep up with the new specs. In addition, the implementations are often incomplete or use one or more optional portions of a specification.

Of course, some formats are more popular and widely used than others. For example, TIFF files on PCs and PICT files on Macs are common formats on those platforms. The longevity of your documents will be placed at risk if you choose an obscure graphics format. Inevitably, you will have to move the document to another system or document processor. At that time, you will be faced with graphics format conversion problems.

Within a project, the selection of a particular format as an internal standard is a good way to reduce problems in format conversion. For example, the computer graphics metafile (CGM) standard is used in the CALS arena to represent vector graphic images. (See *Section 7 • 1 • 3 CALS and Electronic Publishing* in *Chapter 7 • Applying Standards* for more information on CALS.) Another graphics standard used to represent raster (bitmapped) images is the CCITT Group 4 format. This is otherwise know as FAX.

IGES, the Initial Graphics Exchange Specification, is another graphics standard. However, it was developed for a specific technical community— Computer Aided Design (CAD). It, too, has achieved a moderate level of use in the CAD domain as the digital equivalent of blueprints. Far and away the champion of CAD interchange is AutoCAD's DXF. Because of the large installed base of AutoCad systems, it is the predominant exchange format for microcomputer based CAD systems. The main advantages of IGES are that it is not a proprietary specification and that it is often the only reasonable way to exchange information between the higher–end "industrial strength" systems.

FAX Flavors

There are several varieties of FAX protocols. Group 3 and Group 4 FAX are different mainly in their digital interfacing capabilities. Group 3 FAX is meant to communicate on the public switched telephone network—the basic phone lines. Group 4 FAX can communicate over packet-switched and integrated services digital network (ISDN) networks—digital computer networks. In practice, your average everyday FAX machine that you plug into your phone line at home is probably a Group 2 or 3 machine. The FAX modem computer card that you plug into your computer is probably a Group 4 FAX. Occasionally, there can be problems communicating from one to another.

Graphics formats can be classified into three major categories: those dealing with bitmaps, those with geometrically defined objects, and those dealing with both (also known as metafiles). A graphic object means such items as lines, circles, curves, and other manipulable objects (these are often called vector graphics). The PICT format, widely used on the Macintosh, represents graphical objects. However, one of the objects is itself a bitmap, so PICT files are mixtures of bitmaps and objects.

The accompanying table, *Graphics Format Characteristics,* illustrates some of the characteristics of the more popular graphics formats. The column titled Native Platform indicates the original hardware platform for which the format was developed—a good indication of reliable implementations. The "na" stands for not applicable, which is true for all the "real" standards that are developed in an open, platform–independent manner.[11]

11. See the *Encyclopedia of Graphic File Formats 2nd Edition*, by James Murray & William vanRyper, O'Reilly, 1996, for ALL the formats.

Graphics Format Characteristics

Name	Color or Black & White	Bitmaps Objects or Both	Native Platform	MIME type	Notes
CCITT (FAX)	bw	bitmap	na	na	Fax files are based on CCITT group 4
CGM: Computer Graphics Metafile	color	both	na	na	Almost no one actually uses the bitmap portion
DXF: Document Exchange Format	color	objects	PC	PC	AutoCAD's exchange format, the most widely used CAD format
GIF	color	bitmap	Mac	Mac	Originated on the CompuServe network so it has good compression
HAM	color	bitmap	Amiga	Amiga	
IFF	color	bitmap	Amiga	Amiga	
IGES: Initial Graphics Exchange Specification	n/a	objects	na	na	Primarily for CAD applications
JPEG: Joint Photographic Experts Group	color	bitmap	na	na	Very good image compression with almost no loss of image quality
PCX	color	bitmap	PC	PC	Extremely wide use on PCs
PICT	color	both	Mac	Mac	THE graphics format for the Mac
PNG	color	bitmap	na	image/ png	New graphics format generated by Web community to be a patent-free replacement for GIF.
RASTERFILE	bw	bitmap	na	na	Based on Group 4 FAX
TARGA	color	bitmap	PC	PC	Used primarily with video capture boards
TIFF: Tagged Image File Format	color	bitmap	PC	PC	Extremely wide use; too many variations
WPG (WordPerfect)	color	both	PC	PC	File must be bitmap or objects but not both

The Tagged Image File Format (TIFF) is a widely used format for representing bitmap images. The TIFF format description of an image includes the resolution, size, gray level or color or bi-level choices, whether dithering was performed, and what compression scheme was used. A TIFF file may also keep a directory of images, which may correspond to all the page images of a document.

MPEG and Px64

The MPEG (Motion Picture Experts Group) and Px64 (CCITT H.261) standards for motion video are in their second generation. Although these standards seemingly have nothing to do with document processing, some systems allow you to cut and paste movie clips as easily as paragraphs. The compound documents that point to video sequences need to be on systems that can play the video.

Many graphics formats use some form of data compression. Image files are large. Therefore, reliable compression is not just nice; it's a necessity. WYSIWYG publishing systems encourage the use of more and more images, which take up more and more space. Some common compression schemes are run length encoding (RLE), vertical replication, keyed compression (which include Huffman codes used by FAX), and Lempel-Ziv Welch (LZW).

The Joint Photographic Experts Group (JPEG) standard is the most significant image compression standard in a long time. JPEG has caught on as a widely used image compression technology, and Web browsers are starting to support this format natively.

The company C-Cube Microsystems, a leading developer of compression hardware, has defined a standard interface to compression algorithms. Called the Image Compression Interface (ICI), this specification allows conforming software products to work with each other. Using this technique, users may pick and choose from among any number of compression algorithms.[12]

Multimedia systems, the next stage in the evolution of desktop publishing, were the motivation for the creation of these new standards (JPEG and MPEG). Coupled with hardware, these standards will provide the performance required for real-time video on the desktop. Desktop video and multimedia publishing are the next wave of new publishing technologies. Interoperability requires the development and implementation of these standards. The creation of new content–rich documents is expensive and much too valuable to be bound to any single platform.

12. For a good overview of JPEG, see http://www.C-Cube.com/tecno/jpeg.html

6 • 5 Integrating Text and Graphics

The integration of text and graphics is probably the single most problematic issue in electronic publishing. Document processing systems take many different approaches to the problems involved. Some systems import the graphics into the document. Others point to external files. Others convert the graphics into an internal format. Some allow graphics editing; others do not. Invariably, each document processing system has its own level of understanding of the graphics formats it can use. The formats themselves impose restrictions on the ultimate flexibility possible.

It is important to understand the types of graphic formats a particular document processing system can use. The portability—the ability to use the document on more than one computing platform— of the document may depend on this one factor. Graphics formats supported on only one hardware platform will surely cause problems when the document and its associated graphics are transferred to another hardware platform.

Just as document processing systems can be classified as batch or WYSIWYG, the integration of text and graphics can also be accomplished in a batch or WYSIWYG manner. Let's examine both forms of integration and end this section with some thoughts about advice for users.

6 • 5 • 1 Language Oriented Integration

One aspect of a batch approach to text and graphics integration is a reliance on file names. In the typical case, a language–oriented document processor interprets the document and enters some graphics interpretation mode where it expects to see the file name of a graphic. The document containing the file name reference must be correct, and the file containing the graphic must also be correct and must include any conventions about the directory.

File name references are crucial when using a set of files that were moved, for example, from a UNIX to DOS system. DOS has more restrictive naming conventions then UNIX. To guarantee accurate file names, you must restrict the names to the least common denominator— the DOS file names. An alternative approach to restrictive file names is to come up with a file name mapping scheme with some utility programs to automate the process. Either way, the solution is distasteful.

Encapsulated PostScript (EPS) files are the most commonly used format to represent the graphics placed in documents. Virtually all electronic publishing systems, including both the batch and WYSIWYG systems, allow the user to place an EPS file[13].

Both TeX and troff have mechanisms for importing PostScript files. These mechanisms consist of a set of TeX commands or troff macros, that insert the PostScript graphic at the appropriate point in the document.

Encapsulated PostScript Flavors

As the popularity of PostScript increased, it became common to interchange graphics information as PostScript files. This need gave birth to the widespread use of Encapsulated PostScript (EPS). In general, an EPS file is positioned somewhere on a page while using an application. It also became necessary to add a little bit of semantics to the EPS files for the convenience of the interpreting programs. These are such things as a bounding box that identifies the size of the graphic and standardized comments, such as a title, creator name, and the creation date. Inside the EPS data are usually two representations of the image. One is standard PostScript; the other is a bitmap representation used for purposes of display. The bitmap display portion of an EPS file generated on a PC differs from an EPS file generated on a Mac, causing some portability problems.

EPSI is the device-independent interchange flavor of an EPS file. In it, ALL information is in clear text with no hidden or unprintable characters. The bitmap preview section is represented in ASCII–encoded hexadecimal.

13. For the complete specifications and guidelines of EPS files refer to *Encapsulated PostScript Files Specification Version 2.0* available from the PostScript® Developer Tools & Strategies Group of Adobe Systems, Inc.

PostScript, TeX, and Troff

Psfig is a facility that enables authors to include PostScript figures in both troff and TeX documents. The two varieties of Psfig exist in harmony with the customary practices of document development. The troff version of Psfig is a troff preprocessor. The TeX version is an environment. Both allow the author to include and manipulate PostScript figures in a variety of ways. Some of the controls are illustrated below.

TeX

```
\psfig{figure=rosette.ps,

height=.4in,width=1.6in}
\psfig{figure=rosette.ps,

height=.8in,width=1.6in}
\psfig{figure=rosette.ps,
                    height=1.6in}
```

```
figure resslerFace.ps height 1.25i

figure resslerFace.ps height .5i
                      width .8i

figure resslerFace.ps height .25i
                      width .8i
```

A marvelous example of text and graphics integration in the UNIX environment is FaceSaver.[14] It's also an example of the UNIX hacker mentality. Over a period of several years, attendees of USENIX conferences (a popular UNIX conference) had their pictures taken and saved by the people running the FaceSaver project. The idea was to create a repository of faces accessible on the Internet. This has now been accomplished and the faces are stored at UUNET, a widely accessible Internet provider.

Given the existence of this repository of images, it is only natural that a number of "FaceSaver" utilities have been created. One particularly clever set converts the image into PostScript and enables the user to create business cards, labels, a letterhead, or a dartboard.[15]

14. The FaceSaver project was primarily the responsibility of Lou Katz, a former Director of USENIX, although many people had a hand in the success of FaceSaver over the years. A short overview of the project in action is covered in "The FaceSaver Project" in the July/Aug. 1989 issue of *;login:*.

15. For the details on psfig, see *Psfig – A Ditroff Preprocessor for PostScript files*, Internal Report, Computer and Information Science Department, University of Pennsylvania, Philadelphia, PA. The easiest place to get the document is from one of the many Internet archives that provides the psfig software.

FaceSaver in a Document

These pages illustrate the use of FaceSaver images as they are incorporated into a troff document.

LISA IV
October 17-19, 1990
Colo. Springs, Colorado

Kenneth Manheimer – NIST
Barry A. Warsaw – Century Computing
Stephen N. Clark – NIST
Walter Rowe – NIST

The *Depot*: A Framework for Sharing Software Installation Across Organizational and UNIX Platform Boundaries

ABSTRACT

The *depot* is a coherent framework for distributing and administering non-OS-distribution UNIX applications across extensibly numerous and diverse computer platforms. It is designed to promote reliable sharing of the expertise and disk resources necessary to maintain elaborate software packages. It facilitates software installation, release, and maintenance across multiple platforms and diverse host configurations.

We have implemented the *depot* using conventional UNIX subsystems and resources combined with policies for coordinating them. This paper presents the specific aims, structure, and rationale of the *depot* framework in sufficient detail to facilitate its implementation elsewhere.

Keywords: *Depot*, UNIX, sharing, distributed file system, `/usr/local`, installation, third-party.

Introduction

Installing and administering third-party UNIX applications often requires significant investment of time and expertise, precious commodities in any organization. Duplicating this investment is usually not the most efficient way to distribute its benefits. Instead, it s much preferable to share the product of this investment in the form of stable, usable configurations, provided organizational and platform discrepancies between different machines can be overcome. The *depot* is a systematic organization for distributing the products of expert application maintainers efforts in an efficient and unburdensome manner. The foundation of this system is a generalized framework for installation and maintenance of applications that accommodates distribution across multiple platforms in a versatile way.

With the greater distribution that this framework provides, reliability and change-release management become more critical. The *depot* has comprehensive provisions to reduce and sometimes eliminate difficulties inherent in greater operational interdependencies between hosts.

***Depot* Objectives**

The *depot* provides a mechanism for distributing application installations across numerous machines. In order to be successful, it must accomplish this while meeting the following criteria:

Generality: Accommodate diverse UNIX operating systems, hardware platforms,[1] and host configurations as well as diverse application packagings. Commercial, academic, and public domain packages each come with their own often elaborate installation methods and mechanisms and we need to accommodate them all.

Robustness: Provide predictable and consistent services. Formalize procedures for staged release of new packages and new package versions.

Scalability: Provide for incremental addition and commissioning of applications, clients,

[1]To date, the *depot* has been implemented only on various Sun Workstation architectures, but no essential mechanisms are Sun-specific. Our implementation makes extensive use of conveniences like Sun s *NIS* distributed administrative databases and Sun s *automount*[2]. *NIS* is becoming universally available, and automount capability is widely available as *amd*[3] for many UNIX and some non-UNIX platforms.

Lisa IV – Fall 90 **37**

The Depot ... **Manheimer, Warsaw, Clark, and Rowe**

[7] Available from The Free Software Foundation of Cambridge, Massachusetts, further information is available via electronic mail on the Internet from gnu@prep.ai.mit.edu.

Ken Manheimer works as UNIX Systems Support Manager in the Factory Automation Systems division at National Institute of Standards and Technology, where he has shepherded the growth of his divisions UNIX computing from four Sun 1 s (and Eunice on a VAX) to seventy+ UNIX systems. He received a B.A. in Computer Science from Hampshire College. Reach him at NIST; Bldg 220, Rm A127; Gaithersburg, MD 20899 or electronically at klm@cme.nist.gov.

Barry A. Warsaw has just recently joined Century Computing, Inc. as a Data Systems Engineer, where he will be working on an online retrieval system for the National Library of Medicine. Formerly with NIST, he was at times system manager for the Robot Systems Division network of UNIX machines, and developer of user interfaces for robotic and automated machine control systems. He received a B.S. in Computer Science from the University of Maryland. Reach him at Century Computing; 1014 West Street; Laurel, MD 20707 or electronically at baw@fox.gsfc.nasa.gov.

Stephen N. Clark has never been a system administrator in his life, falling instead into the amorphous category of knowledgeable user. He is currently working on tools for building schema-driven applications in support of the National PDES Testbed at NIST. He received an Sc.B. in Math and Computer Science from Brown University. Reach him at NIST; Bldg 220, Rm A127; Gaithersburg, MD 20899 or electronically at clark@cme.nist.gov.

Walter Rowe is currently the System Administrator for the Robot Systems Division of the NIST, where he maintains a network of 30 Sun workstations. He received a BS in Computer Science from Tennessee Technological University and is currently working on a MS in Computer Science at the Johns Hopkins University in Gaithersburg, Maryland. Reach him at NIST; Bldg 220, Rm B124; Gaithersburg, MD 20899 or electronically at rowe@cme.nist.gov.

46 **Lisa IV – Fall 90**

6 • 5 • 2 WYSIWYG Integration

Some document processing systems, usually the higher–end systems, attempt to display the graphic on the screen with the text. The manipulation of these graphics varies widely, ranging from no manipulation to total control. One important characteristic is whether the graphics are treated as an unbreakable block or whether the system supports some amount of graphic editing. In addition, some systems have an internal set of graphics. For example, FrameMaker has, roughly put, the equivalent to MacDraw built in, but without bitmapped image manipulation capabilities.

> ***A Note about "Flow"***
>
> The term flow is used in two distinct ways by a number of document processing/desktop publishing/page layout systems. These can be distinguished as logical and visual flow. The logical flow of text is epitomized by newspaper layouts. The text for a story runs to the bottom of a page and continues on another page. These columns of text are logically connected; that is, they are the same story. Visual flow is exemplified by newsletter and magazine layouts in which text wraps around a graphic. These are also called run–arounds.

The placement of graphics and how the graphics should flow, visually and logically, within the text is a major design issue for page layout and document processing systems. The classic page layout system typified by PageMaker allows a high degree of textual integration with the graphics. You simply drag the graphic into an area of text, and the system will visually flow the text around the graphic. The control of such run-arounds gives the document designer a great deal of freedom. (See *Section 3 • 1 • 4 Page* in *Chapter 3 • Points of View* for an illustration of text flowing around a graphic.)

Some systems allow graphics to be anchored to text; as new text is inserted or deleted, the graphic remains attached to the correct place in the text. Another form of anchoring is to attach the graphic to a particular location on a page, such as the top of the page.

WYSIWYG publishing systems differ in many subtle ways. The ability of a system to incorporate graphics into an integrated document is an area in which these differences can make a real difference in your publishing job. Keep an eye out for the types of graphic manipulations allowed and how the system handles external file references.

6 • 5 • 3 Inline versus External on the Web

As we've just concluded our discussion of language versus WYSIWYG, it is appropriate to compare the two integration mechanisms available for Web browsing. In much the same way that document processing systems have evolved from languages to WYSIWYG, Web browsers are evolving from a collection of loosely integrated "helper" applications to tighter integrated inline systems.

Lost in all the technical whiz-bang demos and slick Web pages we see is the supremely important issue of the user interface. The most significant problem with the external helper application approach is the change in user interface that a user must endure. One second you're happily clicking on links and the next moment some foreign application pops up and you must figure out what to do. Of course, the use of external applications is a good way of distributing new types of data formats before going through the labor of integrating that data type with your browser.

Netscape appears to have a good solution to this problem with the development of an API[16] that formalizes how applications may embed themselves in Web documents. This approach is similar to Microsoft's OLE (Object Linking and Embedding)[17] and the OpenDoc[18] architecture. The concept of "plug-ins," dynamically callable functional additions to an application, is well proven and is used extensively by a wide variety of PC and Mac software vendors. In geek terms, the plug-in architectures really consist of a well–defined Application Programming Interface (API), the interface between an application and externally defined functionality. The first Netscape Plug-in was a Virtual Reality Modeling Language (VRML) browser called WebFX by Paper Software Inc. In fact Netscape liked it so much they bought the company![19] The plug-in is now called Live3D.

16. Netscape developer information is nicely packaged in a proceedings at: http://www.netscape.com/misc/developer/conference/proceedings/.

17. See http://www.microsoft.com/devonly/strategy/ole/ole.htm for a strategic look at OLE technologies.

18. See http://www.astro.nwu.edu/lentz/mac/programming/open-doc/home-od.html for info on OpenDoc.

19. In Feb. 1996, Netscape announced Live3D, a VRML extension to Netscape's Browser, built by acquiring Paper Software Inc.

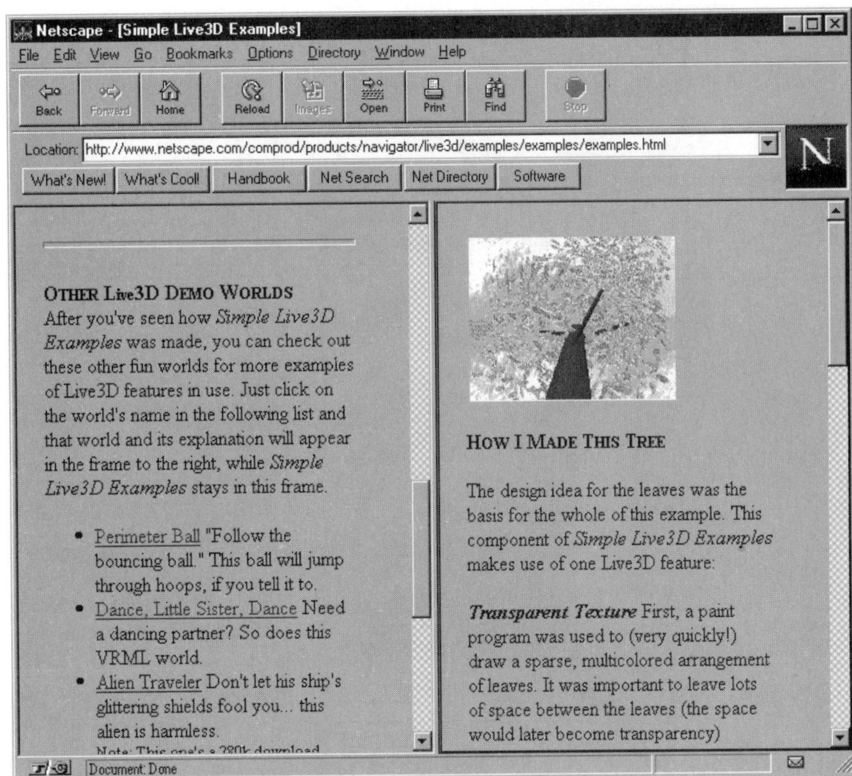

An example at the Live3D simple examples page at Netscape

This particular plug-in example uses the "frames" extension defined by Netscape that allows independently scrollable windows within the context of a single Web "page."

One interesting example of Web application integration is Adobe's Acrobat Amber. It effectively embeds their PDF Reader product into the Web browser. It functions quite nicely, but again, the integration of user interfaces becomes problematic. The icons from the Acrobat Reader product are now presently embedded on top of the PDF page in a strange location for Netscape's Navigator. It is unusual to go to a URL and have another application effectively embed itself in the page. Not terrible, just unusual.

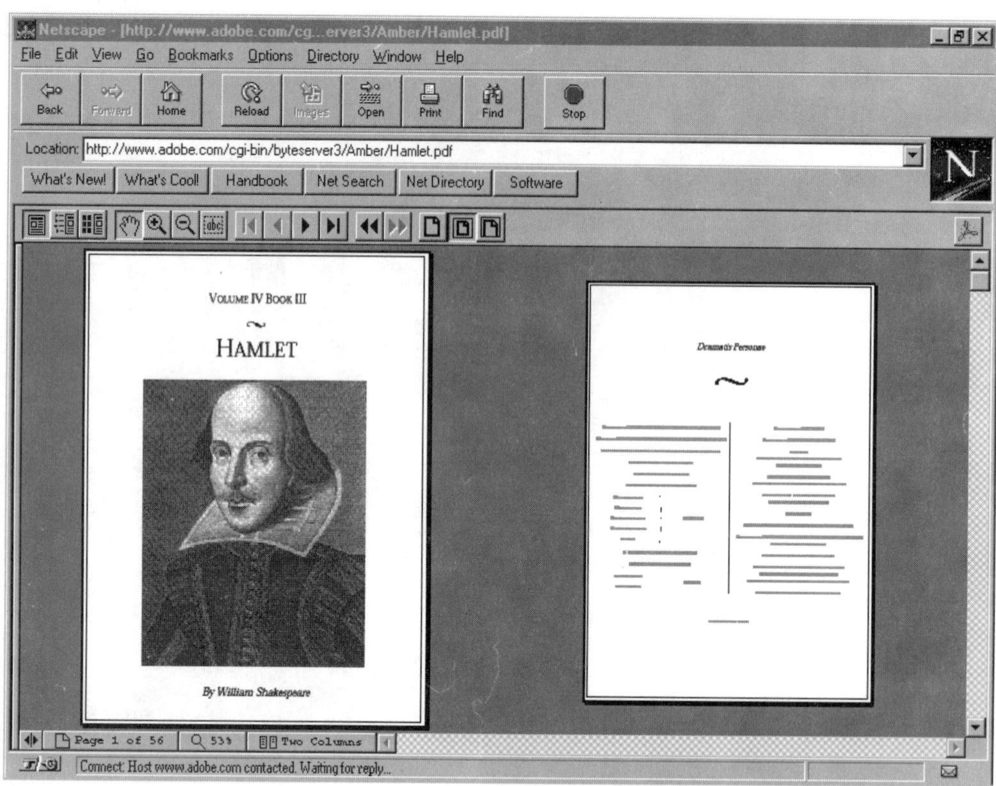

Adobe's Amber PDF Netscape plug-in

Clearly the king of integration, however, is Java. Java represents the first true attempt at an open, fully distributable, neutral, Internet execution machine. Java is powerful for a few key reasons. First, it is highly portable. It is tightly integrated with the Internet and can establish asynchronous threads of communications which stream data across the net. (For more detail on Java, see *Section 2 • 1 Java/HotJava* in *Chapter 2 • World Wide Web—the Next Generation*.)

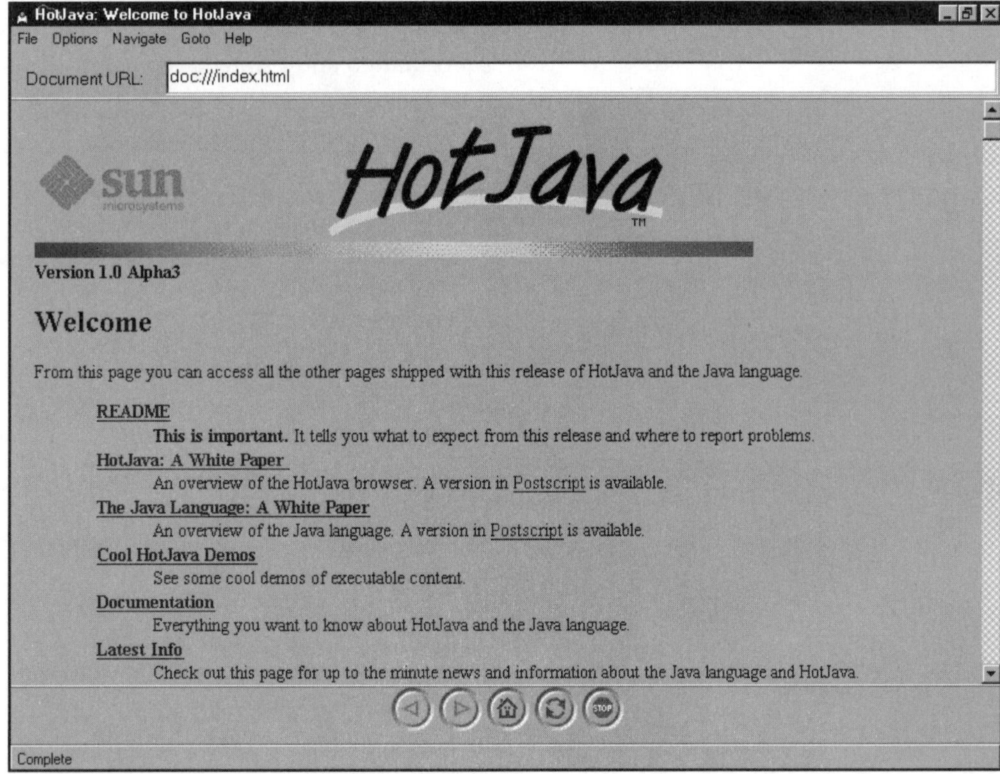

HotJava Sun's Java based Web browser

6 • 5 • 4 Integration Advice

Inevitably, you will be asked for advice on integrating some graphics with some text. Let's look at the problem from a different point of view— the user's.

USER TYPES

The decision to use one particular graphics format over another, or to advise someone else in that decision, has a subtle component— the type of end user. It may be perfectly appropriate to give one person one solution and another person a different solution. Some user types are:

FRANTIC USER: Someone with too many things to do. Word and document processing are just painful things they have to do to get that damn document formatted and printed. Typically, these are front–line managers.

TECHIE USER: A technical professional who is usually focused on one particular job at a time.

SYSTEMS ADMINISTRATOR: Someone who isn't all that familiar with publishing systems, but on whom you depend to keep your computers and network running.

SECRETARY: Someone who is often worth more than the boss and is forced to live with whatever approach the "experts" choose.

PUBLISHING PROFESSIONAL: Someone who is familiar with the primary publishing system, but who is not necessarily all that computer literate.

QUESTIONS TO ASK

In all cases, the format chosen must be usable by the publishing system familiar to the user. Some important questions are:

Will the graphic need to be modified once it is integrated with the text?

If so, how difficult is that process?

Does the integration process convert the native drawing format into another format that cannot be modified?

A conversion from a geometric representation to a bitmapped representation is a one way conversion. After the geometry is converted into a bitmap it would take a lot of trouble to go in the reverse direction, if at all. The not–yet–integrated original geometric graphic must be maintained somewhere if changes are expected, raising the specter of configuration management.

Each type of user will have a different level of understanding and concern about these issues. Your responsibility as the expert is to balance these concerns with the requirements of the tasks at hand. It also pays to help educate the users so that they can eventually make these decisions for themselves or at least appreciate their complexity.

6 • 6 Integrating Sound

The advent of on-line publishing has enabled the introduction of new media such as sound with the rest of the publication. On-line documents can have sounds sprinkled throughout the text. Sounds can start playing either automatically when a page is first viewed, or when the user selects a particular icon, or with other user interface cues.

Many of the issues for integrating sound with a document are analogous to the integration of graphics with text. There are lots of formats and the decision to use one or another will affect the portability and longevity of your content.

First, a simple (very) explanation of the of sound file formats and the types of data and parameters involved. All the sound formats discussed concern the representation of "sampled" sound, not synthetically produced sounds (another topic beyond the scope of this book), such as the commonly used MIDI.

Sampling Rate: Sounds exist digitally as a collection of numbers that are the output of a sampling device over time. In other words, sound goes into a microphone through an A/D converter (analog to digital) and is output as a sequence of numbers. These numbers most directly correspond to the amplitude or loudness of the sound. The frequency of those numbers, i.e., how often each one occurs, is the sampling rate. For example, a sampling rate of 8k or 8Hz or 8000 means that 8000 times a second, a measurement of the sound level was taken and turned into a number.

Encoding: The entire collection of samples can be represented in many different ways. You can imagine that capturing sounds creates a lot of data, so, often, a compression format of some sort is used. The encoding refers to how the actual sample numbers are stored in the file. These can vary by being signed or unsigned, as bytes or short integers in a little-endian or big-endian byte order and so on. The compression, when used, is applied to the samples encoded in a particular way.

Most of the information below comes from a thorough FAQ on Audio File Formats by Guido van Rossum.[20]

One major aspect that distinguishes file formats is whether or not they are self-describing. From the FAQ - "There are two types of file formats: self-describing formats, where the device parameters and encoding are made explicit in some form of header, and 'raw' formats, where the device parameters and encoding are fixed."

Popular sampling rates from Guido van Rossum's audio FAQ are found in the following table:

Table 2: Popular Sampling Rates

Samples/sec	Description
5500	One fourth of the Mac sampling rate (rarely seen).
7333	One third of the Mac sampling rate (rarely seen).
8000	Exactly 8000 samples/sec is a telephony standard that goes together with U-LAW (and also A-LAW) encoding. Some systems use a slightly different rate; in particular, the NeXT workstation uses 8012.8210513, apparently the rate used by Telco CODECs.
11 k	Either 11025, a quarter of the CD sampling rate, or half the Mac sampling rate (perhaps the most popular rate on the Mac).
16000	Used by, e.g. the G.722 compression standard.
18.9 k	CD-ROM/XA standard.
22 k	Either 22050, half the CD sampling rate, or the Mac rate; the latter is precisely 22254.545454545454 but usually misquoted as 22000. (Historical note: 22254.5454... was the horizontal scan rate of the original 128k Mac.)
32000	Used in digital radio, NICAM (Nearly Instantaneous Compandable Audio Matrix [IBA/BREMA/BBC]) and other TV work, at least in the UK; also long play DAT and Japanese HDTV.

20. Available at: ftp://ftp.cwi.nl/pub/audio/.

Table 2: Popular Sampling Rates

Samples/sec	Description
37.8 k	CD-ROM/XA standard for higher quality.
44056	This weird rate is used by professional audio equipment to fit an integral number of samples in a video frame.
44100	The CD sampling rate. (DAT players recording digitally from CD also use this rate.)
48000	The DAT (Digital Audio Tape) sampling rate for domestic use.

Files samples on SoundBlaster hardware have sampling rates that are divisors of 1,000,000.

The name of the format is often just the file extension.

Sound Format Characteristics

Name	Native Platform/ Origin	Sampling Rate	Number of Channels (1 mono, 2 stereo)	Notes
au or .snd	NeXT, Sun	variable	1 or 2	header with info string
.aif(f), AIFF, AIFC	Apple, SGI	variable	1 or 2	header with lots of info, AIFC version has compression
.iff, IFF/8SVX	Amiga	variable	1 or 2	also has 8 bits of instrument info
.voc	Soundblaster	8 bits	1	can use silence detection
.wav, WAVE	PCs - Microsoft	variable	1 or 2	lots of info
.sf	IRCAM	variable	1 or 2	encoding and other info
none, HCOM	Mac	8 bits	1	Huffman compression

Sound Format Characteristics

Name	Native Platform/ Origin	Sampling Rate	Number of Channels (1 mono, 2 stereo)	Notes
none, MIME	Internet			audio/basic 8 bit U-LAW 8000 samples/sec
none, NIST SPHERE DARPA speech community			1024 byte blocked ASCII structure prepended to waveform data. SPHERE package available via anonymous FTP from jaguar.ncsl.nist.gov/ sphere-v.tar.Z	
.mod or .nst, MOD	Amiga	Music files containing 2 parts: (1) a bank of digitized samples; (2) sequencing information, how and when to play the samples.		
Headerless Formats				
.snd, .fssd	Mac, PC	variable	1	8 bits unsigned
.ul	US telephony	8k	1	8 bit U-LAW
.snd?	Amiga	variable	1	8 bits signed

In making the decision to use one sound format versus another, the most important factor will be the ability of your intended audience to listen to the sounds. If, for example, you expect users of mostly UNIX platforms to be the audience, then choosing the WAVE format would be a mistake, as WAVE players are rare. However, if your intended audience is a PC then the WAVE format would most likely be the format of choice. The .au format, originally for Suns, is probably the widest usable choice because the Netscape browser on PC and many UNIX platforms support it.

6 • 7 Integrating Video

Digital Video is perhaps the most whiz-bang of all media types. It's still very cool to see little (but getting bigger) windows of video playing on your monitor. There are several video formats, each, of course, with advantages, disadvantages, and tricky issues.

Probably the most widely used digital video format is Apple's QuickTime. Apple beat all the other players, notably Microsoft, to the market and established a foothold. Wisely, Apple also created a Windows version of QuickTime so video sequences encoded as QuickTime can usually be played back on Macs or PCs.

Microsoft's equivalent is called AVI (Audio Video Interleaved), and the ubiquitous presence of WINTEL (Windows, Intel) machines make this a widely used format. There is, however, little AVI playback software for Macs. In addition, QuickTime players exist for many UNIX platforms, and AVI players don't or are certainly rare. Netscape's new version (3.0) of their browser will playback AVI video's inline.

While QuickTime and AVI are defacto proprietary specifications, Motion Picture Experts Group (MPEG) version 1 and 2 is a real formal standard. Initially, MPEG video files were THE choice for digital video on the Web, and they are still widely used. Unfortunately, the MPEG players rarely include support for sound, and even if they do, the content must have the sound encoded. Still, MPEG is a reasonable choice for silent Web videos.

MPEG hardware is becoming much more widely available for PCs and, in fact, many relatively low cost PCs come with support for MPEG-2. Actually, there are variants of MPEG imaginatively named MPEG-1, MPEG-2, and MPEG-4. MPEG-3 used to exist, but was merged into MPEG-2.

MPEG-1 defines a bit stream for compressed video and audio optimized to fit into a bandwidth of 1.5Mb/sec. This is the data rate of audio CDs and DATS.

The General MPEG Decoding System operates as illustrated in the following:

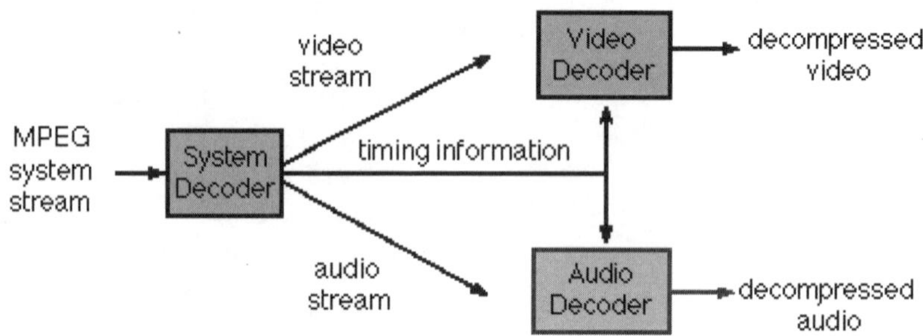

General MPEG Decoding System[21]

The MPEG standard defines a hierarchy of data structures in the video stream as shown schematically in the following figure:

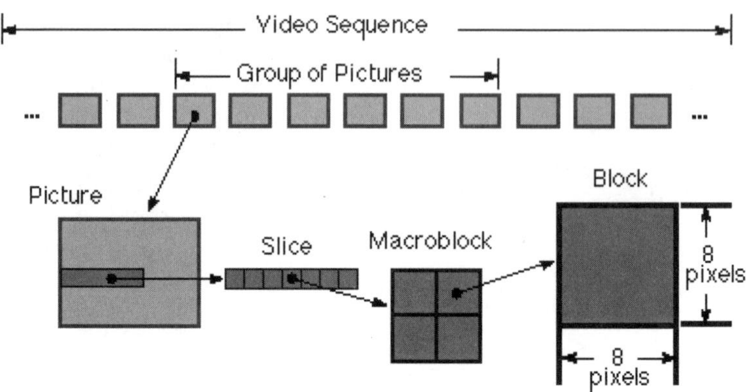

MPEG Data Hierarchy[22]

21. From C-Cube's "Compression Technology" at http://www.C-Cube.com/tecno/mpeg.html.

22. as above

The objective of MPEG-2 is to define a bitstream for video and audio coded at 3-10 Mbits/sec. MPEG uses predictive motion from frame to frame in time. MPEG uses DCTs discrete cosine transforms to organize the redundancy in spatial directions. (Don't worry, I have no clue what DCT is either.)

MPEG-1 audio contains the specification for three different audio encoding methods for three different bit rates. Currently, MPEG-1 and MPEG-2 are finished, and you can buy software/hardware solutions to digitize and playback files. MPEG-4 is still in the works.

CD quality audio is sampled at 44100 samples/sec and 16 bits per sample = 1.4Mbit/sec.

Things, however, get complicated with the business of **codecs**. A codec (short for compressor decompressor) is the actual algorithm used to compress the digital data. Compression is THE big issue for digital video, because the amount of data needed to store 30 frames per second, the normal US (NTSC) video rate, is astounding. Ten seconds can easily take 15-20 Mb. Not a reasonable thing to ask people with modems to view.

When you record a sequence of video, you must then (either in real time or more frequently as a secondary post process) compress the data. By the way, in case you didn't realize it, you need hundreds of Mb of spare disk space to fool around with this stuff. Performance is also a major issue; suffice it to say you need a really fast disk drive as disk I/O is probably the single biggest performance issue.

Codecs generally try to optimize for different types of video content. For example, Apple's QuickTime comes with "Video" and "Animation" codecs. If you had a sequence of computer generated video, use the animation codec. Aside from quality issues, the codec also presents you, the author, with portability problems. If, for example, you digitize some video using the "Indeo" codec, you must ensure that viewers of your document-with-video also have the Indeo codec. No codec, no video.

Digital Video Characteristics

Name	Native Platform/ Origin	Sampling Rate	Number of Channels (1 mono, 2 stereo)	Notes
QuickTime	Macintosh	variable	1 or 2	Apple origin available on PCs variety of CODECs
AVI	PCs	variable	1 or 2	Microsoft origin variety of CODECs
MPEG 1 ISO/IEC 11172	na (standard)	1.5 Mb/sec play-back rate (uncom-pressed audio CDs	1 or 2	frame differencing
MPEG 2 ISO/IEC 13818	na (standard)	intended for broad-cast video	1 or 2 + sur-round sound channels	frame differencing
JPEG Motion Video M-JPEG	NOT a standard		n/a	vendor–dependent implementations (dangerous)

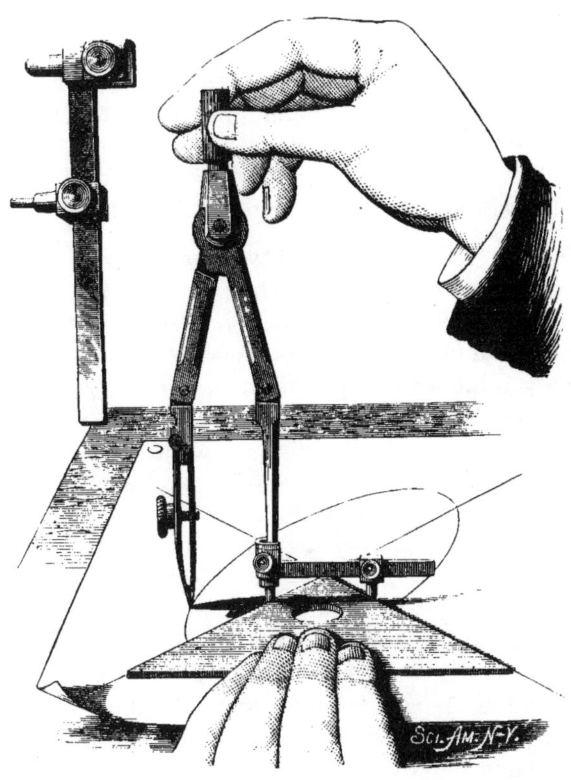

Chapter 7 • Applying Standards

If you cannot convince them, confuse them. —Harry S. Truman

Standards can be used in many ways. Properly used document standards can improve quality and increase productivity. Most important, the proper use of standards will let you keep and reuse your investment in the document's content.

Standards are also an enabling technology. Both document interchange and electronic distribution depend on standards. In this chapter, we examine the use of document and electronic distribution standards.

Before we examine several of the ways in which standards can be used, let's step back from the trees and look at the forest again. What do standards provide and why bother at all?

A single standard cannot possibly satisfy all requirements all the time. To believe that any one standard is a magic bullet is foolish, although technological developments often breed technology bigots. One particular new solution does not automatically negate others. Most standards have some value under certain circumstances. A few are extremely valuable under many circumstances. Value, however, often comes with a price tag—complexity.

For any particular project, you may be the only one who understands the particular requirements. You may be the only one aware of the future uses or potential future uses of the documents. The potential for producing multiple products and using the document's raw content in multiple ways is a powerful reason to pay attention to standards. For example, one vendor can take an SGML document database and turn it into an on-line hypertext document.[1] Of course, some people suggest that you really need a compelling reason not to use HTML. If your project has archival requirements, standards are your best bet for maintaining the integrity of your archive. If none of these concerns is realistic, you may indeed be better off using systems that let you easily accomplish the project, rather than paying too much attention to standards.

Document standards are complex and address many types of document requirements. As is true of any complex technology, document standards can be misused. Usually, the fundamental assumptions of the standard form conceptual boundaries that are very difficult to cross. A good example of these boundaries are the various efforts over the years to provide style capabilities to SGML. SGML does not inherently take into account the visual appearance of a document. To provide such a capability, other standards are being developed with a great deal of effort and complexity.[2]

1. *DynaText,* an electronic book publishing system from Electronic Book Technologies, Inc., can accept SGML text directly. EBT is located at One Richmond Square, Providence, RI 02906 (401) 421-9550 and their Web site is at: http://www.ebt.com.

2. The DSSSL standards, in the ISO domain, and FOSI in the CALS domain, are two efforts at providing styles that work with SGML. There is also the CSS (Cascading Style Sheet) work of the W3O.

7 • 1 Choosing Standards

The first action you must take is to pick a standard. The selection process can become very complex. What is the budget? How long do you have to complete the project? Are new software and/or hardware systems required? Does the staff have sufficient expertise? Will the document be edited by another organization? You should ask these types of questions when deciding among the various document processing standards and systems.

An amazingly large number of complex standards are available. They have complex relationships with each other. A number of significant activities have evolved to pick and choose a set of standards that work together. The methods used by these activities can prove useful for any organization. The following list contains a few suggested questions to ask in the process of picking a document standard and document processing systems for a project.

QUESTIONS FOR STANDARDS SELECTION

Is there a long–term archival requirement?

Some industries have legal requirements that mandate that information must be available for 20 years or more. Airplane manufacturers are one example. In that period of time, all aspects of the computer systems will have changed, such as the hardware, operating system, and retrieval and display programs.

Is there a financial or other need to produce multiple products from the same content?

High up-front investment in content can be spread among several products if there is a mechanism (that is, the proper use of standards) for reusing the content.

What are the document exchange requirements?

Will the document be used by other departments or organizations for further editing or printing? In either case, you must check that the receiving system has the proper environment: the correct collection of software; fonts; and the ability to edit, view, or print any graphics included in the document.

Is there a need to localize (internationalize) the document?

If the document and/or the document processing system must be used in international markets on systems with other character sets, you must check that localized versions of the document processing system exist. In addition, there may be other foreign requirements, either corporate or government, that mandate the use of particular standards.

Is the staff knowledgeable about a particular document processing system?

Ordering a switch from one document processing system to another may be more harmful than helpful. The expense in staff retraining can be significant. One alternative to a forced switch is to investigate document conversion systems or services. Of course, it may be wise to bite the bullet and adapt to newer or better technology.

Let's examine in more detail some aspects of the selection process and the use of standards once selected.

7 • 1 • 1 The Corporate Publishing Standard

We should distrust any enterprise that requires new clothes. —Henry David Thoreau

Many organizations have their own corporate style and publishing guidelines. Two areas that are often standardized are the document style and the document processing system. Within any organization with substantial publishing requirements, it is important to look at the requirements for exchange, style, and systems. Document exchange is easy to overlook and is the source of many problems.

Perhaps the best example of a corporate publishing standard is the *XEROX Publishing Standard: A Manual of Style and Design.*[3] This book encompasses the entire range of printed material for the corporation. More than a specification of document types, it discusses the process of publishing, the structure of documents, writing style, and visual design. While it is

3. *Xerox Publishing Standards: A Manual of Style and Design,* Xerox Corporation, Watson-Guptill Publications, A Xerox Press book, New York, 1988.

an amazingly complete reference for the publishing process and standardized document style, it does not address any document exchange or processing issues.

Many organizations simply pick one system, such as WordPerfect, and declare it as the corporate standard. In some respects, this is a perfectly reasonable approach. It ensures that people can pass documents among one another reliably. It also has the significant downside of tying the organization to a particular software vendor and a particular hardware platform. In addition, your organization may have problems teaming with other organizations that use a different internal standard. It's almost always possible to come up with an ad hoc interchange solution, but eventually the effort required to maintain such a process will be greater than the benefit. Therefore, a careful analysis of document exchange and processing needs should pay off in the long term.

It is important to create an organizational style that is easy and convenient to use by the staff. One straightforward approach of ensuring this is to create an organizational style with a particular document processing system in mind. Doing so should not significantly constrain the document styles you desire, because even the simpler word processor systems have the ability to define sequences of actions (macros) and visual elements (styles). MS Word even has a built in language, called WordBasic, to define complex macros.

Organization–specific styles and commands are useful tools to ensure document consistency throughout an organization. However, be aware that simply specifying a collection of styles and commands is insufficient. A document that lists recommended practices or provides a style guide must also be created and distributed to the staff so that everyone knows how to use the styles and commands.

The corporate style used by an organization can also get into the specifics of font selection. Apple Computer uses particular fonts in all its manuals and even prints the following identification inside the back covers of its manuals: *"Text type and display type are Apple's corporate font, a condensed version of Garamond. Bullets are ITC Zapf Dingbats®. Some elements, such as program listings, are set in Apple Courier, a fixed-width font."*

The specific font choices are not important, but consistency is extremely important. The consistent usage of fonts, headers and footers, document structuring conventions, and layouts will give your organization a more professional look. Readers will also get used to particular visual cues and become tuned to the document elements of interest.

Individual organizations select collections of standards and have the freedom to specify any type of software and hardware to implement and support those standards. Governments often cannot specify a particular vendor's product but must rely on a functional specification. The goal of vendor independence is also valuable for private business.

Any organization is wise not to use a sole source to address a particular problem. This is a well known principle of manufacturing; the manufacturer almost always will seek out multiple sources of components before starting production. This principle is much the same for software. Standards Profiles are one methodology used by the U.S. Government. They present guidelines for the selection of collections of standards that work together, allowing the government to choose from multiple sources of software components that conform to the standards.

7 • 1 • 2 Standards Profiles

In a literal sense, the phrase "using standards" is the subject of profiles. A **profile** is a collection of a particular set of specifications or standards to accomplish some function. The profile may also add restrictions to the exact usage of a standard. For example, military standards (MIL-STDS) can mandate the use of existing national or international standards with additional restrictions or functionality.[4] The Application Portability Profile (APP) is one methodology

4. For example, MIL-STD 28000 points to the IGES standard with the additional concept of application subsets, which are not part of the formal standard.

that is being used by the U.S. Government in the domain of open systems as a framework for systems integration.

From the Executive Summary of *Application Portability Profile (APP) The U.S. Government's Open System Environment Profile Version 3.0*[5]:

> An Open System Environment (OSE) encompasses the functionality needed to provide interoperability, portability, and scalability of computerized applications distributed across networks of heterogeneous, multivendor hardware/software/communications platforms. The OSE forms an extensible framework that allows services, interfaces, protocols, and supporting data formats to be defined in terms of nonproprietary specifications that evolve through open (public), consensus-based forums.
>
> A selected suite of specifications that define the interfaces, services, protocols, and data formats for a particular class or domain of applications is called a profile. The Application Portability Profile (APP) integrates industry, Federal, national, international, and other specifications into a Federal application profile to provide functionality necessary to accommodate a broad range of Federal information technology requirements.

5. See "Application Portability Profile (APP), The U.S. Government's Open System Environment Profile Version 3.0," *NIST Special Publication 500-230*, Feb. 1996. Available from NTIS or the Superintendent of Documents, U.S. Government Printing Office, Washington, DC 20402.

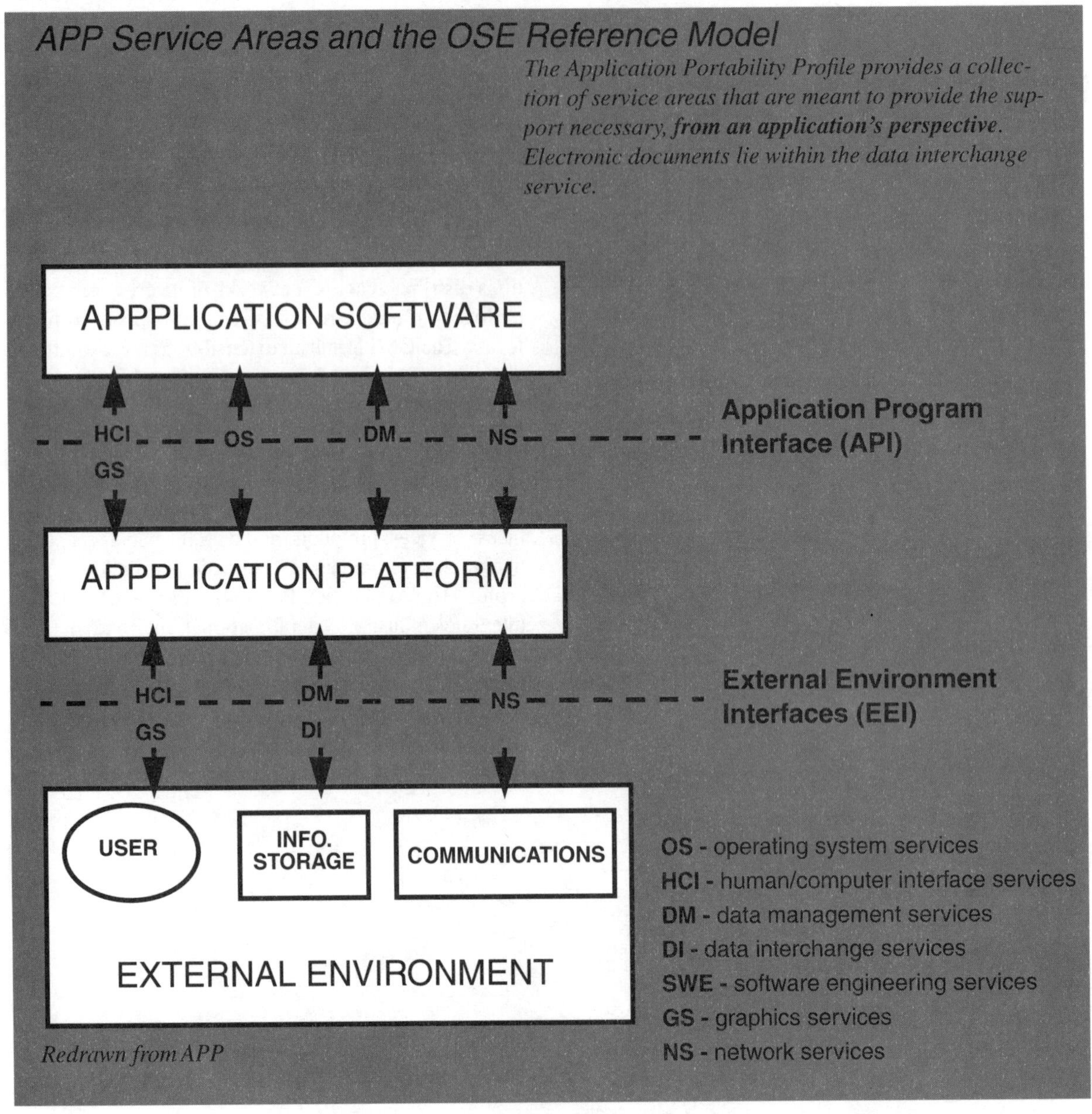

Redrawn from APP

The APP refers both to ODA and SGML as possible document interchange standards. There is no attempt to reconcile differences in functionality; however, both sit in the architectural "slot" of data interchange services.

The entire methodology of profiles makes an amazing amount of sense. The term profiles in this context comes from the formal standards domain. From *The Open Book* by Marshall Rose comes the following explanation:[6]

> A standard often contains many more options than can be implemented altogether. If each vendor implements only a subset of options, there is no guarantee that any two vendors will implement the same subset. The result is systems that are interoperable in theory, but not in practice!
>
> An important pragmatic step is to identify a common subset of options and related practices that can be used effectively. This is the purpose of groups that promulgate functional profiles.

Standards are often meant to operate in areas of very different scope. Profiles provide a framework within which the standards function.

For example, a document archive system may need to function at many different levels. At the system level, there is the operating system; at the database level, there is the query language; at the document level, there are text–retrieval issues; at the document content level, there is structure. In addition, for viewing or printing purposes, there are font issues, and for document interchange purposes, all the above affect the system. Standards exist for each of these domains, and profiles provide guidance for their use.

7 • 1 • 3 CALS and Electronic Publishing

CALS, the Computer-aided Acquisition and Logistic Support project within the Office of the Secretary of Defense (OSD) of the U.S. Government, has had a significant impact on the electronic publishing industry. One key goal of the CALS project is to reduce the use of paper, and this goal has been embraced by virtually all participants.

We're not talking about eliminating a few notebooks, either. Any significant project run by the Department of Defense (DoD) requires warehouses of documents. Extensive documentation is not a fabrication

6. *The Open Book: A Practical Perspective on OSI* by Marshall T. Rose, Prentice Hall, Englewood Cliffs, NJ 1990.

of DoD; instead, it results from the extremely large, complex, interrelated contracts with literally thousands of contractors and subcontractors involved in a single project. Managing such complexity requires careful attention to standards. The careful use of standards is a key element in the quest to reduce the cost of these projects.

SGML is one of the CALS–selected standards for document processing. Likewise, the rapid adoption of SGML by document processing vendors was significantly influenced by the notion of potential CALS customers. There exist several specific CALS document type definitions (DTDs) that define the structure of a CALS–compliant document. Once a body of text has been properly tagged, it can be used in a number of ways. (For a more through discussion on the variety of uses, see *Section 7 • 3 Multiple Use* in this chapter.)

In addition to the work on document processing for printed documents, the CALS[7] arena is experiencing a great deal of interest in creating on-line, interactive documents. This effort is called the Interactive Electronic Technical Manual (IETM). Its concept is to allow engineers with portable computers equipped with CD-ROM drives to interactively browse through maintenance manuals, at the site of a repair (for example, in an aircraft hanger) or in the field.

7. A watershed in the life of CALS was a public declaration by then Deputy Secretary of Defense William H. Taft in August 1988, in the "Taft Memo," which, simply put, said, "Start using the CALS standards."

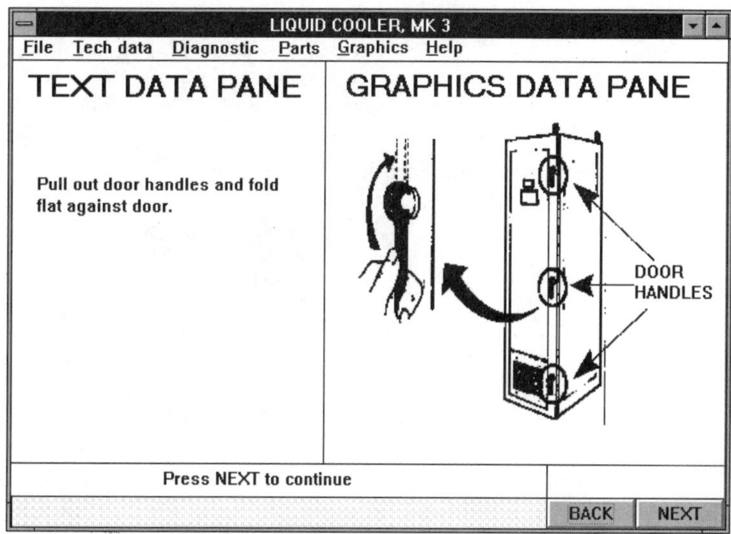

Example IETM application[8]

This work will probably use and spur more implementations of HyTime, a hypermedia standard based on SGML. (See *Section 5 • 3 • 4 HyTime* in *Chapter 5 • Document Standards*.) Given the complexity of requirements in the military, a set of classes or functional levels of IETM manuals has been defined by the Naval Surface Warfare Command Carderock Division (NSWCCD). The classes are "fairly broad," and "The class definitions, however are insufficient for use on contracts." However, they are illustrative of a coherent approach to the creation of complex document requirements.

Following are the IETM class definitions:

Class 1

Electronically Indexed Pages

Display

- Full page viewing
- Page-turner/Next function
- Intelligent index for user access to page images
- Page integrity preserved

Data Format

- BitMap (raster)
- Indexing and header files (Navy Mil 29532)
- MIL-R-28001 or Postscript pages

8. From NAVY CALS WWW at http://navysgml.dt.navy.mil/ietm.html.

- Generic COTS imaging system formats

Funtionality

- Access pages by intelligent index/header info
- View page with pan, zoom, etc., tools
- Limited use of hot-spots
- Useful for library or reference use

Class 2

Electronically Scrolling Documents

Display

- Primary view is scrolling text window
- Hot-spot access (Hyper-links) to other text or graphics
- User selection and navigation aids (key-word search, on-line indices
- Minimal text-formatting for display
- User selectable call to (launch) another process

Data Format

- Text - ASCII
- Graphics -whatever viewer support (e.g., BMP or CALS)
- Can be SGML tagged - no page breaks (browser)
- Access/index often COTS dependent with Hypertext browser
- Generic: COTS with Hypertext browser

Funtionality

- Browse through scrolling info
- User selection of graphics or hot-spot reference to more text
- Hot-spot and cross-reference usually added after original authoring

Class 3

Linearly Structured IETMS

Display

- View smaller logical block of text—less use of scrolling
- Interaction through dialog boxes
- Interaction per MIL-M-87268 to extent possible
- Text and graphic simultaneously displayed in separate window when keyed together EXAMPLE

Data Format

- Linear ASCII with SGML tags
- SGML with content vice format tags
- Maximum use of MIL-D-87269
- Generic: SGML tags equivalent to MIL-D-87269

Funtionality

- Dialog-driven interaction
- Logical display of data in accordance with content
- Logical NEXT and BACK functions
- User-selectable cross-refs and indices
- Content-specific help available

Class 4

Hierarchically Structured IETMs

Display

- View smaller logical block of text—very limited use of scrolling
- Interaction through dialog boxes with user prompts
- Interaction per MIL-M-87268
- Text and graphic simultaneously displayed in separate window when keyed together EXAMPLE

Data Format

- Fully attributed DB elements (MIL-D-87269)

- MIL-D-87269 content tags with full conformance with Generic Level
- Object Outlines (architectural forms)
- Authored directly to database for interactive electronic output
- Data managed by a DBMS
- Interactive features "authored in" voice added-on
- Generic: COTS equal to MIL-D-87269 data definition and tags

Funtionality

- Dialog-driven interaction
- Logical display of data in accordance with content
- Logical NEXT and BACK functions
- Useful as interactive maintenance aid
- User-selectable cross-refs and indices
- Content specific help available

Class 5

Integrated Data Base (IETIS)

Display

- Same as Class 4 for IETM function
- Interactive electronic display per MIL-M-87268
- Expert system allows same display session and view system to provide simultaneous access to many differing functions (e.g., supply, training, troubleshooting)

Data Format

- IETM info integrated at the datalevel with other application info
- Does not use separate databases for other application data.
- Identical to Class 4 standards for IETM applications data per
- MIL-D-87269
- Coding for Expert Systems and AI modules when used
- Generic: COTS equal to MIL-D-87269 data definition and tags

Funtionality

- Single viewing system for simultaneous access to multiple info sources
- Same as Class 4 for IETM functions
- Expert system to assist in NEXT functions, based on info gathered in session

A Motivation for Electronic Documents

Repairmen of all types of complex equipment, from airplanes to cars to tanks, must wade through a veritable sea of paper manuals. Electronic documents often stored on CD-ROMs, viewed with portable computers, will reduce the clutter.

The stack of maintenance manuals for the M1A1 tank, stacked up, is nearly as tall as a soldier! This situation is serious motivation for a movement toward electronic documents.

Photo courtesy Roy Morgan.

One prime motivation behind the selection and development of a series of standards is the desire for meaningful exchange of documents. Contractors and subcontractors would certainly work together more efficiently if they could exchange documents electronically. Document exchange is a deceptively complex problem, as we will show in the next section.

7 • 2 Document Exchange

Conceptually, document exchange is very simple. Two people who need to collaborate on a document must be able to read, write, and edit the document. The system that each individual uses must be able to manipulate the electronic form of the document. The textual information is usually not a problem, but the document's formatting and structural elements are another matter. If the two parties really need to work with a visually identical document, they must use the same collection of publishing applications, operating system, and operating system resources. Furthermore, they must use these resources in the same way.

The fundamental difficulty is that text, graphics, and images must all be used and understood by different systems in the same way. Words, paragraphs, pages, graphics, images, and so on are objects with which we associate meaning—semantics. Words, for example, may be hyphenated in one system and not in another. Graphics may be editable or not. Paragraphs may be automatically numbered. All these semantically meaningful operations are difficult to transfer from one system to another. In reality, no one has been able to figure out a practical way to accomplish transfers across multiple applications and multiple platforms. Standards ameliorate the problems, but don't eliminate them.

Compound documents containing information from several applications make the exchange problem more difficult. The more dynamic aspects of such technologies as "live" links, "active" documents, object linking and embedding (OLE), Java, Visual Basic scripts, and so on exacerbate the exchange problem. The exchange of these new types of documents is an unsolved problem, and the electronic publishing world must solve it.

7 • 2 • 1 Types of Document Exchange

Because document exchange is such a difficult problem, it is instructive to break the problem up into different types of exchange. One useful classification is the exchange of a document from a purely visual point of view. Another view is the exchange of logical or structural information. This classification is similar to the two types of information dealt with in the ODA standard: layout (visual) information and logical (structural) information.

VISUAL

Document exchange focusing on the visual elements of a document typically concentrates on font problems, at least for starters. The system used by one person may have a different set of fonts installed than for the second person. Usually, the system will substitute one font for another, and that may be just fine. However, the document will probably change in subtle ways. The page count and line breaks will probably be different because of the change in fonts. Even in the simplest case of document exchange, in which both parties use the same system (for example, WordPerfect), documents will not necessarily exchange identically if the parties did not agree on font usage. Document fidelity, the way a document looks, may or may not be important when two individuals collaborate; either way, it is useful to be aware of these differences.

The following story illustrates an exchange problem that was due to a lack of semantics:

> I needed to simply take a small portion of one document (we'll call it the *old* document) and place it into another document (we'll call it the *new* document). A simple cut and paste job. Unfortunately, the old and new documents were written using different word processing systems. Well, no problem, in theory. I normally use a workstation with a robust window system and select and cut the portion of text I need from the old document and save it as a file. Then I go into

the new document by using the second word processor and import the small file. I was NOT expecting to maintain any formatting information whatsoever; all I wanted was the text. Funny thing though: in the new document, I wound up with a bunch of words with hyphens in strange places. You see, the document processor used for the old document "understood" hyphenation but the window system didn't. When I selected the text using the mouse and window system, it simply selected the words and treated the hyphens as just more text rather than as a meaningful break in words.[9]

Matching Fonts

Differences in the size and shape of fonts (font metrics) are one of the fundamental technical problems for document exchange. Multiple Master Fonts, a new font technology from Adobe, can be used for font substitution because it retains the original font metrics.

Multiple Master Fonts

Because a Multiple Master font can produce a wide range of typeface variations, it can precisely match the copyfit of a document created in an entirely different typeface, even though designs of the characters in the Multiple Master font might have little in common with those of the font it's trying to match.

Figure A: *The original document uses a mix of serif and sans serif fonts.*

```
Multiple Master Fonts

Because a Multiple Master font can
produce a wide range of typeface
variations, it can precisely match
the copyfit of a document created in
an entirely different typeface,
even though designs of the char-
acters in the Multiple Master font
might have little in common with
those of the font it's trying to match.
```

Figure B: *Using the default printer font results in the loss of the original look of the document.*

Multiple Master Fonts

Because a Multiple Master font can produce a wide range of typeface variations, it can precisely match the copyfit of a document created in an entirely different typeface, even though designs of the characters in the Multiple Master font might have little in common with those of the font it's trying to match.

Figure C: *Multiple Master font technology retains the metrics of the original fonts to preserve the look and spacing of the original document.*

Reprinted with permission, from "Matching Fonts", *BYTE Magazine*, June 1992.

9. This happened to yours truly, the author.

LOGICAL

The second major type of document exchange is the exchange of logical or structural information. The logical or structural information in a document is rarely exchanged well. Conversion programs manage to keep paragraphs separate, and maybe even some of the paragraph numbering, but usually little else. Page layouts and such items as master pages and styles sheets are often lost. Carefully chosen tag and style names are usually converted (if at all) into numerical sequences such as `para0`, `para1`, `para2`; these names are not all that meaningful. When many of these items are actually converted, the results usually need so much editing that the conversion process becomes extremely painful.

When exchanging structural information, SGML seems to be a natural solution. After all, SGML captures and codifies the structure of a document extremely well. Unfortunately, most documents are not SGML documents, and converting documents into SGML may or may not be simple. If the documents are not consistently structured, conversion to SGML will be as problematic as conversion to any other format. If by chance you do have an SGML document or can easily convert to it, the logical and structural information should convert easily into a publishing system; however, the visual information will now be the problem. The association of visual elements, such as font families and sizes, master pages, and document layout, depends on a particular interpretation of the SGML elements. That interpretation must also be converted if a complete visual and logical document exchange is to be successful. We can see similar problems as everyone trys to figure out how to convert their favorite format to HTML for the Web. This is a difficult problem!

7 • 2 • 2 Document Components

Now let's look at the various pieces of a document that must go through the exchange process.

A document usually consists of several types of information. Again, it is useful to think of the two categories, visual and logical. You can also think of this as form and content.

A document *looks* a certain way because of the way it was composed, designed, and laid out. The various pieces of a document that look a particular way also fit into the structure of the document. A document *means* something because of its content.

As discussed in *Chapter 5 • Document Standards*, SGML and ODA take two approaches on how the visual and logical information should be related to each other. SGML mostly ignores the issue, but allows you to define associations that can be interpreted by an application. DSSSL and the continuing work on DSSSL for the Web (called DSSSL Online) is attempting to address the issues of a document's visual appearance. ODA provides an architectural framework that integrates both the visual and logical information. However, ODA has a limited set of visual elements that have been defined for use with its architecture.

FONTS

Font usage is one of the most important aspects of document exchange. If you expect a visually identical document to come out the end of an exchange process, you must pay attention to fonts. PostScript solves many of the practical problems of page layout. A page represented with PostScript is portable to any PostScript device. This is because PostScript is proprietary. Only one company, Adobe, licenses the technology. PostScript clones have now appeared and generally work quite well. One area of difficulty is that of font usage. When a PostScript document is moved from one machine or printer to another, it is important to know what fonts are available in the printer or system. If a font used in the original document is not available on the destination system, either you're out of luck or the font must be included with the PostScript file, which will increase the file size tremendously.

In the simplest case, a document composed with more than the four original Apple LaserWriter fonts cannot be printed on a LaserWriter unless the host machine also has that outline font available for downloading to the printer. As more and more fonts are used, the destination equipment, computer host, and printer must be contacted about font availability. Fortunately, once a particular font is identified as available, it should print just fine.

When you want to take a document to a service bureau for high–quality printing, your choice of fonts better match what the service bureau can print. You can usually embed the fonts in the document, but you have to be conscious of these issues. The problem is worse now since the introduction of new font technologies, such as TrueType and Master Type. The service bureau must also have a collection of TrueType and Master Type fonts.

These problems are exacerbated when dealing with a WYSIWYG system. The fonts displayed on the screen are often special variations of the fonts used in the printer, and there are several flavors of screen fonts. Adobe solves the problem with Adobe Type Manager (ATM) available for both the Mac and PC platforms. ATM creates screen fonts from the same Type 1 format used for printing. TrueType, spearheaded by Apple and Microsoft, uses the same font description both for printing and display.

PARAGRAPH TAGS AND STYLES

In many systems, the paragraph is treated as a distinct entity. It is a convenient portion of a document in which to associate visual with structural information. Some systems call the format of a paragraph a style; others, a tag. Either way, they are named entities that can be used as a mechanism for style or tag association. For example, all paragraphs tagged with the name, `SectionHeading`, can be given the same font, size, and positioning.

The transfer of a document from one system that uses styles and tags, to another usually results in a visually reasonable document on the receiving system. Unfortunately, it also usually loses the tag and style names, because they were all renamed and converted in a simplistic way. This level of document exchange is incomplete and is the result of incompatible document exchange, which converts the visual, but not logical, information. The user will probably need to rename and identify all the tags or styles by hand. Although this is a much better starting place then no conversion at all, it is a problem worth noting. These incomplete conversions take a significant amount of labor to correct, and discourage the overall use of conversion systems. More importantly, they prevent automatic conversion.

GRAPHICS AND MULTIMEDIA

Documents that contain graphics introduce another level of complexity in the document exchange process. Exchanging the graphics embedded inside a document is difficult. (See *Section 6 • 4 Standards and Formats* in *Chapter 6 • Media and Document Integration* for more information on graphic standards and the integration of various media types with text.)

The new forms of electronic publishing, which include sound annotations and video clips, raise the level of complexity for document exchange even higher. Issues of data formats must be addressed. The role of operating system and hardware resources takes on greater importance. To take a simple example, Apple now provides the ability to play little movies inside documents with their QuickTime operating system facility on the Macintosh. If I write a document heavily dependent on QuickTime, it won't be usable on another platform. However, if vendors create QuickTime viewers for other hardware platforms, and they have, the documents may be usable on other platforms. The same is true for sound annotations: the document must be viewed online and on a system that can handle the particular sound format.

All these new data types increase the functionality of the document, increase the complexity of document exchange, and decrease the portability of the document. Work in progress will standardize many of these elements. (See *Section 6 • 4 Standards and Formats* in *Chapter 6 • Media and Document Integration* for information on these standardization efforts.)

7 • 2 • 3 Direct versus Standardized Interchange

We've examined *what*; now let's examine *how* information is exchanged to achieve complete document interchange. One tried and true method to accomplish reliable interchange is to write direct translators between two systems. This method greatly increases the probability of an accurate translation since every type of information in one system is hand–tailored to a corresponding piece of information on the other. People who write translators interpret the semantics of items in one system into items in another with semantics that match completely or in part. The two major drawbacks of this method are that (1) you are locked into those two specific systems and (2) each time a new system is introduced, several translators must be written. The number of translators goes up geometrically (actually n^2–n) as the number of systems increases.

Using a single common interchange format, new systems may be added, and only the input and output translators (pre– and postprocessors) must be added.

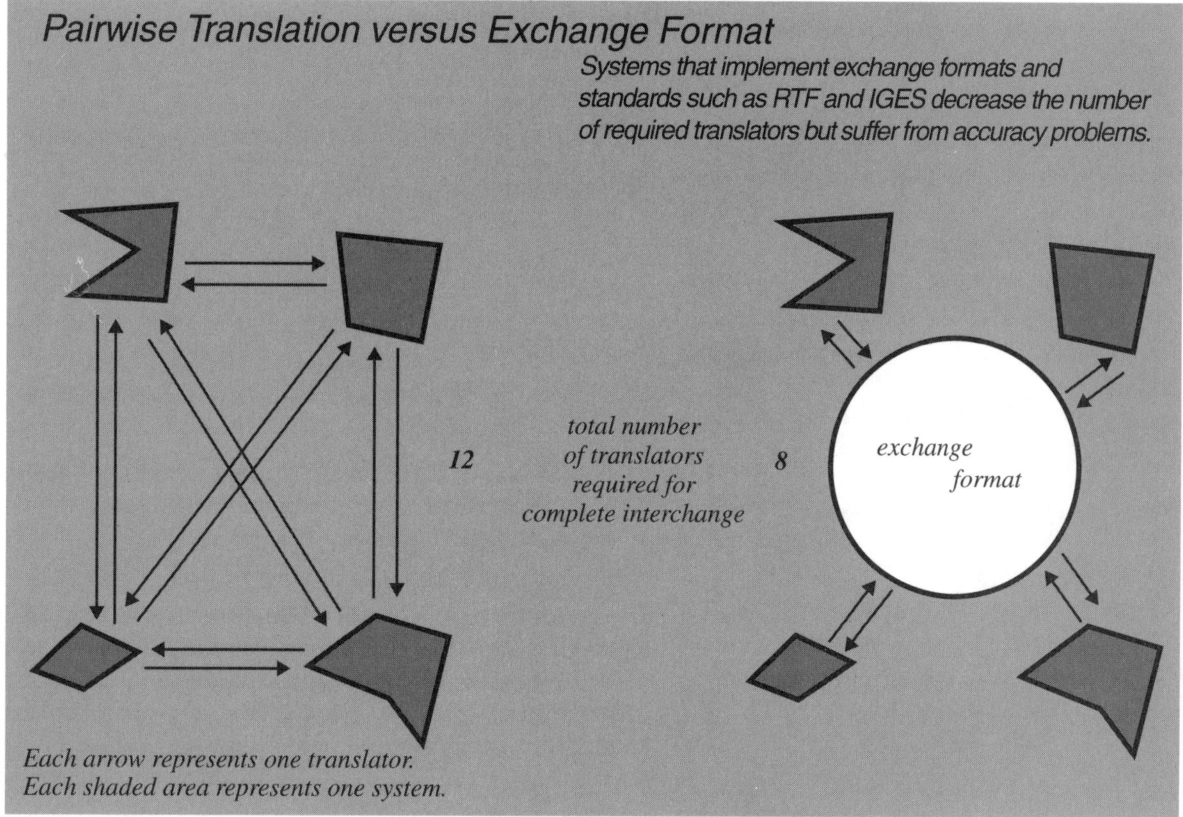

Pairwise Translation versus Exchange Format
Systems that implement exchange formats and standards such as RTF and IGES decrease the number of required translators but suffer from accuracy problems.
12
total number of translators required for complete interchange
8
exchange format
Each arrow represents one translator.
Each shaded area represents one system.

7 • 3 Multiple Use

Facilitating document interchange is only one reason to use standards. Another compelling reason to use a standard document representation is that it allows you to use document content in more than one way.

The proper use of standards enables the creation of documents that may be used in several ways: for printing, presentations, and on-line viewing. Several products can be based on a single repository of content. It is possible, indeed desirable, to automate the usually manual cut–and–paste process. A CD-ROM electronic encyclopedia and the printed version can be created from the one collection of information.[10]

10. The *Hutchinson Encyclopedia*, a printed document, was created from an on–line database. In addition, a CD-ROM was produced and packaged with Sun workstations sold in the United Kingdom.

Document components can be extracted for the purpose of generating automatic summaries. Indexes and automatic cross references can be created with the consistent use of tagging schemes.

In the CALS domain, a significant project that is addressing the issue of multiple use is the Interactive Electronic Technical Manual (IETM) project. The IETM project is concerned mainly with the delivery and use of on-line hypertext/hypermedia documents. However, it will be possible to generate paper copies of the document from the same electronic information.

7 • 3 • 1 Data Preparation

The process of preparing information for distribution in a number of electronic forms is called data preparation.

The creation of electronic documents invariably requires a clear, organized structure for the data. The tagging and markup mechanisms used by SGML and procedural markup systems greatly aid the data preparation process. Usually, the data preparation involves identifying certain structural elements of the document. The elements chosen can become a form of outline that can be used as a user interface mechanism for on-line browsers. The Table-of-Contents used as a front end for a document is common and useful.

Key tagged elements can also be used to create automatic cross-references. Creating semantically meaningful links across a large collection of text is a significant authoring task, which should not be underestimated. Tags and markup can be used to jump–start the process by automating some of the link creation.

7 • 3 • 2 TeX's Weave and GNU Emacs' Texinfo

Two interesting and practical examples of multiple use are TeX and GNU Emacs. TeX is one of the most widespread batch–oriented typesetting languages. (See *Section 4 • 1 Types of Document Processors* in *Chapter 4 • Form and Function of Document Processors.*)

GNU (Gnu's Not Unix) Emacs is one of the popular text editing environments for UNIX and is available for free from the Free Software Foundation (FSF). Both systems use information for two different purposes.

Oh, What a Tangled Web We Weave

The implementation of TeX is as interesting as the program itself. Literate programming, the creation of source code that is readable (that is, literature), is a concept championed by Donald Knuth of Stanford University. To support the concept, a language (WEB) and two programs (tangle and weave) were created to work as a literate programming system. TeX was written in WEB. The illustration below shows how they work together. This WEB is different from the World Wide Web.

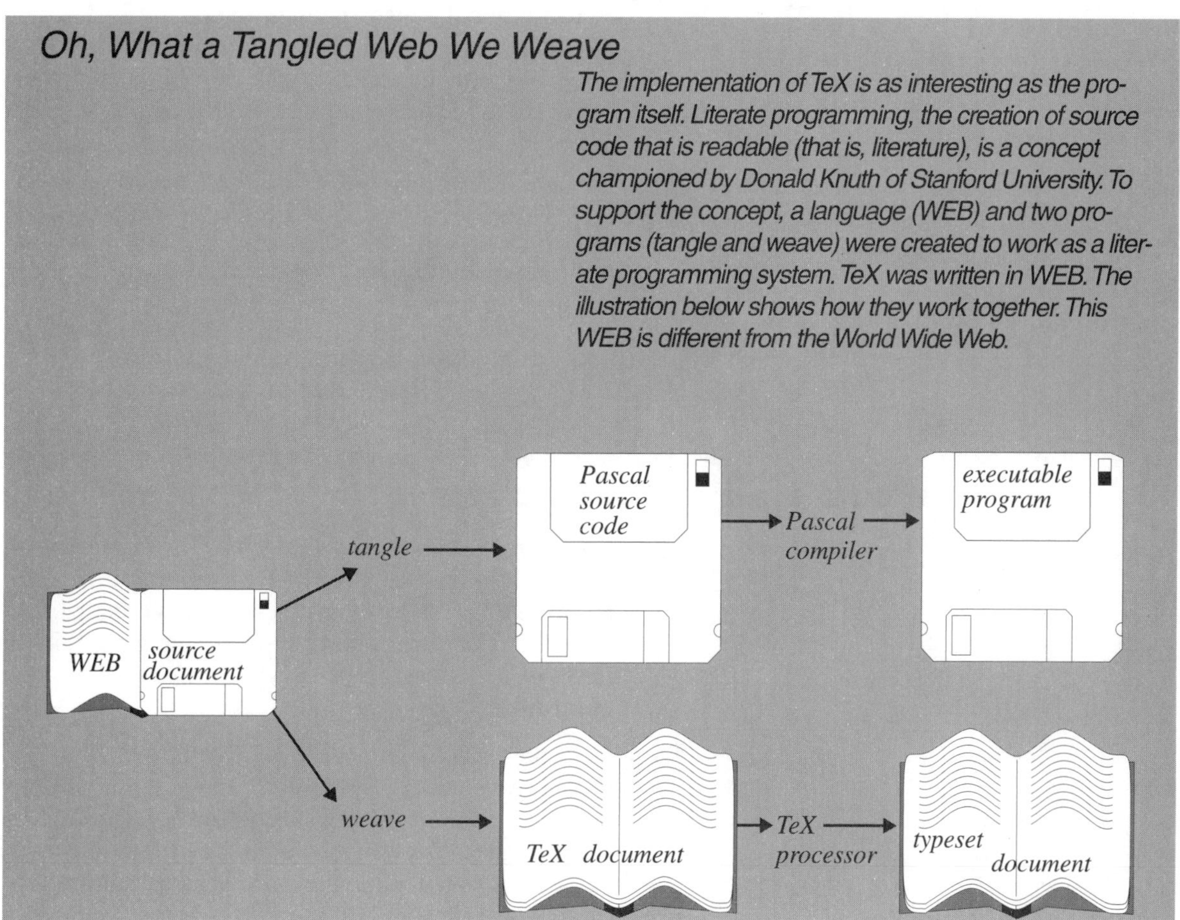

Another format with multiple uses is the `texinfo` format used in GNU's Emacs. GNU Emacs is as much a user's environment as it is a text editor. Just name a bizarre, complicated, baroque function you wish to accomplish in a few keystrokes, and Emacs probably has a built–in function for just such a purpose.

One of the more interesting features of Emacs is the *info* system. It provides Emacs users with a robust hypertext help system. It is an Emacs mode, which allows the interactive browsing of a tree–structured collection of documentation. The info system is used as one of the principal means of documenting many of the internal Emacs modes, as well as just about anything else you like. Paper documentation is also quite nice: so, in order to kill two birds with one stone, the GNU folks have created the texinfo format. Texinfo is a collection of specific TeX macros. The texinfo document can be run through TeX to create a typeset document for printing. In addition, the texinfo document can be processed through a texinfo program, an Emacs function, to create an info system online document. The bottom line is that an author can create a single document that can be printed with high–quality typesetting and browsed online. Clever folks!

7 • 4 Electronic Distribution

Electronic distribution depends on the proper use of standards. Whether electronic or paper, documents must be distributed to people to achieve their main purpose, communication. Distribution mechanisms for electronic documents are vital to the evolution of publishing.

Electronic documents can be distributed in many more ways than can their paper counterparts. Although much of this section is applicable to software and data in general, the techniques discussed are useful distribution mechanisms for electronic documents.

Resources such as the mail response programs and other network services discussed later in this section are possible only because of network standards. In fact, the entire domain of electronic document distribution is a good example of the proper use of standards for a particular function. The underlying standards that make these services possible are the technological glue needed by people trying to communicate. Before we examine various sorts of on-line communications, let's take a look at one significant relatively new storage mechanism, CD-ROMs.

7 • 4 • 1 CD-ROM

Compact Disc Read Only Memory or CD-ROM is the fortunate spin-off of the audio CD used at home to listen to high–quality music. Music on CDs is recorded digitally. Back in the mid 1980s, people realized that the data used to represent music could represent anything else. Thus, the CD-ROM and standards for representing files were born. The international standard ISO 9660 for volume and file structure has enabled the CD-ROM to become a widely used data distribution mechanism. Approximately 660Mb of data can fit on one CD-ROM.

The cost of CD-ROM replication has dropped to under $1.50 per CD-ROM because of the high volume of audio CDs. Of course, the true costs in mastering a CD-ROM are hidden in the data preparation phase. The cost of CD-ROM players has also dropped dramatically and is currently in the $100-$400 ballpark. You pay a price premium for the faster players, and players able to hold several CDs at once.

SIGCAT Text Retrieval CD-ROM

SIGCAT, an odd name for a group focusing on CD-ROMs, is the largest organization of people with an interest in CD-ROMs. The organization has produced a CD-ROM with twelve text retrieval engines on the same body of text. It is a tremendously convenient way of comparing the user interface for each system. It should not be considered a benchmark test of speed comparisons between the systems, but it is a unique resource.

Typically, a collection of documents will be prepared for a CD-ROM by using a full-text retrieval system. These systems create a database that allows the end user to search for any word appearing in the documents and to retrieve the documents quickly. These systems vary widely in their pricing structure, and typically, some sort of run-time royalty must be paid to the developer of the text retrieval engine.[11] (For a list of vendors of these systems, see *Section Text Retrieval* in the Appendix Resources.)

CD-Write Once (CD-WO) technology enables true desktop CD-ROM production, reducing even the initial mastering cost to under $20 (after the cost of the machine). These machines allow the user to write data to the optical disk (but only once) and to take that disk and play it on any CD-ROM drive.

11. SIGCAT, which stands for Special Interest Group on Computer Aided Technology, is the largest organization of CD-ROM users in existence. Please see *section Professional Organizations* in the *appendix Resources* for the complete address. Visit their Web site at: http://www.sigcat.org.

CD-ROMs have become the preferred mechanism for software and document distribution for one simple reason: it saves money. CD-ROMs are also more convenient from the customer's point of view. Rather then sifting through a shelf full of documentation, an online document browser can be used. Apple, Sun, IBM, DEC, and HP, to name a few, distribute software and software documentation on CD-ROMs. CD-ROMs are THE most cost–effective mechanism for distributing electronic information.

In addition, the read-only limitation is actually a valuable feature. The information provider does not have to worry about changes made by the users because they can't make any. CD-ROMs have become the medium of choice for electronic publishing and distribution.

DVDs - Next Generation CD-ROM

The revolution in digital storage and delivery spawned by the audio CD industry is about to be repeated. A second generation CD, called DVD (digital video disk) or HD-CD-ROM (High Density CD-ROM) is expected to be released in late 1996.[12]

The breakthrough in this technology was the agreement in September of 1995 to a single standard from what was two competing specifications. The two groups Sony/Phillips and Toshiba/Warner, were each proposing incompatible formats. These two groups wisely sought to avoid previously costly format battles such as the VHS versus Beta for video in the early 80's. They eventually created a unified format for the new CDs.

CD-ROMs meet the Internet

Another fascinating trend is the use of CD-ROM is collaboration with data on the Internet. These so-called hybrid CD-ROM go for the best of both worlds. Lots of data, delivered to a desktop user, and updated via the net. Compton's Encyclopedia lets its owners get updates from AOL.[a]

a. See *CD-ROMs Start Talking to the Net,* Business Week, Feb. 26, 1996.

In addition, these groups clearly recognize the value of a single standard in the creation of a market. The CD-audio disc followed by the ISO 9660 standard for data created the CD-ROM industry.

The new disk will (going out on a limb here) replicate much of the phenomenal growth of the audio CD. Video tape will, in several years, disappear as a rental media and be replaced by DVDs. The DVDs will use the MPEG-2 standard to encode high quality video and audio.

12. See "DVD Gets Rolling," Patricia Casey, *AV Video* Dec. 95, Vol. 17, #12.

Similarly, HD-CD-ROMs will replace regular CD-ROMs. All of this is made possible by the increased storage capacity of the new discs. The preliminary specs of the unified format will be as follows: it will have 2 sides, each side can have 2 layers, each layer can have 4.7GB. Eventually the discs full capacity of 17GB will be reached. Systems are expected to hit the market in 1998 or 1999.

The specification allows for existing audio and CD-ROM discs to be played in the new players. The size will be the same as current audio discs, 120mm. According to a market research firm called InfoTech in Woodstock, Vermont, it is expected that three main applications will arise: linear video (a replacement for video tape playback), multimedia PCs, and interactive TV set-tops (video-game consoles). Probably the first to gain in the market with be for the PC desktop, which has an insatiable appetite for storage capacity and where the initial expense ($500-$800) of the new units can more easily be absorbed.

By 1998, an erasable version called HD-CD-E is expected to open up all sorts of possibilities. Even if this revolution occurs at the same phenomenal rate as audio CDs, it will take at least 5years, so don't get rid of your VCR yet.

7 • 4 • 2 Electronic Page Delivery

The maintenance of page fidelity is one of the most difficult issues standards committees and vendors have tried to solve. The old problem of structure versus style is the major issue. Standards such as SGML and ODA along with document processing systems such as troff and TeX provide strict structural definitions and mappings between structure and the visuals (style). In the last few years, several efforts have met with considerable success.

Page delivery systems attempt to solve the document interchange problem, while maintaining page fidelity. They offer varying features, such as searching and the level and types of editing allowed. Certainly the clear winner in the battle of these systems is Adobe's Acrobat suite of products. Adobe, using a combination of marketing and technical prowess, is attempting to market PDF as the premier page interchange file format.

Adobe's Acrobat

Adobe's answer to the demands of on-line publishing comes in the form of an updated form of PostScript called the Portable Document Format (PDF). The Acrobat product suite offers users a robust and flexible mechanism for on-line publishing and very convenient tools—with some important restrictions. Simply put, the PDF form of a document maintains page fidelity and allows for cost–effective distribution of those pages. A kind of electronic paper. Any word/document processing system that can output PostScript can convert the output to PDF. The PDF files can be viewed using a freely distributable viewer. You cannot, however, edit the content of the PDF document. In addition, not all font problems have been solved.

> ***Acrobat beats out SGML***
>
> This headline was a front page story in the Nov. 20, 95 issue of Federal Computer Week. The Defense Printing Service (DPS), part of the US military, had the formidable task of converting millions of paper document into electronic form. The project involved about 20 million text pages. The DPS decided, for cost reasons, to use Acrobat as a major component of the conversion effort. It turned out that previously, the efforts focused on SGML with an eye toward ease of authoring. They discovered that the material doesn't really change that much, so the more static nature of PDF was appropriate and more cost effective.

The folks at Adobe Systems are attempting to create a new "revolution" in document interchange. Adobe's approach has two phases. First, create a technology that allows the document to be transmitted, viewed, and printed. Once this is accomplished and users commonly interchange electronic documents, the assumption is that market forces will drive vendors to use the PDF format as building blocks for new editing applications that understand the semantics of the objects that make up the document.

Any document that can be printed can be converted into a PDF document. Users will be able to view, print, attach notes, search for words, and create links between items of these documents. Adobe's approach is to let the market decide whether successful vendors will create applications that allow complex editing. Only time will tell if this approach will work

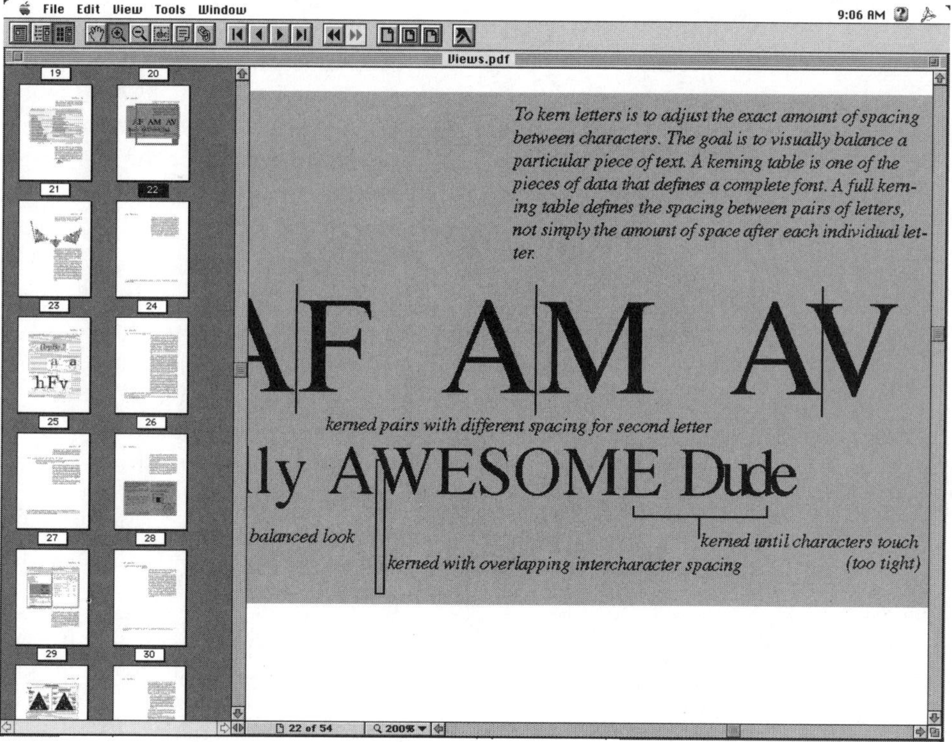
File Edit View Tools Window
9:06 AM
Views.pdf
To kern letters is to adjust the exact amount of spacing between characters. The goal is to visually balance a particular piece of text. A kerning table is one of the pieces of data that defines a complete font. A full kerning table defines the spacing between pairs of letters, not simply the amount of space after each individual letter.
AF AM AV
kerned pairs with different spacing for second letter
lly AWESOME Dude
balanced look
kerned until characters touch (too tight)
kerned with overlapping intercharacter spacing
22 of 54
200%

Adobe Acrobat Exchange viewer with thumbnails and enlarged section of page.

The PDF format itself has been published by Adobe, and there don't appear to be any proprietary tricks up their sleeves. The Acrobat viewer is being integrated with Netscape's Web browser as another plug-in. Speaking of the Web, Acrobat's relationship with the Web brings up some interesting issues. The Adobe Acrobat Plug-in is called Amber and can be downloaded from either the Netscape or Adobe Web site.

The hypertext linking capability of Acrobat has been enhanced by Adobe to allow links that are URLs. In the early days of Acrobat/Web integration, you could, in a properly configured Web browser, select a link which would point to a PDF file. Acrobat would launch as a helper application, and that was it. Afterwards, you would be left in Acrobat with no integrated way of getting back to the browser, other than through the window system. Typical helper application stuff. Now, however, you can link to a PDF document and, inside Acrobat, select a link that is really a URL, causing the Web browser to go to the new URL. This presents the user with a powerful browsing capability. It may also be somewhat confusing to the user who now has to cognitivly switch between the user interface of the Web browser and the user interface of Acrobat.

Common Ground is one of the other major contenders in page delivery systems. Acrobat and Common Ground were introduced at about the same time. Common Ground gave away its viewer for free, and Adobe charged about $50 for the Acrobat Reader. This nominal fee was sometimes a problem for educational institutions and other non-profits that wanted to ensure the lowest cost and widest possible distribution of their documents. Eventually, Adobe saw the light and changed its policy; they now give away the viewer. (You can find it at http://www.adobe.com).

A third electronic page delivery system is called Envoy from, folks at WordPerfect. With the turmoil brought on, no doubt, by the sale (twice) of WordPerfect to Corel, it remains a bit player.

7 • 4 • 3 Bulletin Boards

Electronic bulletin board systems (BBS) are still a widely used mechanism to distribute electronic documents. Using a modem, users simply dial up to the BBS of interest, poke around, find some files of interest, and start downloading—transferring a file from a remote system to your local system.

Bulletin boards have become widespread because they are extremely inexpensive. All that's required is an inexpensive PC, a modem, and some BBS software (widely available for free). Any local PC users group can provide more information on bulletin boards.

Perhaps the greatest benefit of bulletin boards is that they can put you in touch with technical experts in virtually any domain. For example, if you were having a nasty technical problem with PageMaker, simply locate a bulletin board with a discussion group about PageMaker, post your problem, check back in a few days, and maybe someone has posted an answer. The large commercial bulletin boards, like CompuServe, are ideal for this type of interaction because they have discussion groups (forums) on all sorts of topics. The commercial bulletin boards are relatively expensive to use but are invaluable for this type of access to expertise. You might also want to hunt down an appropriate USENET newsgroup for technical questions.

> ***The Breaking News Network***
>
> FLASH! This just in from "Fast Forward" April 1996, a monthly magazine published with the Washington Post — Alan Henney, listening to radio scanners of police and fire broadcasts, types out the news on his computer system. The system relays the news to subscribers of the BNN, Breaking News Network, who carry pagers. Reporters, free-lance photographers, and people who need to get a life follow the action. Ahhh...strange and wonderful things happen when technologies integrate. Contact Henney at: henney@gwis2.circ.gwu.edu.

As a distribution mechanism, a BBS is just like the electronic equivalent of the physical bulletin board at the supermarket. On both media, you can see ads, information blurbs, requests for help, and items for sale. One limitation, some would say benefit, of this form of communication is its passive nature. People must take the action to dial the BBS and look for information. Electronic mail–based systems can be set up to interrupt and inform you about important new documents or actions that must be taken.

Clearly the days of BBSs are numbered. The Web has certainly overtaken BBS is terms of sheer numbers, however, it's still much simpler to set up a BBS than a Web server. Small organizations with little or no technical support and a well defined community of users would be wise to take a look at BBS technology, it may be just the right solution to their needs.

7 • 4 • 4 Electronic Mail

Electronic Mail (e-mail), that modern staple of office communications, is also an effective way to distribute documents and coordinate a group's activities. Worldwide e-mail service has greatly improved in recent years to the point where many different e-mail networks are interconnected.

There are two main ways of using e-mail as a distribution mechanism. The first is an Electronic Mail Response Program (EMRP), and the second is a mailing list server. Let's examine each of these in turn.

An **electronic mail response program**, also known as archive servers or mail servers (and some other names), is a clever use of electronic mail. An EMRP is a program that reads mail and responds to requests

E–mail Conventions

Throughout this book and in many magazines and on networks, an individual's e–mail address is often as important and, in fact, more useful, than their phone number. Addressing conventions vary with the network. In the case of Internet mail, an address is composed of two pieces of information: their user ID (their identification to the mail system, typically the same as their login ID) and the name of the network location of their mail domain. For example, the address

`sandy@ability.net`

means that my mail ID is sandy and the domain that understands my ID is ability.net.

Mail addressing gets confusing when you try to send mail from one network to another. For example, users of the MCImail commercial network can send mail to users of the Internet. A gateway connects the two networks. MCI-mail users must go though some added complexity to accomplish this connection, but it's a small price to pay for this added functionality. Users of the Internet who wish to send mail to MCImail users simply have to use an address that looks like

`user@mcimail.com`

The gateway does the proper addressing conversion to turn the Internet address into an MCImail address. The existence of a number of gateways among several major networks has greatly increased the number of interconnected e–mail users.

specified in the mail. Usually, the EMRP can respond only to a limited set of commands. The primary command is usually `send`. It is usually followed by a file name. The exact syntax of these commands varies with the particular mail server; however, they are all simple to use and functionally very similar.

Virtually all mail servers can interpret the command `help` (if not, they certainly should) and respond with useful information. Typically, the mail server contains an index that points to directories, individual files, or both. You can request the files.

The second e-mail distribution mechanism is a **mailing list manager** (MLM). The two principle MLMs are LISTSERV and majordomo. A good comparison of the different MLMs can be found at: ftp://ftp.uu.net/usenet/news.answers/mail/list-admin/software-faq. A mailing list manager is a program that maintains a list of user addresses and lets remote users access and/or send information to these addresses. Mailing list managers allow interested users to participate in discussions about topics of interest. Once you subscribe to a list, you receive all mail sent to the list. One of the more popular MLMs is called LISTSERV. The functionality of LISTSERV is really a superset of an EMRP, as well as a simple mailing list manager. LISTSERV is very robust, with facilities for secure access, packaging of files into related groupings of information, and mailing list maintenance.

From an introductory file describing the Revised LISTSERV:

> Although the primary function of LISTSERV is to distribute mail and files to predefined distribution lists, it may often be desired to provide the subscribers of the list with a set of data or program files to be peri-

> odically maintained by a particular person or set of persons. Apart from the obvious example of list "notebooks" (archives), working groups might want to provide minutes of internal meetings held by some of the subscribers, technical groups might want to share application programs related to some software they are all using, etc.
>
> It was decided that the most convenient way of meeting these needs was to provide basic, non-specialized fileserver functions along with the mail-processing function of LISTSERV. Those functions would have to provide powerful yet list-based file access control and remote file updating facilities, under the control of both the list owner and the LISTSERV management.
>
> Automatic distribution of updated materials to subscribers was another major concern, since it makes this distribution more efficient whenever the list is supported by more than one peer server, and relieves the file maintainer of the burden of preparing the list of subscribers. The users request such distribution directly from the server without any intervention from the file maintainer.[13]

E-mail access is probably the widest of all distribution mechanisms. More people can access more information via e-mail than with any other electronic mechanism. The downside, however, is slow access speed and the sometimes limited ability to transfer large information files. E-mail is generally a nonreal-time process. It usually takes a few hours, and sometimes days, for e-mail to go from one site to another because of the many gateways involved. Mail systems are typically configured to send mail at some fixed interval, such as once an hour or at night when phone rates are least expensive. Fast, real-time access and the ability to conveniently transfer large files requires a true network.

13. From "Revised LISTSERV: File Server Functions," by Eric Thomas, <ERIC@FRECP11.BITNET> of Ecole Centrale de Paris, 1987.

7 • 4 • 5 Resource Discovery Tools

As the Internet becomes larger and more interconnected finding information is becoming one of the most challenging issues. Often one is struck by thoughts such as "I know I saw something about the new netWizard product...but where was it?" An entire discipline has been created called resource discovery.[14] Resource discovery is the formal study of net surfing.

One of the more serious problems, which is only recently being addressed, is finding information on the "net." A combination of funded efforts, clever programming, and better interconnectivity is leading to a tamer Internet. The rest of this section discusses some of these projects.

Internet Society

The Internet Society is an international professional membership organization. The organizers of the Internet Society include the Corporation for National Research Initiatives (CNRI), EDUCOM, and the Internet Activities Board (IAB). The society began operation in January 1992. The society is an educational, nonprofit organization supporting the technical evolution of the Internet, the education of the public on the use of the Internet, and the educational and scientific use of the Internet by educational institutions, industry, and the public at large. The society also provides a forum for new Internet applications and fosters broader use of the Internet. Its Web site is at: http://www.isoc.org.

14. Michael F. Schwartz, Alan Emtage, Brewster Kahle, B. Clifford Neuman, "A Comparison of Internet Resource Discovery Approaches", *Computing Systems*, Vol. 5, No. 4, Fall 1992.

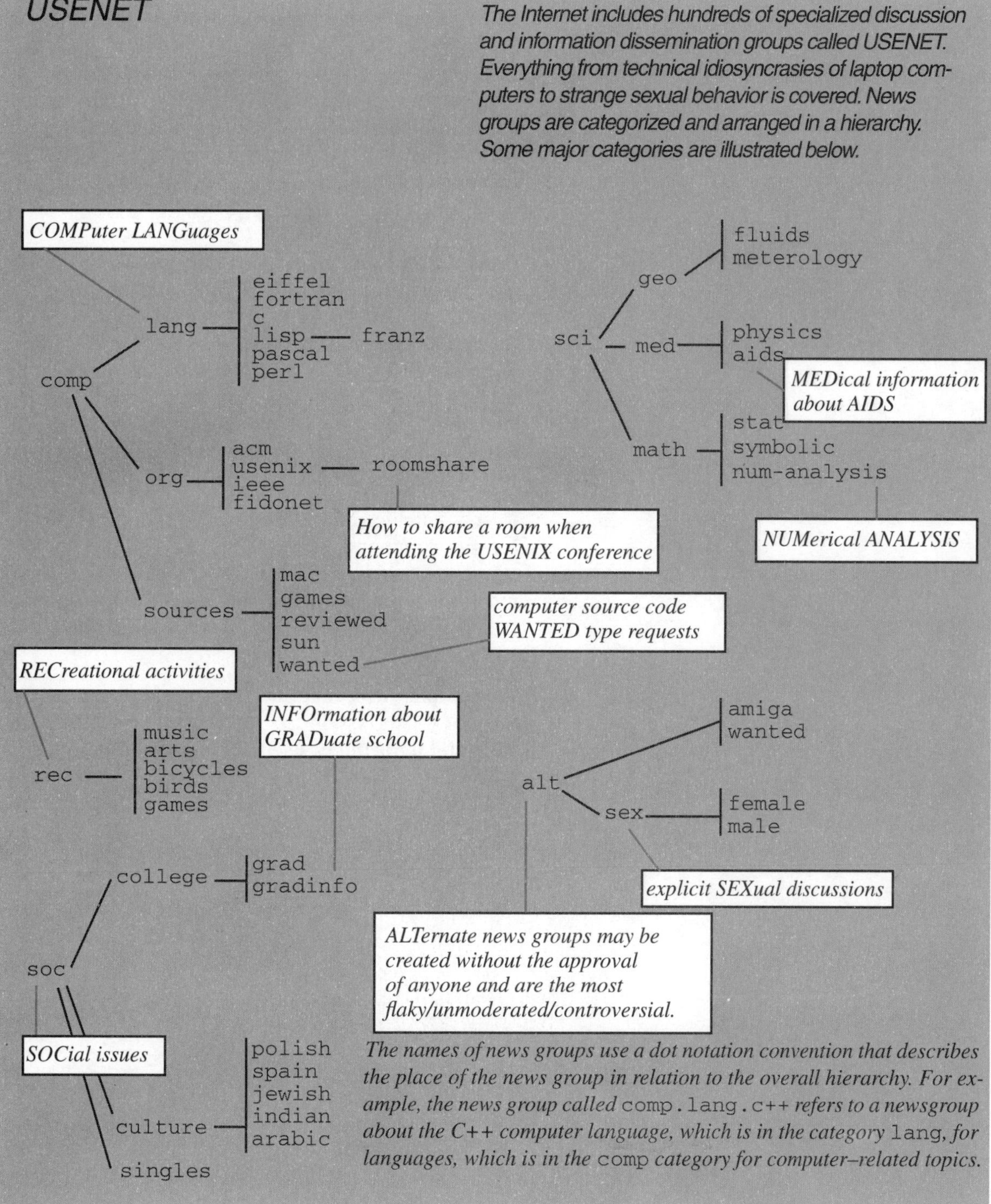
USENET
The Internet includes hundreds of specialized discussion and information dissemination groups called USENET. Everything from technical idiosyncrasies of laptop computers to strange sexual behavior is covered. News groups are categorized and arranged in a hierarchy. Some major categories are illustrated below.
COMPuter LANGuages
comp
lang
eiffel
fortran
c
lisp
franz
pascal
perl
org
acm
usenix
roomshare
ieee
fidonet
How to share a room when attending the USENIX conference
sources
mac
games
reviewed
sun
wanted
computer source code WANTED type requests
RECreational activities
rec
music
arts
bicycles
birds
games
INFOrmation about GRADuate school
soc
college
grad
gradinfo
SOCial issues
culture
polish
spain
jewish
indian
arabic
singles
sci
geo
fluids
meterology
med
physics
aids
MEDical information about AIDS
math
stat
symbolic
num-analysis
NUMerical ANALYSIS
alt
amiga
wanted
sex
female
male
explicit SEXual discussions
ALTernate news groups may be created without the approval of anyone and are the most flaky/unmoderated/controversial.
The names of news groups use a dot notation convention that describes the place of the news group in relation to the overall hierarchy. For example, the news group called comp.lang.c++ refers to a newsgroup about the C++ computer language, which is in the category lang, for languages, which is in the comp category for computer–related topics.

ARCHIE

Some clever people at McGill University in Canada created one of the best early means of locating information on the Internet. They created an electronic mail response program called "archie." Archie maintains a database of archive sites and the names of their contents. The command used for searching functions follows:

prog <reg expr1> [<reg exp2>...]

in which `prog` is a keyword that means to find or search. A search of the "archie" database is performed with each <reg exp> (a regular expression) in turn, and any matches found are returned to the requestor. Note that multiple regular expressions may be placed on one line, in which case the results will be mailed back to you in one message. If you have multiple "prog" lines, then multiple messages will be returned, one for each line.

Users of archie simply send e–mail requests containing the command `prog` using the syntax specified above to search for particular programs or documents of interest. Archie e–mail sends a response, telling you where to go to find the item you requested.

A friendlier user interface exists via the program `xarchie`. An X window system program, xarchie lets you interactively select the database sources and pose queries. Xarchie returns the results of the query in a list with the most relevant items on the top of the list.

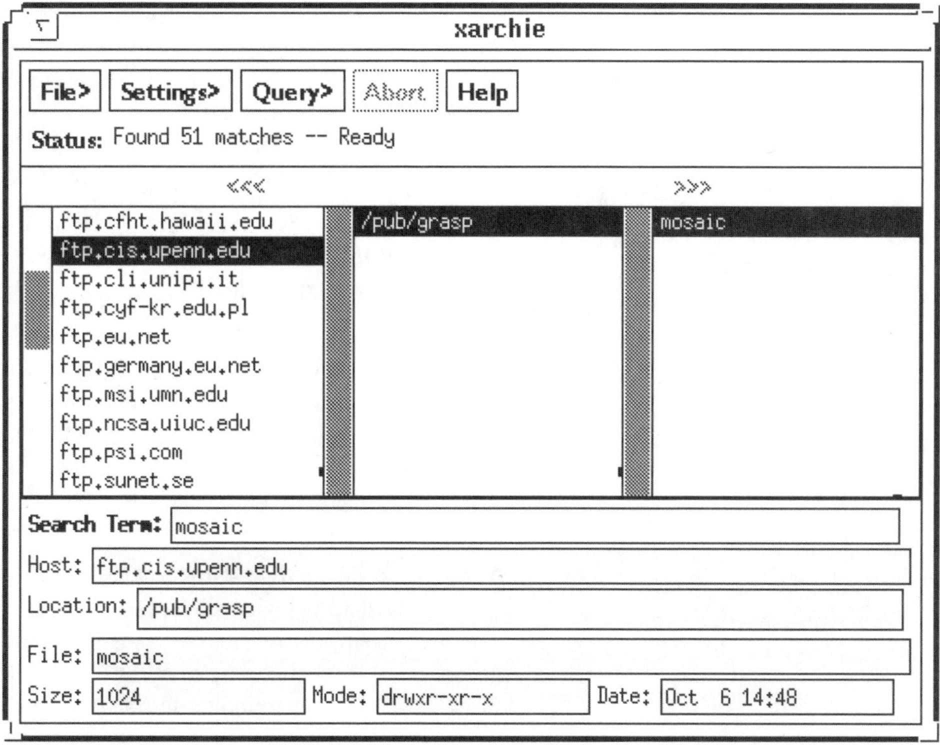

XARCHIE - the X Window System User Interface to archie[15]

An archie site runs a program that maintains the database by using anonymous ftp. The archie program checks the contents of several hundred archive sites over approximately 1 to 2 months. Lots of sites run archie servers.[16] Some sites allow interactive queries of the archie database via TELNET,[17] eliminating the delay inherent in e–mail.

15. A nice overview of Xarchie is available at: http://www.vis.colostate.edu/software/Xarchie/xarchie_ov.html.

16. Archie servers are now located all over the world. They include archie@cs.mcgill.ca (the original site of the developers of archie at McGill School of Computer Science in Canada), archie@pucc.princeton.edu (Princeton University), archie.funet.fu (Finland/Europe), cs.huji.ac.il (Israel), archie.au (you may log in as archie with no password for an interactive version of archie present at many sites).

17. TELNET is a commonly available program that allows one to have an interactive session with a program at a remote system on the Internet. The TELNET specification exists on the Internet as "Telnet Protocol RFC 854." It is also specified as the military standard MIL-STD 1782.

WAIS

The Wide Area Information Service (WAIS) is an effort to make possible network–wide document retrieval. The project started as a joint effort of Thinking Machines Corporation, Dow Jones News/Retrieval, and Apple Computer. Now WAIS Inc. is a subsidiary of America OnLine (AOL).

The WAIS project leader, Brewster Kahle, tells some of the history and functionality of WAIS in this overview written in 1991:

> The Wide Area Information Servers system is a set of products supplied by different vendors to help end-users find and retrieve information over networks. Thinking Machines, Apple Computer, and Dow Jones initially implemented such a system for use by business executives. These products are becoming more widely available from various companies.
>
> *What does WAIS do?* Users on different platforms can access personal, company, and published information from one interface. The information can be anything: text, pictures, voice, or formatted documents. Since a single computer-to-computer protocol is used, information can be stored anywhere on different types of machines. Anyone can use this system since it uses natural language questions to find relevant documents. Relevant documents can be fed back to a server to refine the search. This avoids complicated query languages and vendor specific systems. Successful searches can be automatically run to alert the user when new information becomes available.
>
> *How does WAIS work?* The servers take a user's question and do their best to find relevant documents. The servers, at this point, do not "understand" the user's English language question, rather they try to find documents that contain those words and phrases and rank them based on heuristics. The user interfaces (clients) talk to the servers using an extension to a standard protocol Z39.50. Using a public standard allows vendors to compete with each other, while bypassing the usual proprietary protocol period that slows development. Thinking Machines is giving away an implementation of this standard to help vendors develop clients and servers.

What WAIS servers exist? Even though the system is very new, there are already several servers:

* Dow Jones is putting a server on their own DowVision network. This server contains the Wall Street Journal, Barons, and 450 magazines. This is a for-pay server.

* Thinking Machines operates a Connection Machine on the internet for free use. The databases it supports are some patents, a collection of molecular biology abstracts, a cookbook, and the CIA World Factbook.

* MIT supports a poetry server with a great deal of classical and modern poetry. Cosmic is serving descriptions of government software packages. The Library of Congress has plans to make their catalog available on the protocol.

* Weather maps and forecasts are made available by Thinking Machines as a repackaging of existing information.

* The "directory of servers" facility is operated by Thinking Machines so that new servers can be easily registered as either for-pay or for-free servers and users can find out about these services.

How can I find out more about WAIS?

Contact Brewster Kahle for more information on the WAIS project, the Connection Machine WAIS system, or the free Mac, Unix Server, and X Window System interfaces. There is a mailing list that has weekly postings on progress and new releases; to subscribe send an email note to
wais-discussion-request@think.com.

Brewster Kahle
Project Leader Wide Area Information Servers
Brewster@Think.com

It is important to note that the communications to the WAIS servers are accomplished using the ANSI standard protocol for database retrieval applications, Z39.50. The decision to use a public standard is what makes this communications method truly open.

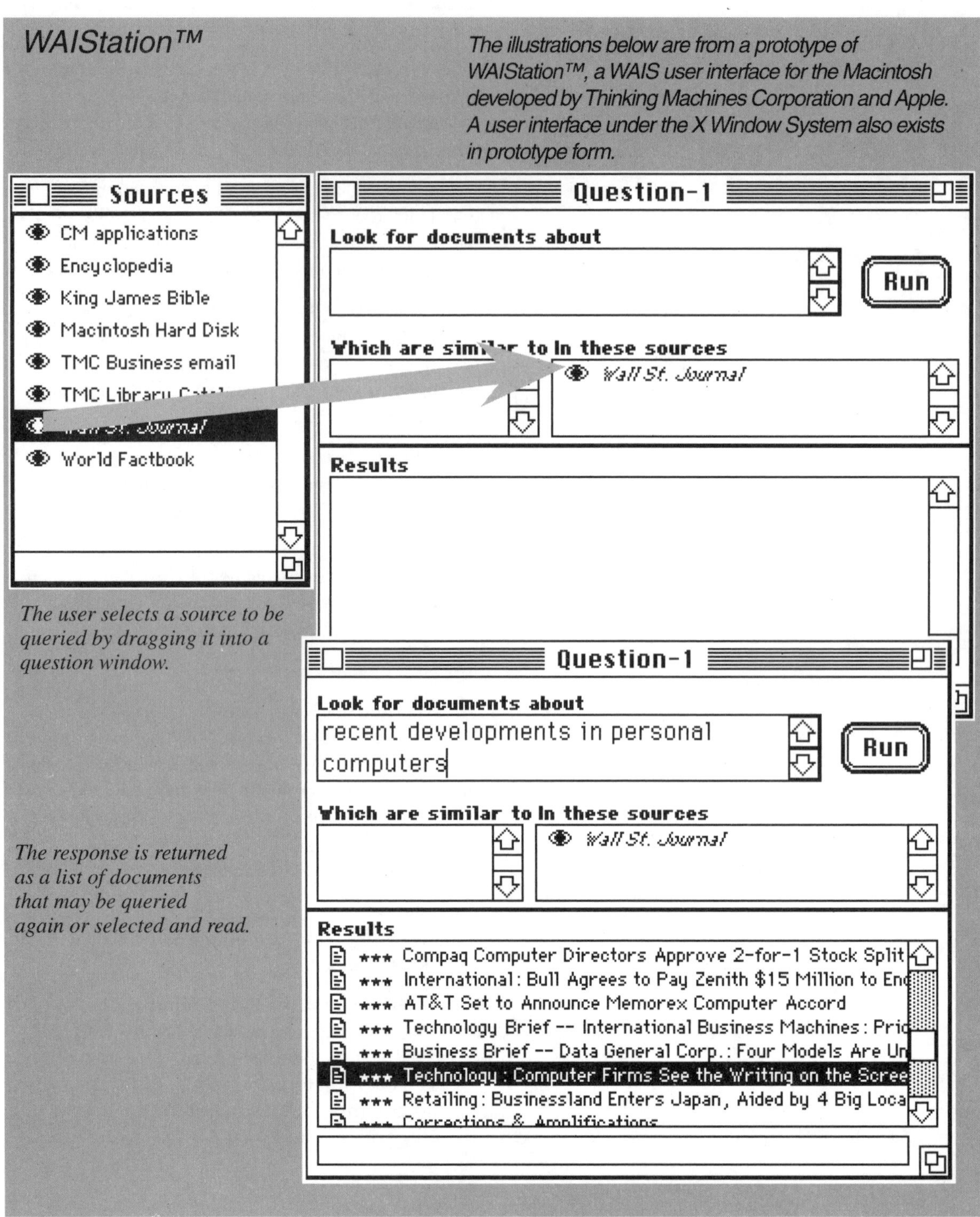

WAIStation™

The illustrations below are from a prototype of WAIStation™, a WAIS user interface for the Macintosh developed by Thinking Machines Corporation and Apple. A user interface under the X Window System also exists in prototype form.

The user selects a source to be queried by dragging it into a question window.

The response is returned as a list of documents that may be queried again or selected and read.

GOPHER

Gopher is a widely used method for browsing through documents on the Internet. Originated at the University of Minnesota, Gopher usage has exploded from around 1992-1995. Usage has tapered off with the explosion of the Web. The appeal of Gopher, however, is that it is text–only, allowing more ubiquitous access to the information.

One way of locating information on the Internet is to use Gopher servers. Gopher servers maintain collections of documents with the additional ability of full-text searching. The Gopher protocol and concept are due to the effort of the people at the Microcomputer and Workstation Networks Research Center at the University of Minnesota. One of the appealing aspects of Gopher is the simplicity with which it presents itself to the user. You, the user, are presented a "file system" just like any hierarchically organized file system, except that this file system covers all information known to the particular Gopher server. It's a simple, elegant, and powerful approach.

Client systems through which a user "speaks" to the Gopher server can have a number of user interfaces. One of the clients on UNIX systems is based on `curses` and will function on any terminal.

According to Mark McCahill, member of the Gopher development team:

> The Internet Gopher is a distributed document delivery service. It allows a neophyte user to access various types of data residing on multiple hosts in a seamless fashion. This is accomplished by presenting the user a hierarchical arrangement of documents, a menu, and by using a client-server communications model. In addition to browsing through hierarchies of documents, Gopher users can submit queries to Gopher search servers. The search servers typically have full-text indexes for a set of Gopher documents; the response to a query is a list of documents that matched the search criteria.
>
> Internet Gopher servers accept simple queries (sent over a TCP connection) and respond by sending the client a document or a list of documents. Since this is

Information Grazing

From Howard Rheingold in *Publish* magazine:

> Information grazing is part skill, part social contract, part file management and part serendipity... .A different set of skills come into play when you know what you are looking for. If you have a specific question about a subject, no matter how esoteric, you can post a question in the right place and then harvest the answer when you log back on an hour later.[a]

a. From "I Want to Turn You On-line," by Howard Rheingold, in *Publish* magazine, Feb. 1992.

> a distributed protocol there can be many servers but the client software hides this fact from the user. We currently use this technology at the University of Minnesota to help support microcomputer users... a couple of Gopher servers have 6000-7000 computer Q&A items that users can search for answers to their questions. In addition, there are also Gopher servers with recipes and other fun stuff.

Conceptually, a user might see something like the following illustration.[18]

A Gopher's eye view of available information is presented as a typical directory structure on a Macintosh.

About internet Gopher
Around the University of Minnesota - Offices and Services
Courses, Schedules, Calendars
Events
Microcomputer News & Prices
Student-Staff Directories
University Relations Information and Forms
Weather for the Twin Cities

In the case of an interaction with Gopher servers, however, these directories may exist anywhere on the Internet. Furthermore, the user doesn't really care where the information is, as long as it's accessible in a timely manner.

Client systems through which a user "speaks" to the Gopher server can have a number of user interfaces. One of the clients on UNIX systems is based on `curses` and will function on any terminal.

18. From "Notes on the internet Gopher protocol" by Alberti and others, Spring 1991, Microcomputer and Workstation Networks Research Center, University of Minnesota, Minneapolis.

MISCELLANEOUS INTERNET SERVICES

Along with the services already discussed, a few dozen more also exist. As the reliability and speed of the Internet increases, these resources are becoming increasingly valuable, especially since the Web integrates them all. Indeed, the spread of this technology raises important questions about the future of academic journals, libraries, and publishing.

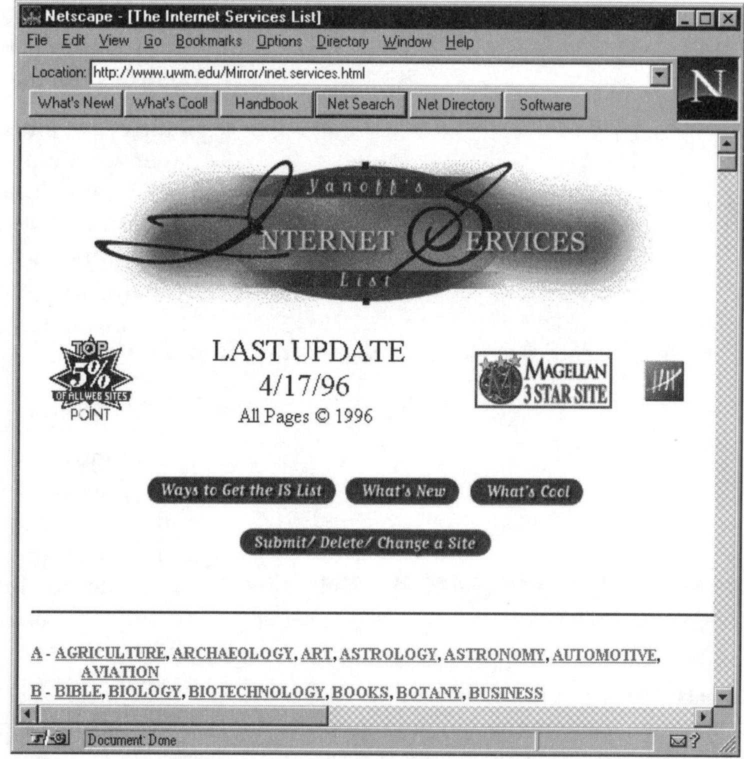

Scott Yanoff has for many years provided lists of various Internet Services, this has now evelved into a valuable Web site, that you can find at: http://www.uwm.edu/Mirror/inet.services.html.

7 • 4 • 6 Electronic Journals

Another trend that is taking advantage of the improved connectivity of networks and e-mail is the rise of the electronic journal. An electronic journal is, as the name implies, simply a genuine academic journal that is published and disseminated primarily via electronic media. These media primarily consist of archives accessible via ftp and listservers. Electronic journals represent the maturing of network connectivity.

Given the distributed nature of networks with worldwide geographic coverage and literally thousands of places where information hides, it is a challenge to find information "out on the net." One great place to find electronic journals is the "Directory of Electronic Journals and Newsletters." It was compiled by Michael Stangelove of the University of Ottawa, Canada.[19] A more up-to-date directory is published by the Association of Research Libraries.[20]

Some of the journals are peer reviewed just like their paper counterparts. They cover a wide range of topics, ranging from fine art to issues concerning the handicapped, to library science and ethnomusicology. It appears that the world of electronic networks is finally growing up!

7 • 4 • 7 FAX Boards and Modems

Well, if I called the wrong number, why did you answer the phone?— James Thurber

The ubiquitous FAX is no longer limited to hard copy. Special FAX boards can be plugged into PCs and workstations to send and receive FAX documents without ever having to scan or print paper. CCITT Group 4 is the standard for representing FAX documents, and these devices can transmit and receive purely electronic FAX documents. FAX modems are widely available for a little more money than simply a modem. These days, it's hard to find a modem card that doesn't have FAX capabilities. Using this technology, electronic distribution systems can be easily set up. (See *Section 6 • 4 Standards and Formats* in *Chapter 6 • Media and Document Integration* for more information on FAX).

FAX Distribution

Many companies will distribute your documents via FAX. A company called FaXLand Corporation in Falls Church, Virginia has computers set up to send up to 100 faxes at a time. In the Washington, D.C. area, the service is being used by companies that put out daily newsletters about Congressional activities, where timeliness is what counts.

The relationship between FAX software computers and the normal printing functions on the computer is very interesting. For example, on most computers with window systems, FAX modems are usually

19. The directory is available at http://www.w3.org/hypertext/DataSources/Journals.html.

20. The ARL directory is available at: gopher://arl.cni.org/11/scomm/edir.

FAX®-IT-BACK

The magazine *Portable Office* has taken reader service cards to new heights with a service called FAX®-IT-BACK. Instead of having to mail in a postcard requesting information on a particular product you can, for some of the products, request a FAX. You call an 800 number and have a dialog with a machine. You key in the product number and your FAX machine number. In a few minutes, the information requested gets FAXed back to you, and it didn't cost you anything!

implemented as a printer device. This means that the FAX appears to the operating system as just another printer. When running an application, you simply print something and the currently selected printer, in this case the FAX modem, receives the output. The printing dialog box presents the user with various options concerning phone dialing, and soon the document is on its way as a FAX. The seamless substitution of a FAX device for a printer is very appealing.

Another interesting approach is taken by vendors of FAX software for workstations. Often they come with a PostScript interpreter, that takes a PostScript file, images it in the same way that a printer images PostScript information, and then ships the image out via FAX.

As FAX hardware gets ever closer to printing software, the distinctions start to blur. Device drivers treat FAX devices as printers. Page description languages are used to create FAX images. FAX printing and distribution are midway between electronic and traditional document distribution.

Another FAX possibility is the integration of a FAX server with a local area network or e-mail. Some FAX servers can be sent text files or some other well–defined format, such as PostScript. It is quite feasible to set up mail distribution lists, such as those discussed in the earlier section on electronic mail, to send FAXs to additional people who don't have e–mail.

Finally, of course, someone has figured out how to marry the Web with FAX. The folks at Universal Access Inc. have a service called WebFaX which (yes you heard it here first) lets you surf the Web via your FAX machine. You dial their FAX number, spell out the server on the touch tone keypad, and voila, the Web page gets faxed back to you. Actually it's not quite so simple or complete. They only have a few thousand of the more popular Web sites, and it works best if the site has a unique ID assigned by the WebFaX people. The WebFaX system is being packaged up into a more complete communications system. Stay tuned; it's a neat idea with some useful possibilities.

Related to FAX and Web integration, we also have NetPhonic Communications Web-On-Call Voice Browser. That's right; once these folks get their software up and running, you will be able to surf the net with your telephone. So when you are at the airport away from your computer, don't worry, a voice synthesizer can read those pages to you. Actually, it can send email or a FAX of the page, so it might actually be useful. We'll see.

7 • 4 • 8 The Internet Appliance

On one side of the Internet boxing ring, we have Microsoft and its allies. On the other, we have Oracle, Sun, and Netscape. The battleground is the future of the Internet. The weapons: the Web, Java and microkernal operating systems versus the Windows desktop model of computing. The battle is over the future of an extremely low–cost device called the Internet Appliance, WebPC, or Network Computer, which will cost under $500 and allow access to the Internet.

The Internet Appliance represents a convergence of several technologies. First is the Web, which has effectively tamed the unruly Internet, somewhat, for the masses. Second is Java as a mechanism to provide network downloadable applications that are portable to many platforms. Third is a network centric operating system a microkernal operating system to execute the applications.

In a cover story "Inside the WebPC" in *BYTE* magazine of March 1996, Tom Halfill, the author points out the convergence and requirements for such a WebPC. The *BYTE* article also include high bandwidth access, via cable modems, ISDN, or ATM, as another necessary technology.

Clearly, the history of hardware design points to the high probability of a $500 or less WebPC, not as a likelihood but as an inevitability, and soon. The increasing sophistication of chips with super computer class compute and I/O processing capabilities is astonishing. Again, according to the *BYTE* article LSI Communications Products Division is already working on an "Internet on a Chip" to enable the affordable pricing of the Internet Appliance.

Another interesting development in this domain is Apple's apparent shift of the "Pippin," originally a set-top box, towards this concept of the Internet Appliance. In fact, Bandai, a Japanese corporation known for the Power Rangers, is going to manufacture the Pippin under the Power Player name. In December of 1995 Apple and Bandai "demonstrated a Power Player browsing the World Wide Web with Netscape Navigator."

Low–cost Internet access and affordable hardware have tremendous potential. It is also a case where this type of technological advance can help bring computing resources to people who simply can't afford the $3000 PC. If this takes off, the social impact could be enormous.

7 • 4 • 9 The New World Order of Communications

As the technology for document distribution and communications races into the future, the legal system is ill prepared to deal with the many issues these technologies raise. In an effort to address these issues as well as their ethical implications, two organizations have been created: the Electronic Frontier Foundation (EFF) and the Computer Professionals for Social Responsibility. EFF issued the following press release as its opening announcement:

> FOR IMMEDIATE RELEASE
>
> Contact: Cathy Cook (415) 759-5578
>
> NEW FOUNDATION ESTABLISHED TO ENCOURAGE COMPUTER-BASED COMMUNICATIONS POLICIES
>
> Washington, D.C., July 10, 1990 -- Mitchell D. Kapor, founder of Lotus Development Corporation and ON Technology, today announced that he, along with colleague John Perry Barlow, has established a foundation to address social and legal issues arising from the impact on society of the increasingly pervasive use of computers as a means of communication and information distribution. The Electronic Frontier Foundation (EFF) will support and engage in public education on current and future developments in computer-based and telecommunications media. In addition, it will

support litigation in the public interest to preserve, protect and extend First Amendment rights within the realm of computing and telecommunications technology.

Initial funding for the Foundation comes from private contributions by Kapor and Steve Wozniak, co-founder of Apple Computer, Inc. The Foundation expects to actively raise contributions from a wide constituency.

As an initial step to foster public education on these issues, the Foundation today awarded a grant to the Palo Alto, California-based public advocacy group, Computer Professionals for Social Responsibility (CPSR). The grant will be used by CPSR to expand the scope of its on-going Computing and Civil Liberties Project.

Because its mission is to not only increase public awareness about civil liberties issues arising in the area of computer-based communications, but also to support litigation in the public interest, the Foundation has recently intervened on behalf of two legal cases.

The first case concerns Steve Jackson, an Austin-based game manufacturer who was the target of the Secret Service's Operation Sun Devil. The EFF has pressed for a full disclosure by the government regarding the seizure of his company's computer equipment. In the second action, the Foundation intends to seek amicus curiae (friend of the court) status in the government's case against Craig Neidorf, a 20-year-old University of Missouri student who is the editor of the electronic newsletter, Phrack World News....

"It is becoming increasingly obvious that the rate of technology advancement in communications is far outpacing the establishment of appropriate cultural, legal and political frameworks to handle the issues that are arising," said Kapor. "And the Steve Jackson and Neidorf cases dramatically point to the timeliness of the Foundation's mission. We intend to be instrumental in helping shape a new framework that embraces these powerful new technologies for the public good."

> The use of new digital media — in the form of on-line information and interactive conferencing services, computer networks and electronic bulletin boards — is becoming widespread in businesses and homes. However, the electronic society created by these new forms of digital communications does not fit neatly into existing, conventional legal and social structures.
>
> The question of how electronic communications should be accorded the same political freedoms as newspapers, books, journals and other modes of discourse is currently the subject of discussion among this country's lawmakers and members of the computer industry. The EFF will take an active role in these discussions through its continued funding of various educational projects and forums.
>
> An important facet of the Foundation's mission is to help both the public and policy-makers see and understand the opportunities as well as the challenges posed by developments in computing and telecommunications. In addition, the EFF will encourage and support the development of new software to enable non-technical users to more easily use their computers to access the growing number of digital communications services available.

In Feb. of 1996 the EFF conducted an online "Blue Ribbon Campaign." The campaign protested a portion of a telecommunications deregulation bill, which passed the US congress and contained a ridiculously unenforceable and illconcieved restriction on free speech on the Internet. Web masters throughout the country were asked to place "blue ribbon" images on their Web pages which linked to information about the bill and it's problems. Political activism has met the Web.

The EFF can be reached at the Internet mail address eff@eff.org. Their Web site is, you guessed it: http://www.eff.org.

Chapter 8 • Document Management

A memorandum is written not to inform the reader but to protect the writer.
—Dean Acheson

The creation of large quantities of documents usually involves many people and processes. Eventually, management or the technical staff will recognize the need for good working practices for the document creation, development, and maintenance processes.

Like the management of any complex set of tasks, document management can benefit from sound general management practices. However, some notable practices specifically apply to document management. Two of these are the creation of project standards and the use of configuration management. These two practices apply to a variety of document creation and maintenance tasks. Good management principles apply to any type of electronic document project, whether delivered on paper or on-line. This chapter explores the application of these tools and techniques to document management.

You Said How Many Pages!!!

This graph illustrates the explosion of information needed to support modern aircraft.

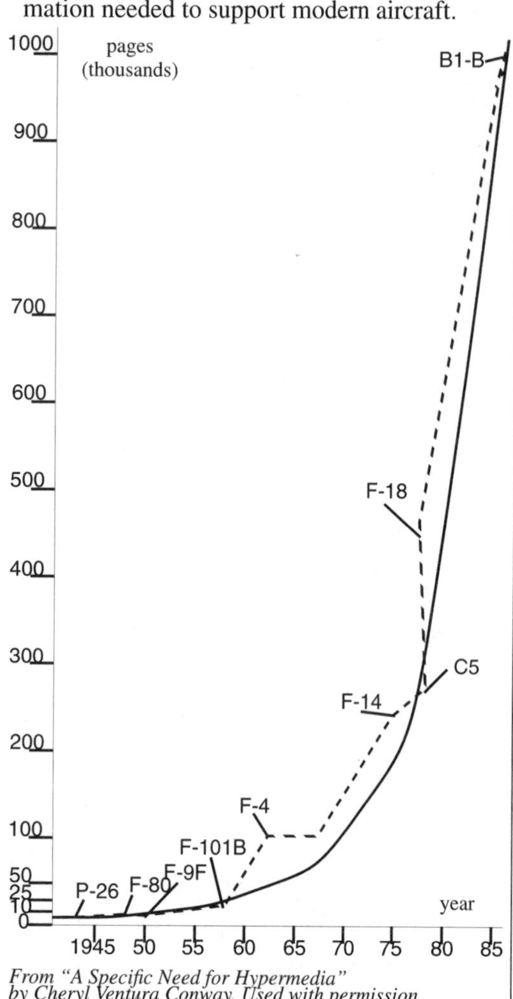

From "A Specific Need for Hypermedia" by Cheryl Ventura Conway. Used with permission. Allied-Signal Inc., Bendix Test Systems Division 1990.

The creation and production of documents in any large project takes a great deal of time, effort, and, ultimately, money. How can the process be controlled? What kinds of issues need to be examined? What parts of the document creation, production, and maintenance process must be managed?[1]

Let's break the document management problem into three areas (1) **process**: specific functions that must occur in a specific order to complete a document; (2) **organization**: functional responsibilities of people and management structure; and (3) **system**: technicalities of the electronic publishing system(s).

In the rest of this chapter, we examine project standards, configuration management, collaborative work, and document imaging. Each of these topics relates in various ways to the process, organization, and system issues outlined above.

Project standards form a bridge between the elements that make up a document and the capabilities of a publishing system. Project standards can also help clarify the publishing process. **Configuration management** defines the process used to create, maintain, and manage the documents. In addition, configuration management works within the bounds of the functional responsibilities of the people on the project. **Collaborative work** is the application of new technologies that help to integrate the work process of many people in a controlled manner. Finally, **document imaging** is a technological systems–oriented solution to problems with the management of existing document archives. Document imaging can help improve the management, use, and accessibility of these archives.

8 • 1 Project Standards

Establishing and using a set of project standards are the simplest things you can do to do improve the efficiency and quality of a project. An organization that produces documents that all follow consistent

1. See the paper "Towards Document Engineering" V. Quint, M. Nanard and J.André EP90 *Proceedings of the International Conference on Electronic Publishing, Document Manipulation & Typography*, Sept. 1990, Cambridge University Press, New York.

visual and structural conventions looks professional. Projects of any size, especially those that must be coordinated with a variety of departments and activities, can benefit from the use of project standards.

The term project standards, as used here, covers two areas: (1) those relating to the document themselves, such as layout and structural conventions and (2) those relating to the process of creating and producing the documents. The process–oriented aspects of project standards are closely related to configuration management, covered in the next section.

Let's examine the specifics of what a project standard is and how to establish the usage of the standard. Realize that simply defining a project standard will not necessarily cause it to be used. Several components are needed to make an effective set of project standards. These are:

- *The project standard definition document.*
- *An example that uses the standard.*
- *Templates or style files in one or several electronic publishing formats.*
- *Guidelines specific to the publishing system.*
- *Environmental specifications such as fonts, printers, and operating system services.*

Let's examine each of these components in turn.

DEFINITION DOCUMENT

The project standard definition document should be a reference manual in which users can quickly find answers to specific questions on formatting and style. It's desirable, if this manual is rarely used. Most of the time style files and the examples should be the main ways to use the standard.

EXAMPLES

Examples of the project standards should cover all the optional aspects of the design. For example, if either bullets or a bold font are acceptable for lists of information, present both alternatives. Along with the examples, there should be clear statements about recommended practices. For example, for software documentation, you may recommend that a brief description of each subroutine always precede the subroutine. These are not stylistic issues as much as issues relating to the actual content of your documents. Therefore, a separate "recommended practices" document may be necessary.

TEMPLATES OR STYLE FILES

Templates or style files allow users to "jump right in," creating documents that conform to the project standard. They are one of the simplest and most effective ways to improve the image of an organization's documents. A corporate look will give your project an aura of professionalism and make that first impression a good one.

Hire a graphic designer or consult your internal art department to design the look of reports, memos, and manuals. Don't assume you can do it alone. When a group of people work together, even loosely, it is possible to give an entire collection of documents visual coherence by using common styles. Common report covers and formats can, at the very least, give the impression that separately produced documents were coordinated and produced in a well–thought–out fashion, even if they weren't.

The templates are much more than a mere convenience to users, although convenience is an important factor in gaining use of the standard. Templates provide a convenient way of encapsulating the project standard. Just as important, they encourage the use of the standard. Of course, if you have the luxury of mandating the use of the project standard, encouraging usage is not an issue. However, management chains are often not straightforward, especially in large organizations.

One individual should maintain the template files. Many people may have opinions about the style of the document. However, if versions of the templates start to proliferate, the project standard can disintegrate. Again, these issues relate closely to the configuration management of the documents.

PUBLISHING SYSTEM–SPECIFIC GUIDELINES

Every document processing system has its own terminology and capabilities. The standardized usage of these capabilities will not necessarily translate well among various systems. Different systems may simply use different names for similar functionality. For example, WordPerfect styles are almost the same as FrameMaker tags. These systems provide different capabilities in the use of styles and tags, but the concept is fundamentally the same. Tags and styles are named, format–specific constructs. The consistent and meaningful use of names is important.

Meaningful names will help people who are unfamiliar with the particular document styles use those styles more quickly. For example, naming a particular font style "emphasis" rather than "zowie" will help the uninitiated. Personal, "cutesy" names quickly become tiresome and are usually only meaningful to the select few people familiar with your idiosyncrasies.

Meaningful names are appropriate for virtually anything that requires a name. Thoughtful naming can make files, paragraph styles and tags, user variables, font variations, and other items more intelligible.[2]

In addition to meaningful names, publishing systems often have other capabilities you may wish to use. You can develop a project–specific dictionary to ease spell checking. You can also create catalogs of styles and tags and make them centrally available. Specifying these items and providing easy access to them will make usage of these standard components convenient and prevent a proliferation of ad hoc solutions created by enterprising staff members. Again, these issues are part of an overall configuration management solution.

2. For an amusing and thoughtful article on naming conventions, see "Choosing a Name For Your Computer" D. Libes, *Communications of the ACM*, Nov. 1989.

ENVIRONMENTAL ISSUES

Finally, let's examine the environmental component of a project standard. Environmental components are the operating system resources, printers, and publishing system installation options that are specific to your computer.

Probably, you work on one particular computer and use one particular printer, operating system, and publishing system. Most complex publishing systems have a variety of installation options such as languages, dictionaries, fonts supported, and so on. Different sites—even those that use the same electronic publishing system—may have differences in operating environments. These differences can result in documents that are difficult to transfer from one site to another.

The environmental issues are insidious, because they are hidden from the user. Even experienced users are often not aware that these issues even exist.

The most common environmental differences are those concerning fonts. Don't assume that another location has all the fonts you are using. The project standard should specify the fonts, and you should make sure that all sites have access to the correct set of fonts. Printer description languages may be important if, for example, one site has all HP printers (PCL) and another site uses PostScript printers.

The five components of a project standard outlined above are not absolute requirements. Each project will have unique constraints and circumstances. You should view them as useful guidelines in the creation of your own project standards. Common sense is usually worth a shelf full of guidelines.

Along with the establishment of conventions for particular document processing systems, it is useful to establish procedures on how systems should be used. The process a document goes through is often as important as the content. Sign-offs, approvals, hand-offs, and so on are simply process conventions that clarify who is in control of what and when. Management must usually sign off and add feedback.

Clear procedures and identification of what exactly must and must not be approved form the basis of an effective configuration management capability.

8 • 2 Configuration Management

Command is getting people to go the way you want them to go—enthusiatically.
—General William Westmoreland

In engineering domains, a configuration is a particular arrangement of parts that reflect a real–world instance of a product. For example, one configuration is the particular choice of options and colors for a car. Version control, revision control, and change control are all names for activities closely related to configuration management. All these terms point to slightly different viewpoints of the way information is controlled, as well as changes over time. **Configuration Management** is a tool to manage a process for the creation of products—in this case, electronic documents.

The configured items that must be managed change over time. A configuration management system helps manage this change. Changes take place as a part is redesigned or a technical manual is revised for a new edition.

As projects grow more complex, formal configuration management will become necessary. Let's examine some of the basic functions that must be accomplished in creating a technical document. We will then look at how documents are managed during creation and what types of software can help coordinate and manage the process.

It is vital not to delude yourself into thinking that a configuration management system is going to solve your management problems. The system is only one portion of an overall solution. A clear set of organizational procedures and a clear understanding of exactly what needs to be configured are far more important parts of a managerial solution.

8 • 2 • 1 Configuration Items

The first thing to do when planning a configuration management system is to determine exactly what is to be configured. List these so–called configuration items and tailor them to your project. If you don't make this list, the various steps in the document development process will be a waste of time. The configuration items will be associated with products in the development process—master copy, working copy, and so on. [3]

Basic Configuration Management Files

In the article "Configuration Management: Getting the Facts Right," Michael Morris sketches out a succinct, albeit oversimplified, description of the types of information that need to be managed.

Master files: information sets that are retained for revision.

Working files: information sets released to people for the purpose of revising or modifying the information.

Released files: information sets that contain revisions and have been authorized for implementation.

Configuration files: information sets that reflect the current status of the real world.

Archive files: information sets that record the history of configuration changes. Archive files are not subject to revision.

These files represent five different perspectives on engineering documentation. The pilot of an airplane is interested primarily in the configuration file, which describes the plane to be flown that day. The pilot might also be interested in design changes on the drawing board that might make flying easier or safer, but they are not his primary concern. Tomorrow's changes have no effect on how that plane flies today. On the other hand, people in the maintenance section are interested in these released files, because they have to incorporate those changes when the plane comes to the hangar next week. Meanwhile, the lawyer is interested in the archive files describing a plane involved in an accident that occurred several years ago.

Configuration management becomes complicated when the individuals involved work with different systems. Authors in different organizations will often be working with different document processing systems. When their work must be integrated into a final report or other product, the complexities can become tremendous. Careful planning that identifies the configuration items, can prevent this problem. If you know ahead of time that two different

3. From "Configuration Management: Getting the Facts Right," Michael Morris, *Inform*, May 1991.

types of graphics must be integrated, you can plan reasonable methods to integrate the two in the final document.

In addition, make sure that the original graphics and diagrams are appropriately saved in the configuration management system for future modifications. Be sure to capture the original editable versions of illustrations, tables, and graphics. It is easy to lose the original *editable* versions of graphics and diagrams, especially when one organization produces the graphics and another integrates them into the final product.

8 • 2 • 2 Roles and Functions

During the creation, production, and publication of a document, one person may take on many roles. In larger organizations, separate individuals may perform these roles. In any case, it is important to delineate *who* is responsible for *what* and *when*. It is useful to clearly understand these roles and how a "configuration management system" can and cannot solve certain problems. Each person has a specific role.

The *author(s)* create the document content and collaborates with others.

The *editor* changes stylistic and grammatical aspects of the document, but not the content.

The *manager* approves the document, often making editorial changes.

The *producer* merges illustrations and text (cut and paste) to produce camera–ready output *or* electronic merging, assembly, and printing.

At each stage in the development of a document, a person performing a particular role must be in control of the current version of the document. When one person performs most of the roles, life is simple. However, in larger organizations and with complex documents, it is important to be clear about who owns a document and what precisely is the current document.

Document Management Cycle

A prototypical sequence in the creation, approval and production of a document. This sequence has many variations.

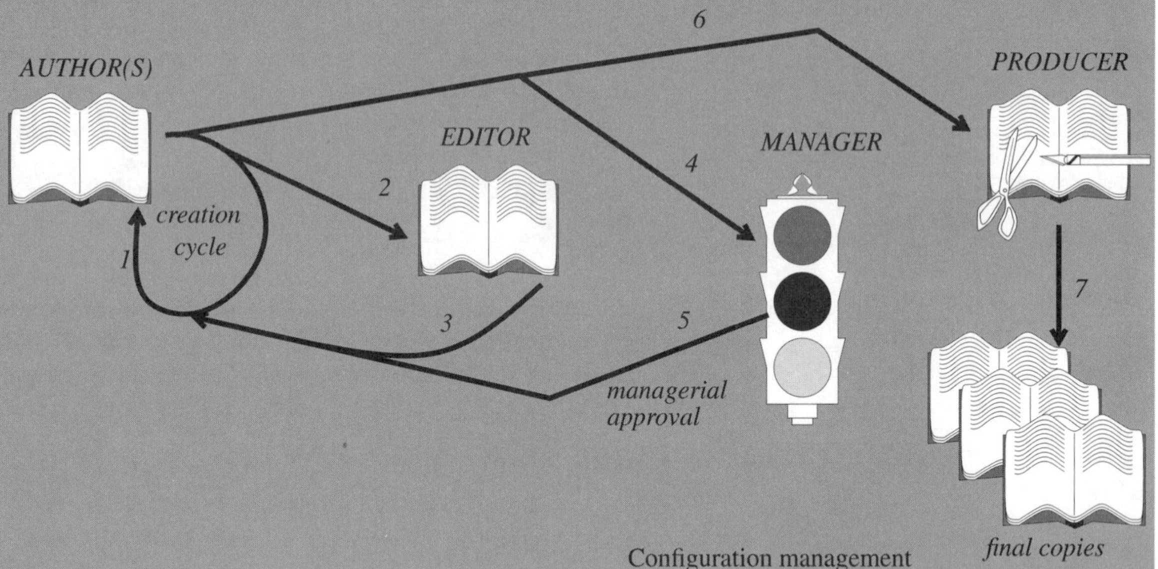

Sequence descriptions

1. The AUTHORS write and edit collaboratively, until draft is complete.
2. The EDITOR makes stylistic and grammatical changes.
3. The EDITOR's output is passed back to the AUTHORS for approval.
4. The AUTHORS send the document to the MANAGER for approval (or rejection).
5. The MANAGER approves/rejects and possibly comments, adding more changes to the document, and sends it back to AUTHORS.
6. The AUTHORS send document to the PRODUCER with illustrations, which may or may not be separate from the document.
7. The document is assembled for printing and binding.

Configuration management system activities at each step

1. Version numbers on files incremented and ownership passed back and forth between AUTHORS.
2. Files, including graphics and images, grouped for release to EDITOR and ownership changed. The group of files is the entire document.
3. Group marked as "Edited" and ownership changed.
4. Group sent as "Draft Author Approved" to MANAGER.
5. Group sent back to AUTHOR as "Draft Approved" or "Draft Disapproved."
6. Group sent to PRODUCER as "Management Approved."
7. Group sent to Archive as "Final" and published.

A configuration management system should help you manage and use the concepts of document ownership, signature authority, and security. In addition, the system should allow the grouping of files into a unit (often, a release of some sort) assigned a name or status such as DRAFT or RELEASE 7.

The configuration management system itself is primarily a management tool. It helps manage the complexity and coordination of many people working with shared information.

Now that we have identified the items to configure and understand the flow of these items through the organization, let's examine some software issues in configuration management.

8 • 2 • 3 Configuration Software

A wide variety of configuration management software systems are available. Similarly, a wide variety of document processing systems are available. Systems that integrate the two are not nearly as common. The ones that do exist are expensive, high-end "solutions."[4]

The range of configuration management systems is analogous to the range of electronic publishing systems. Publishing systems run the spectrum from batch–language–oriented to WYSIWYG. Similarly, configuration management systems run the spectrum from suites of utilities to complete systems. Suites of utilities are functional. Some examples are those using the UNIX configuration control utilities Revision Control System (RCS) or Source Code Control System (SCCS), intended for source code control. These systems will require more of your technical staff's time to tailor them for document processing.

Databases can be used to add configuration management functionality to your document processing system. Information about what task is being performed and who is in control of the documents, along with status information, can be used to monitor the progress of the document's production. A database

4. Xyvision's Parlance Document Manager (617) 245-4100 is a $100,000 to $300,000 system that integrates document processing and configuration management. A fully configured version of Interleaf Publisher also integrates these capabilities.

can add the additional functionality missing from a document processing system for configuration purposes. Security, shared access, and traceability are some of the capabilities that you can add by integrating a database with your publishing practices.

The integration of a database with the publishing system does not have to be a technical challenge. A perfectly reasonable solution is to assign a secretary or other staff member the responsibility of updating information in the database. You must also establish proper management practices to ensure that information about the changing document status is passed along promptly. Clear, reasonable organizational practices are much more important than the features of any particular configuration management system.

Let's turn our attention to those aspects of the document processing system that can be used to help the configuration management process. Invariably, publishing systems have a variety of features that can be used for configuration management, even if they were not intended for such use.

TYPOGRAPHIC AIDS

All electronic publishing systems allow a variety of typographic controls. Strikeouts, underline, overline, outlines, shadows, font changes, and change bars can all indicate visually the changes to a document. Online reviews can use color as effective feedback. Before you select a particular convention, be sure that all members of the work group can use the particular visual cue. It is useful to establish a few guidelines and perhaps a key to identify the sources of the comments and the markup. Keep in mind that the purpose of a visual markup system is to allow traceability on the printed page.

Decide on what you want to indicate with the visual changes. Two possibilities are (1) to indicate who is making a commentary on the document and (2) to indicate a change in the document's content on a version by version basis. When too many fonts and strikeouts are used, the page quickly becomes unreadable. The following figure is functional but ugly. A mechanism for rebaselining and cleaning up the document should be part of the configuration process.

Here are three sets of hypothetical comments, by three reviewers of an essay.

Key to Comments

Comment by Sabulosus

Comment by Joesuphus

Comment note by Taxinius

Mirum est ut animus agitatione motuque corporis excitetut. Iam undique silvae et solitudo ipsumque illud silentium quod venationi datur magna cogitationis incitamenta sunt. Proinde cum venabere, licebit, auctore me, ut panarium et laguncularn sic etiam pugillares feras. Experieris non Dianam magis montibus quam Minervam inerare. Vale.

This paragraph is the biggest bunch of crap!!

Ad retia sedebam: erat in proximo non venabulum aut lancea, sed stilus et pugilares: meditabar aliquid enotabamque, ut, si manus vacuas, plenas tamen ceras reportarem. Non est quod contemnas hoc studendi genus.

Meditabar aliquid enotabamque, ut, si manus vacuas, plenas tamen ceras reportarem. Non est quod ~~contemnas~~ contemponisti hoc studendi genus.

Ad retia sedebam: erat in proximo non venabulum aut lancea, sed stilus et pugilares; meditabar aliquid enotabamque, plenas tamen ceras reportarem.

Ridebis: ~~Mirum est ut animus agitatione motuque corporis excitetut. Iam undique silvae et solitudo ipsumque illud silentium quod venationi datur magna cogitationis incitamenta sunt. Proinde cum venabere, licebit, auctore me, ut panarium et laguncularn sic etiam pugillares feras.~~ Mirum est ut animus agitatione motuque corporis excitetut. Iam undique silvae et solitudo ipsumque illud silentium quod venationi datur magna cogitationis incitamenta sunt. Proinde cum venabere, licebit, auctore me, ut panarium et lagunculam sic etiam pugillares feras. **Non est quod contemnas hoc studendi**

The more capabilities a document processing system has, the more possibilities there are for various types of visual indications. Don't take this too far, however. A document with half a dozen types of markup will probably be unreadable. The purpose of a visual indication of change is to give the reader an easy way to review the changes.

Simple Visual Indicators

The following text from a reference document about LISTSERV illustrates effective and simple conventions.

```
         Conventions
      The following typographical conventions have been made in this
  document to improve its readability:

 | Recent changes in the publication are indicated by a vertical bar in
 | the left margin.

 !     Intermediate changes between two releases of the document
 ! ("Prereleases") are flagged with an exclamation point in the left
 ! margin. Features described in this fashion should be considered as
 ! not documented and not officially supported until the exclamation
 ! point is removed.

 >     Temporary restrictions or circumventions are marked with a
 > "greater than" sign in the left margin. This sign may also be used to
 > signal obsolete features for which support will be dropped in the next
 > release.

      >>>>>>>>>>>>>>>>>>>>>>>>>>>>>>>>>>>>>>>>>>>>>>>>>>>>>>>>>>>>>>>>
  >
         This manual duplicates some parts of the Revised LISTSERV:
  User's Guide (Document Number U01-001) for easier reference. Those
  excerpts are delimited by runs of ">>>" and "<<<" signs.
      <<<<<<<<<<<<<<<<<<<<<<<<<<<<<<<<<<<<<<<<<<<<<<<<<<<<<<<<<<<<<<<<
 + <
 +
 +     Paragraphs marked with a '+' sign in the left margin contain
  detailed explanations for experienced users and can be skipped at
  first reading.
```

From "Revised LISTSERV: File Server Functions, " Eric Thomas, <ERIC@FRECP11.BITNET> Ecole Centrale de Paris, 1987.

The field of on-line review and commentary is also gaining momentum. Products such as Lotus Notes and Adobe's Acrobat let groups mark up documents for review. The Computer Aided Logistics Support (CALS) program industry support group and the Institute of Electrical and Electronics Engineers (IEEE) have committees looking into electronic review of standards and specifications.

One interesting line of research in the area of on-line commentary and annotations has drawn inspiration from 15th–century glossed bibles. The visual principles used in these works have provided fertile ground for research in hypertext and computer–supported cooperative work.[5] Just as monks over the centuries made comments upon biblical passages, your boss can make comments on your work.

Groupware, the coordinated work of many individuals, has been heralded as the next computer revolution. (See *Section 8 • 3 Groupware* in this chapter for more information on Groupware.)

5. The user interface of the *prep* editor created by a group of researchers at Carnegie–Mellon University was designed by Todd Cavalier, a graphic designer, and was based on 15th–century illustrated manuscripts.

Learning from the Past

This illustration of the experimental system PREP for collaborative work highlights the value of knowledge from noncomputer fields of study. The layout and commentary systems used in glosses are the inspiration for modern-day collaborative workstation software. See color plate 8 for a sample page from an original glossed bible.

Plan (representation of intent) — *Content (the focus of discussion)* — *Comments (different users opinions)*

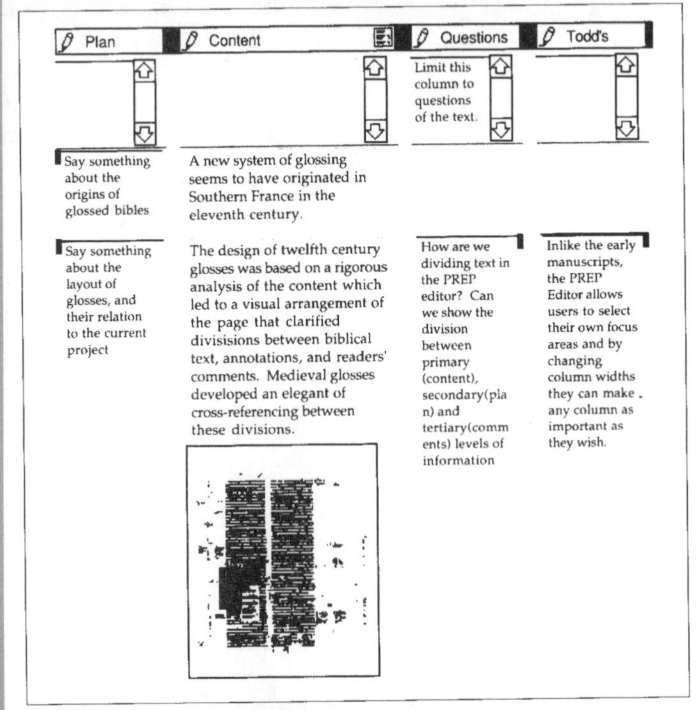

Columns that visually connect three types of information.

Reprinted from Graphic design for a collaborative workstation: columns for commenting and annotation by Todd Cavalier and Ravinder Chandhok, *Information Design Journal* 6/3, 1991. Reprinted with permission.

Research systems such as PREP (see previous illustration) and commercial products such as Rapport, Lotus Notes, BBN's Slate, and Instant Update are pointing the way into this largely uncharted territory. (Please see *section Groupware* in the *appendix Resources*.)

PAGE NUMBERING

Another low-tech configuration management device is the page number. If you produce a large set of documents that change periodically, you certainly don't want to republish everything just because of a change in page numbers. Two common techniques to avoid this problem are to use chapter-page numbering and point pages.

Point pages are simply inserted pages. For example, page 23.1 might be a new page inserted between pages 23 and 24. This technique does not require any reprinting of pages, and the reader may simply insert the page where it belongs. Once a year or so, the point pages are consolidated into "real" pages, and the document is republished.

Chapter-page numbering sequentially numbers all pages within one chapter. For example, page 4-23 refers to page 23 of chapter 4. This numbering scheme can also be used for figures and tables. New pages simply force the republication of individual chapters (or sections), rather than the entire document.

USER–DEFINED ATTRIBUTES

Some electronic publishing systems allow the user to define an attribute and associate that attribute with portions of text. A good example of this is a capability called *conditional text* in the FrameMaker publishing system.

Conditional text can be used to maintain different configurations of a document. For example, a TOP SECRET document can be maintained as both secret and public versions by marking all the secret portions with a tag `secret`. The secret sections can be hidden and printed out only when required. A single document is maintained that contains both versions.

FrameMaker's Conditional Text

Conditional text is text that can be selectively displayed or hidden. The following sample pages illustrate the three possible views of a document with two different conditional tags in a FrameMaker document.

Enjoying your new Loading the

DynaLoadster Sedan

Pickup Truck

Your *DynaLoadster* Sedan Pickup Truck is designed to carry passengers a payload anywhere you need to go. With 4-wheel drive, extra high clearance, and the new DynaPower 6-cylinder engine, you can take your passengers load past any obstacleCover your loadIt is against the law in many states to carry an uncovered load. Cover your load and secure it with *DynaLoadster* Tiedowns (optional).

Sedan and Pickup Truck conditional text shown.

Enjoying your new

DynaLoadster Sedan

Your *DynaLoadster* Sedan is designed to carry passengers anywhere you need to go. With 4-wheel drive, extra high clearance, and the new DynaPower 6-cylinder engine, you can take your passengers past any obstacle

Sedan text shown
Pickup Truck text hidden.

Loading the

DynaLoadster Pickup Truck

Your *DynaLoadster* Pickup Truck is designed to carry a payload anywhere you need to go. With 4-wheel drive, extra high clearance, and the new DynaPower 6-cylinder engine, you can take your load past any obstacleCover your loadIt is against the law in many states to carry an uncovered load. Cover your load and secure it with *DynaLoadster* Tiedowns (optional).

Sedan text hidden
Pickup Truck text shown.

Illustrations used with permission of Frame Technology Corporation.

The user–defined attributes can associate comments with specific individuals. Thus the attribute `Larry-Comments` can be used to identify Larry's comments. Depending on the system's capabilities, you may be able to print or view only the portions of the text associated with a particular attribute. This kind of usage leads naturally to groupware types of applications.

8 • 2 • 4 ISO 9000

One important set of international standards for quality assurance and management is called ISO 9000. As part of the ISO 9000 suite, document management is required.[6] It includes:

6. Much of the ISO 9000 material is borrowed from an excellent overview by Interleaf at: http://www.ileaf.com/isoguide.html.

- *A standard language for documenting quality practices.*
- *A system to track and manage evidence that these practices are instituted throughout the organization.*
- *A third-party auditing model to review, certify and maintain certification of organizations.*

Document management is critical to the successful completion of ISO 9000 certification. "Your organization shall control all your quality systems documents to assure availability of documented information to those who require it," states ISO Standard 9001.

The ISO 9000 quality assurance system includes 20 system elements documented in a pyramid of policies, procedures, and work instructions. Notice that many of these elements place requirements on a document management system. From the QBS Web site[7]:

The 20 ISO 9000 Quality Assurance System Elements

An ISO 9000 compliant quality assurance system includes up to 20 system elements documented in a pyramid of inter-connected policies, procedures and work instructions. Of the three system models (ISO 9001, 9002, and ISO 9003), ISO 9001 requires all 20 system elements. The following summary is condensed from the International Standard document ISO 9001, second edition, reference number ISO 9001:1994(E).

1. *Management responsibility:*

   to define, document, and implement a policy for quality.

2. *Quality system:*

   to establish, document, and maintain a quality system which includes a quality manual, system procedures, and quality planning.

3. *Contract review:*

   to establish and maintain documented procedures for contract review.

7. The ISO 9000 element descriptions are taken from Quality Business Systems (QBS), quality management consultants, Web site at: http://fox.nstn.ca/~qbs_ott/.

4. *Design control:*

   to establish and maintain documented procedures to control and verify the design of the product to ensure conformance to specified requirements.

5. *Document and data control:*

   to establish and maintain documented procedures to control all documents and data (including hard copy and electronic media), including such documents as standards and customer drawings.

6. *Purchasing:*

   to establish and maintain documented procedures to ensure that purchased product, associated documents, and data conform to requirements. Sub-contractors are to be evaluated and selected on their ability to meet subcontract requirements and the type and extent of control exercised by the supplier over sub-contractors is to be defined.

7. *Control of customer-supplied product*

   to establish and maintain documented procedures for the control of verification, storage and maintenance of customer-supplied product provided for incorporation into the supplies or for related activities.

8. *Product identification and traceability:*

   where appropriate, to establish and maintain documented procedures for identifying the product from receipt and during all stages of production, delivery and installation.

9. *Process control:*

   to identify and plan the production, installation and servicing processes which directly affect quality, and to ensure these processes are carried out under controlled conditions.

10. *Inspection and testing:*

    to establish and maintain documented procedures for inspection and testing activities to in order to verify that the specified requirements for the product are met.

11. *Control of inspection, measuring and test equipment:*

    to establish and maintain documented procedures to control, calibrate and maintain inspection, measuring and test equipment (including test software) used by the supplier to demonstrate the conformance of product to the specified requirements.

12. *Inspection and test status:*

    the inspection and test status of product shall be identified and maintained throughout the production, installation and servicing of the product to ensure that only product that has passed the required inspections and tests (or released under an authorized concession) is dispatched, used or installed.

13. *Control of non-conforming product:*

    to establish and maintain documented procedures to ensure that product that does not conform to specified requirements is prevented from un-intended use or installation.

14. *Corrective and preventive action:*

    to establish and maintain documented procedures for implementing corrective action in the handling of customer complaints, product non-conformities, and the application of controls to ensure corrective action is taken and that it is effective. Preventive action procedures will detect, analyze, and eliminate potential causes of non-conformities.

15. *Handling, storage, packaging, preservation and delivery:*

    to establish and maintain documented procedures to prevent damage or deterioration of product.

16. *Control of quality records:*

    to establish and maintain documented procedures for identification, collection, indexing, access, filing, storage, maintenance and disposition of quality records. Quality records shall be maintained to demonstrate conformance to specified requirements and the effective operation of the quality system.

17. *Internal quality audits:*

    to establish and maintain documented procedures for planning and implementing internal quality audits to verify whether quality activities and related results comply with planned arrangements and to determine the effectiveness of the quality system.

18. *Training:*

    to establish and maintain documented procedures for identifying training needs and provide for the training of all personnel performing activities affecting quality. Appropriate records of training shall be maintained.

19. *Servicing:*

    where servicing is a specified requirement, to establish and maintain documented procedures for performing, verifying and reporting that the servicing meets the specified requirements.

20. *Statistical techniques:*

    the supplier identify the need for statistical techniques required for establishing, controlling and verifying process capability and product characteristics, and shall establish and maintain documented procedures to implement and control their application.

The ISO 9000 documentation pyramid

The 20 quality assurance elements, or fewer elements in the case of ISO 9002 and ISO 9003, are incorporated in an interconnected documentation pyramid. The documents are indexed so that changes at one level do not require changes at a higher level, but may require changes at a lower level.

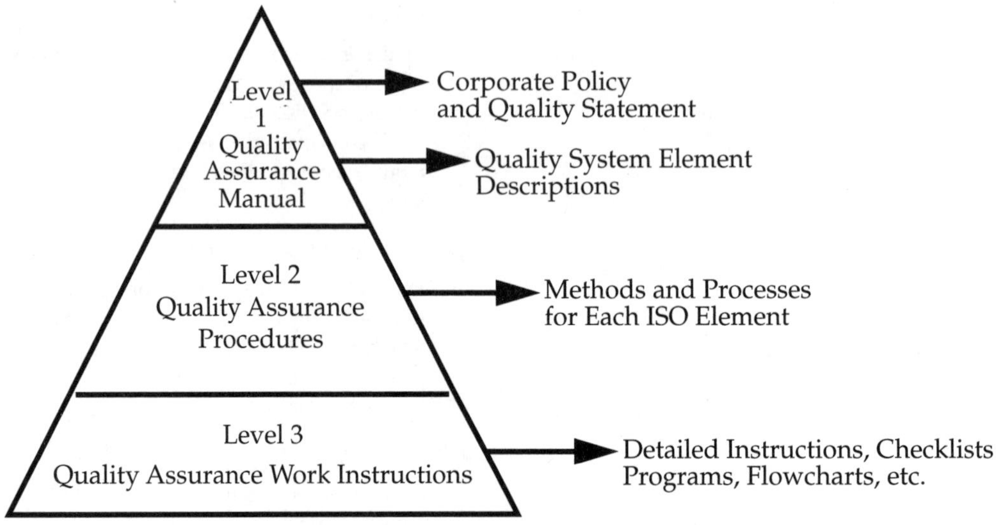

ISO 9000 Documentation Pyramid

Level 1: the quality manual and quality system elements

At the top of the pyramid is the quality assurance manual, which contains the corporate policy and statement on quality. Also included are brief statements describing how each of the applicable system elements are implemented in accordance with the company quality policy. The primary function of the 40–to–50 page quality manual is to succinctly define the company's quality assurance system to employees, management, and the ISO 9000 Registrar. It also acts as an excellent sales tool. The quality manual can be included with responses to proposals and other sales initiatives. It clearly confirms to prospective clients that they will be dealing with a quality organization that can provide goods or services in conformance with the clients' requirements.

Level 2: quality assurance procedures

The second level of the documentation pyramid contains quality assurance procedures that describe how, when, and where the quality system element activities are conducted, along with who is responsible for conducting them. Typically, each procedure is a few pages long.

Level 3: quality assurance work instructions

The third documentation level includes the detailed instructions for the performance of the work done by the company or organization. The work instructions include design specifications, drawings, service instructions, operating procedures, process sheets, etc.

8 • 3 Groupware

"I'm not good in groups. It's difficult to work in a group when you're omnipotent."
- Q, Star Trek

Groupware,[8] the software that assists in the collaboration of groups of people, is one of the latest application areas to get into the mainstream. It has been

8. For a good overview of how Groupware and the Internet are coming together, see the Dec. 1995, *BYTE* magazine, "Groupware the Internet" by Peter Jerram.

around, most notably with Lotus Notes for a while but the Web and ubiquitous access to the Internet is fueling its grown.

Clearly, the grand-daddy of groupware products is Lotus Notes. Notes, however, provides much more than is currently viable with the Web. Enterprises use Notes in secure environments to support business processes. Product development, sales, order processing, and technical support need the support of sophisticated work-flow software. Routing information through discrete phases and through a management chain is the key. Web/Notes interoperability is moving towards this end with the InterNotes product, which can publish a Notes database on the Web.

"Groupware Grows Up," the cover story of the March 4, 1996 issue of *Information Week*,[9] points out that Lotus Notes is not the only game in town any more. Products from Netscape, Microsoft, Novell, and Hewlett-Packard all address this growing market. In addition the links between collaborative work products and the Internet are getting stronger.

Microsoft is going after Lotus Notes with its Exchange product. Clearly, Exchange is not as robust as the time–tested Notes. However it does have clear advantages in its integration with Microsoft Office. Most significantly, the Notes server can run on several types of platforms, whereas the Exchange server is tightly bound to Windows NT. "Exchange Versus Notes" by Sean Gallagher also in the March 4, 1996 issue of *Information Week* does a thorough comparison of the two.

Netscape's acquisition of Collabra Software with CollabraShare conferencing software gives Netscape a running start in this frenzied market. Collabra Share lets you organize information into a set of "forums." In each forum, groups can discuss relevant topics. Information discussed in the topics can later be retrieved via a search engine, and related topics can be linked. An important feature is the flexibility

9. Article by Stephanie Stahl and John Swenson. More groupware info available at: http://techweb.cmp.com/iw/center/default.html.

of forum management. The forums can allow anonymous input and moderated information and can be used for brainstorming or customer support.

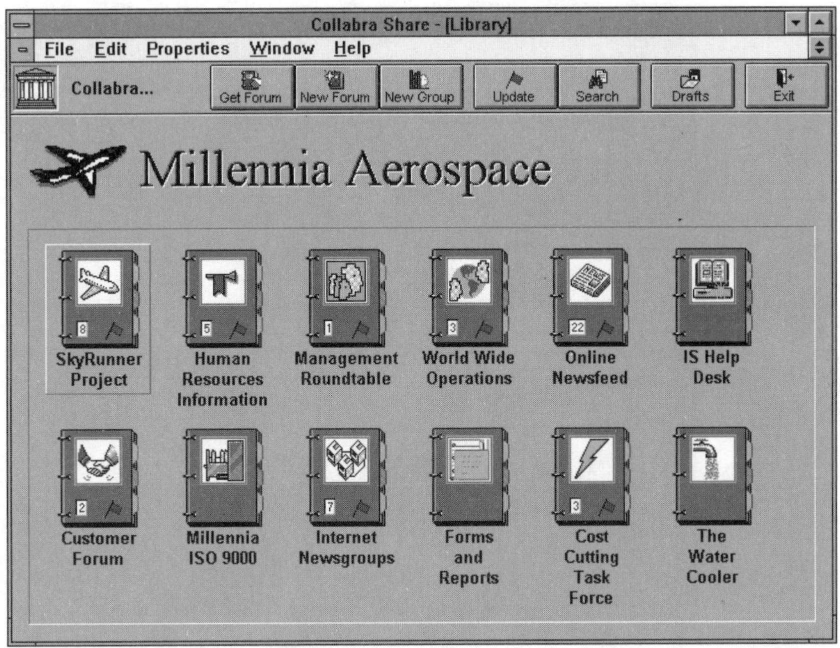

Collabra Share's presentation of "forums" for collaborative discussions

DEC is also entering this market with the Workgroup Web product. It, too, allows for on-line conferencing. It also provides tools for reaching consensus and decision making, such as a real-time polling feature to give a group instant voting results. It works with many existing Web browsers and servers. An interesting development feature is the Software Development Kit (SDK), which is based on the Tcl scripting language (widely used in the UNIX and X windows world).

A new product called CoolTalk by InSoft is being bundled with the new Netscape Navigator (version 3) called Atlas. CoolTalk is a suite of utilities for collaborative computing. It contains a real–time audio facility like the various Internet phone programs.

More significantly, it includes a whiteboard so people can draw on a shared surface and see what each other is doing.

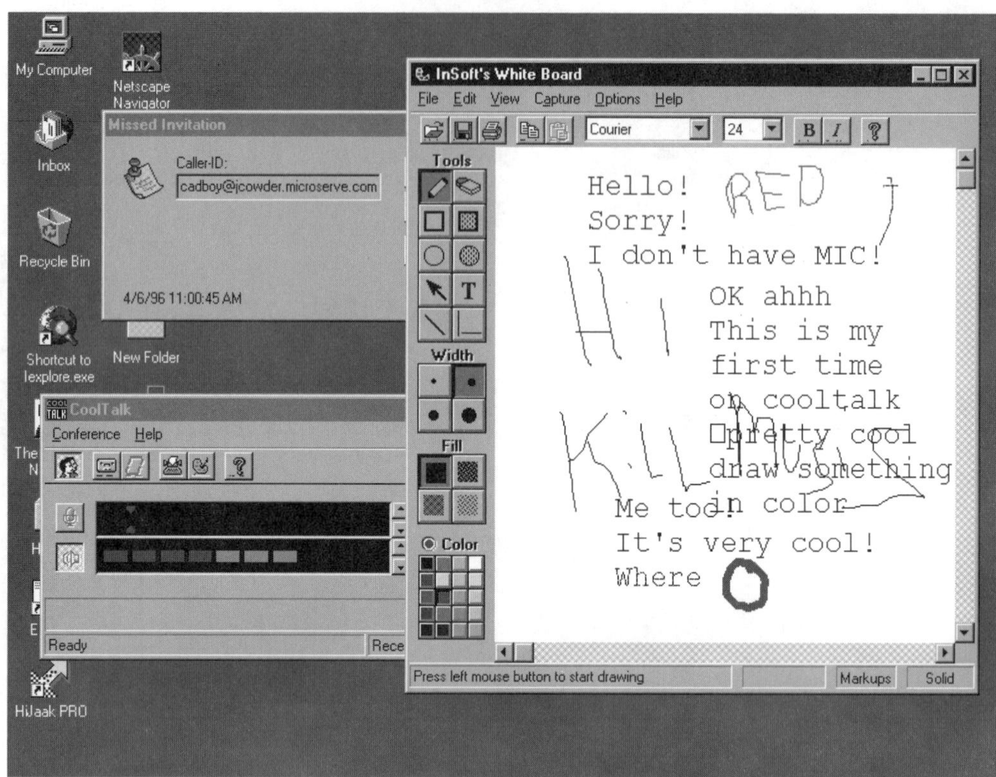

CoolTalk utilities, audio tool, and shared white board

The ability to communicate using audio and shared data spaces like a white board should improve communications among geographically–dispersed groups. The amazing part is that this all functions on a PC! Only a few short years ago, these capabilities cost many thousands of dollars, and you had to have a high-end workstation.

8 • 4 Intranets

Intranets, an internal Internet Web of documents and information restricted to employees of an organization, are becoming a major tool for enterprises. More than one in five large corporations now run Intranets, according to Forrester Research, Inc., in Cambridge, Mass.[10]

Security concerns are a key motivation for the creation of an Intranet. Simply put, the Internet is not very secure and probably won't be for some time. A security infrastructure is slowly being deployed however, vendors and users alike are not used to authentication, single-use password, and encryption as a normal part of doing business on the Internet. Security concerns aside, Intranets are an effective and relatively simple mechanism to improve communications within an enterprise.

According to a Feb. 26, 1996 *Business Week* cover story, "Here comes the Intranet," some example of Intranets in use are:

- *Kiosks at Compaq Computer Corp. where employees can check on benefits, savings and 401(k) plans.*
- *DreamWorks SKG (the new Spielberg, Katzenberg and Geffen studio) has Netscape browsers on all desktops so production managers and artists can check on the daily status of projects and coordinate scenes.*
- *Ford Motor Co., where an Intranet links design centers in Asia, Europe and the U.S., and engineers collaborated on the design of the 1996 Taurus.*
- *FedEx, learning from its highly successful public Web, (which is estimated to save $2 million a year) has 60 intranets created by and for employees. They are equipping all 30,000 office employees with Web browsers to provide access to the slew of news sites.*
- *Silicon Graphics, with an Intranet called "Silicon Junction," allows employees to access more than two dozen corporate databases.*

Netscape's Web site has an extensive set of "company profiles" and demos that highlighting "Intranets in Action." Their impressive list of companies using Intranets includes: 3M, Allen-Bradley, AT&T, Electronic Arts, Eli Lilly, Genentech, McDonnell Douglas, Mobil, National Semiconductor, and more.

10. From "Your Worst Nightmare," *Information Week*, Feb. 19, 1996 by Bob Violino.

The explosion of Intranets will cause a corresponding explosion for Web server software. Zona Research estimates that by 1998 revenue for Web server software, the backbone of any Intranet, will be at $8 billion compared with $2 billion for Internets.

Many companies already have the infrastructure necessary for Intranets. A Local Area Network (LAN), a Web server with browsers for the desktop, and a firewall to keep people out are the core elements of an Intranet. The Web, which has already provided a unifying view of the Internet, can provide the same service to an enterprise.

Most organizations have jumbled collections of information technologies serving different functions. Payroll, accounting, engineering, purchasing, employee benefits, travel expenses, and so on can often be found to function on separate, so–called "islands of automation." The Web presents a unique opportunity to unify these systems into an apparently single system. Unification of these systems is not simple, but a path now exists, an architecture of sorts, which, if followed, can give users better more timely access to company–wide data, improving communications on the way.

8 • 5 Document Imaging

People are turning to document imaging in an effort to manage the mountains of paper generated every day in this age of the so-called paperless office. In part, document imaging can be viewed as paper management in electronic form. Properly used, however, document imaging can become much more than electronic paper. Electronic documents created from document images can be indexed, searched, and accessed in a variety of ways to make their information more useful and valuable.

One particularly interesting document imaging software system is Adobe's Acrobat Capture. Its idea is to scan documents and have them converted into PDF (Adobe Acrobat format) files. Of course, document imaging systems can rarely recognize all the text and convert it to computer text, so Acrobat takes an interesting approach. Basically it punts and if the system can't figure out what a character is, it replaces it with the image of the character. Using this approach, the document will keep the correct look, although, of course, there may be problems with searches. It's a clever trade-off

Before you embark on an imaging conversion project it would be useful to consider the following questions:

- *Did you determine what you intended to do with the images?* Your use of the documents will affect the storage and processing of the images.
- *Do the images meet all your legal requirements?* Some industries require documents that are valid from a legal standpoint. Documents may sometimes be required as evidence, and electronic documents may not be valid.[11]
- *Does your organization have the infrastructure to support the new types of skilled staff needed to work with the new system?* Your existing staff may need more technical training. A training budget should be part of the project, and retraining should be part of the project plan and organizational goals.

To become involved in document imaging, you presumably already have a large collection of paper documents. These documents must be converted into electronic images in a process known as backfile conversion. According to one particularly practical article, this process involves the following five steps:[12]

Document Preparation—Organize and discard old documents.

Scanning—Purchase an appropriate scanner for your documents. Autofeed scanners are a myth; hands-on feeding is a reality.

11. Other than a lawyer, you can see "Legal Requirements for Microfilm, Computer and Optical Disk Records, Evidence, Regulation, Government and International Requirements," Donald S. Skupsky, J.D., CRM Information Requirements Clearinghouse, 3801 East Florida Ave., Suite 400, Denver, CO 80210. (303) 691-3600.

12. From "How to Successfully Convert Your Backfiles," Greg Bartels, in *Imaging*, May 1992.

Indexing—Create all potential identifiers, using current technology such as autoindexing, OCR, and bar codes. Where possible, use existing databases to retrieve additional information, such as employee information from an ID.

Quality Assurance—Manage the process carefully; conversion is tedious and difficult. Get it right the first time, because reprocessing is expensive.

Image Integration—Your goal is a system to handle daily throughput. Service bureaus may be appropriate for the backfile work while you focus on the future system.

Scanning House Calls

Imagine the problems involved using a scanning service bureau when you've got a warehouse full of documents. What are you supposed to do? One enterprising company will park a "scanmobile" trailer at your doorstep with a complete mobile document conversion facility. This approach is also feasible for documents you want to keep secret.

As part of the document conversion process, paper documents are scanned, and images are converted into electronic files and kept in large electronic filing cabinets.[13] The document images may be recognized by optical character recognition (OCR) software and converted into computer interpretable text, which can be indexed and searched.

According to the news magazine *Imaging World*, "office workers spend 60% of the day dealing with paper documents and U.S. businesses continue to create over one billion pages of paper each day."[14] That's a lot of trees. The same article categorizes the imaging market into five components:

- *image input*
- *image storage*
- *image management and processing*
- *image communications*
- *image output and display*

Let's examine three aspects of these components. First, the OCR part of the input component; second, text retrieval, part of the management and processing component; finally, the media issues that are part of the storage component.

13. See "Who's Who in Service Bureaus, and How They Can Help," Peter Meade, *Imaging Magazine*, May 1992. International Imaging of Azusa, CA, operates the "scanmobile."

14. From "Imaging comes of age," Charles Pesko, *Imaging World* Feb., 1992.

8 • 5 • 1 OCR

> ***OCR via FAX***
>
> If you don't have the need or the money to purchase OCR software and hardware, you can use one service bureau's approach. Just FAX the document to them and they will, in a few hours, send you back a word processing file, via modem.

Paper documents consisting mainly of text represent a document conversion opportunity. It would be nice to get that text into your computer in a manipulable form such as ASCII text.[15] The two ways to do this are to retype the information or to use OCR (Optical Character Recognition). Retyping is not as absurd as it may seem at first glance. Scores of "offshore" workers provide inexpensive labor and a number of companies provide this service. (see *section Appendix A • Resources* in the *appendix Resources* for more information.) You can imagine that proof reading the material is excruciating. Nevertheless, rekeying is a cost–effective option.

The more civilized approach, OCR, has come a long way. Software and hardware packages are now available for all classes of computer equipment, from PCs to workstations. Recognition systems can interpret a wide variety of fonts. The accuracy of some systems can be improved by training them to recognize particular fonts and the specific characteristics of the documents.

15. The OCR via FAX service is offered by ViaPhone of Albany NY at (800) 321-7466. See "OCR for Rent" in the March 1992, *Imaging* magazine for more information.

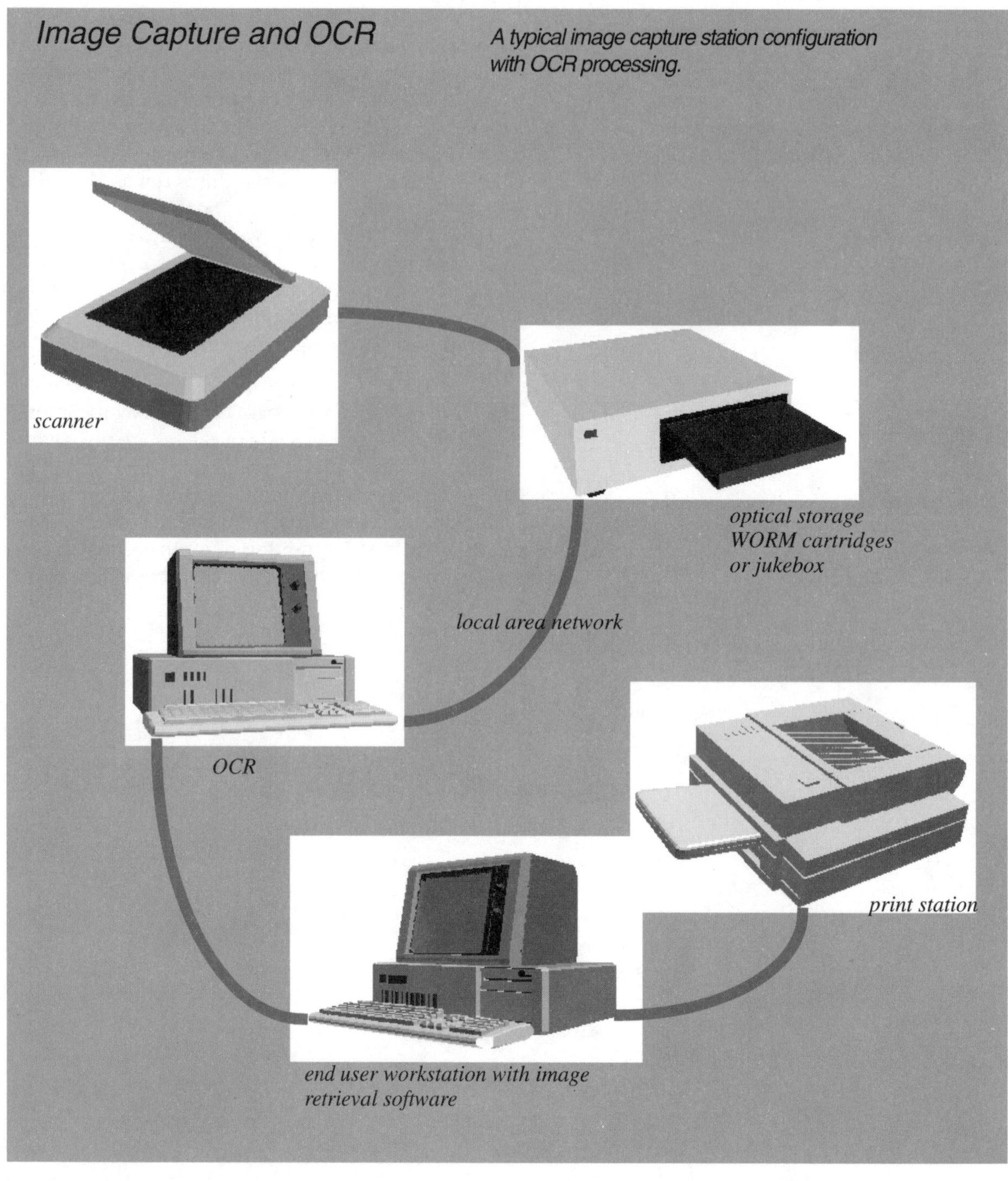
Image Capture and OCR
A typical image capture station configuration with OCR processing.
scanner
optical storage
WORM cartridges
or jukebox
local area network
OCR
print station
end user workstation with image
retrieval software

8 • 5 • 2 Text Retrieval

A basic reason to convert paper documents into electronic files is to improve access to the information. After a set of documents has been scanned and the text recognized and converted into ASCII, what's next? Indexing and the creation of a full–text retrieval database is one possibility.

What is a full–text database, and how is one used? As the name implies, a full–text database allows you to search the entire text of a document. Every word is indexed for rapid retrieval. Often, the index takes up as much space as the text. Storage media like CD-ROMs with over 600Mb of available space are perfect for these types of databases. However this involves the classic trade-off between speed and space.

To build a full–text database, you go through the following steps:

1. *Assemble all text into a common area, such as a single directory.*
2. *Identify and possibly mark up, in any required format, the headings, sections, and subsections that provide a hierarchical structure to the document. (Typically, this is used for the user interface of the text retrieval engine.)*
3. *Identify the "kill list" words you do not wish to search, such as "the," "and," and so on.*
4. *Run the database builder software to create the indexes and generate the user interface for the particular set of data.*

In a typical case, the textual information that originated with a set of documents is processed by the database builder software to produce a searchable database. A user interface or run-time system—as opposed to the builder system—is used to search through the text in a variety of ways. The searching flexibility is an important characteristic of full–text retrieval systems. (Please see *section Text Retrieval* in the *appendix Resources* for some references to these products.)

Textual searching can take many forms. The complexity of searching can range from a simple word search to boolean queries with proximity distance and regular expressions. OK, I'll explain that obnoxious jargon.

A **boolean query** (or search) is something like the following:

```
Find all occurrences of the words
"your mother wears" AND
("army boots" OR "high heel shoes")
```

The query above would find the phrases:

```
"your mother wears army boots"
```

```
"your mother wears high heel shoes, what a
fashion statement"
```

The query would not find:

```
"your mother wears some funky army boots"
```

A proximity search is a way of specifying words that you want to locate that are not necessarily next to each other. They would have to be within some specified distance of each other. Distance is described as a stated number of words.

Regular expressions are a formal way of using a pattern to represent many letters. You are probably already familiar with the concept of *wild carding* for file names. For example, in DOS, when you ask to list all files names that start with the letter F, you type the command:

```
dir F*
```

The * is a simple "regular expression" that means match 0 or more of any character. More complex regular expressions are commonly used in the UNIX operating system and as a way to specify text for retrieval and editing.

These types of searches were previously used only by techno-geeks. Now however with the advent of the Web doing them is becoming a more important skill. Many of the Internet Starting point services, such as Yahoo and Open Text, can take advantage of more complex queries, helping you to find what you're after faster.

8 • 5 • 3 Storage Media

In any discussion of document imaging, we must also talk about mass storage. The images captured by scanners take a lot of space. Currently, the preferred media is the optical disk. The advent of economical, high–capacity optical disks was one of the critical technological advances that enabled the imaging industry to become a reality. The main technology used in the imaging domain is called WORM for Write Once Read Many. WORM disks can store from 1.2 to 10 gigabytes of data on a single cartridge. The write–once limitation may actually be an advantage. The data are physically impossible to erase, an advantage for most imaging applications with an archival function.

The other optical technologies, MO or Magneto Optical and CD-ROM, are not appropriate for document imaging applications, but the prices are always going down, so check the costs. MO disks allow reading and writing many times, but they are probably too expensive for the high data volumes needed. This may change in the future. CD-ROMs require a factory to master and replicate the information. But CD-ROMs are *the* media of choice for the distribution of many copies of large volumes of information. Actually, desktop CD-ROM production is now a reality, and low–volume production is practical.

Significant imaging applications often require terabytes of on-line storage. The cost–effective solution for keeping all this information accessible is to use optical jukeboxes. Just like the old Wurlitzer in the corner diner, the optical jukebox contains a set of cartridges. They are swapped, one at a time, into the drive. A wide variety of jukeboxes are available. They range in size from a toaster to a refrigerator. Some jukeboxes hold WORM cartridges, some hold MO (rewritable), and some contain both types. Jukebox capacities are largely dependent on the number of cartridges they can hold—from 10 to 2000. The storage capacities can go as high as 12 terabytes for a single jukebox. A jukebox this large is larger than desktop size, however.

> ***Aperture Cards***
>
> An aperture card is a wonderful jury-rigged solution to the management of engineering drawings. It looks like a punch card with a big square hole in the middle. In the hole is a microfilm transparency of the drawing. The cards have a numeric code that allows crude searching and cataloging. Organizations such as the military have millions of these cards, requiring warehouses for storage. This is the reason for digitizing the images for optical disk storage and easier access. Using this process, the data do not turn yellow and deteriorate over time.

Let's also remember the wonderful world of micrographics. COM (Computer Output Microform) systems are still alive and kicking. Even today, images can be stored in a cost–effective way using microfilm, microfiche, and the ever–popular aperture card. Microfilm is accepted throughout the world as a legal archival copy.

Access to images stored in these analog media is labor intensive and basically awkward. You can't even do simple text searches. Digital information will be able to take advantage of new storage technologies. You can't shrink microfilm images, but as digital storage technology improves, more and more information can be packed into less and less space. Witness the new development in next generation CD-ROMs. (See *Section 7 • 4 • 1 CD-ROM* in *Chapter 7 • Applying Standards* for more information on DVDs.) Some far-out technologies mentioned in the press are digital paper and holographic memory, with storage capacity several orders of magnitude greater than existing optical media.

The capabilities of document imaging systems are constantly expanding. Coupled with the improvements in text retrieval and networks, it seem likely that imaging systems present us with an important opportunity—to add value to the information.

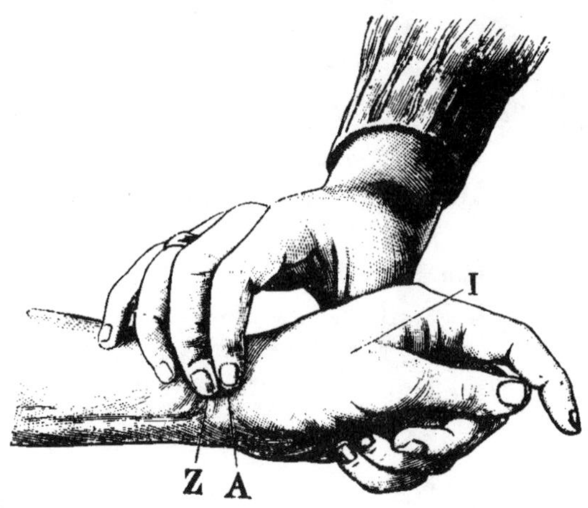

Chapter 9 • Case Studies

"Few things are harder to put up with than the annoyance of a good example."
—Mark Twain

In this chapter we will take a brief look at a number of real life projects. Each project has its own idiosyncrasies and unique constraints, but so do all publishing efforts. These case studies shed some light on the actual experiences of completed projects. These are not toy projects but full–fledged productions with real–world deadlines and problems.

The initial information on many of these projects was came from participants' answers to variations of the questions shown on the next page.

Case Study Questionnaire

Case Study Questionnaire

1.0 Background

Please give a brief statement of the background of the project.

2.0 Goals

What were the overall goals of the project?

Was there a specific design phase to the project and how was it conducted?

Was distribution of your material an important consideration and if so how did you address this concern?

3.0 Systems Used

What types of hardware were used to implement the system(s)? Web server?

What types of software were used in the system(s)?

4.0 Standards

Were any project wide standards used?

If any formal or defacto document standards were used what is your opinion of them?

5.0 Web Issues

What type of Web server do you use?

What is your business model?

How do you deal with issues of scale?

Do you use a Web crawler or other automated means to gather your information?

6.0 Unique Circumstances

Were there any unique circumstances involved with the project?

7.0 Management

What type of management structure was used to initiate, implement and maintain the project?

8.0 Staffing

What was the staffing level?

9.0 Work Flow

Was there a typical work flow involved in the preparation of material, if so please describe.

10.0 Resources

Was this a self supporting project? If not what types of resources were used?

11.0 Other Constraints

Were there any specific constraints which impacted the project, such as time, money, skill or other limitations?

12.0 Lessons Learned

What lessons did you learn and what advice can you give to people desiring to do similar efforts?

What was unexpected during the creation process?

13.0 Other Comments

In some cases, the information came from e-mail conversations, published documents, Web sites, the Internet, or other mass–media sources.

In each case study, quotes are in indented paragraphs and editorial comments [like this comment] are placed in brackets. For example,

> The end result of the project was totally mind blowing. It will revolutionize [in the project manager's opinion] the chicken farming business making it one of the growth industries of the 90's.

In several cases I simply paraphrased the material from acknowledged sources. In a few cases, I did some minor editing of quotes send in an informal style. In all cases, I did not change the meaning.

9 • 1 The CAJUN Project

SUMMARY

The CDROM Acrobat Journal Using Networks (CAJUN) project is an experiment in publishing journal articles using Acrobat. Dissemination of the resulting PDF files occurs via network and CD-ROM.

BACKGROUND

The CAJUN and it's follow–on, the CAJUN II projects, are efforts to move the publication of electronic journals toward a genuine technical and business reality. The project is a collaboration between the Electronic Publishing Research Group at the University of Nottingham in the United Kingdom and John Wiley & Sons, Ltd., the publishers. Initially the Wiley journal *Electronic Publishing—Origination, Dissemination and Design (EP-odd)* was the focus. A second journal, Chapman and Hall's *Optical and Quantum Electronics* (OQE) as a non-computer science journal, was also used for the project. The bulk of this case study comes from the paper *"Journal publishing with Acrobat: the CAJUN project"* by Philip N. Smith, David F. Brailsford, David R. Evans, Leon Harrison, Steve G. Probets and Peter E. Sutton, in the *Proceedings of Electronic Publishing 94*, Darmstadt Germany. The authors are all members of the Electronic Publishing Research Group at the University of Nottingham in the UK.

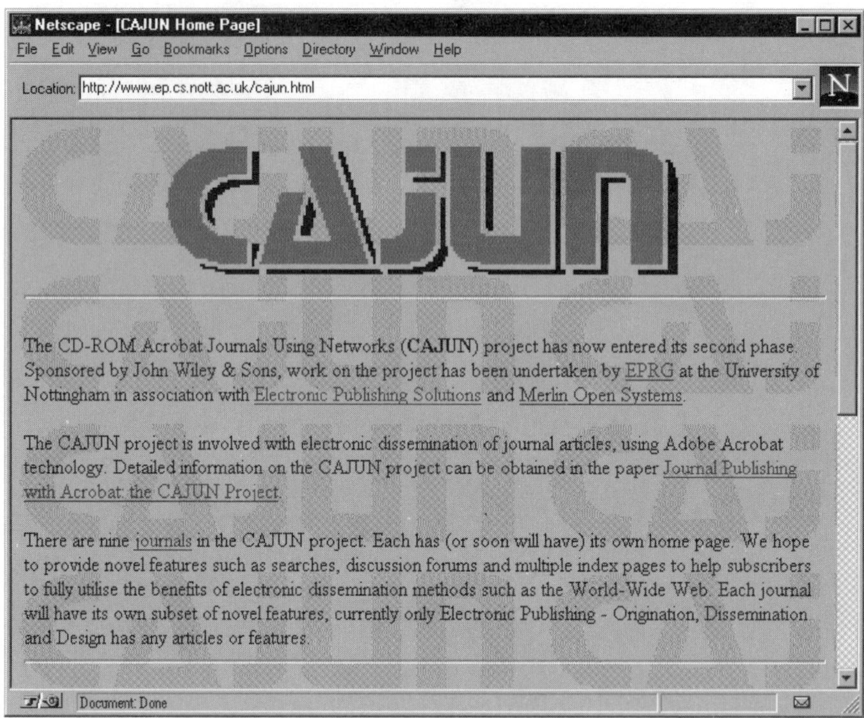

The CAJUN Project home page at the University of Nottingham

The CAJUN project has expanded to a set of nine journals. These can be found at: http://www.ep.cs.nott.ac.uk/wiley/journals/. Each journal has or soon will have its own home page:

- *Electronic Publishing - Origination, Dissemination and Design*
- *Software Practice and Experience*
- *Internetworking*
- *Software Testing Verification and Reliability*
- *Software Maintenance*
- *Visualisation and Computer and Animation*
- *Concurrency, Practice and Experience*
- *Software Process - Improvement and Practice*
- *Network Management*

ACROBAT

Acrobat was chosen for the project because it had the potential of being a flexible, platform-independent standard, documented in the public domain, rather than yet another proprietary system. The Acrobat publishing process is also capable of using existing PostScript documents. The following figure, redrawn from the previously cited paper illustrates the Acrobat publishing process:

The Acrobat publishing process

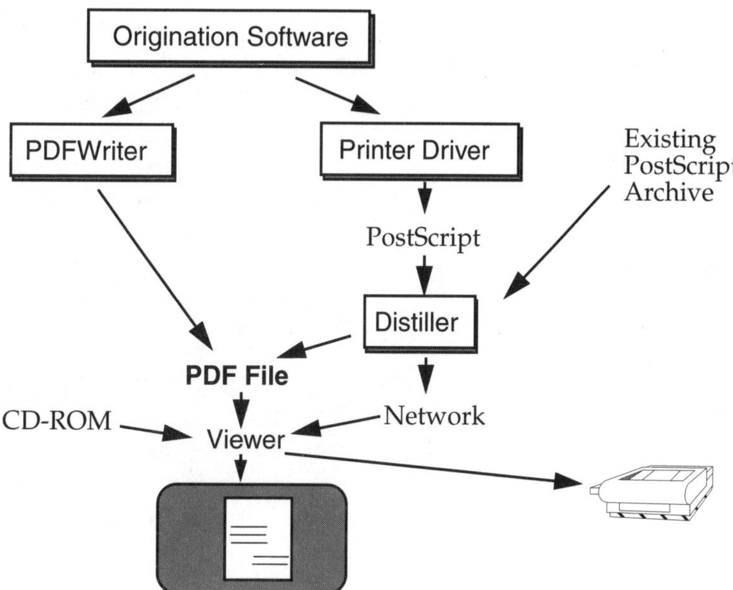

HYPERTEXT

Acrobat has the ability to support hypertext links. These links in the Acrobat viewer application are displayed as text; a black box is drawn around the text. This default display is ugly and clashes with surrounding text. The CAJUN team decided to add PostScript color to the linked text and effectively replace the default display. This was accomplished using the **`pdfmark`** PostScript operator, part of the PDF enhancements to PostScript. After beta–testing the displays, the CAJUN team decided on the following:

> Buttons for links should be displayed in dark blue rather than being enclosed in a box. The shade of blue chosen is easy to distinguish on screen yet is dark enough to print clearly on a 300-dpi monochrome printer. Users of monochrome screen displays, probably small in number, will find it hard to distinguish the coloured text, but will at least know that all textual references are linked up.
>
> Link destinations should bring up a view of the document with the target material positioned at the top of the screen. The view should be at the current magnification, as this is the most comfortable for the reader.
>
> PDF bookmarks should be provided for all section heading at all levels. The destination view, after following a bookmark, should be the same as for other links (i.e., beginning of section at top of page and current magnification).

One "principal aim of the project is to automate the process of generating pdfmarks from the troff or LaTeX source."

> The solution we have adopted involves delving into the output routines of TeX to intercept the page just before output. ...when version 2 of pdfmark becomes available, with an optional argument for 'source page number,' it will be possible to position all pdfmarks at the image of the PostScript file.
>
> Generation of pdfmarks for bookmark entries also requires extra processing in order to arrange them into a hierarchy reflecting that of the sections in the paper. This is also done with extra PostScript procedures defined in the prologue.

CONCLUSIONS

Clearly the CAJUN project has demonstrated the feasibility of automatically generating electronic documents that retain page fidelity. The process, however is not simple. It required experienced document processing professionals. It was research, however, the lessons learned will apply to a wide range of practical publishing problems. As Acrobat becomes more widely available and integrated with the Web, the procedures the CAJUN project has invented will become even more valuable.

9 • 2 Text Encoding Initiative

SUMMARY

The Text Encoding Initiative (TEI) illustrates how a large complex set of document specifications and standards were created for the humanities.

BACKGROUND

Most of the information about this project came from through publicly available information sources, particularly the TEI ListServer at the University of Illinois at Chicago. In addition, useful pointers and information were provided by Nancy Ide, a member of the TEI steering committee and organizer of the original planning conference, and Lou Burnard, one of the two editors of the guidelines.

> The Text Encoding Initiative (TEI) arose out of a planning conference convened by the Association for Computers and the Humanities (ACH) at Poughkeepsie, New York, in November 1987. It is an international research project, sponsored jointly by the ACH, the Association for Computational Linguistics (ACL), and the Association for Literary and Linguistic Computing (ALLC), with the further participation of several other organizations and learned societies.
>
> From this meeting there emerged there emerged a set of resolutions upon the necessity and feasibility of defining a set of guidelines to facilitate both the interchange of existing encoded texts and the creation of newly encoded texts. The resolutions stated that the guidelines would specify both what features should be encoded and also how they should be encoded, as well as suggesting ways of describing the resulting encoding scheme and its relationship with pre-existing schemes. Compatibility with existing schemes would be sought where possible, and in particular, ISO standard 8879, Standard Generalized Markup Language (SGML), would provide the basic syntax for the guidelines if feasible.
>
> After the Vassar meeting, ACH, the Association for Literary and Linguistic Computing (ALLC), and the Association for Computational Linguistics (ACL) joined as co-sponsors of the project and defined a four-year work plan to achieve the project's goals.

Funding for the works plan has since been provided by substantial grants from the American National Endowment for the Humanities and the European Economic Community.

GOALS

The goal of the TEI is to develop and disseminate a clearly defined format for the *interchange* of machine-readable texts among researchers, so as to allow easier and more efficient sharing of resources for textual computing and natural language processing. This interchange format is intended to specify *how* texts should be encoded or marked up so that they can be shared by different research projects for different purposes. The use of specific types of delimiters to distinguish markup from text, the use of specific delimiter characters, and the use of specific tags to express specific information, are all specified by this interchange format, which is closely based on the international standard ISO 8879, *Standard Generalized Markup Language* (SGML).

In addition, the TEI has taken on the task of making *recommendations* for the encoding of new texts using the interchange format. These recommendations give specific advice on *what* textual features to encode, when encoding texts from scratch, to help ensure that the text, once encoded, will be useful not only for the original encoder, but also for other researchers with other purposes. In these Guidelines, the requirements of the interchange format are expressed as imperatives; other recommendations, which are not binding for *TEI-conformant* texts, are marked as such by the use of such phrases as 'should' or 'where possible.'

The current Guidelines thus have two closely related goals: to define a format for text interchange and to recommend specific practices in the encoding of new texts. The format and recommendations may be used for interchange, for local processing of any texts, or for creation of new texts.[1]

Some of the design goals are that the guidelines should:[2]

1. From *Guidelines for the Encoding and Interchange of Machine-Readable Texts*, edited by C. M. Sperberg-McQueen and Lou Burnard. Document Number TEI P1. Draft Version 1.1, Oct. 1990.

1) suffice to represent the textual features needed for research

2) be simple, clear, and concrete

3) be easy for researchers to use without special-purpose software

4) allow the rigorous definition and efficient processing of texts

5) provide for user-defined extensions

6) conform to existing and emergent standards

PROJECT ORGANIZATION

The TEI is a project of significant size and scope, so it requires a formal structure. The project has three organizational units: a Steering Committee, an Advisory Board, and Working Committees.

A six–member steering committee with two representatives from each of the three sponsoring organizations guides the project.

The advisory board includes representatives from the American Anthropological Association, American Historical Association, American Philological Association, American Society for Information Science, Association for Computing Machinery-SIG for Information Retrieval, Association for Documentary Editing, Association for History and Computing, Association Internationale Bible et Informatique, Canadian Linguistic Association, Dictionary Society of North America, Electronic Publishing SIG, International Federation of Library Associations and Institutions, Linguistic Society of America, and Modern Language Association. The advisory board will be asked to endorse the guidelines when they are completed.

Two editors coordinate the work of the project's four Working Committees.

Committee 1: Text Documentation

Committee 2: Text Representation

Committee 3: Text Analysis and Interpretation

2. From TEI Listserver document "Basics of the TEI, part 1: design goals," by Michael Sperberg-McQueen, Aug. 1990.

Committee 4: Metalanguage and Syntax Issues

The organization and process that created the guidelines are similar to those for the development of national and international standards. The process is open; public comments are solicited and encouraged. The Guidelines emerge from a consensus reached in the Working Committees.

> From the outset, the TEI has sought to involve the community of potential users in shaping the content and format of the Guidelines. Before the final report is published, it is essential that diverse groups of scholars and others involved in the encoding of literary and linguistic materials be given the opportunity to test and comment on our proposals. This draft begins the first of what we know will be several cycles of recommendation, review, and revision.[3]

The Document Type Definition (DTD) development process was mostly accomplished by the two individual who are the editors of the Guidelines, C.M. Sperberg-McQueen and Lou Burnard. The TEI committees, in especially the Metalanguage Committee provided a great deal of support and help.

The tools to develop the DTDs were "Every SGML editor we could lay our hands on: specifically MarkIt, Author/Editor, Exoterica, and more recently VM2."[4]

RESOURCES

An initial four–year grant from the U.S. National Endowment for the Humanities, the European Economic Community, and the Andrew K. Mellon Foundation, got the project off the ground. The project is jointly sponsored by the ACH, ACL and ALLC (see *BACKGROUND* section). Substantial new funding was obtained for Phase 2 of the project.

PROJECT OUTPUTS

A significant draft of TEI Guidelines entitled *Guidelines for the Encoding and Interchange of Machine-Readable Texts* was published in 1990. The second version of the TEI Guidelines was published in mid-1992.

3. From the Preface of Draft Version 1.1 of TEI Guidelines.

4. Personal communication from Lou Burnard.

Given the works scope and scale, the second version (known as P2) was distributed as a series of parts. Each part is made available when completed through the usual distribution channels (for example, ListServer and direct requests to the project).

Version 3, (known as P2) is distributed on the TEI Web site at: http://www-tei.uic.edu:80/orgs/tei/. The guidelines are available in SGML or plain ASCII. In addition you can now purchase a CD-ROM of the guidelines which includes DynaText browsing software for the Mac and MS Windows PCs.

Along with the Guidelines, a series of DTDs was produced. These DTDs are as follows:

`TEI.1` - The main DTD, which:

> ...defines some useful entities, then defines the element TEI.1 and includes files with various specialized parts of the document type definition.
>
> `TEIhdr1 - Header for TEI documents`
>
> A TEI header comprises a file description, a set of encoding declarations, and a revision history (change log).
>
> `TEI.wsd - Header for TEI writing system declaration`
>
> A TEI writing system declaration documents the character set being used in a document, whether for local work or for interchange.
>
> `TEIbase1 - Basic structure for conventional prose.`
>
> TEIfron - Element declarations for front matter.
>
> Front matter comprises a title page and a series of other front-matter elements. Generic "front.part" tags may be used for other pieces which occur in a given text; they can occur before or between any others.
>
> TEI.1 - Main document type declaration file.
>
> Definitions for phrase-level elements
>
> `TEIcrys1 - Declarations for paragraph-level crystals.`

Citations, Structured Citations, Lists of Citations occur between or within paragraphs.

`TEIling1 - Declarations for linguistic analysis.`

`TEIrend1 - Declarations for typographic rendition.`

TEItc - Declarations for critical apparatus

`TEIdram1 - Basic structure for dramatic texts` (An alternate base DTD to be used in lieu of TEIbase1)

Several working papers are available. The Metalanguage Committee has a definition of "TEI conformance, " a topic of concern to potential developers of TEI-conformant software.

DISTRIBUTION MECHANISMS

The Guidelines were mailed to interested parties at no cost. An electronic mail also plays a major role in the dissemination of documents and timely information. The address of the listserver is: `listserv@UICVM.BITNET` or `listserv@uicvm.uic.edu`.

Send a mail message with the line GET TEI-L FILELIST to obtain a list of currently available information. (See *Section 7 • 4 • 4 Electronic Mail* in *Chapter 7 • Applying Standards* for more information on listservers.)

The Guidelines and the DTDs that have been completed are available to the public via this listserver.

Meetings take place approximately twice a year, to coordinate participants activities. The meetings alternate between the United States and Europe.

MANAGING SCALE

Given the very large scale of the TEI Guidelines, tutorial and introductory material was needed. Two documents in particular define TEI subsets which aim to gently introduce users to the full TEI tag set. First a version called "Bare–Bones SGML" which is a skeletal but clean subset of the full TEI encoding scheme. Familiarity with this minimal tag set should lead to the second subset called "TEI Lite."

TEI Lite: An Introduction to Text Encoding for Interchange, by Lou Burnard and C.M. Sperberg-McQueen is a document (on the TEI Web site) describing a useful subset of TEI. It states:

> The present document describes a manageable selection from the extensive set of SGML elements and recommendations resulting from those design goals, which is called TEI Lite.
>
> In selecting from the several hundred SGML elements defined by the full TEI scheme, we have tried to identify a useful 'starter set', comprising the elements which almost every user should know about. Experience working with TEI Lite will be invaluable in understanding the full TEI DTD and in knowing which optional parts of the full DTD are necessary for work with particular types of text.

LESSONS LEARNED

Getting a large collection of researchers to agree on anything is a monumental task. While there may be disagreements on the content of the Guidelines, it is clear that very substantial progress has been made toward the goals initially set at the start of the project. SGML was used, as it should be, as an enabling technology. There was no reason to reinvent a markup scheme when a rich extensible one already existed. Furthermore, the TEI community was able to take advantage of commercially available tools. In fact, donation of SGML parsing tools by the SEMA Group and Software Exoterica significantly aided the development of the Guidelines.

CONCLUSIONS

To date, the TEI Guidelines are the most significant large–scale effort at developing a semantically meaningful tag set. The use of the tags is up to the users. The Guidelines are, in effect, an extension of markup technology. The meaningful use of these tags is not dictated by the tags. They enable meaningful analysis.

The project and its results should both serve as a models for other projects involved in aspects of text analysis. The open participatory methods used by the project, along with a number of key funded positions, enabled the project to produce real results in a reasonable time frame. The tags and DTDs form a good basis for discussing the issues of textual analyses.

9 • 3 SGML: The Standard and Handbook

SUMMARY

This case study is about the production of two intimately related documents. The first document is *SGML*, the ISO standard itself. The second document is *The SGML Handbook*, a book about the ISO standard.

BACKGROUND

The product of any standards–making activity is a document. Since SGML is a standard for the electronic publishing industry, it was only fitting (and elegant) that the ISO standard document be produced with the aid of SGML. *The SGML Handbook* (hereafter called the *Handbook*) is a book published six years after the ISO standard that contains the entire text of the SGML standard. The *Handbook*, presents the SGML standard in two complete ways: in its original order with annotations and in a logically structured overview. In addition it presents SGML with tutorial material explaining basic and advanced concepts.

THE STANDARD

SGML started out as an ANSI project called "Computer Languages for the Processing of Text" back in 1978. IBM's Charles Goldfarb made a presentation to the project committee, which eventually changed focus to the development of a language for the description, rather than processing, of text. The project was eventually taken over by the ISO committee TC97/SC18/WG8.

The technical development and evolution of SGML was the result of the work of many people. However, during the entire development cycle, Charles Goldfarb was the principal designer and editor. Coordination of the document was handled through conventional mailings of printed output, phone conversations, and working group meetings. The actual document processing system used for most of the process was IBM's Document Composition Facility (DCF), which used GML (Generic Markup Language), the predecessor to SGML. GML provided a head start in the development of SGML, but it was by no means the same thing. Toward the end of the development process, it was possible for a conversion program to translate GML into SGML.

Approximately one year before completion of the standard, Goldfarb went to the ISO Central Secretariat to clarify some language issues and formatting concerns. This meeting laid the groundwork for changing the way ISO does business. Goldfarb, Anders Berglund, of CERN, and Keith Brannon, of ISO, clearly demonstrated the true value of the SGML approach. They formatted the marked–up text of the standard in five different ways in a period of about 30 minutes without touching the contents. Today, ISO is committed to producing all its standards using SGML.

The famous proof-of-the-pudding SGML story goes roughly as follows: Goldfarb shipped the unformatted standard to Anders Berglund at ISO via a computer network (Internet). Three days later, Goldfarb boarded a plane to Geneva. Upon arriving at the Geneva Hilton, he was greeted with, "Oh, Dr. Goldfarb, there is a package here for you." It was the complete, SGML standard, formatted to ISO specifications.

THE HANDBOOK

Although the production of the SGML standard was an SGML first, many of the *Handbook's* formatting requirements were more demanding and interesting.

The SGML Handbook was published in 1990 by Oxford University Press. The books editing and formatting were done mainly by Yuri Rubinsky, the late president of SoftQuad Inc., a major SGML vendor. The *Handbook* is unusual in several ways. First and foremost, it contains the entire text of ISO 8879, the SGML standard.

Second, it contains a novel cross-referencing system, which consists of roughly 3000 visual "buttons" that look like **[128]** *410:17* and are quite effective. In the button illustrated here, the **[128]** refers to a syntax production (parts of the definition of the standard), the *410* is a page number, and the *17* is a line number of ISO text. ISO text is text that originated in the actual standard and is typographically distinct from the new material in the *Handbook.* The cross-referencing mechanism is made more usable by the book's physical construction, which includes two ribbon bookmarks. The original "syntax production with built in cross-reference" idea came from Harvey Bingham of Interleaf Corporation. David Slocombe of SoftQuad, Inc., improved it with formatting-for-readability of the syntax productions.

The integration of several ISO–owned texts with new material is unique. The SGML standard was originally tagged with SGML, and the same tagged text was imported into this book.

A new DTD for the book was developed that contained all the structure used by the standard and the new structure needed. The ISO text was not modified in any way, with the exception of the addition of the cross-reference buttons. Most of these buttons were generated automatically from the SGML markup; Yuri Rubinsky the editor, added the rest.

LEGAL ISSUES

Standards are explicit codifications of technology or a set of knowledge. They are written with precision and are generally difficult to read. The strict legalese in which they are written is necessary because standards can become legally binding. In addition, the standards-making process forces a certain structure and style upon the document. The *Handbook* is a reorganized version of SGML with readable explanations and commentary throughout. The primary contribution of this book is to make a difficult topic accessible.

The *Handbook* includes three sources of ISO–owned information, which are interwoven with new material.

1. The entire text of ISO 8879.

2. The 1988 amendment to ISO 8879.

3. The document "ISO/IEC/JTC1/SC18/WG8/N1035: Recommendations for a Possible Revision of ISO 8879."

From a legal point of view, the text of an ISO standard is copyrighted by ISO. The legal nature and use of standards require that ISO be protect its standards to ensure that no unauthorized changes of content or intent are introduced. ISO also must continue to obtain revenue from the sale of standards. Like all organizations it must have resources.

Two major legal issues were resolved to bring the book into existence. First ISO receives a significant royalty from *Handbook* sales. This seems reasonable; since the book contains the entire text and commentary, why would anyone buy a copy of the standard directly from ISO? Second, and technically much more interesting, is the use and formatting of the three ISO documents. ISO had to be convinced that the content of the standard was not going to be modified in any way when it appeared in the *Handbook*. Technically, this was accomplished by using the same SGML-marked-up electronic files used to create the standard.

The 1988 amendment to the standard, which contains a small number of replacement sections, and the recommended changes from the N1035 document, are used in the structured overview and annotations. Change bars indicate that the material came from the amendment or N1035, rather than the 1986 standard.

FROM STANDARD TO HANDBOOK

The standard and much of the *Handbook* were keyed in using IBM's DCF system. A program written by Wayne Wohler of IBM was used to convert the original GML documents into SGML documents.

The *Handbook* was actually produced by Yuri Rubinsky. Rubinsky was sent dictation tapes for much of the new material for the *Handbook*. These were transcribed into SoftQuad's Author/Editor (an SGML–sensitive word processor). The resulting files, a collection of the original ISO 8879 standard, the amendment and N1035, and the new material were merged. The merged files were validated both by Goldfarb, using a parser he wrote during the development of the SGML, and by SoftQuad's SGML parser. This ensured that the files were conformant to SGML.

The final formatted version of the *Handbook* was produced using SoftQuad's Publishing Software. The publishing software provides the connection between the structural representation captured in SGML and the visual representation of the document. In fact this software converts SGML markup into troff (See *Section 4 • 1 • 2 Language Characteristics* in *Chapter 4 • Form and Function of Document Processors* for more information on troff.)

CONCLUSIONS

The SGML Handbook sets a new standard for the publication of standards. One aspect of the *Handbook* is clear; it demonstrates the way all standards should be treated when printed. The re–publication of standards by knowledgeable participants should be encouraged by the standards–making organizations. ISO, Goldfarb, and Rubinsky all deserve congratulations for breaking new ground with publication of the *The SGML Handbook*.

9 • 4 Project Gutenberg

Now this is a project with a mission. Almost single–handedly, Michael Hart, an English professor at the University of Illinois campus in Urbana-Champaign (UIUC), has assembled and continues to assemble a collection of electronic texts for simple and wide distribution.

BACKGROUND

According to a an article about the project:[5]

In describing the genesis of Project Gutenberg, Mr. Hart waxes lyrical. It was 1971, he was a student at the University of Illinois, and through computer-operator friends, gained access to its mainframe from midnight to 8 a.m. 'The old computer rooms had an aura of mystery, church and magic,' he recalls. 'You were a computer god.' But what to do with all those millions of microseconds ticking away? Fishing around in his backpack, he found a copy of the Declaration of Independence, began typing, and Project Gutenberg was born.

GOALS

The purpose of Project Gutenberg is to encourage the creation and distribution of English language electronic texts. We prefer the texts to be made available in pure ASCII formats so they would be most easily converted to use in various hardware and software. A file of this nature will also be made available in various markup formats as it is used in various environments. However, we accept files in ANY format, and will do our best to provide them in all.

Our goal is to provide a collection of 10,000 of the most used books by the year 2000, and to reduce, and we do mean reduce, the effective costs to the user to a price of approximately one cent per book, plus the cost of media and of shipping and handling. Thus, we hope the entire cost of libraries of this nature will be about $100 plus the price of the disks and CDROMS and mailing.

This project makes use of a list server that is at `LISTSERV@UIUCVMD.BITNET`. (See *Section 7 • 4 • 4 Electronic Mail* in *Chapter 7 • Applying Standards* for more information on list servers.)

Of course, a number of Web sites now point to the texts, and several FTP sites make the texts available.[6]

5. See "Plug In, Sign On And Read Milton, An Electronic Classic," Ellen Graham, *Wall Street Journal*, Oct. 29, 1991.

6. Go to: http://www.vuw.ac.nz/non-local/gutenberg/obtaining.html for a list of sites with Gutenberg texts.

PROJECT ORGANIZATION

Project Gutenberg has evolved into a mini crusade. There is no real organization, just one determined individual leading the rest. When it comes to resources, most of the work has been done over the years by volunteers either typing or scanning the material. In some cases, Hart paid some people out of pocket. The equipment has been scrounged, and computer time has been borrowed from UIUC.

CONSTRAINTS

All text entered into the system must be free of copyright restrictions. This is a fairly stiff constraint; in fact, several almost–completed books had to be canceled due to copyright restrictions.

DOCUMENT PROCESSING AND WORK FLOW

In general, the flow of work consisted of finding the work, checking copyright, input via typing or scanning spell checking, proofing, and proofing again.

PROJECT OUTPUTS

A publicly accessible collection of copyright–free text. Some representative examples of the texts are:

- *Alice's Adventures in Wonderland* - Lewis Carroll
- *Through the Looking Glass* - Lewis Carroll
- *The World Factbook* 1990 - CIA
- *The Night Before Christmas (A Visit from St. Nicholas)* - Clement Clarke Moore
- The U.S. Constitution in troff format

DISTRIBUTION MECHANISMS

Project Gutenberg uses shareware and public domain distributions. Speeches also spread the word. Over the years the distribution has, along with the technology become more sophisticated. Walnut Creek CDROM, a CDROM publisher, sells a CD of all the Gutenberg texts. It's also updated twice a year. You can find them at: http://www.cdrom.com. Many texts are in scattered places on the Web. Simply use your favorite Internet search mechanism to find a few. You could start with the Walnut Creek FTP site, which has just about everything at: ftp://ftp.cdrom.com/pub/gutenberg/.

LESSONS LEARNED

> The world insists that you go slooooowly. The "NOT INVENTED HERE" syndrome is HUGE. Lots of people resist for other reasons.

One interesting lesson of this project is that sometimes persistence and missionary zeal do bring about converts. After 20 years of typing away in obscurity, Michael Hart's 15 minutes of fame came with a recent front page article in the *Wall Street Journal*. That article marked the first time the Internet appeared on the front page of a major national or international paper. His conviction that lots of text should be available free seems to be catching on. The press has had dozens of articles about the project. In fact an online file lists 125 articles.[7]

9 • 5 Oxford English Dictionary

The Oxford English Dictionary (OED) is *the* definitive English dictionary used by scholars and linguists. In 1989, the long-awaited Second Edition of the OED was completed. Production of the dictionary, which is a 20–volume set, is a monumental task. It is now available both in hard copy and in two electronic forms, a CD-ROM and as a manipulable database.

Most of the information for this case study comes from an interview with Frank Tompa, a professor at the University of Waterloo in Canada. Tompa is intimately familiar with the software used in the development of the Second Edition of the OED.

IN THE BEGINNING

Back in 1983, the folks at Oxford University Press (OUP), which owns the OED, put out a request for proposals to create the Second Edition of the OED. The goal of the New Oxford English Dictionary

7. Located at: ftp://ftp.cdrom.com/pub/gutenberg/articles/biblio.gut.

Project was to integrate and update the Oxford English Dictionary and Supplement. The Supplement was a four–volume set of new material. Printed and electronic forms of the dictionary were to be produced. The project was eventually broken out into three parts all coordinated by OUP: data capture, integration, and database management.

THE RAW MATERIAL

The entire project involved the manipulation of three sets of data: (1) the original 1st edition, (2) a supplement to the first edition, and (3) the new material that would form the changes for the second edition.

DATA CAPTURE

The initial task was to place the three sets of data into an electronic form. International Computaprint Corporation (ICC), a subsidiary of Reed International, won the contract for data capture. The entire text was keyed in, and the staff at OUP handled the editing, proofreading, and overall quality control. The keyboarding work took 18 months and more than 120 keyboarders. The proofreading effort was massive. The text was tagged with an ICC propriety procedural markup form, which contained a lot of information concerning the look and layout of the document.

DOCUMENT INTEGRATION

The second portion of the project was to take the three separate data sets and integrate them into a single document, the 2nd edition OED. This task was accomplished primarily through a significant donation of hardware, software, and people by IBM. Database tools and more than 20 people sorted, merged, and massaged the data into the final form of the Second Edition over a period of two to three years.

DATABASE MANAGEMENT

Until this point, the data capture and document integration parts of the project were concerned primarily with the production of a printed product, OED's 20 volumes. Database management consisted of turning the procedurally marked up text into a more maintainable descriptive and structurally marked–up database. The product of this phase was not simply a single product, but a set of data and tools with which to maintain and manage the data.

Staff members of the University of Waterloo were primarily responsible for the database management. Waterloo has a research staff devoted to text databases and a long history of research in this domain.

SOFTWARE TOOLS

The University of Waterloo staff created and used three software tools. These are PAT, a text–searching utility; LECTOR a text–display utility; and TTK, a translation utility.

In fact, during the project's first stage OUP used the PAT text–searching tool to help proofread the material. For example, readers could enter the correct abbreviation for obscure as *Obs.* and ensure that the abbreviation was spelled correctly throughout a section of text, clearly a tedious and error–prone task if conducted purely by eye.

TTK, the Transduction ToolKit utility, is a tool that allowed the staff at Waterloo and OUP to convert the procedural markup into a structural/descriptive markup. The structural/descriptive markup of the Second Edition is the source of the other electronic products.

Some view the text–manipulation tools as useful enough to sell. A small spin-off company has been created in Waterloo called the Open Text Corporation (OTC). You can purchase PAT, LECTOR, TTK, and the PAT text database management system from the OTC.[8]

BENEFITS

The staff at OUP maintain the database, and now they have the flexibility to check out and make changes to sections of the text. Simple and straightforward principles of good configuration management can now be applied to the dictionary. The

8. Open Text Corporation, Suite 550, 180 Kind St., South Waterloo, Ontario, N2J1P8. (519) 571-7111, Fax: (519) 571-9092, http://www.opentext.com.

dictionary is now manageable as a database. In the future, additional printed and electronic products can be easily derived from the data.

Currently, the OED is available in two electronic forms. The first, a CD-ROM with an MS WINDOWS front end, was created using the descriptive marked–up text as its source. Second the raw descriptive marked up text is available and is a widely used source of material for linguistic researchers and lexicographers.

A new product based on the database is, of course, a Web site. The site is under development at the time of writing, but you can visit and find out what's going on at http://www.oed.com. You will be able to subscribe to the OED, which will allow you to search for entries in the dictionary using sophisticated linguistic tools such as PAT.

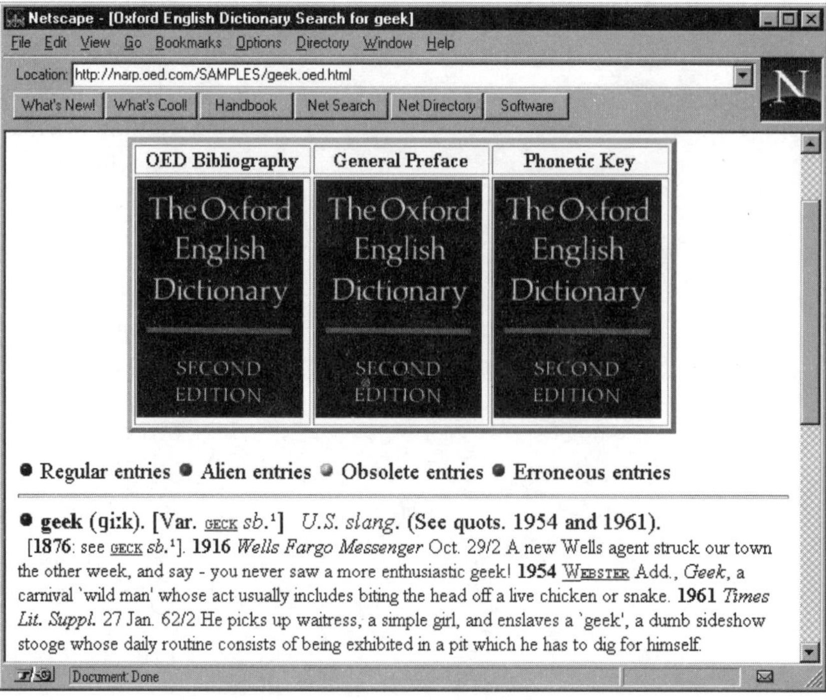

From the experimental Oxford English Dictionary server, under development.

LESSONS LEARNED

Clearly, Oxford University Press had the courage and foresight to take the plunge and convert a venerable product into an electronic form. Production of the Second Edition of the OED was a massive job, culminating in a 20–volume set containing 22,000 pages of material, and defining over a half million words. I would also bet that the CD-ROM version of the OED is a popular product and that the ease with which new products can be generated from a maintainable database will pay the investment many times. Access via the Web is the next logical extension of the electronic database and provides new business opportunities.

9 • 6 Voyager Expanded Books

BACKGROUND

The Voyager Company in Santa Monica, California has created a product line called *Expanded Books*. This effort is tightly coupled with the introduction, success, and "feel" of the Apple's laptop computer, the PowerBook. The material for this case study comes from the article "Books in a New Light" by Joe Matazzoni in the October 1992 issue of *Publish* magazine and from press release information provided by The Voyager Company. Although this was quite some time ago, Voyager remains the only producer of mass market electronic books.

THE FEEL OF A BOOK

> In the spring of 1991, Apple Computer sent The Voyager Company a prototype of its PowerBook portable computer, which completely changed the equation," says producer Michael Cohen. As Cohen remembers, someone "put a few pages of a favorite novel up on screen. As he passed it around, people were saying, 'Damn if that doesn't look kind of like a book.' Within an hour, the Expanded Books project was born.

Voyager, in the early years produced them at the rate of three per month. You really have to wonder why anyone want to read a book on a computer screen. Voyager folks say, "To be honest, we're not entirely sure yet."

> One reason is what he [Cohen] calls the "argument from gravity," He explains: If you travel with a PowerBook, "you can carry ten books with you as easily as one."

HYPERCARD FOUNDATION

The principal software technology used is Apple's HyperCard program. HyperCard presents the user with a "Card" that is on a stack. You can think of a stack of cards as a book. Paging from one card to another, by clicking with the mouse, is similar to flipping the pages of a book. The staff at Voyager has created an elegant user interface on top of the foundation HyperCard provided. Most of all, the page is simple. Unlike many other HyperCard stacks and hypertext programs, there are not a lot of cryptic looking symbols and buttons that often perform unexpected actions.

The book metaphor is maintained in several ways. You can dog-ear the page corners to mark a page and place electronic paper clips for fast access to specific pages. You can scribble (type) in the margins also, a valuable for writing your own commentary. A small palette of controls is clear and simple. It lets the user page forward and backward, search for entries, and retrace where in the books they have visited. Every single word can be selected. Selecting a word brings up a menu indicating whether you want to search for the next or all occurrences of that word.

TOOLKIT

> Voyager's Expanded Books are aimed at Apple's PowerBook but will work on any Macintosh with the all-purpose multimedia language HyperCard. ... As a page layout tool, though, HyperCard leaves a lot to be desired. For example, text doesn't flow from one card to another when you add or delete. And forget about more advanced functions like the ability to detect paragraph widows.

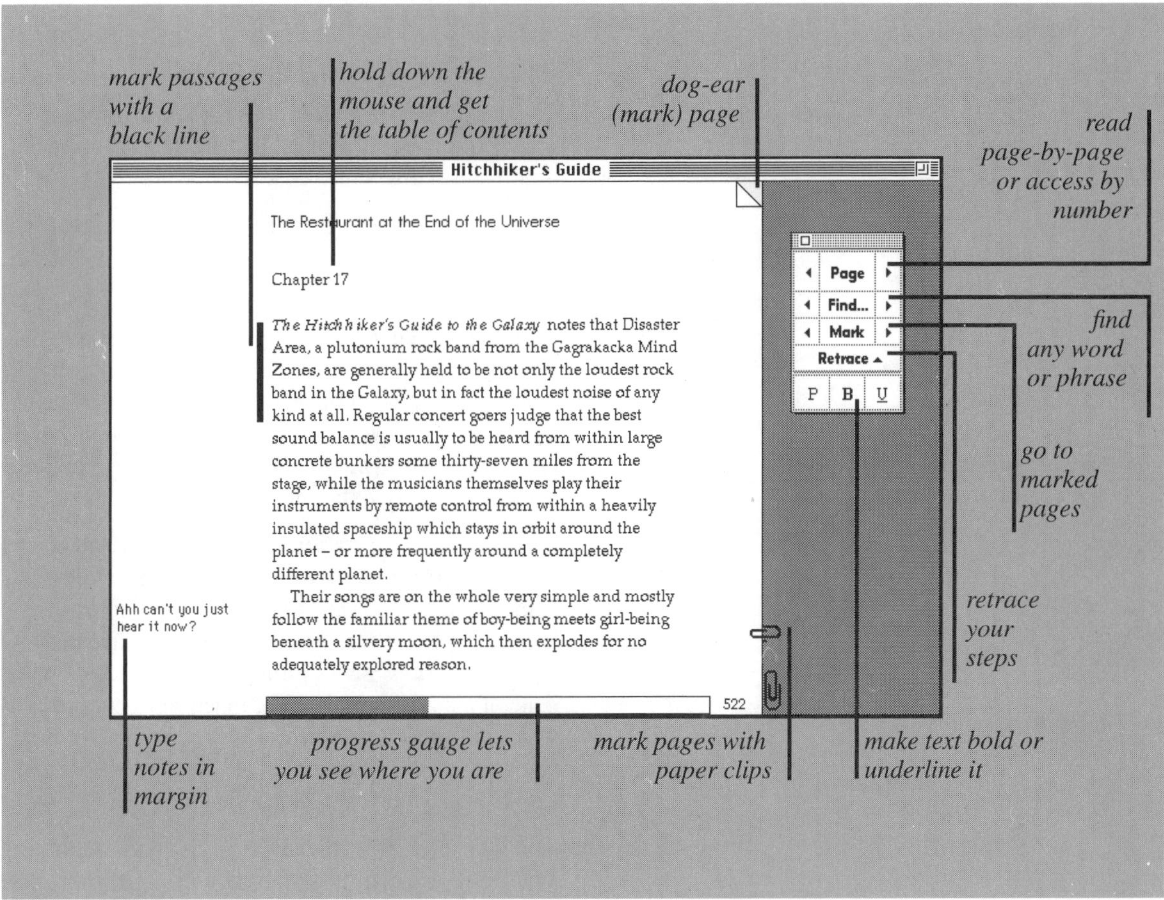
mark passages with a black line
hold down the mouse and get the table of contents
dog-ear (mark) page
read page-by-page or access by number
Hitchhiker's Guide
The Restaurant at the End of the Universe
Chapter 17
The Hitchhiker's Guide to the Galaxy notes that Disaster Area, a plutonium rock band from the Gagrakacka Mind Zones, are generally held to be not only the loudest rock band in the Galaxy, but in fact the loudest noise of any kind at all. Regular concert goers judge that the best sound balance is usually to be heard from within large concrete bunkers some thirty-seven miles from the stage, while the musicians themselves play their instruments by remote control from within a heavily insulated spaceship which stays in orbit around the planet – or more frequently around a completely different planet.
Their songs are on the whole very simple and mostly follow the familiar theme of boy-being meets girl-being beneath a silvery moon, which then explodes for no adequately explored reason.
Ahh can't you just hear it now?
522
Page
Find...
Mark
Retrace
P B U
find any word or phrase
go to marked pages
retrace your steps
type notes in margin
progress gauge lets you see where you are
mark pages with paper clips
make text bold or underline it

In true frontier fashion, the staff at The Voyager Company built what it couldn't buy. The designers created a HyperCard program called the Toolkit that provides text flow and widow detection as well as extensive features for building annotations and functions like printing a font report (useful if you must include fonts with your documents).

The Toolkit is available as a separate product. Clearly this company "does things right." The Toolkit can be used by organizations wishing to create their own Expanded Book series or, more importantly, as a relatively simple way to create on-line hypertext documents that will function on any Macintosh.

SELLING

The Expanded Book series is a business venture. Products must sell in order to continue.

> Voyager sells Expanded Books for about the same price as hardbound books. Most are $19.95, and a few multiple-titled volumes cost $24.95.

It is still an unknown if there is a real market or if these are just a novelty.

> Bob Stein, another Voyager partner, cites success of another type when evaluating the project to date. "I never thought it would get such broad acceptance among traditional publishers." he says. "A year ago, they didn't get it at all. Now every major publisher is either planning to publish something or has a high-level task force looking into it."
>
> Stein's biggest frustration is the lack of a retail channel for electronic books. Most of Voyager's sales come through the firm's mail-order catalog. A few bookstores in the Los Angeles area sell Expanded Books, but, says Stein, selling electronic books to the general public "doesn't make much sense until Apple wants to support their efforts with some kind of hardware in the bookstores or some sort of point-of-sale display— it could even be cardboard."

Clearly, however, the distribution aspects is picking up. It is not uncommon to see a rack of Voyager Expanded Books in a bookstore. You can also see sections of and purchase Expanded Books, at the Voyager Web site at: http://www.voyagerco.com.

THE DREADED LEGAL STUFF

> "Book publishing has a reputation for being conservative when it comes to new technology. But Voyager partner Jonathan Turrell says he had no problem negotiating Expanded Book deals with 'about a dozen' rights holders ranging 'from independent authors who hold one book to Random House and everything in between."
>
> The reason for his success, says Turrell, is that although the form his books take may be novel, the contracts he negotiates are not: "Basically, these deals look very familiar to people in the publishing indus-

> try. They're all royalty deals, so if they're successful, everyone shares in the success." Turrell says that publishers have been "very understanding about this being a beginning market" and have not demanded excessive advances. The royalties that Voyager pays, he says, are standard for the book industry.
>
> "It's wrong to think that this is such a departure for publisher," Turrell observes. "They've been fragmenting their rights for a long time. I also think the publishing industry believes that, at some point, electronic publishing is going to be real. Expanded Books give them an interesting way to explore that market."

CONCLUSIONS

The fortuitous match of the PowerBook with Expanded Books is a classic case of 1 + 1 = 3. The clean integration of software and a friendly portable computer is a winning system. The Voyager staff clearly recognizes the value of traditional paper books and is not out to replace them.

> "You'd be surprised at how many people assume that we are on a satanic mission to destroy the libraries and bookstores of the world." says Cohen [product producer Michael Cohen]. "In fact, we love books. This place is full of books. We're just trying to provide another way to enjoy them."

9 • 7 Books In Print

SUMMARY

The Books In Print (BIP) case study illustrates how one company, R. R. Bowker, has taken an existing print product and created a separate value–added electronic product.

BACKGROUND

When you're looking for a book one indispensable item is *Books in Print*. Produced by R.R. Bowker, it is present in every bookstore and library. Finding information in it, however, can be a problem if you don't know enough relevant items like the complete name of the author, book, or publisher. Obviously an on-line version is immensely useful. Reed Reference Electronic Publishing publishes a CDROM called *"Books In Print PLUS."* Thousands of independent book stores, small and large chains, including Barnes & Nobel and Borders use this CD-ROM, to locate and order books. Most of the information for this case study was provided by Skip Slawson of Reed Technology and Information Services Inc. (RTIS), and Marty Brooks of Reed Reference Publishing.

DATABASE

The BIP database contains 1.6 million entries of active titles, with another 700,000 inactive titles. There is also another 70,000 entries of publishers and a linked database of subject headings.

The database itself exists in a proprietary format called Bowker Power. The information is stored in a standard relational database. Information gets entered into the database via on–line keying, off-line keying and EDI transmissions from the publishers.

The paper book is created by processing the database via a proprietary composition program. After printing the pages are proofed.

CD-ROM PRODUCTION

The paper and CD-ROM versions of *Books In Print* are released monthly. Following is the description of the CD-ROM production process:

> The CD-ROM database is processed via a proprietary premastering and indexing program at RTIS-Online Computer Systems. Data is output at Bowker in "Bowker Power" format and sent to RTIS via overnight delivery. Records are built for the bibliographic data, the publisher data, and the full-text review data. Subject files are incorporated. Nineteen indexes are created. In addition, inventory data from Ingram is added. The result is mounted on a VAX computer and is checked by the staff. Each index is checked and statistics are compiled for the number of entries in each index and the total number of hits in each index and compared to the previous month. Then, Bowker staff compiles the final root directory software and sends it to RTIS via the Internet. They create a WORM, ship it

back to us at the same time they send a final tape to our disc pressing facility. We approve the WORM and release the tape for manufacture.

QUALITY CONTROL

Quality Control (QC) is an important part of any data processing operation, such as the production of this CD-ROM. Every stage has the potential for error. QC procedures are numerous and occur at all stages of data input and CD-ROM creation. As one example, when a new record is entered the ISBN (a unique book identification number) is checked against another database. If the ISBN does exists it is checked against the author/title information to see whether it is really the same record as an existing one or a new intellectual work with an incorrect ISBN number.

In addition there is a large staff of database editors who correct and update information. Reed receives tapes and EDI transmissions from publishers, usually on a monthly basis. Weekly data feeds also occur occasionally.

SOFTWARE

An experimental Windows version of the Books In Print CD-ROM product integrates the BIP software with the rest of the PC.

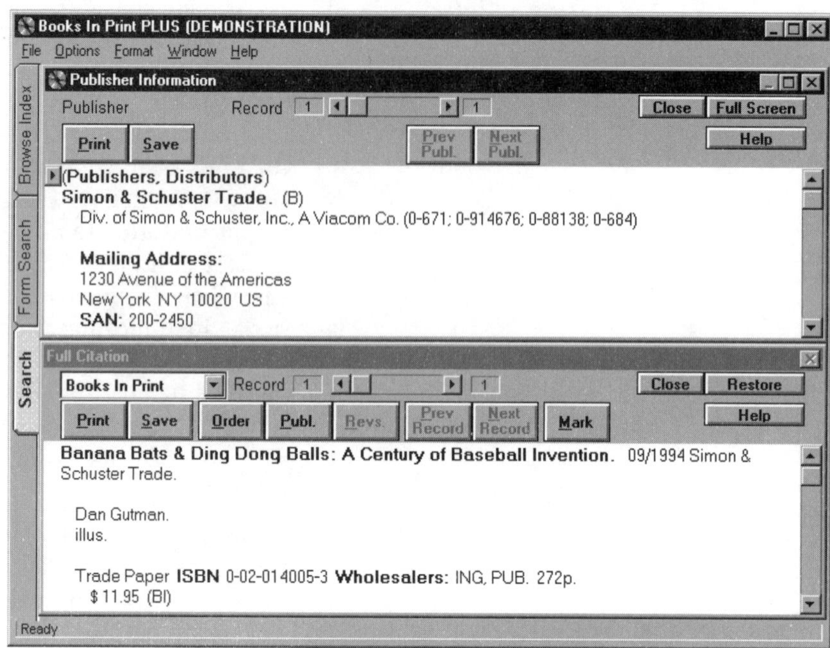

Books In Print PLUS information output.

PRICING

There are several variations of the product. Books In Print PLUS costs $1095 per year and is updated monthly. Books In Print with Book Reviews PLUS costs $1595 per year. The Book Review version of the CD-ROM contains brief reviews of many books. INGRAM-Books In Print PLUS has weekly updates. INGRAMs is a major supplier of books to bookstores. The CD-ROM contains information about inventory and warehouse locations. Ordering software is integrated with the CD-ROM in both versions.

THE WEB

Taking advantage of the value of their database Reed Publishing is starting to move their information to the Web. (Their Web site is at http://www.reedref.com.) Currently they have available for free the Books Out of Print database. At some time in 1996 the Books In Print database will be available, for a fee, on the Web. In addition the Web site will be available in certain situations on booksellers own Web sites, although with restricted information.

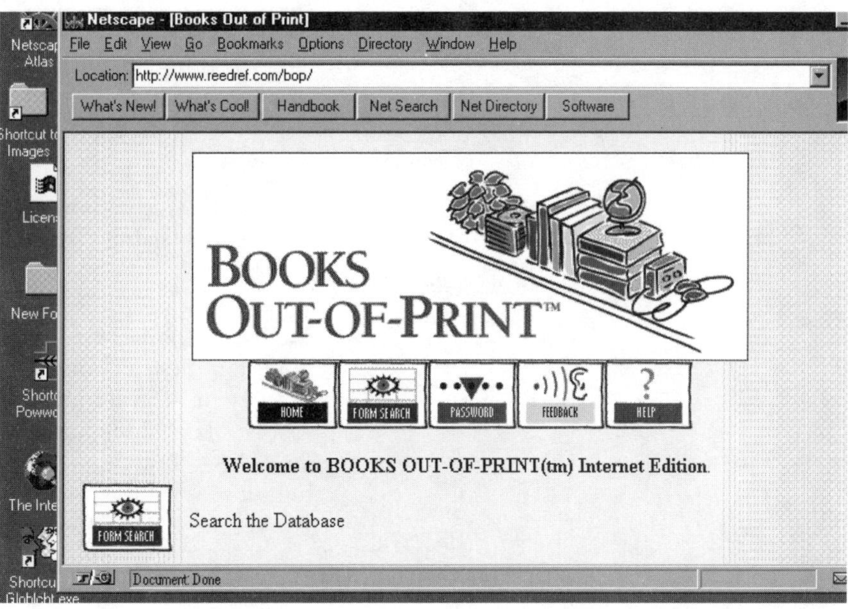

The Books Out-Of-Print page on the Reed Reference Publishing Web site.

IN THE STORE

The CD-ROM product is intended for bookstores, not the mass market. In addition to a searchable version of Books In Print, an ordering system is built in. Book stores can, order the books they find, from a wide variety of suppliers. Of course, they must have accounts with these suppliers, but that is a normal part of the book business.

A company called MUZE has recently licensed the Books In Print database and will have versions available in kiosks for retail stores. MUZE currently has kiosks in music and video stores all over the world. Their Web site can be found at: http://www.muze.com.

CONCLUSIONS

Reed Reference Publishing is starting to exploit the value of their database in several ways. What was formerly a print only product has turned into a series of CD-ROM products, a Web site, and a licensable resource. This represents data reuse at its best.

9 • 8 Bethesda Softworks

SUMMARY

This case study shows how a medium sized game company is using the Web to promote it's products.

BACKGROUND

Bethesda Softworks is the fourth–largest private entertainment PC publisher. It has produced a wide variety of PC titles including The Terminator: Future Shock, The Elder Scrolls: Arena, The Tenth Planet, and PBA Bowling. Chris Weaver, President, provided most of the information presented here.

STATISTICS

The site, began operation in January 1995, receives approximately 30,000 hits per week. They receive approximately 250 email messages per day, with over 2000 a day during product launches. Sample games available on the site are downloaded at the rate of about 20-30 per hour.

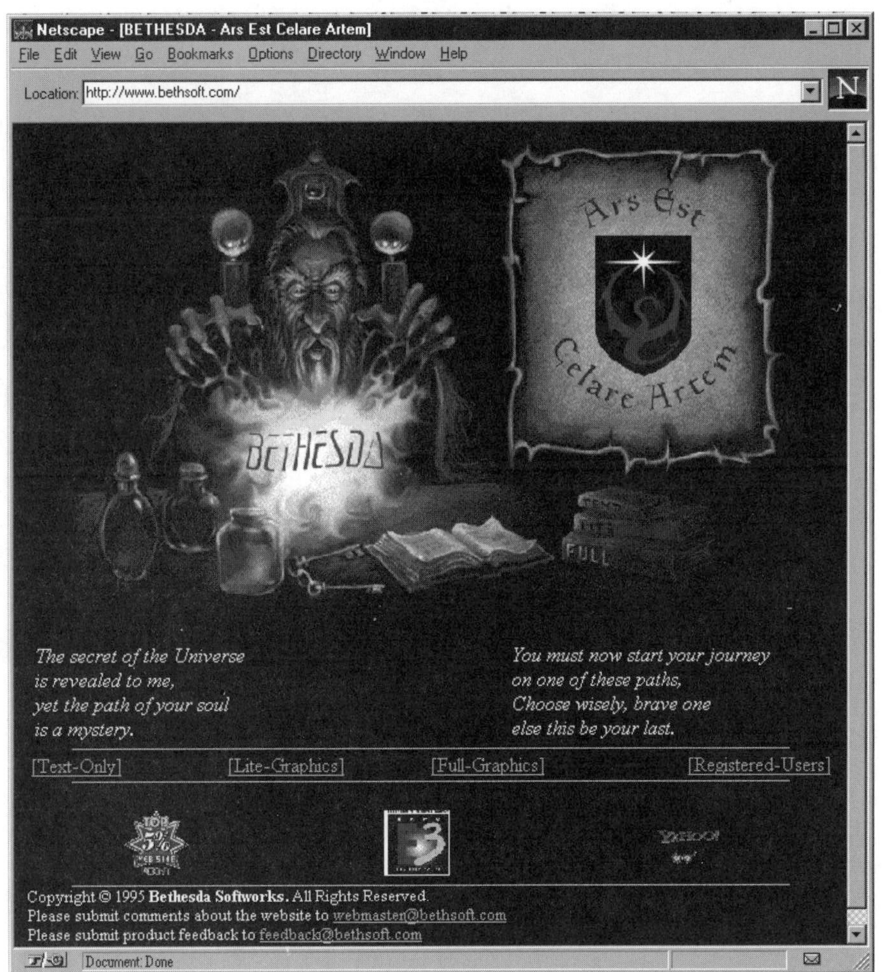

The Bethesda Softworks Home Page

WEB STRUCTURE

Much of Bethesda Software's success is due to its highly detailed role–playing–games (RPG) such The Elder Scrolls: Arena and its sequel Daggerfall. Following this line of thought, the Web site itself is structured as a self–guided tour through a medieval land, complete with detailed descriptions of the surrounding areas. The illustrations of the sites are highly detailed and follow medieval tones. For example, location names include: Archives, Castellan, Cauldron, Cistern, Courtyard, Tavern, and Tourney Field.

These locations often lead to "real" information about products, demos, press releases, and employment opportunities. Clearly the goal is to provide an entertaining Web site that also points to "serious" content.

CONTENT

The site contains information about each of the companies game products as well as teaser images of soon-to-be-release games and demo versions. The Web site functions as an inexpensive recruiting mechanism with a "Billboard" of current job opportunities.

Through a registration process, you can register with the site. Registration has obvious benefits to the company, such as an ever growing list of names interested in the products. The benefits to the user, however, are questionable; the user must be enticed to register.

Bethesda accomplishes this by telling people, "Registering will make your stay here more comfortable, by allowing you to carry coin and by remembering which site you last visited. It will also reveal to you may secrets of Bethesda that would otherwise remain hidden to your eye." The coins registered users can collect can be used to get discounts on real Bethesda products.

CUSTOMIZATION

One immediately noticeable aspect of the site, is that the URLs for each of the pages don't seem quite normal. This is because all of the pages are dynamically generated by cgi–scripts. This allows Bethesda to serve up "text-only," "lite-graphics," "full-graphics," and pages for "registered-users," all from one common set of information. As you travel around the text is dynamically altered to reflect places visited and "coins" you have acquired. These "coins" can be used as discounts for Bethesda products.

DESIGN

The initial site design, developed by a group of people, took approximately 2 weeks. Maintenance takes about 3 to 4 hours per day, primarily due to the volume of email.

As the "winner" of a Point 5% top Web site award, and being selected as a Yahoo! cool site, clearly this site has accomplished many of it's design objectives. It's fun, interesting to experience, and provides useful content.

CONCLUSIONS

With the volume of email and downloads the site is clearly a powerful mechanism to distribute information. The site does, in a cost effective manner, distribute patches and help support existing customers as well as advertise and entice new ones. Future plans include tighter linkages to actual games and more advanced Web technologies.

9 • 9 Towson Art Supply

SUMMARY

This case study illustrates how an art supply company is able to advertise and sell its products via the Web. It is also shows how a small Web service provider has combined automated data base management with Web page design and electronic commerce.

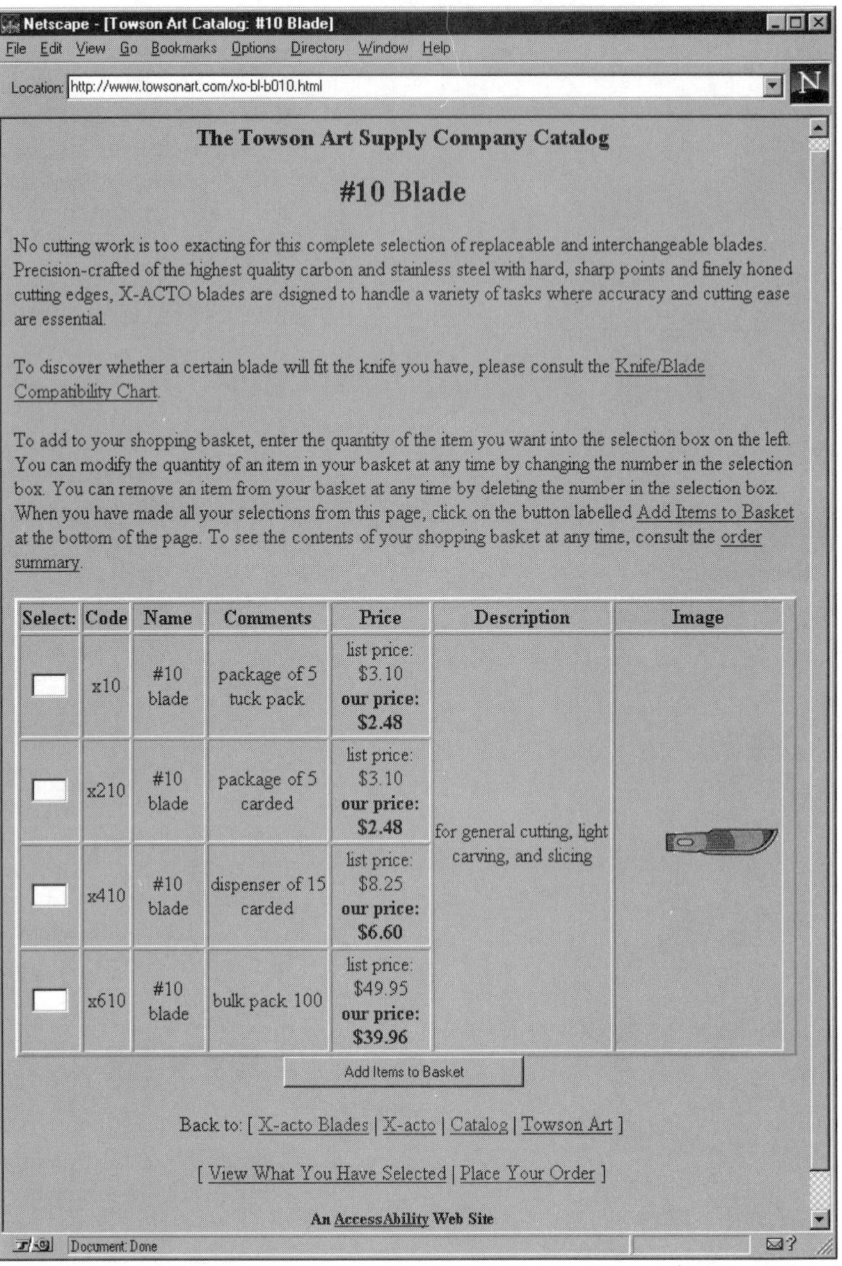

Netscape - [Towson Art Catalog: #10 Blade]

File Edit View Go Bookmarks Options Directory Window Help

Location: http://www.towsonart.com/xo-bl-b010.html

The Towson Art Supply Company Catalog

#10 Blade

No cutting work is too exacting for this complete selection of replaceable and interchangeable blades. Precision-crafted of the highest quality carbon and stainless steel with hard, sharp points and finely honed cutting edges, X-ACTO blades are dsigned to handle a variety of tasks where accuracy and cutting ease are essential.

To discover whether a certain blade will fit the knife you have, please consult the Knife/Blade Compatibility Chart.

To add to your shopping basket, enter the quantity of the item you want into the selection box on the left. You can modify the quantity of an item in your basket at any time by changing the number in the selection box. You can remove an item from your basket at any time by deleting the number in the selection box. When you have made all your selections from this page, click on the button labelled Add Items to Basket at the bottom of the page. To see the contents of your shopping basket at any time, consult the order summary.

Select:	Code	Name	Comments	Price	Description	Image
	x10	#10 blade	package of 5 tuck pack	list price: $3.10 **our price: $2.48**	for general cutting, light carving, and slicing	
	x210	#10 blade	package of 5 carded	list price: $3.10 **our price: $2.48**		
	x410	#10 blade	dispenser of 15 carded	list price: $8.25 **our price: $6.60**		
	x610	#10 blade	bulk pack 100	list price: $49.95 **our price: $39.96**		

Add Items to Basket

Back to: [X-acto Blades | X-acto | Catalog | Towson Art]

[View What You Have Selected | Place Your Order]

An AccessAbility Web Site

Document: Done

One catalog page at Towson Art Supply

PROCESS

This Maryland retail operation is entering the Web and electronic commerce in a big way. The concept is to create an on-line database both to manage products and to be used as the direct source of data for Web page generation. This system is called the "AccessAbility's Integrated Catalog." The Web designers and implementors are AccessAbility Internet Services Inc. Most of the information presented here comes from Scott Bodarky and Don Krapf of AccessAbility.

Store employees enter data via a convenient form-based interface. The structure of the data is flexible enough to accommodate virtually any product identification system already used by a merchant. An automated suite of programs automatically generates the actual Web pages. This is critical as data in the catalog changes frequently.

The concept is to give Web site developers access to an integrated database and Web site development suite. A custom designed database works in concert with Web page generation software to automatically produce the Web pages, once a database has been created. The process is iterative, allowing refinement of the site design and database management. The following sections discuss the process from the point of view of the three principal types of people using the site.

WEBMASTER

The Webmaster, the individual responsible for implementing the catalog, uses a form-based tool to create "prototype" files. These files, a combination of a style sheet and database definition are created by selecting the "Catalog Profile" section of the form. Often the Webmaster and Merchant will be the same person, depending on the scale of the operation, of course.

MERCHANT

The merchant is responsible for data entry and catalog updates. The catalog software is set up to handle catalog pages, detail pages, and images. Detail pages describe, in as much detail as desired, the product. One or several images can also be associated with the product. These images are named according to a merchant selected naming scheme for automated referencing.

From the AccessAbility's Integrated Catalog User's Guide:

> What the merchant sees:
>
> The integrated catalog system can be viewed as a series of interacting components. All the products in a catalog are stored in the *product database*. The products are displayed on the web via the *catalog display* system. Information which applies to the catalog, rather than the products, such as how to calculate shipping and handling, is part of the *catalog configuration*. The integrated catalog system also provides a series of *enhanced HTML resources* which enable the site to perform a number of nifty functions, such as detect which browser someone is using.
>
> The catalog is managed from the catalog control page, which provides access to all the components of the catalog. Orders are managed from the *ordering administration page*.
>
> The merchant is responsible for creating and maintaining the product database (via the catalog control panel), writing and installing the prototype pages (again via the catalog control panel), and filling orders. All the shopping basket and ordering functionality is handled by the integrated catalog.

CUSTOMER

In typical Web site fashion, the customer can browse around the store adding or removing items from a shopping basket. An additional custom feature called "Smart Links," implemented as cgi scripts working with the server, enables the customer to go back to places previously visited. Customers can even leave the session and come back on another day to continue the shopping. The "Smart Links" feature is also a facility for the Web site designer as it eases navigation issues. The designer can simply place a "back" link in the page and the user will go back to wherever they were, even if using frames. More unusual, the customer can create a record of purchases and locations in the virtual store, which can be used on subsequent visits to speed their way through. Finally, the customer can actually purchase the products via a secure Web server.

ENHANCED HTML

One final capability provided by AccessAbility is a technology they call "Enhanced HTML." Simply put, they have designed additional control commands which can be embedded within normal HTML. An enhanced HTML file is first interpreted by a program which works with the Web server, an Apache server, and the HTML is sent back to the client. An example application of this is to embed "if-then-else" type of control within the Web document. At run time the server, knowing the state of a user's travel's can decide, according to the enhanced HTML commands, to present the user with a particular Web page. This flexibility is only possible at run time and cannot be predesigned.

From the AccessAbility Enhanced HTML User Guide:

> Let's look at some examples of the IF command. Suppose you are operating an online catalog, and wish to display special instructions for international customers. Your order form might have two checkboxes, one for customers who live in the US and one for customers who don't. Let's say that the name of the selector is "LOCATION", and that selecting "US" produces a value of 0, while selecting "non-US" produces a value of 1. We could test for this and provide conditional instructions as follow:

```
<!--*IF @LOCATION = 1 -->
   <P>
   For international shipping, the
   carrier we use varies depending
   on the destination. The shipping
   will be calculated and automati-
   cally added to your bill.
   </P>

<!--*ELSESKIP-->
   <P>
   Your order will be shipped via
```

```
UPS.
</P>

<!--*ENDSKIP-->
```

SUMMARY

While new, the Towson Art Web site, is an interesting experiment in integrated database and Web site management. The success of the site is as yet, untested, however the concepts have proven workable. In addition, Self service (Please see *Section 1 • 3 Web Maintenance* in *Chapter 1 • World Wide Web* for more discussion of self service Web services) clients of AccessAbility can take advantage of this powerful facility by designing their own catalogs using the many tools provided.

9 • 10 WEBster & HPCWire

SUMMARY

Here we see how one company leverages good old–fashioned email to get its message to customers.

Most of the information presented here is from email correspondence with Dianna Husum, Editorial Director of Tabor Griffin Communications, who was kind enough to answer my pesky questions.

BACKGROUND

How long have you been in business? Tabor Griffin has been publishing on the Internet since 1990. We started with the electronic version of the now–defunct hard–copy *Supercomputing Review.* Eventually this evolved into HPCwire. In September 1994, we launched WEBster--The Cyberspace Surfer.

How long have you been publishing weekly? HPCwire has been weekly since its inception. WEBster is currently published every other week with plans to expand to weekly coverage.

AUTHORING

How do you get your articles originally. (i.e. are they from wire services, or originally authored for WEBster?) We use a combination of wire services and freelance reporters.

Do you have any company standards for the process of getting the information into the central distribution point? We are set up like a traditional "newspaper" operation, in which certain editors are responsible for certain sections of each publication. We maintain a central database for notes, back issues and other research items.

How do you coordinate the work of all the authors? Again, it's pretty much a standard newsroom setup. The managing editor is responsible for coordinating magazine content and freelance assignments. We operate on a query basis with freelance writers. Each week our staff "meets" via phone, e-mail, or conferencing to discuss issues, coverage, and deadlines for the next edition.

Are the "News Briefs" section articles primarily from press releases, and if so do you have any automation or semi-automation systems to help in the overall selection process? Articles in the news brief section do originate from press releases and newswire services. We use Compuserve as our news feed and set up filtered folders that capture files that contain specific key words. For WEBster we are viewing about 200 articles a day. For HPCwire it is only about 80. Then our editors view the capture files, pulling out those items that we plan to include in the issue. So automation is minimal, and a lot of hands–on copy editing and enhancement takes place prior to publication.

SYSTEMS

What kind of computing equipment to you use? Our editorial/production department operates on 486s; back office, advertising, marketing, and accounting are on a combination of PCs and Macs and systems; and our Internet server is run off an SGI Indy and DEC station. So you could say we have a very heterogeneous network going.

What kind of mail system do you have as the server, or is it custom or a combination? We use a modified list serve.

```
From: news@newsmaster.tgc.com (Automated Mailer)
To: sressler@interramp.com
Subject: WEBster Table of Contents: February 6
Content-Length: 9877

Gentle Reader,
As a member of WEBster's mailing list you may retrieve all articles indexed
with a number series starting with 6, 7 or 9. Plus you may retrieve the
following WEBnews article:

 69028) MDG ADDS DATABASE TRACKING TO MACINTOSH WEB SERVER
        Database integration is par for the course with MDG Computer
        Services release of Web Server 4D, a new server for the Macintosh.

)\\\\\\\\\\\\\\\\\\\\\\\\\\\\\\\\\\\\\\\\/////////////////////////////////////////

                          ____   ___
           \    /\    /  |      |   )
            \  /  \  /   |===   |===]ster  --   The Cyberspace Surfer
             \/    \/    |____  |___)  the e-zine for the design team

Vol. 2: No. 11                                                  Feb. 6, 1996
~~~~~~~~~~~~~~~~~~~~~~~~~~~~~~~~~~~~~~~~~~~~~~~~~~~~~~~~~~~~~~~~~~~~~~~~~~~~~
~
  Runner-Up Best Online Publication 1994 Computer Press Association Awards
~~~~~~~~~~~~~~~~~~~~~~~~~~~~~~~~~~~~~~~~~~~~~~~~~~~~~~~~~~~~~~~~~~~~~~~~~~~~~
~
                   This issue of WEBster is sponsored by:

                     95015) Quarterdeck(R) WebAuthor(TM)
          Instantly create or convert HTML documents for the World Wide Web!

                              I N   T H I S   I S S U E
~~~~~~~~~~~~~~~~~~~~~~~~~~                          ~~~~~~~~~~~~~~~~~~~~~~~~~~
~  SPOTlight : WEAVING THE WEB INTO YOUR MARKETING PLAN                      ~
~  WEBnews   : DATABASE TRACKING ADDED TO MGD MAC WEB SERVER                  ~
~  HOTlist   : WELCOME TO THE ROBOTIC GARDEN                                 ~
~~~~~~~~~~~~~~~~~~~~~~~~~~~~~~~~~~~~~~~~~~~~~~~~~~~~~~~~~~~~~~~~~~~~~~~~~~~~~
                              TWO WAYS TO READ WEBster
          Send e-mail to  i-want-it@webster.tgc.com  In subject line,
          type the number immediately adjacent to the desired article
          or section. No message text is required. Example appears at
          end of this file.

          Or check out our Web page at http://www.tgc.com/webster.html

*****************************************************************************
*
   FOR A FREE TRIAL SUBSCRIPTION TO WEBster: E-mail 4free@webster.tgc.com
*****************************************************************************
*

SPOTlight (10155 this number retrieves entire section)~~~~~~~~~~~~~~~~~~~~~
 10156 ) WE'RE WIRED. NOW WHAT DO WE DO ?...............................8.34K
         by Cynthia Kurkowski, contributing editor
         As D-Day approaches for getting California's schools hooked-up to
         the Internet, it's becoming more apparent that hardware and software
         represent only half the equation. Can NetDay96 and all its good
```

intentions scale the brick wall of reality ?

10157) WEB@WORK: EXPLORING WEB MARKETING TECHNIQUES - PLANNING........7.24K
by Carl Kline, contributing editor
O.K. you've done all the research. Now its time to put all the information gleaned from those surf sessions to work. Here's how to integrate the Web into your business plan.

10158) DEBUNKING MYTHS ABOUT INTERNET COMMERCE........................10.2K
Guest Commentary by Ravi Kalakota
It is time to debunk once and for all a powerful myth that is taking root about Internet commerce: that secure payment processing is what ultimately makes Internet commerce popular among consumers.

10159) NCSA OPENS SCIENCE FOR THE MILLENNIUM WEB SITE.................3.99K
Three years in the making, Science for the Millennium is now officially open to the public. Through a video-rich, prototype online science exposition, visitors can explore advances in computing, networking and virtual reality.

WEBnews(20608)~~~~~~

20609) DeltaPoint QuickSite Promises to Speed Web Site Construction...3.54K
20610) Sizzler Plug-in Allows Users to Play Live, Real-Time Animation.1.33K
20611) MDG Adds Database Tracking to Macintosh Web Server.............1.73K
20612) First Union Plans to Offer Online Banking Via Internet.........2.28K
20613) AOL Buys Compression Technology Developer, Johnson-Grace.......2.38K
20614) Collaboration Delivers Publishing System for Mamoth Web Event..5.36K
20615) Netscape Will Award $5,000 for Best Gold-Created Home Page.....7.13K
20616) Hummingbird Ships Columbus Intranet Desktop....................2.83K
20617) Sun Introduces Microprocessor Optimized for Java...............4.91K
20618) I/PRO & net.Genesis Collaborate on Web Measurement Product.....1.24K
20619) CyberCash Rolls Out Mac Wallet Secure Payment Service..........2.30K
20620) NCSA Study Says 600 U.S. Communities Are Now on the Web........3.80K
20621) Netscape Closes Year with $80.7 Million in Revenues............2.31K
20622) ThinkQuest Attempts to Bring Drama of Internet to School.......5.75K
20623) Superscape Introduces Super VRML Viewer........................2.80K
20624) WebCube Series P Delivers Plug & Play for ISPs.................3.30K
20625) Frontier Technologies Optimizes CyberSearch 2.0 for Windows 95.2.96K
20626) Online Briefs: A Digest of Recent Developments.................12.6K
20627) New Kids on the Block: A Look at Who Just Got on the Web.......28.1K

HOTlist(40248)~~~~~~

40249) ARTS, ENTERTAINMENT & LEISURE.................................1.25K
Spectacle: a new pinnacle in creative content and mind voyages
The Art Studio Department at UCSB: where art and technology intersect
SportsWorld: worldwide sports information

40250) BUSINESS & COMMERCE...2.05K

```
   The Computer Information Center: an IT treasure trove
   Report on Rights Management Technologies: authoritative information
   dbHOTlinx: client-server information at your fingertips

40251) GOVERNMENT, HISTORY, POLITICS & ACTIVISM......................1.56K
   Best Direct & Electronic Democracy Solutions: tested tools of democracy
   This Week in Bosnia-Hercegovina: Bosnia Action Coalition's newsletter
   Royal Canadian Mounted Police: all there is to know about the RCMP

40252) MATH & SCIENCE................................................1.27K
   The Tele-Garden: plant your seed and watch it grow
   The UMBC Agents Subpage on Security: papers on security issues
   Neuropsychology Central: resources for professionals and laypersons alike

40253 ) TOOL BOX.....................................................1.39K
   WMRL: over 700 carefully selected annotated web sites for learning HTML
   @LearnSkills: take an online authoring course
   Review on the Interpretation of the Joint Evolution of Browsers

40254 ) THE MINI LIST................................................7.67K
   An index of all the URLs published in this edition of WEBster.

40021) THE MASTER LIST: all the URLs ever printed in WEBster...........89.8K
       Note: this file must be ordered separately.

DATEbook (65112 )~~~~~~~~~~~~~~~~~~~~~~~~~~~~~~~~~~~~~~~~~~~~~~~~~~~~~~~~~~~~
 65001 ) Conference Listings (updated Feb. 5, 1996)....................27.2K

************************ A B O U T   W E B s t e r ***********************
*                                                                        *
*  90001) Subscription Information                                       *
*  90002) Contribute Your News, Tips & Information                       *
*  90003) Meet the Staff                                                 *
*  90004) Let's Do the Time Warp Again -- Access WEBster's Back Issues   *
*  95000) WEBster Sponsorship Information                                *
**************************************************************************

RETRIEVAL EXAMPLE:  To: i-want-it@webster.tgc.com
                    From: reader@xyz.com
                    Subject: 90000 40001 10000
                    NO MESSAGE TEXT REQUIRED

 _____________________________S P O N S O R S_____________________________
|                                                                          |
|   95004 ) Silicon Graphics, Inc.        95006 ) DCI                      |
|   95016 ) Simware Inc.                                                   |
|__________________________________________________________________________|

     FOR SUBSCRIPTION INFORMATION: E-Mail such-a-deal@webster.tgc.com
    TO GET OFF OUR MAILING LIST: E-Mail leave-me-alone@webster.tgc.com

! HELPHELPHELPHELPHELPHELPHELPHELPHELPHELPHELPHELPHELPHELPHELPHELPHELP !
HELP            Help me! I've ordered and I can't retrieve            PLEH
ELPH            For help with retrieval problems send an              LPHE
LPHE            e-mail message to sos@webster.tgc.com or              EHPL
PHEL            human@webster.tgc.com for human intervention          HELP
! HELPHELPHELPHELPHELPHELPHELPHELPHELPHELPHELPHELPHELPHELPHELPHELPHELP !
?
```

BUSINESS ISSUES

What type of business model do you follow? We follow the model of a paid subscription magazine, essentially a traditional publishing model.

How many subscribers do you have? We essentially have two levels of subscription: paid/full access and unpaid/limited access. The paid group has full access to all articles ever published by that specific magazine. The unpaid group receives all of our mailings, but can only retrieve specific articles.

WEBster has about 38,000 addresses on its mailing list and about 6,000 paid subscribers. HPCwire has about 17,700 addresses on its mailing list and about 5,000 paid subscribers.

What other businesses are TGC involved in? We define ourselves primarily as a publishing house, but we also offer Internet and WWW consulting as well as publishing services for other businesses; (i.e., we have produced live publications for international events such as the G7 Ministerial Conference held last year in Brussels, and Internet publishing services for non-competing publications and internal newsletters for large corporations.)

Are you considering repackaging some of your archived material into other forms for sale? We have at times discussed this issue, but have not yet made any firm decisions.

What is your pricing structure? We have individual, group, and site license rates. HPCwire is priced at $97 per year for individuals or $49 per year for each member of a group of 3 or more. WEBster is $29 per year. These are flat rates and offer readers unlimited access in terms of numbers of articles ordered.

Can institutions get site-licenses? Yes, we have site license programs for each publication. These are based on a flat rate for a specific number of subscribers. The more subscribers you have, the lower the individual rate.

FUTURE DIRECTIONS

Are you seriously considering using any type of MIME data types such as audio or video in the future? We are always open to new content development or ways of presenting our material. However, the actual file type depends on our readers. We recently committed, our resources to Web delivery for both publications, this emerged from an overwhelming request from our readership. The difficulty with MIME and other specific data types is accessibility. When evaluating these technologies, it is important to keep in mind the mission of the publication (entertainment vs. information) as well as the nature of the readers. Our readers are primarily busy executives who are more interested in mission–critical information delivered in a timely, easy–to–read format rather than all the bells and whistles. Also at issue is portability. There is a lot to be said for good ol' ASCII. Everyone can accept ASCII files. Not everyone has MIME compatibility. So the key is determining the lowest common denominator for your readership and designing around that specification.

What do you see as the relationship between the HTML and email version? Our use of the e-mail version is two-fold. First, it serves as a reminder that new information is available. Think of it in terms of having your newspaper delivered to your front door every morning. A web page by itself is a very passive animal. The e-mail dynamic makes it more proactive.

Second, a large portion of our readership prefers reading the publication via e-mail as opposed to on the Web. So it remains an important delivery channel.

What is the hardest part of putting the publication together? I would have to say that the most challenging aspect is making sure that all the components of the process are in place and functioning in tandem — from customer service to editorial, advertising to systems administration, and keeping the lines of communication open between those areas.

On the production side, the most difficult aspect is converting from ASCII to HTML, double checking all the links and all the other nitty gritty unglamourous details that suck up huge amounts of time and push you past deadline. Each issue of WEBster contains between 100 and 150 live outside links and about 100 "tgc" links.

What is the most surprising part of putting the publication together? With WEBster it would have to be the joy of discovery...the Web is growing so quickly that you never really know what waits at the end of the next link. The other surprise from both publications is the amount of feedback from readers. Coming from the "hard copy" publishing world, I am always amazed at the amount and extent of reader mail we receive and the "ownership" many readers feel toward these publications.[9]

CONCLUSIONS

The people at Tabor Griffin have clearly gone the low-tech route. Email provides a simple information dissemination method. Rather than try to create lots of new whiz-bang, content-free material, Tabor Griffin decided to stick with the real content and cost-effective distribution technology. The weekly summaries provided by both e-zine's get to the point and provide easy methods for article retrieval. Clearly, this type of distribution mechanism can be an effective tool for the dissemination of timely content.

9 • 11 The Internal Revenue Service (IRS)

SUMMARY

The Internal Revenue Service (IRS) provides an example of how a large information provider, (tax forms and publications) uses the Web in coordination with the Internet to give people easy access to a large quantity of necessary information.

BACKGROUND

The Internal Revenue Service (IRS) an often despised government agency, actually has a sense of humor! Starting in early January of 1996, the IRS has created

9. Dianna Husum, Editorial Director Tabor Griffin Communications Publishers of HPCwire & WEBster--The Cyberspace Surfer dianna@tgc.com http://www.tgc.com 619-625-0070 619-625-0088 (fax). For free trial subscriptions trial@hpcwire.tgc.com (HPCwire) 4free@webster.tgc.com (WEBster).

a Web site that's downright friendly. It's chock full of useful information and a terrific example of the imaginative use of advanced Web features. Most of the material for this case study was from information generously provided by Linda Wallace part of the Web team at the IRS.

A team of four IRS technicians (one part-time) and two research assistants develops and provides IRS electronic information services to the public. These products and services increase the responsiveness of IRS services and reduce costs. All the IRS applications for the Internet were conceived and laid out in-house.

The site was developed by contracting with Fed-World, part of the Department of Commerce's National Technical Information Service (NTIS), to provide operations and maintenance. NTIS then contracted with Websys, a small northern Virginia company specializing in Internet services, to develop the software and overall design. The content, applications and overall newspaper style layout was specified by the IRS staff.

In addition to the friendly 1950's art deco style the page features a globe that spins and a marquee of information. The opening screen lets the user select between a graphics or text–only version of the Web. The site actually detects browser types and adjusts the type of HTML delivered to the capabilities of the browser.

The Digital Daily - IRS Web site

TEXT MANAGEMENT

Before the Web site design and implementation, the IRS team benchmarked with a number of leading companies in electronic text management services to find industry best practices. They relied heavily on evaluation factors used in the Baldrige National Quality Award as they researched these best practices. Over the past ten years the IRS has had a strong commitment to SGML. They feel that without this strong foundation it would not have been possible to build this 3000 page Web site so quickly and accurately. The IRS text and graphics repository was a key component to the effective management of their data. The core business products, such as tax forms and publications, were moved into a self-help electronic access facility, the Web site.

More important than the Web site is the information it leads to. The IRS has placed *all* of their forms on-line in four formats. You can obtain the forms in PDF (Acrobat Reader format), PCL (Hewlett Packard's printer format), PS (PostScript) and SGML (Standard Generalized Markup Language).

The files themselves are located on an FTP site maintained by FEDWORLD, the premier disseminator of U.S. government information in electronic form.

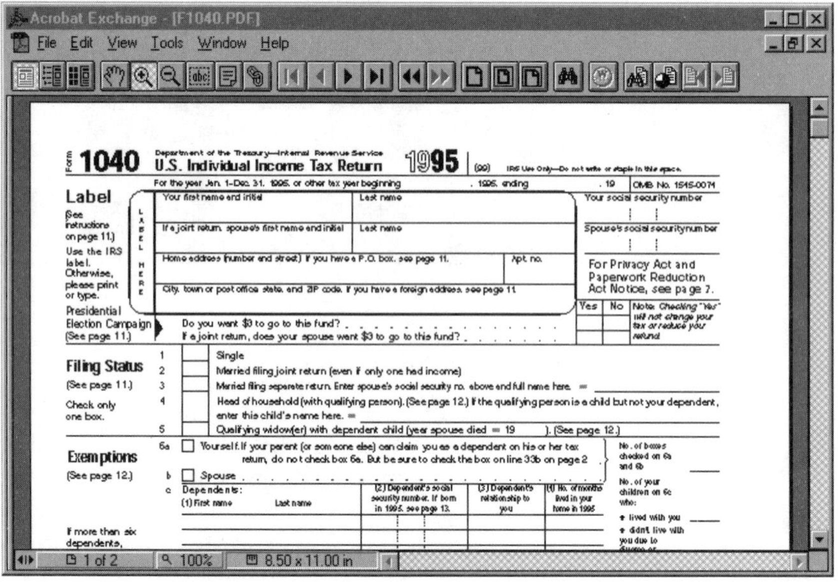

Display of a 1040 form in PDF format using Adobe Acrobat

In addition to the forms themselves, there are two versions of regulations on-line. One is the full text of various incomprehensible regulations. The second is a plain English version of the tax regulations for simple folk, like me. The plain English version exists as nicely formatted HTML pages.

INFRASTRUCTURE ISSUES

In addressing the issues of business process and infrastructure, Linda Wallace (of the IRS) says:

> The IRS staff concentrates primarily on applications development, identifying core business products and matching them to electronic media, and building infrastructure which will move the IRS into more multimedia service delivery. According to the Electronic Information Services staff, the infrastructure issue is the most difficult. It means changing the way people build business products. Another challenge was helping internal business functions look at their products and services to find those that lend themselves to self-help electronic format and that are the top customer priorities.

CUSTOMIZATION

As a customer driven organization the IRS really tries hard to keep their Web site responsive to, and focused on, the customer. One technical method they use is to make several Web browser interfaces available to the customer. These browser interfaces help people with "new and not-so-new technology and for persons with disabilities." Access to as–wide–as–possible a customer base is very important. This must be balanced with the desire to present the most attractive Web site possible, which usually requires newer technologies, such as Java for example. Every Web page exists as HTML 3.0, HTML 1.0 and text only versions. In addition a variety of interactive applications, navigational metaphors, and search techniques make the search at hand easy and interesting for the novice and expert user.

STATISTICS

Needless to say, a lot of people need to deal with the IRS. During the last week of the filing season (April 1996) the Web site was getting over 1 million hits every day. On the last day April 15th 1996 almost 1.9 million hits were logged. During the early time period of site deployment they were averaging 25,000 file downloads every day., and on the final day of the 96 tax season, over 100,000 files were downloaded. These include tax forms and publications.

SUCCESS

The IRS Web site has in a short three month of operation received a great deal of (well justified) praise. They have won over 30 industry awards and great feedback from the media. A major accomplishment give most people's usual view of the IRS.

These award have included:

- *Wired - Hot Spots*
- *Yahoo Internet Life, four start rating (of four)*
- *Money - Top Web Site*
- *USA Today - Net Sites of Note*
- *Magellan - four stars (of four)*

The New York Times said "Innovative and useful," and CNN reports, "Colorful, easy to use, and funny."

According to the IRS there have been over 52 million hits in about 3 months and most amazingly "people are actually writing in to say 'thank you' to the IRS." Imagine that!

CONCLUSIONS

The success of the IRS Web sites illustrates how to move a bureaucracy toward the future. Wide use of the information on this site, saves money, in this case taxpayer dollars. It's much cheaper for the IRS to provide information electronically than via traditional means. Technology is rarely the problem when introducing new services, usually old business practices are the enemy. Any large organization, government or private, has people with vested interests and resistance to change. This site above all else shows that it is possible to make real changes in established organizations and to do so with style.

9 • 12 Banana Bats & Ding Dong Balls

SUMMARY

This case study is a little special. Mostly it represents an attempt by yours truly to take material from one media, print, and transform it into another, the Web. First of all, the process has only barely begun. Initially, I was going to place the whole book with figures on the CD-ROM and Web site for this book. Time pressure and technical issues conspired to change the original project into another (more interesting) one.

Over the course of several months I will be turning the book into an integral part of the Case Studies section of this book's Web site at Prentice-Hall. I will document the process and problems encountered so that we may all learn from the process. I would especially like to thank Dan Gutman for letting me play with his book in this way.

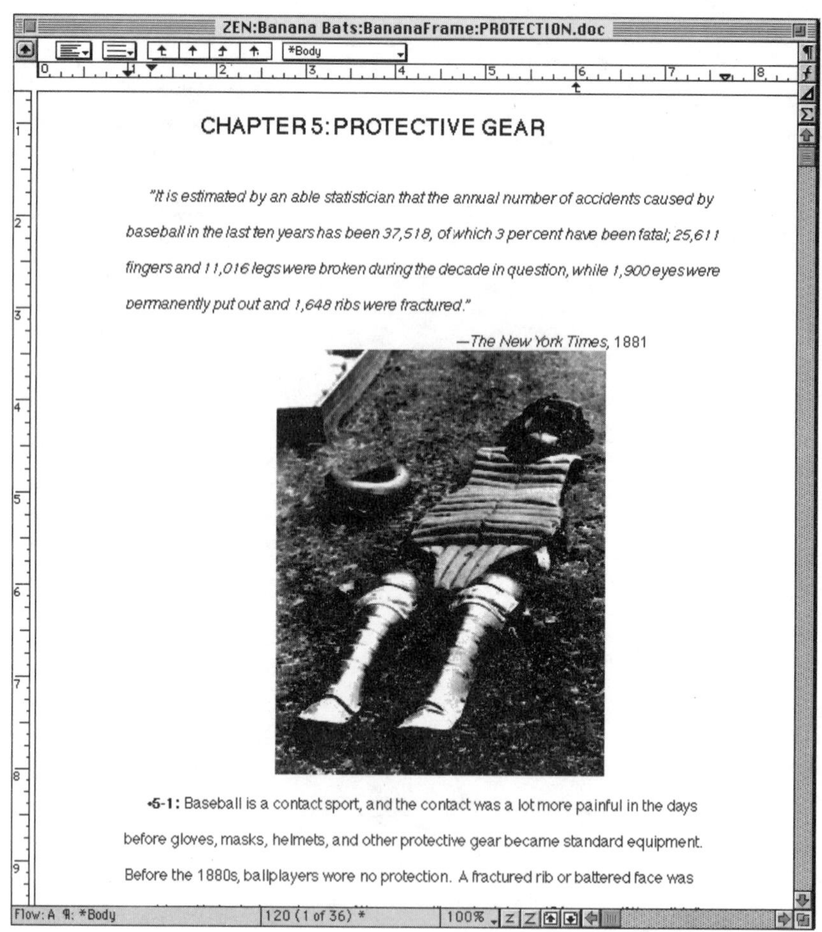

CHAPTER 5: PROTECTIVE GEAR

"It is estimated by an able statistician that the annual number of accidents caused by baseball in the last ten years has been 37,518, of which 3 per cent have been fatal; 25,611 fingers and 11,016 legs were broken during the decade in question, while 1,900 eyes were permanently put out and 1,648 ribs were fractured."

—*The New York Times,* 1881

•5-1: Baseball is a contact sport, and the contact was a lot more painful in the days before gloves, masks, helmets, and other protective gear became standard equipment. Before the 1880s, ballplayers wore no protection. A fractured rib or battered face was

Banana Bats and Ding-Dong Balls undergoing transformation

Banana Bats & Ding Dong Balls: A Century of Baseball Invention by Dan Gutman is a traditional paperback book. It also represents an experiment, in putting existing material intended for one medium into electronic form.

I avoided the first problem, legal rights, because Dan Gutman is a friend who owns the copyright and I knew he could be persuaded, to let me experiment on his book. Next, I had to get the electronic form of the book. It turned out to exist in MacWrite format. Another reason for selecting this book is that it is a bunch of stories, and not a novel or piece of fiction that must be read from start to finish. It seemed to have potential for lots of hypertext links and jumping around.

Please stop by and visit our Web site at: http://www.prenhall.com to check on the progress. Finally it is my intent to continue to produce case studies and place them on the Web. If you feel that you'd like to explain how you put together a Web site, CD-ROM or other electronic publication please write to me at sandy@ability.net.

Appendix A • Resources

All I know is just what I read in the papers.—Will Rogers

An amazing variety of services and software available to help you in virtually any electronic publishing task. The information in this chapter will lead you to these sources. It is categorized into a number of useful topics. In addition the conspicuous lack of Web resources is because the Web itself is a much better source than any printed document. Simply go to one of the Internet Starting Points and look around a little. (See *Section 1 • 9 Internet Starting Points* in *Chapter 1 • World Wide Web* for pointers to these sites.) Inclusion in this chapter is by no means an endorsement of the specific company or product, just an attempt to save you some legwork and make your life a little easier.

Clip Art

Clip art seems like a simple enough topic. You wouldn't think of having too many kinds. But hard as it may be to believe, there are all sorts of clip art categories. Funny, serious, industrial, medical, borders, textures, 3D, and so on, are some of the many varieties of clip art you can buy.

From a technical point of view, the format of the artwork is the important factor. One critical distinction is whether the artwork is scalable (EPS is scalable) or not. If the ability to scale the image is not important, just go with a convenient format, assuming you're satisfied with the content, of course. Most important, is a determination that you can use the clip art with your publishing software.

If you're concerned about producing documents with everyone else's "same old clip art," you can try the subscription approach. Subscription clip art services provide monthly supplies of clip art. These services provide up-to-date topical or seasonal art for a price.

Not exactly clip art, but worth knowing about, is the existence of special papers for laser printers. Colorful gradations and patterns can be used for dramatic impact. Certificates, and awards, already embossed and ready for the laser printer, are also available.

There are also two YAHOO catagories for Web access which are at:

http://www.yahoo.com/Business_and_Economy/Companies/Computers/Software/Clip_art

http://www.yahoo.com/Computers_and_Internet/Multimedia/Pictures/Clip_Art

Assorted

3G Graphics, 11410 N.E. 124th St. Suite 6155, Kirkland, WA 98034
(206) 367-9321, (800) 456-0234

ArtRight, 1130 Morrison Dr., Ottowa, Ontario K2H 9N6
(613) 820-1000, FAX (613) 820-2651

Image Club Graphics, Inc., Suite 5, 1902 Eleventh St. SE,
Calgary, Alberta, Canada T2G 3G2
(403) 262 8008, FAX (403) 261-7013
Regular upgrades to keep current

Metro Imagebase
18623 Ventura Blvd., Suite 210
Tarzana, CA 91356
(800) 525-1552

T/Maker, 1390 Villa Street, Mountain View, CA 94041
(800) 395-0195, FAX: (415) 962-0201

Cartoon

Freemyers Design, 575 Nelson Ave., Oroville, CA 95965
(916) 533-9365
AD/ART Plus, Cartoon Designer, Architectural Graphics, Laser Art/Borders

Sandhill Arts, P.O. Box 7298, Menlo Park, CA 94026
(800) 854-0717

Government Symbols/Maps

One Mile Up, Inc., 7011 Evergreen Court,
Annandale, VA 22003
(703) 642-1177
http://www.onemileup.com
Federal Clip Art

Cartesia Software, 5 S. Main St. PO Box 757,
Lambertville, NJ 08530
(800) 334-4291
MapArt (PC and Mac)

Specially Printed Paper

Baudville Computer Products, 5380 52nd Street SE,
Grand Rapids, MI 49512
(616) 698-0888, (800) 728-0888
Awards, Certificates

Desktop Graphics, 268 East 16th St.,Suite 6, Costa Mesa,
CA. 92627
Awards, Certificates

Queblo Images, 131 Heartland Blvd, Brentwood, NY
11717
(800) 523-9080
Exotic and preprinted paper

Subscription Service

Dynamic Graphics, Inc., 6000 N. Forest Park Dr., PO
Box 1901, Park Dr., Peoria IL 61656-9941
(800) 255-8800, FAX (309) 688-5873
Designer's Club (subscription service)

Textures

Artbeats, Inc., P.O. Box 20083, San Bernadino, CA 92406
(714) 881-1200

Impact Communications, 13412 Galewood St., Sherman Oaks CA 91423
(213) 479-4377

Progressive Desktop Publishing, 13A Park Ave., Gaithersberg MD 20877
(301) 948-3047

Three-D

SwivelArt

NEC Technologies, Inc., 1255 Michael Dr., Wood Dale, IL 60191-1094
1-800-NEC-INFO

NEC Clip Art 3-D

Macromedia, 600 Townsend, San Francisco, CA 94103
(415) 442-02001, FAX: (415) 442-0190

SwivelArt, Anatomy Collection: Clip Art with Guts including the heart, liver, lungs, kidneys, and articulated skeleton.

Copyrights, Stock, and Syndicates

Stock photographs are a great source of professional, high quality images...for a price. Prices vary primarily on how you want to use them. A syndicate is an organization through which you may obtain legal permission to use cartoons, photographs and so on.

The pricing is usually based on the type and quantity of publication and on types of distribution, that is, American or world rights. On YAHOO there is: http://www.yahoo.com/Business_and_Economy/Companies/Law/Intellectual_Property/Copyrights and for stock photography,

http://www.yahoo.com/Business_and_Economy/Companies/Photography/Stock_Photography.

Bettmann Archives & News Photos, New York
(212) 777-6200

Copyright Clearance Center, Inc., 27 Congress St.
Salem, MA 01970
(508) 744-3350
http://www.copyright.com

A nonprofit organization helping photocopy users comply with the copyright law. They have a register of over 1,000,000 journals, books, magazines, and newsletters.

Comstock, New York
(800) 225-2727

The Image Bank, New York, Chicago, Los Angeles and others
(212) 529-6700

TIME Picture Syndication
(212) 522-3352
LIFE Picture Service
(212) 522-4800

Images from the huge collection of Time and Life magazines.

Universal Press Syndicate, 4900 Main St., Kansas City, MO 64112
(816) 932-6600

Typical costs for use in a book: (cartoon)
American rights $175 to $250, world rights $275-to $325. Costs vary widely based on source material and usage. They will provide a stat (camera–ready copy).

Data Translation, Format Conversion

Advanced Computer Innovations, 30 Burncoat Way, #C5, Pittsford, NY 14534-2216
(716) 383-1939, FAX (716) 383-8428

R-Doc/X, bidirectional conversions between over 25 word processor programs. $149.00 MS-DOS

Blueberry Software, 7207 Bodega Ave., Sebastopol CA 95472
(707) 829-5443

Filtrix

DataViz Inc., 55 Corporate Drive, Trunbull, CT, 06611
(203) 268-0030, FAX: (203) 268-4345, http://www.dataviz.com.

MacLink Plus, conversion utilities that work with the Apple File Exchange program provided by Apple. Converts between Macintosh and MS-DOS data for many file formats.

Design Software Technologies, Inc., 19808 Nordhoff Place, Chatsworth, CA 91311
(312) 231-4540

Word for Word (DOS), bidirectional conversions between over 30 word processor formats. Batch processing utility. ASCII or EBCDIC files accepted.

Inset Systems, 71 Commerce Drive, Brookfield, CT 06804-3405
(800) 828-8088

HiJaak & HiJaak P, screen capture and format conversion

Shaffstall Corporation, 7901 East 88th Street, Indianapolis, Indiana 46256-1293
(800) 248-3475, FAX: (317) 842-8294

SGML Translator, 6000 Media Conversion System, Hardware and software full media conversion system. The full system has over 1000 formats. Good for setting up a service bureau. It can handle 3 1/2", 5 1/4" , and 8" floppies.

Document Capture

Data Entry (including off-shore services)

Data Development, Inc., 3595 SW Corporate Parkway, Palm City, FL 34990
(407) 288-SCAN, FAX: (407) 288-2775

Equidata Data Entry Services, Equidata Building, 3200 S., Arlington St., Suite One, Akron, OH 44312

OCR

Caere, 100 Cooper Court, Los Gatos, CA 95030
(800) 535-SCAN

OmniPage product family

Calera Recognition Systems, 2500 Augustine Drive, Santa Clara, CA 95054
(408) 986-8006

Expervision, 3590 North First Street, San Jose, CA 95134
(800) REA-DTYPE

Infinite Images International, 360 Herndon Parkway, Suite 2100, Herndon, VA 22071
(703) 803-9000

Inovatic, 1901 Ft Meyer Drive, Arlington, VA 22209
(703) 522-3053

OCRSystems, 1800 Bayberry Road, Suite 1405, Huntingdon Valley, PA 19006
(215) 938-7460

Progressive Technologies, 19650 Club House Road, Suite 106, Gaithersburg, MD 20897
(301) 590-0900

Xerox Imaging Systems, Kurzweil Products, 185 Albany St., Cambridge, MA 02139
(800) 248-6550

Document Processors

ArborText, Inc., 1000 Victors Way, Suite 400, Ann Arbor, MI 48108
(313) 996-3566, FAX: (316) 996-3573
SGML•Publisher

CYGNET Publishing Technologies, 411 Seventh Ave., Suite 1175, Pittsburgh, PA 15219
(412) 471-2070, FAX: (412) 391-7215
Scribe

Frame Technology Corp., 1010 Rincon Circle, San Jose, CA 95131
(800) 843-7263, FAX: (408) 433-1928
FrameMaker, multiple platform publishing system

image network, 140 S. Whisman Road, Mountain View, CA 94041
(800) TO-XROFF, FAX: (415) 967-0543

Xroff, one of many implementations of troff available from many sources including public domain clones from the Free Software Foundation. This is one particularly widely used commercial vendor.

Intergraph Corp., One Madison Industrial Park, Huntsville, AL 35894-0001
(800) 826-3515, FAX: (205) 730-2461

Interleaf, Inc., 9 Hillside Ave., Prospect Place, Waltham, MA 02154
(800) 456-5323, FAX: (617) 290-4943
Interleaf 5, multiple platform publishing system

Island Graphics Corp., 4000 Civic Center Dr., San Rafael, CA 94903-4178
(800) 255-4499, FAX: (415) 491-0402
IslandDraw, IslandWrite, IslandPaint, workstation equivalent of PC oriented packages

Personal TEX Inc., 12 Madrona Ave., Mill Valley, CA 94941
(415) 388-8853, FAX: (415) 388-8865

PC TEX and an extensive collection of supporting software such as printer drivers for PCs.

Ventura Software, Inc., 15175 Innovation Drive, San Diego, CA 92128
(800) 822-8221

Ventura Publisher

Education and Training

The following companies offer a variety of education and training courses in the area of electronic publishing. There are, of course, many, many more; just watch your junk mail.

InfoDesign Corporation, One Prince Stree, Suite 300, Alexandria, VA 22314
(703) 799-0932, FAX: (703) 519-9775

SGML training and consulting

Lou Williams Seminars, Two Prudential Plaza, 180 N. Stetson Ave., #1500, Chicago, IL 60601
(800) 837-7123, FAX: (312) 565-1770

Course: 1day, "Design for Destop Publishing"

LearnKey Inc., 93 S. Mountain Way Dr., Rm X, Orem, UT 84058
1-800-937-3279

Software Training Videos: Ventura Publisher, WordPerfect.

Patricia Seybolds' Office Computing Group, 148 State Street, 7th Floor, Boston, MA 02109
(800) 826-2424

Market research, Newsletters and Reports

Ragan Communications Seminars, 407 S. Dearborn Street, Chicago, IL 60605
1-800-878-5331

Course: 1 day, "Effective Design for Desktop Publishing"

USLynx, 853 Broadway, New York, NY 10003
(212) 673-3210

SGML training and DTD consulting

VideoTutor, 110 Wild Basin Road, Suite 280, Austin, TX 78746
1-800-252-1225
Videotape self paced tutorials (PageMaker, Ventura Publisher, Graphic Design (see below)

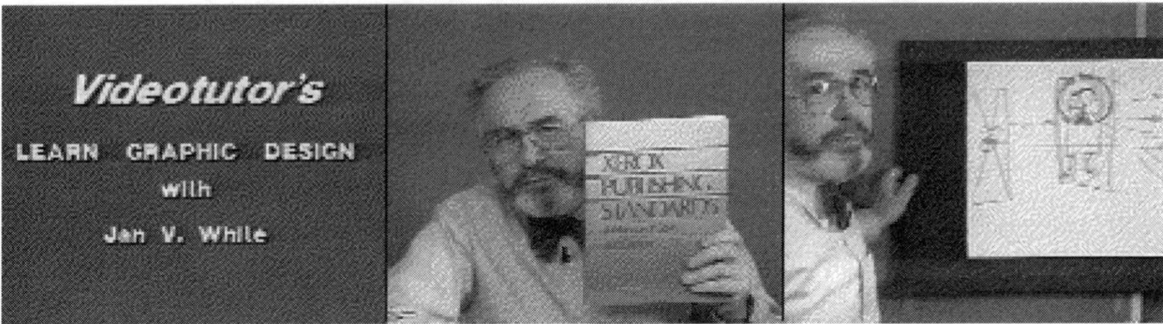

Fonts

The following companies all provide fonts. Some also sell font manipulation and management software. For information on the particulars of font formats and types of equipment they work with, contact the individual companies.

Some of the vendors have fonts packages for particular applications such as Faxes, Newsletters, and Presentations.

Adobe Systems, Inc., 1585 Charleston Rd., Mountain View, CA 94039
(800) 833-6687
Fonts, Adobe TypeAlign, Adobe Type Manager, and more

Agfa Compugraphic, 90 Industrial Way, Wilmington, MA 01887
(800) 424-8973
Fonts

Altsys Corp., 269 W. Renner Rd., Richardson, TX 75080
Fontographer, Metamorphosis

Bitstream, Inc., 215 First St., Cambridge, MA 02142
(800) 522-3668
Fonts, BitStream MakeUp, FaceLift

Broderbund Software Inc., 500 Redwood Blvd., Novato, CA 91355
(805) 257-1797
TypeStyler

Linotype-Hell Co., 425 Oser Ave.,
Hauppauge, NY 11788
(800) 633-1900

Fonts

Monotype Typography Inc., 53 W. Jackson Blvd.,
Ste. 504, Chicago, IL 60604
(800) 666-6897

Fonts

The Font Company, 12629 N. Tatum Blvd.,
Phoenix, AZ 85032
(602) 998-9711

Fonts

Groupware

This new software classification describes products that let groups of people work in a collaborative manner. Check out Yahoo's list at:

http://www.yahoo.com/
Business_and_Economy/Companies/Computers/
Software/Communications_and_Networking/
Groupware

http://www.yahoo.com/
Computers_and_Internet_Software/Groupware.

BBN Software Products, 150 Cambridge Park Dr.,
Cambridge, MA 02140
(800) 251-1717, FAX (617) 873-4020

BBN/Slate was the first UNIX–based computer–supported cooperative work product. As the name implies, it presents users, in different locations, a virtual slate or white board in which they can share.

Clarity Software Inc., 2700 Garcia Ave.,
Mountain View, CA 94043
(800) 235-6736

Rapport

Lotus Development Corp., 55 Cambridge Parkway,
Cambridge, MA 02142
(800) 343-5414

Lotus Notes

Microsoft Corp., 1 Microsoft Way, Redmond, WA 98502, (206) 882-8080, FAX (206) 936-7329

Windows for Workgroups (WFW) makes PC–based groupware a reality. It provides convient mechanisms to share files, devices such as printers and a tool called Schedule+ to coordinate personal planning and meeting schedules among a group of people. It's a significant move foward, but this is brand new stuff so I'd take a show–me attitude for a while.

ON Technology, Inc., 155 Second Street,
Cambridge, MA 02141
(617) 876-0900

Instant Update is one of the first successful groupware products for the Mac. It allows a group of people to simultaneously work on a document. If flags conflicts when users attempt to edit the same paragraph and provides a mechanism to resolve the conflicts.

SunSolutions, Sun Technology Enterprises, Inc., 2550 Garcia Ave., MS MTV02-208,
Mountain View, CA 94043
(415) 336-4567, FAX (415) 962-9421

ShowMe, interactive conferencing on workstation

Miscellaneous

AccessAbility Internet Services, 12515 Greenbriar Rd., Potomac MD 20854
(301) 983-3547, FAX (301) 983-4899
info@ability.net http://www.ability.net

Self service Web site hosting facilities with extended HTML services.

Macbeth, P.O. Box 230, Newburgh, NY 12551-0230
(914) 565-7660, FAX (914) 561-0267

Munsell Color materials

Macbeth provides numerous products and services based on the Munsell color standard. Your can obtain the Munsell books, software conversion between CIE and Munsell and even a Munsell tree of your very own!

Mulberry Technologies Inc, 1714 Tweed St.
Rockville, MD 20851
(301) 231-6930

SGML Content Modeler

Creating SGML DTDs is not a trivial task. Teaching other people is even more difficult. This is exactly where the SGML Content Modeler comes it. Created by Tommie Usdin formerly of the ATLIS Consulting Group, it consists of a series of jigsaw puzzle pieces. The pieces of the puzzle are labeled with a number of document elements, such as Book, Front, Chapter, and Section, and can be connected together with pieces that specify whether the elements are required, optional, or repeatable. The modeler is available from GCA.

SGML the Movie (see SoftQuad entry under SGML)

A campy, informative video introduction to SGML. This videotape is a light introduction to the basic concepts of SGML with a nonthreatening humorous style. It's light on technical content but useful for the uninitiated (for example, managers). Produced by SoftQuad, Inc., it's always a pleasure (and much too rare) to see an explanation of technology that doesn't take itself too seriously.

CDROM bonus - this movie is on the CD-ROM accompanying this book as a series of QuickTime files.

Network Connectivity

You don't have to be a student or employed at a large corporation to enjoy the variety of information sources available on the Internet. You can actually just pay for it. There are literally hundreds of "ISPs" Internet Service Providers pick up any computer related magazine for a list. The vendors listed are not necessarily good for your needs and are present merely to help you get started.

Internet

The following companies offer Internet connectivity or USENET (bulletin board–type discussions) feeds or both.

This information came from a USENET posting by Jonathan Kamens (jik@MIT.Edu), the MIT Information Systems/Athena Moderator of the USENET newsgroup `news.answers`.

AlterNet, a low cost approach for access to the Internet by UUNET (see entry below).

Anterior Technology, P.O. Box 1206,
Menlo Park, CA 94026-1206
(415) 328-5615, Fax: (415) 322-1753,
info@fernwood.mpk.ca.us

CERFnet (California Education and Research Federation Network), San Diego Supercomputer Center, P.O. Box 85608, San Diego, CA 92186
(800) 876-CERF, help@cerf.net

Low cost dial-up access to the Internet

MSEN, Inc., 628 Brooks Street, Ann Arbor, MI 48103
(313) 741-1120, info@msen.com

MV Communications, Inc., P.O. Box 4963,
Manchester, NH 03108-4963
(603) 429-2223,
Data: (603) 429-1735 (log in as "info" or "rates")

Netcom - Online Communication Services,
P.O. Box 20774, San Jose, CA 95160
(408) 554-8649, bobr@netcom.com

Performance Systems International, Inc., 11800 Sunrise Valley Drive, Suite 1100, Reston, VA 22091
(800) 827-7482, Computerized info: all-info@psi.com
Human-based info: info@psi.com

SURAnet, 8400 Baltimore Blvd., College Park, MD 20742
(301) 982-3214, Fax: (301) 982-4605
news-admin@sura.net

UUNET Technologies, Inc., 3110 Fairview Park Drive, Suite 570, Falls Church, VA 22042
(703) 876-5050, Fax: (703) 876-5059
info@uunet.uu.net

UUNORTH, Inc., Box 445, Station E, Toronto, Ontario Canada M6H 4E3
(416) 225-UNIX, Fax: (416) 537-4890
UUCP & Connectivity across Canada and the Northern USA

Internet Information (official)

SRI International, Room EJ291, 333 Ravenswood Ave., Menlo Park, CA 94025
(800) 235-3155, nic@sri-nic.arpa
Network Information Center (NIC), DDN Network Information Center,

BBN Laboratories, Inc., 10 Moulton St., Cambridge, MA 02238
(617) 497-3400, nnsc@nnsc.nsf.net
NSF Network Service Center (NNSC)

Professional Organizations

AIIM, Association for Information and Image Management, AIIM Publication Sales, 1100 Wayne Ave, Suite 1100, Silver Spring, MD 20910
(301) 587-8202, FAX: (301) 587-2711
http://www.aiim.org
The AIIM Bookstore contains an excellent selection of books, standards, and related information on the imaging industry. This includes various specialized material on electronic document systems.

EPSIG, c/o OCLC, 6565 Frantz Rd., Dublin, Ohio 43017-3395
(614) 764-6195
The Electronic Publishing Special Interest Group (EPSIG) is a collaboration between the Online Computer Library Center, Inc. (OCLC), and the American Association of Publishers (AAP). From "EPSIG News" the organizations newsletter: "EPSIG membership is open to all individuals and organizations with an interest in learning more about, using, implementing, maintaining, updating, and expanding the Electronic Manuscript Standard, SGML and related standards, and electronic publishing in

general. The main goals of EPSIG are helping members to use the Electronic Manuscript Standard and promoting its widespread and further development."

Graphic Communication Association, 100 Daingerfield Rd., Alexandria, VA 22314-2804
(703) 519-8160, FAX: (703) 548-2867
http://www.gca.org

The GCA has been one of the leading proponents of SGML over the years. Their "InfoTech Resource Listing" is also the single best source of SGML and related information including books, periodicals, and a variety of miscellaneous material.

The HTML Writers Guild
http://www.hwg.org/

The focus of The HTML Writers Guild is on the World Wide Web publishing process as controlled by the HTML markup language.

National Association of Desktop Publishers, *462 Old Boston St., Topsfield, MA 01983*
(800) 874-4113, FAX: (800) 887-6117

The National Association of Desktop Publishers (NADTP) is a large trade association, serving the needs of professional desktop publishers. They produce a monthly journal the NADTP Journal and have a discount purchase program.

SIGCAT, E.J. (Jerry) McFaul, U.S. Geological Survey, 904 National Center, Reston, VA 22092-9998
http://www.sigcat.org

The Special Interest Group on CD-ROM Applications & Technology (SIGCAT) is a user group sponsored by the U.S. Geological Survey that is devoted to the investigation of CD-ROM technology and its myriad applications. This group provides an ongoing forum for the exchange of ideas, information and experiences on CD-ROM for the benefit of all concerned.

SGML Users Group, Stephen Downie, Secretary, c/o SoftQuad, Inc., 56 Aberfoyle Crescent, Suite 810, Toronto,, Ontario, Canada, M8X2W4
(416) 239-4801, FAX: (416) 239-7105
http://www.sgmlopen.org/sgml/docs/library/usergrp.htm

An international group devoted to the promotion and exchange of information about SGML.

SGML SIGhyper, Steven Newcomb, Chairman c/o TechnoTeacher, Inc., 1810 High Rd., Tallahassee, FL 32303-4408
(904) 422-3574, FAX: (904) 386-2562
email: srn@cmr.fsu.edu

"The SGML Users' Group Special Interest Group on Hypertext and Multimedia (SGML SIGhyper) is interested in the promulgation of information about the ISO/IEC "HyTime" Hypermedia/Time-based Structuring Language (ISO/IEC Draft International Standard) 10744) as a worldwide standard technical framework for integrated open hypermedia. We hope that all information processing industries will evaluate HyTime as a standard toward which they can migrate in an orderly and profitable fashion. The intent is not to inhibit competition, but to help create a new arena for it, and to help to train and equip the players."

Society for Technical Communication (STC), 901 North Stuart St., Suite 304, Arlington, Va 22203
(410) 528-8555

The Society for Technical Communication is a non-profit educational organization. It publishes a quarterly magazine called Technical Communication filled will practical information for technical writers.

TeX Users Group (TUG), P.O. Box 9506-BR, Providence, RI 02940
(401) 751-7760, FAX: (401) 751-1071
email: cvl@Math.AMS.com

The TeX Users Group hosts an annual conference and provides technical information to users of TeX. They deal with many of the important yet practical issues concerning document processing.

Publications

Advanced Imaging, PTN Publishing Co., 445 Broad Hollow Rd., Melville, NY 11747

A monthly magazine covering the imaging industry. Reasonably in depth technical articles. Not just fluff.

CALS Journal, 14407 Big Basin Way, Saratoga, CA 95070-6008
(408) 867-8600, FAX (408) 867-9800

A quarterly journal devoted to a wide range of topics of interest to the CALS community. These include business issues, standards, technology, and research.

CALS Report, Knowledge Base International,
13939 Northwest Fwy., Ste. 270, Houston, TX 77040
(713) 690-7644

Latest and greatest gossip, rumors, and up-to-the-minute CALS trends.

Digital Video Magazine, Active Media Inc, IDG Communications,
600 Townsend St., Suite 170E, San Francisco CA 94103
(713) 690-7644

The world of digital video is covered including systems, formats, tools and software.

EPodd, Electronic Publishing Origination, Dissemination and Design, Dept JP/EPodd, John Wiley & Sons Ltd., Baffins Lane, Chinchester,
West Sussex, PO19 1UD, England

One of the few scholarly journals dedicated to the interdisciplinary field of electronic publishing. The range of papers cover a sufficiently wide domain of topics related to the publication process. The rather ungainly subtitle of the journal does accurately express the subject matter— the origination, dissemination and design of electronic documents.

Imaging Magazine, 12 West 21 Street,
New York, NY 10010
(800) 542-7279

A monthly magazine focusing on imaging and related technologies. "Written for information professional who buy, implement and manage imaging products and services." Good for broad overviews of particular technologies relevant to the imaging industry.

Imaging World, IW Publishing, Inc., Bayview St. at Sharp's Wharf,
Camden, ME 04843
(207) 236-8524, FAX (207) 236-6452
http://www.cardinal.com/iw

A monthly large format news magazine covering the entire imaging industry. Lots of short overview–type news-briefs. Few in depth articles.

InterActivity, 411 Borel Ave., Suite 100,
San Mateo, CA 94402
(415) 358-9500, FAX (415) 655-4360
interactivity@mfi.com

A monthly magazine covering the wide variety of computer based interactive topics such as the Web, digital video, computer based training and animation.

Internet Business Report, Jupiter Communications
627 Broadway, New York NY 10012
(212) 780-6075, FAX (212) 780-6060
http://www.jup.com

An expensive ($495) publication with valuable Internet business data. Published monthly. Jupiter also offers a variety of special reports covering the Web, Online services and Internet in depth.

NewMedia Magazine, 901 Mariners' Island Blvd., Suite 365, San Mateo, CA 94404
(415) 573-5170, FAX (415) 573-5131
http://www.hyperstand.com

A monthly magazine about multimedia trends. It is relativly light on in-depth technical details, but does a good job covering both the Mac and PC markets. Reviews tend to be honest early evaluations of products, rather than simple gee-whiz technobabble.

<TAG>: The SGML Newsletter,
Graphic Communications Association,
100 Daingerfield Rd., 4th Fl.,
Alexandria VA. 22314-2888
(703) 481-8700, FAX (703) 548-2867

This newsletter was the first to focus entirely on the SGML industry. Provides valuable and timely news on trends and topics. It remains the principal source of news about SGML and related topics and also contains informative technical articles.

WebWeek, MecklerMedia Corp.,
20 Ketchum St., Westport CT 06880
http://www.iworld.com/ww-online

This large format news magazine published monthly does an excellent job covering the exploding technologies surrounding the Web. With an terrific format including Web links for each page, this magazine covers this domain well.

SGML

Many vendors of SGML products also offer consulting services.

Agfa Corporation, 200 Ballardvale St.,
Wilmington, MA 01887
(508) 658-5600, FAX (508) 658-2648

Agfa CAPS

Avalanche Development Company, 947 Walnut Street,
Boulder CO 80302-9885
(303) 449-5032

FastTAG (Automated Markup Software)
Proof Positive (Writing Tools)

Database Publishing Systems Ltd., 608 Delta Business Park, Swindon, Wiltshire SN5 7XF, UK
(+44) 793-512-515, FAX: (+44) 793-512-516

DMA (Document Management Architecture)

Datalogics, 441West Huron St., Chicago, IL 60610
(312) 266-4444, FAX: (312) 266-4473

Electronic Book Technologies, One Richmond Square,
Providence, RI 02906
(401) 421-9550, FAX (401) 421-9551
http://www.ebt.com

DynaText (Hypertext using SGML)

Mulberry Technologies Inc, 1714 Tweed St.
Rockville, MD 20851
(301) 231-6930

SGML Consulting

Oster & Associates, Inc., 125 N. Main Street, Bel Air,
MD 21014
(301) 838-1908, FAX: (301) 838-1913

IPEX, Yard Software (MARK-IT), Sobemap parser

SEMA Group/Yard Software Systems Ltd., Avonbridge House, Bath Road, Chippenham, Wiltshire SN15 2BB
(+44) 249-656-194, FAX: (+44) 249-655-723

MARK-IT, OEM SGML parser, Sobemap parser

SoftQuad, Inc., 56 Aberfoyle Crescent, Suite 810,
Toronto,, Ontario, Canada, M8X2W4
(800) 387-2777
http://www.sq.com

Author/Editor

Software Exoterica Corporation, 383 Parkdale Ave., Suite, 406, Ottawa, Ontario K1Y 4R4, Canada
(613) 722-1700, FAX: (613) 722-5706
XGML

Standards (Defacto & Formal)

This section contains information on where to obtains standards. The entries in this section are ordered by the colloquial names commonly used to refer to these standards. Their complete formal names, usually unwieldy, are in the reference.

On the Web look at yahoo's:
http://www.yahoo.com/Reference/Standards

http://www.yahoo.com/
Computers_and_Iternet/Standards

Sources of Standards

American National Standards Institute Inc.,
1430 Broadway, New York, NY 10018
(212) 354-3300
General Sales: (212) 642-4900
International Publications: (212) 642-4995
http://www.ansi.org
You can purchase both ANSI and ISO standards from ANSI. The information on international standards is available from their International Publications department.

IETF, Internet Engineering Task Force
CNRI (Corporation for National Research Initiative) is the Secretariat
1895 Preston White Drive, Suite 100
Reston, VA 22091, USA
(703) 620-890, FAX (703) 758-5913
http://www.ietf.cnri.reston.va.us
The real Internet standards folks.

CCITT, International Telegraph and Telephone Consultative Committee, Place des Nations, CH-1211 Geneva 20
Switzerland
You can purchase the CCITT standards here.

National Computer Graphics Association, 2722 Merrilee Drive, Suite 200, Fairfax VA 22031

NCGA has a great deal of information on graphics available and also offers the latest versions of IGES (V5.0 and later).

National Information Standards Organization, P.O. Box 1056, Bethesda, MD 20817
(301) 975-2814

NISO handles the "Z" standards, including the Z.39 protocol used as the basis of the WAIS protocol.

National Technical Information Service
5285 Port Royal Rd., Springfield VA 22161
(703) 487-4650, FAX: (703) 321-8547
http://www.doc.gov/resources/csd/csntis.html

You can obtain U.S. government FIPS (Federal Information Processing Standards) and CALS specifications and standards from NTIS. The list of FIPS is available through "NIST Publications List 58." NTIS is the primary source of U.S. government technical documents and software.

CALS

The order numbers are for purchase through the National Technical Information Service (NTIS).

NTIS offers a subscription service for many of the CALS specifications called the CALS Automated Update Service.

1840A, Automated Interchange of Technical Information, MIL-STD-1840A Dec. 1988.
Order #: PB91-962001LFF.

28001A, Markup Requirements and Generic Style Specification for Electronic Printed Output and Exchange of Text, MIL-M-28001A, July 1990.
Order #: PB91-962201LFF.

28000, Digital Representation for Communication of Product Data: IGES Application Subsets, MIL-D-28000, Dec. 1988.
Order #: PB91-962101LFF.

28002A, Raster Graphics Representation in Binary Format, Requirements for MIL-R-28002A, Nov. 1990.
Order #: PB91-962301LFF.

28003, Digital Representation for Communication of Illustration Data: CGM Application Profile, MIL-D-28003, Dec. 1988.
Order #: PB91-962401LFF.

CALS on Disc, CALS standards and technical reports on CD-ROM. Available on a quarterly subscription basis.
Order #: PB92-592140BCU.

CALS Products Fact Sheet
Order #: PR-898/897 (no charge).

Introduction to CALS Kit
Order #: PB-91-780148LFF (includes 1990 CALS videotape).

CITIS, Contractor Integrated Technical Information Service (CITIS), Functional Requirements, MIL-C-CITIS (Draft), Order #: PB91-962601LFF.

Handbook-59A, DoD CALS Program Implementation Guide, MIL-HDBK-59A, Sept. 1990, Order #: PB91-962501LFF.

Character and Data Formats

ASN.1, ISO 8824 Information processing systems — Open Systems Interconnection — Specification of Abstract Syntax Notation One (ASN.1)

ISO 646, Information processing — ISO 7-bit coded character set for information interchange (1983)

Latin 1, ISO 6937 Information processing—Coded character sets for text communication - Part 1: General introduction (1983)
Information processing— Coded character sets for text communication - Part 2: Latin alphabetic and non-alphabetic graphic characters (1983)

ISO 9541, Information processing—Font and character information interchange - Part 1: Architecture
Information processing— Font and character information interchange - Part 2: Interchange format

Document

These references to what are usually considered software are to the specifications themselves.

AAP, Standard for Electronic Manuscript Preparation and Markup, Electronic Markup Series, Association of American Publishers, Washington, D.C., August 1987

DSSSL, ISO 10179 Information Processing — Text and office systems —Document Style Semantics and Specification Language (DSSSL)

EPSF, Adobe Systems, Inc., Encapsulated PostScript File Format (EPSF Version 1.2), March 1987

HyTime, ISO/IEC 10744, Hypermedia/Time-based Document Structuring Language

LaTeX, Leslie Lamport, LaTeX: A Document Preparation System, Addison-Wesley, Reading, MA, 1986

ODA, ISO 8613 Information Processing — Text and office systems — Office Document Architecture (ODA) and interchange format

PostScript, Adobe Systems, Inc., Postscript Language Reference Manual, Addison Wesley, Reading, MA, 1985

SCRIBE, B. Reid, "Scribe: A Document Specification Language and its Compiler," PhD. Dissertation, Carnegie Mellon University, Pittsburgh, PA October 1980

SGML, ISO 8879 Information processing — Text and office systems — Standard Generalized Markup Language (SGML)

SDIF, ISO 9069 Information Processing — SGML Support Facilities — SGML Document Interchange Format (SDIF)

SPDL, ISO 10180 Information Processing — Text and office systems —Standard Page Description Language (SPDL)

TeX, D.E. Knuth, *TeX and METAFONT: New Directions in Typesetting*, Digital Press and the American Mathematical Society, Bedford MA and Providence RI, 1979

TIFF, Aldus Corporation, "Tag Image File Format Specification Revision 6.0," Seattle, WA 98104, June 1989.

TROFF, J. F. Ossanna, "NROFF/TROFF User's Manual," Bell Laboratories: Computing Science Technical Report No. 54, April 1977

Type 1 Fonts, Adobe Systems, Inc., "Adobe Type 1 Font Format, March 1990

Graphics

CGM, ANSI X3.122-1986 American National Standard for Information Systems - Computer Graphics - Metafile for the Storage and Transfer of Picture Description Information (also exists as ISO 8632)

FAX, CCITT Recommendation T.4: Standardization of Group 3 facsimile apparatus for document transmission (1988)
CCITT Recommendation T.6: Facsimile coding schemes and coding control functions for Group 4 facsimile apparatus (1988)

GKS, ANSI X3.124-1985, American National Standard for Information Processing Systems - Computer Graphics - Graphical Kernel System (GKS) Functional Description, Also the international standard ISO 7942.

IGES, Y14.26-1989, Initial Graphic Exchange Specification (IGES 4.0).

PHIGS, ANSI X3.144-1988, American National Standard for Information Processing Systems - Programmer's Hierarchical Interactive Graphics System (PHIGS) Functional Description, Archive File Format, Clear-Text Encoding of Archive File.

Information Retrieval and CDROMs

ISO 9660-1988, Information Processing—Volume and file structure of CD-ROM form information interchange

SQL, ANSI X3.135-1989, Database Language

Z39, Z39.50-1988: Information Retrieval Service Definition and Protocol Specification for Library Applications. National Information Standards Organization

Text Retrieval

There exist a number of full–text retrieval engines. Most of them are oriented toward the production of CD-ROMs but their use is not restricted only to CD-ROMs.

Dataware Technologies, Inc., 222 Third St., Suite 3300, Cambridge, MA 02142
(800) 344-5849, FAX: (617) 621-0307
Full Text Build

Fulcrum Corporate Headquarters, 785 Carling Ave. Ottawa, Canada K1S 5H4
(800) 447-7702

Ful/Text - indexing and retrieval software

Lotus Development Corp., 55 Cambridge Parkway, Cambridge, MA 02142 (800) 831-9679

SmartText 2.0 for Windows, Lotus Magellan

Knowledge Access International, Inc., 2685 Marine Way, Suite 1305, Mountain View, CA 94043
(800) 252-9273, FAX: (415) 964-2027

KAware

KnowledgeSet Corp., 888 Villa St., Suite 410, Mountain View CA, 94041
(800) 456-0469, FAX: (415) 968-9962

Online Computer Systems, Inc., 20251 Century Blvd., Germantown, MD 20874
(800) 922-9204, FAX: (301) 428-2903

Reference Technology, Inc., 5775 Flatiron Parkway, Boulder, CO 80301,
(800) 345-9569

Reference Set, CD-ROM development tools

SunSoft, Inc., 2550 Garcia Ave., Mountain View, CA 94043
(800) 227-9227

SearchIt, integrated text retrieval

Verity, 1550 Plymouth, Mountain View, CA, 94043
(415) 960-7600

TOPIC & TOPIC Real-Time

ZyLab, 100 Lexington Drive, Buffalo Grove, IL 60089
(708) 459-8000

ZyIndex (DOS, Windows, UNIX)

Appendix B • The CD-ROM

This Appendix contains instruction and information about the CD-ROM and a description of the contents. A README.TXT file in the top level directory of the CD-ROM also describes the CD.

Following are the directories and their contents:

ACROBAT

Contains Windows and Mac versions of Adobe's Acrobat Reader 2.1. In addition included is Adobe's Movie Player Acrobat plug-in which must be installed to view the QuickTime video's on the CD. To obtain QuickTime extensions please see Apple's QuickTime Web site at: http://quicktime.apple.com. for Windows or Mac versions of QuickTime.

ARTPDF

This book as a set of PDF files. The files can be viewed on any platform with an Adobe Acrobat Reader program, available for free at: http://www.adobe.com, and on the CD-ROM.

BOOKMARK

This directory contains a file called hotlist.htm, which was generated as a Netscape HTML bookmark file. It can be used with any Web browser and contains a list of interesting Web sites organized according to book chapters.

FM2HTML

fm2html is a suite of scripts, for translating FrameMaker files into HTML. fm2html was written by Jon S. von Tetzcher from Telnor (at the time), and Duncan Fraser, of MacDonald Detwiler. It can run on most UNIX platforms with the typical set of GNU and XWindows utilities.

QTVR

Some example QuickTime VR files which can be viewed using Apple's QTVR Player available for free at http://qtvr.quicktime.apple.com.

SGMLMOV

This directory contains the entire movie "SGML The Movie" in a series of QuickTime files. The video's can be viewed by simply playing them in whatever QuickTime player you have handy. It should be possible to view these on PCs, Macintosh's and UNIX platforms.

VIRTUS

Virtus' Voyager a VRML viewer from Virtus Inc. On the CD are versions for the Mac and Windows plus an assortment of VRML (.wrl) files. Other goodies from the Virtus Web site (http://www.virtus.com) are also included.

Index

"There is was, hidden in alphabetical order." - Rita Holt

C

D

E

I

J

K

L

M

N

O

P

Q

R

S

T

U

LICENSE AGREEMENT AND LIMITED WARRANTY

READ THE FOLLOWING TERMS AND CONDITIONS CAREFULLY BEFORE OPENING THIS CD PACKAGE, *HANDS-ON NETSCAPE CD—WINDOWS 3.1.* THIS LEGAL DOCUMENT IS AN AGREEMENT BETWEEN YOU AND PRENTICE-HALL, INC. (THE "COMPANY"). BY OPENING THIS SEALED CD PACKAGE, YOU ARE AGREEING TO BE BOUND BY THESE TERMS AND CONDITIONS. IF YOU DO NOT AGREE WITH THESE TERMS AND CONDITIONS, DO NOT OPEN THE CD PACKAGE. PROMPTLY RETURN THE UNOPENED CD PACKAGE AND ALL ACCOMPANYING ITEMS TO THE PLACE YOU OBTAINED THEM FOR A FULL REFUND OF ANY SUMS YOU HAVE PAID.

1. **GRANT OF LICENSE:** In consideration of your purchase of this book, and your agreement to abide by the terms and conditions of this Agreement, the Company grants to you a nonexclusive right to use and display the copy of the enclosed software program (hereinafter the "SOFTWARE") on a single computer (i.e., with a single CPU) at a single location so long as you comply with the terms of this Agreement. The Company reserves all rights not expressly granted to you under this Agreement.

2. **OWNERSHIP OF SOFTWARE:** You own only the magnetic or physical media (the enclosed CD) on which the SOFTWARE is recorded or fixed, but the Company and the software developers retain all the rights, title, and ownership to the SOFTWARE recorded on the original CD copy(ies) and all subsequent copies of the SOFTWARE, regardless of the form or media on which the original or other copies may exist. This license is not a sale of the original SOFTWARE or any copy to you.

3. **COPY RESTRICTIONS:** This SOFTWARE and the accompanying printed materials and user manual (the "Documentation") are the subject of copyright. The individual programs on the CD are copyrighted by the authors of each program. Some of the programs on the CD include separate licensing agreements. If you intend to use one of these programs, you must read and follow its accompanying license agreement. You may not copy the Documentation or the SOFTWARE, except that you may make a single copy of the SOFTWARE for backup or archival purposes only. You may be held legally responsible for any copying or copyright infringement which is caused or encouraged by your failure to abide by the terms of this restriction.

4. **USE RESTRICTIONS:** You may not network the SOFTWARE or otherwise use it on more than one computer or computer terminal at the same time. You may physically transfer the SOFTWARE from one computer to another provided that the SOFTWARE is used on only one computer at a time. You may not distribute copies of the SOFTWARE or Documentation to others. You may not reverse engineer, disassemble, decompile, modify, adapt, translate, or create derivative works based on the SOFTWARE or the Documentation without the prior written consent of the Company.

5. **TRANSFER RESTRICTIONS:** The enclosed SOFTWARE is licensed only to you and may not be transferred to any one else without the prior written consent of the Company. Any unauthorized transfer of the SOFTWARE shall result in the immediate termination of this Agreement.

6. **TERMINATION:** This license is effective until terminated. This license will terminate automatically without notice from the Company and become null and void if you fail to comply with any provisions or limitations of this license. Upon termination, you shall destroy the Documentation and all copies of the SOFTWARE. All provisions of this Agreement as to warranties, limitation of liability, remedies or damages, and our ownership rights shall survive termination.

7. **MISCELLANEOUS:** This Agreement shall be construed in accordance with the laws of the United States of America and the State of New York and shall benefit the Company, its affiliates, and assignees.

8. **LIMITED WARRANTY AND DISCLAIMER OF WARRANTY:** The Company warrants that the SOFTWARE, when properly used in accordance with the Documentation, will operate in substantial conformity with the description of the SOFTWARE set forth in the Documentation. The Company does not warrant that the SOFTWARE will meet your requirements or that the operation of the SOFTWARE will be uninterrupted or error-free. The Company warrants that the media on which the SOFTWARE is delivered shall be free from defects in materi-

als and workmanship under normal use for a period of thirty (30) days from the date of your purchase. Your only remedy and the Company's only obligation under these limited warranties is, at the Company's option, return of the warranted item for a refund of any amounts paid by you or replacement of the item. Any replacement of SOFTWARE or media under the warranties shall not extend the original warranty period. The limited warranty set forth above shall not apply to any SOFTWARE which the Company determines in good faith has been subject to misuse, neglect, improper installation, repair, alteration, or damage by you.

EXCEPT FOR THE EXPRESSED WARRANTIES SET FORTH ABOVE, THE COMPANY DISCLAIMS ALL WARRANTIES, EXPRESS OR IMPLIED, INCLUDING WITHOUT LIMITATION, THE IMPLIED WARRANTIES OF MERCHANTABILITY AND FITNESS FOR A PARTICULAR PURPOSE. EXCEPT FOR THE EXPRESS WARRANTY SET FORTH ABOVE, THE COMPANY DOES NOT WARRANT, GUARANTEE, OR MAKE ANY REPRESENTATION REGARDING THE USE OR THE RESULTS OF THE USE OF THE SOFTWARE IN TERMS OF ITS CORRECTNESS, ACCURACY, RELIABILITY, CURRENTNESS, OR OTHERWISE.

IN NO EVENT, SHALL THE COMPANY OR ITS EMPLOYEES, AGENTS, SUPPLIERS, OR CONTRACTORS BE LIABLE FOR ANY INCIDENTAL, INDIRECT, SPECIAL, OR CONSEQUENTIAL DAMAGES ARISING OUT OF OR IN CONNECTION WITH THE LICENSE GRANTED UNDER THIS AGREEMENT, OR FOR LOSS OF USE, LOSS OF DATA, LOSS OF INCOME OR PROFIT, OR OTHER LOSSES, SUSTAINED AS A RESULT OF INJURY TO ANY PERSON, OR LOSS OF OR DAMAGE TO PROPERTY, OR CLAIMS OF THIRD PARTIES, EVEN IF THE COMPANY OR AN AUTHORIZED REPRESENTATIVE OF THE COMPANY HAS BEEN ADVISED OF THE POSSIBILITY OF SUCH DAMAGES. IN NO EVENT SHALL LIABILITY OF THE COMPANY FOR DAMAGES WITH RESPECT TO THE SOFTWARE EXCEED THE AMOUNTS ACTUALLY PAID BY YOU, IF ANY, FOR THE SOFTWARE.

SOME JURISDICTIONS DO NOT ALLOW THE LIMITATION OF IMPLIED WARRANTIES OR LIABILITY FOR INCIDENTAL, INDIRECT, SPECIAL, OR CONSEQUENTIAL DAMAGES, SO THE ABOVE LIMITATIONS MAY NOT ALWAYS APPLY. THE WARRANTIES IN THIS AGREEMENT GIVE YOU SPECIFIC LEGAL RIGHTS AND YOU MAY ALSO HAVE OTHER RIGHTS WHICH VARY IN ACCORDANCE WITH LOCAL LAW.

ACKNOWLEDGMENT

YOU ACKNOWLEDGE THAT YOU HAVE READ THIS AGREEMENT, UNDERSTAND IT, AND AGREE TO BE BOUND BY ITS TERMS AND CONDITIONS. YOU ALSO AGREE THAT THIS AGREEMENT IS THE COMPLETE AND EXCLUSIVE STATEMENT OF THE AGREEMENT BETWEEN YOU AND THE COMPANY AND SUPERSEDES ALL PROPOSALS OR PRIOR AGREEMENTS, ORAL, OR WRITTEN, AND ANY OTHER COMMUNICATIONS BETWEEN YOU AND THE COMPANY OR ANY REPRESENTATIVE OF THE COMPANY RELATING TO THE SUBJECT MATTER OF THIS AGREEMENT.

Should you have any questions concerning this Agreement or if you wish to contact the Company for any reason, please contact in writing at the address below.

Robin Short

Prentice Hall PTR

One Lake Street

Upper Saddle River, New Jersey 07458